Nelson Glueck's 1938–1940 Excavations at Tell el-Kheleifeh
A Reappraisal

American Schools of Oriental Research

Archaeological Reports

Larry G. Herr, editor

Number 03
NELSON GLUECK'S 1938–1940
EXCAVATIONS AT TELL EL-KHELEIFEH
A REAPPRAISAL

by
Gary D. Pratico

Nelson Glueck's 1938–1940 Excavations at Tell el-Kheleifeh

A Reappraisal

Gary D. Pratico

with contributions by: Robert A. DiVito
Frank L. Koucky
Nathan Miller
Pamela Vandiver

SCHOLARS PRESS   •   ATLANTA, GEORGIA

28222294
DLC

3-31-98

Nelson Glueck's 1938–1940 Excavations at Tell el-Kheleifeh

by
Gary D. Pratico

© 1993

American Schools of Oriental Research

Library of Congress Cataloging in Publication Data
Pratico, Gary Davis.
    Nelson Glueck's 1938–1940 excavations at Tell el-Kheleifeh: a
reappraisal/ by Gary D. Pratico; with contributions by Robert A.
DiVito... [et al.].
        p. cm. — (American Schools of Oriental Research
archaeological reports; no. 03)
    Includes bibliographical references.
    ISBN 1–55540–883–4 (alk. paper)
    1. Ezion-geber (Extinct city) 2. Excavations (Archaeology)—
Jordan.   I. DiVito, Robert A. II. Title.   III. Series.
DS154.9.E83P73   1993
    33—dc20   93–24736
                                            CIP

Printed in the United States of America
on acid-free paper

To Mary
My Beloved
the Joy of My Life

Nelson Glueck

Contents

Early Iron Age

Chapter Three
The Identification of Tell el-Kheleifeh

Chapter Four
The Architecture

Chapter Five
The Pottery

Chapter Six
The Tell el-Kheleifeh Inscriptions
Robert A. DiVito
Loyola University of Chicago, Chicago, Illinois

Chapter Seven
The Metal Objects from Tell el-Kheleifeh
Frank L. Koucky and Nathan R. Miller
College of Wooster, Wooster, Ohio

Chapter Eight
Summary

Abbreviations

AASOR	*Annual of the American Schools of Oriental Research*
AASOR 14	See N. Glueck 1934
AASOR 15	See N. Glueck 1935
AASOR 18-19	See N. Glueck 1939e
AASOR 25-28	See N. Glueck 1951
AASOR 36-37	See F. V. Winnett and W. L. Reed 1964
AASOR 38	See O. Sellers 1968
AASOR 39	See W. F. Albright and J. Kelso 1968
AASOR 40	See A. D. Tushingham 1972
ADAJ	*Annual of the Department of Antiquities of Jordan*
AJA	*American Journal of Archaeology*
AS	Assyriological Studies
AS IV	See E. Grant and G. E. Wright 1938
AS V	See E. Grant and G. E. Wright 1939
ASOR	American Schools of Oriental Research
AUSS	*Andrews University Seminary Studies*
BA	*Biblical Archaeologist*
BAR	*Biblical Archaeology Review*
BASOR	*Bulletin of the American Schools of Oriental Research*
Beer-Sheba I	See Y. Aharoni 1973
BIA	*Bulletin of the Institute of Archaeology* (University of London)
BMH	*Bulletin of the Museum Haaretz* (Tel Aviv)
CBZ	See O. Sellers 1933
EAEHL	*Encyclopedia of Archaeological Excavations in the Holy Land*
EI	*Eretz Israel*
Gezer I	See W. G. Dever et al. 1970
Gezer II	See W. G. Dever et al. 1974
Gezer III	See S. Gitin 1990

HA	*Hadashot Arkheologiyot* (Hebrew)
Hazor I	See Y. Yadin et al. 1958
Hazor II	See Y. Yadin et al. 1960
Hazor III-IV	See Y. Yadin et al. 1961
HUCA	*Hebrew Union College Annual*
IEJ	*Israel Exploration Journal*
IJNAUE	*International Journal of Nautical Archaeology and Underwater Exploration*
ILN	*Illustrated London News*
JAM	*Jordan Archaeological Museum*
JBL	*Journal of Biblical Literature*
JJS	*Journal of Jewish Studies*
JNES	*Journal of Near Eastern Studies*
JSOT	*Journal for the Study of the Old Testament*
JTS	*Journal of Theological Studies*
LA	*Liber Annuus*
Lachish III	See O. Tufnell et al. 1953a, 1953b
Lachish IV	See O. Tufnell et al. 1958a, 1958b
Lachish V	See Y. Aharoni 1975c
Megiddo I	See R. S. Lamon and G. M. Shipton 1939
Megiddo II	See G. Loud 1948
PAM	Palestine Archaeological Museum
PEFA	*Palestine Exploration Fund Annual*
PEQ	*Palestine Exploration Quarterly*
PSAS	*Proceedings of the Seminar for Arabian Studies*
QDAP	*Quarterly of the Department of Antiquities of Palestine*
RB	*Revue Biblique*
RR I	See Y. Aharoni 1962a
RR II	See Y. Aharoni 1964a
Samaria	See G. A. Reisner et al. 1924
SS III	See J. W. Crowfoot et al. 1957
TA	*Tel Aviv*
TBM I	See W. F. Albright 1932
TBM III	See W. F. Albright 1943
TN I	See C. C. McCown 1947
TN II	See J. C. Wampler 1947
VT	*Vetus Testamentum*
VTS	*Vetus Testamentum Supplement*
ZAW	*Zeitschrift für die alttestamentliche Wissenschaft*
ZDPV	*Zeitschrift des deutschen Palästina-Vereins*

Tables

Plates

Introduction

The low mudbrick mound known today as Tell el-Kheleifeh is located approximately 500 m from the northern shore of the Gulf of Aqaba, roughly equidistant between modern Eilat and Aqaba. It was first surveyed in 1933 by Fritz Frank, who identified Tell el-Kheleifeh with biblical Ezion-geber. Nelson Glueck directed three seasons of excavation there between 1938 and 1940. Accepting Frank's identification, Glueck discerned five major periods of occupation, which he dated between the tenth and fifth centuries B.C.E. The biblical site provided the historical and cultural context for the interpretation of Tell el-Kheleifeh's archaeological data.

The final results of Glueck's three seasons were never published, although he did produce a series of preliminary reports. The present study reappraises his excavations with special attention to the site's stratigraphy, architecture, pottery traditions, and inscriptional materials. The data suggest that Tell el-Kheleifeh was occupied in two major phases: casemate fortress and fortified settlement. The term "offsets/insets settlement" will also be used for the later phase. The pottery and inscriptional materials suggest an occupational history from the eighth to the sixth centuries B.C.E. with a postscript of uncertain duration. Given the exceptionally lean data for the post-sixth century occupation, our study will focus primarily on the Iron Age casemate fortress and fortified settlement.

As detailed in chapters 2 and 3, any reappraisal of older excavation materials inevitably confronts problems that impose limitations on the extent to which the archaeological history of a site can be written accurately. Tell el-Kheleifeh is certainly no exception.

It must be emphasized that this study is not intended as a final excavation report. Certain aspects of Tell el-Kheleifeh's material culture presented here, such as the small finds, must be complemented by several of Glueck's publications. As a result of sketchy archaeological documentation and the inadequacies, by modern standards, of the original excavation's methodology and recording system, our presentation must be selective, focusing on those areas that allow meaningful comment on the site's history, chronology, and identification.

This project and its personnel were first announced in the American Schools of Oriental Research *Newsletter* (No. 6 [March 1982]: 6-11) and in the *Biblical Archaeologist* (45 [1982]: 120-21). An introductory article was also published in the *Bulletin of the American Schools of Oriental Research* (259 [1985]: 1-32). Reappraisal of Tell el-Kheleifeh's stratigraphy, architecture, and pottery was my responsibility. Robert A. DiVito (Loyola University of Chicago) prepared the inscriptions; Frank L. Koucky (College of Wooster, Wooster, Ohio) was responsible for the technical presentation of the metals in the context of regional mining activity; Nathan Miller, a graduate student at the College of Wooster, assisted Koucky; Pamela Vandiver (Smithsonian Institution, Washington, D.C.) prepared the technical pottery descriptions; Beth Alpert Nakhai, a doctoral student at the University of Arizona, served as draftsperson for the pottery collections, and Karl Kruschen (Toronto, Ontario) deciphered Jacob Pinkerfeld's architectural notes and reworked the site plans.

Several years of research, including three visits to the site, have generated a lengthy list of acknowledgments. I am especially grateful to Helen Glueck, widow of Nelson Glueck, for her generous support and patience with this project. I am also indebted to Eleanor K. Vogel, who was Nelson Glueck's archaeological secretary for many years and who was responsible for the ordering and preservation of the excavation records. I also thank Adnan Hadidi, former director general of the Department of Antiquities of Jordan, for his support and facilitation of various dimensions of research in Jordan, and James Sauer, former director of the American Center of Oriental Research, for his interest, support, and expertise. Dr. Sauer read the pottery from the 1980 survey.

My first exposure to Tell el-Kheleifeh artifacts was in the presence of Ze'ev Meshel (Institute of Archaeology, Tel Aviv University), who was on sabbatical at Harvard University when the Tell el-Kheleifeh records and artifacts arrived at the Harvard Semitic Museum. I have benefited greatly from his knowledge, advice, and friendship through the past decade. The same may be said for Yigal Shiloh, whose generosity and friendship will be long remembered.

A number of scholars have generously shared their time, encouragement, and expertise, including Frank M. Cross and Michael Coogan, my dissertation advisers at Harvard University; Carney Gavin and the staff of the Harvard Semitic Museum; Rudolph Cohen, Department of Antiquities and Museums, Jerusalem; Benjamin Mazar, Amihai Mazar, and Trude Dothan, Institute of Archaeology, Hebrew University; Ruth Amiran, Israel Museum, Jerusalem; Avraham Biran and his assistants at the Nelson Glueck School of Biblical Archaeology of the Hebrew Union College-Jewish Institute of Religion in Jerusalem; Seymour Gitin, director of the Albright Institute of Archaeological Research, Jerusalem; Ze'ev Herzog, Miriam Aharoni, and several staff members of the Institute of Archaeology, Tel Aviv University; Bruce Zuckerman, University of Southern California; Beno Rothenberg, Institute of Archaeo-Metallurgical Studies, Institute of Archaeology, University College, London; Virginia R. Grace, American School of Classical Studies, Athens; Nancy Lapp, Pittsburgh Theological Seminary; and the late Crystal M. Bennett, director of the excavations at Buseirah, Tawilan, and Umm el-Biyara.

Several individuals helped with the mechanics of bringing this manuscript to fruition. I am grateful to Larry Herr and Robert Schick for their editorial suggestions and to Larry for his communications with regard to the Tell el-'Umeiri excavations; to Kathleen Mallak for her editing and work with the ASOR collection of Tell el-Kheleifeh materials at the Harvard Semitic Museum; to Tammy Peterson, Corinne Languedoc, Frank Vanlandingham, Wes Blood, and Tom Charlton for their labors on computer, and to my wife, Mary, for typing two earlier drafts with painstaking precision. Most importantly, however, I am grateful to Mary for her encouragement, support, and patience with this long-term project.

Chapter One

Tell el-Kheleifeh 1937-1940:
A Summary of the Work of Nelson Glueck and Architect Jacob Pinkerfeld

I. INTRODUCTION

The Jordanian site of Tell el-Kheleifeh is located approximately 500 m from the northern shore of the Gulf of Aqaba, roughly equidistant from modern Eilat and Aqaba (pls. 41, 46A-47B, and 48B). The site was first surveyed in 1933 by the German explorer Fritz Frank, who identified Tell el-Kheleifeh with biblical Ezion-geber (Frank 1934: 243-45). In November 1937, Nelson Glueck and others from the American School of Oriental Research in Jerusalem conducted a surface survey of the low mudbrick mound, determining its outlines and postulating an occupational history no later than the eighth century B.C.E. (Glueck 1938a: 3-4).[1] Glueck directed three seasons of excavation at Tell el-Kheleifeh between 1938 and 1940 (Glueck 1938a: 3-17; 1938c: 13-16; 1939a: 8-22; 1939b: 37-41; 1940a: 2-18), discerning six periods of occupation between the Iron I and Persian periods. He accepted Frank's identification of Tell el-Kheleifeh with biblical Ezion-geber. Though some uncertainty is reflected in his preliminary reports and field records, the Tell el-Kheleifeh/Ezion-geber equation remained the underlying premise for the interpretation of the site's occupational history.

A brief survey of the 1938-1940 seasons, with reference to subsequent publications by Glueck and others, will provide data for our reappraisal.

II. THE SITE AT THE BEGINNING OF THE 1938 SEASON

The excavated area of Tell el-Kheleifeh, which corresponds roughly to the size of the site, was ca. 80 m north-south and ca. 72 m east-west (pls. 1 and 2). The area consequently was about 5760 m² (Frank 1934: 243-45), or almost six metric dunams. The surface surrounding the tell was quite flat, covered with sand and sparse desert flora (pl. 48A).

The corner of a neighboring fence wall was chosen for the site benchmark. Its height was 3.99 m above the north shore of the Gulf of Aqaba. That fixed point level is indicated in the sections as a comparison horizon ±0 (pls. 9, 10).

The surface of the mound was very even, with a level fluctuating between -0.36 and -0.38 m. The foundations of the casemate wall (at G:10, 11 and H:10, 11) constituted the deepest points of the excavation (pl. 2). For the western perimeter of the casemate fortification, the lowest points of the walls reached -1.45 m in Room 107, -1.46 m in Room 111, and -1.53 m in Room 113.

The highest point of the tell was south of its center, in the group of Rooms 47, 38, 50, 110, and 125. The highest level was in Room 110 at +2.84 m, corresponding to an absolute height above sea level of +6.83 m. The difference in height between the deepest wall foundation in Glueck's Period I and the upper edge of the preserved walls from the later periods is 4.37 m. That difference also marks the limits between the lowest and the uppermost levels of the excavation.

The following summary of Glueck's three seasons of excavation, together with his revisions after the conclusion of the 1940 season, are taken from his field notebooks and preliminary reports (see Glueck 1938a; 1938b; 1938c; 1939a; 1939b; 1940a; 1940f; 1965a; 1967a; 1969; 1971a; 1971c; and 1977). The summary of Glueck's conclusions is complemented by observations from architect Jacob Pinkerfeld. There are a few inconsistencies in the level designations Glueck utilized as his interpretation of the site's occupational history evolved through the three seasons. Unfortunately, neither the excavation records nor Glueck's publications reflect a resolution of those problems.

III. THE 1938 SEASON

The first season, conducted during March through May 1938, saw the removal of more than one-third of the site's northern perimeter, comprising some 45 rooms (pl. 42). The mound's most impressive structure, uncovered in the northwest corner, was a building complex consisting of three small rooms at the northern end and three larger rectangular rooms at the southern end (pls. 3, 51A, 51B). The building is clearly visible in the aerial photograph taken at the end of the 1938 season (pl. 42). The walls of the complex were perforated with two horizontal rows of apertures. The lower course penetrated the walls (pls. 52A-54A); Glueck described the upper course as leading into an air channel that extended the length of the wall (Glueck 1938a: 5-6). At that time, the structure was considered to be a copper-refining plant and the two courses of apertures were interpreted as flues. The lower row of apertures, Glueck reasoned, permitted the transfer of heat between chambers while the upper course provided the necessary draft. He described the smelting process in this way:

> . . .pottery crucibles were placed on loosely packed masses of clay debris which had been burned to the consistency of intensely fired bricks by the heat which permeated through them from the charcoal fires built on them. The already "roasted" ore placed in the pottery crucibles over the hard-baked clay debris, was fired by packing charcoal around and over the crucibles in the furnace rooms, which were not roofed over. The strong drafts of air coming through the flue holes would fan the flames to a furious heat. The charcoal was furnished in part by burning palm wood from the vicinity, but most of it was undoubtedly imported from the wooded hills of Edom proper. The height of the level of the hard-baked, loosely packed clay debris, which was practically uniform in all the furnace rooms of the refinery, rose in time to a few cm. above the line of the lower rows of flues. Whether gases or air could infiltrate through this debris, and then through the flue holes from one room to another is still a moot question with us (1938a: 10).

The "crucibles" to which Glueck referred are the coarse, handmade vessels known today as Negevite ware.

Interpreting the complex as one of the largest and most elaborate refineries in the ancient Near East provided Glueck an explanation for the choice of this unlikely building spot.

> ...the builders of Ezion-geber had in mind the needs of the large refinery they were planning to erect, and chose after careful examination the one site in the centre of the south end of the ʿArabah where the winds blew strong, and constantly, and from an almost un-varying direction. They needed a constant draft from a known quarter to work the furnaces of the refinery. Without this draft, for the sake of which they were willing to endure frequent sandstorms, they could not

have erected such a large and elaborate refinery, and would have had to rely upon the primitive bellows-system in vogue before (1938a: 7-8).

Glueck considered the refinery and the poorly defined adjoining buildings to be pre-Solomonic and constructed by or for the Edomites.

The next major period in the refinery evidenced architectural features that reflected a radical change in the methods of smelting. Though the plan of the structure was altered with partitions in several rooms, the feature considered most significant was the plastering of the exterior walls, which covered the flues. Glueck commented on the metallurgical technology of that period:

> It was a period of intense industrial activity, to judge from the numerous crucibles in the various furnace rooms of the refining plant. Why the system of flues and air-channels was discarded in favor of what seems to be a cruder system is not clear. We can only suggest that perhaps too many of the flues had got out of order by fragments of brick and mortar falling into them from inside the walls to enable the working of the original system without extensive rebuilding. Rather than do that, the elaborate system of flues and air-channels was scrapped, and a different, if cruder system adopted. The new period marked by the radical change in the refining system may, we believe, be associated with the time of Solomon, when, in all probability, a spurt of new industrial activity took place (1938a: 11).

The handmade pottery, thought to be a tradition of the tenth and early ninth centuries B.C.E. (Glueck 1938a: 14; 1940a: 17; 1971a: 45-56), constituted the dating criterion. Though Glueck provided data relative to contiguous architecture, the site's early stratigraphy was determined, in large measure, by the major architectural changes in the so-called refinery.

From the perspective of preserved architecture, the following level was the richest discerned during the first season of excavation. This new town, assigned to the eighth century B.C.E., was constructed over the ashes and debris of the Solomonic level. Excavation records and the preliminary report for the 1938 season provide significantly fewer stratigraphic, architectural, and ceramic details for this and the final phase, dated to the seventh century B.C.E.

The 1938 season thus discerned an occupational history extending from the 11th through the seventh century B.C.E. Apart from the site's largest structure in the northwest corner, field records and publications provide few data relating to adjoining architecture. Glueck never produced period plans for the 1938 season, and excavation records concentrate on cultural and historical reconstruction. Glueck outlined four primary activities at Tell el-Kheleifeh/Ezion-geber: the smelting and refining of copper and iron; the manufacture of copper and iron implements; sea trade, including shipbuilding and fishing; and caravan trade with Sinai, Egypt, Edom, Judah, and Arabia.

While emphasizing the uniqueness and regional character of the Tell el-Kheleifeh ceramic repertoire, Glueck noted similarities with examples from Early Iron Age Palestine and Transjordan. On the handmade pottery Glueck wrote:

> Particularly striking are the large quantities of crude hand-made, friable, smoke-blackened pots, many of which were built up on a mat, and most of which have various simple types of horn and ledge-handles, or combinations of both. It was difficult to believe at first, when numerous ledge-handles appeared in the excavations, that Tell el-Kheleifeh was not an Early Bronze Age site. When, however, after a comparatively large number of rooms had been opened up, and in each one of them ledge-handles had been found together with other pottery which could only be Early Iron Age, we were forced to the conclusion that the peculiar ledge-handles of Tell el-Kheleifeh belonged to a type of Early Iron Age pottery hitherto unknown in Palestine and Transjordan. The uniqueness of this type of pottery, however, is not the only difference that sets the pottery of Tell el-Kheleifeh, by and large, into a category of its own. The forms and decorations of much of the finer pottery also do not fit exactly into any known category. The closest resemblance on the whole is to the Early Iron Age pottery of Edom, and there is much ware that cannot be distinguished from the Early Iron Age (1938a: 14).

IV. THE 1939 SEASON

The second season, conducted during April and May 1939, provided significant refinement of the site's occupational history (pls. 43, 44). The possibility of an original Edomite settlement was abandoned and the earliest remains were dated to the tenth century B.C.E. During the 1938 season, the stratigraphic relationship between the first refinery and adjoining architecture was unclear. During the 1939 season, the earliest construction of the copper-smelting plant was phased with the earliest architecture in the town proper, the two constituting a carefully integrated industrial complex. Who was responsible?

> There was, so far as we know, only one man who possessed the strength, wealth, and wisdom capable of initiating and carrying out the construction of a

highly complex and specialized site, such as the factory town of Ezion-geber in its first and greatest period. This was King Solomon. He alone in his day had the ability, the vision, and the power to build an important industrial center and sea-port so comparatively far from Jerusalem. With the building of a new Ezion-geber, Solomon was able to have smelted and refined and worked up into finished products the ores extracted from his great copper and iron mines in the 'Arabah, and was then able to export them directly by sea and by land in exchange for the spices and ivory and gold and precious woods of Arabia and Africa. The wise ruler of Israel was a copper king, a shipping magnate, a merchant prince, and a great builder (Glueck 1939a: 12).

As a result of the 1938 season, Glueck had described the site as "an open, unwalled town, with one large smelting and refining plant, and some adjoining workshops, houses, store-rooms, and slave quarters, separated by several alleys, and including probably somewhere in its complex a market place" (1939a: 12). The small size of the mound, the rather extensive area of excavation in the northern perimeter and the lack of visible traces of walls around the site seemed to preclude the existence of an outer fortification system. In 1939, in an effort to confirm the unwalled character of the complex, Glueck probed the area beyond what appeared to be the outer limits of the site's architecture. An impressive fortification complex emerged, the outer wall of which was characterized by pronounced offsets, especially at the corners. That solid wall was traced on the eastern, southern, and western sides of the mound (pls. 4-6, 58B, 62B). The northern section would await the 1940 season.

The gate complex, constructed on the four-chambered plan, was uncovered in the southwest corner of the site (pls. 4, 8, 63B-66B). Glueck described the entryway:

> There were three gates in this entrance way built at intervals one behind the other, the first two of which opened respectively into separate sets of guard-rooms behind each gate, with one room on each side of the entrance-passage. Thus if the first gate were broken down, the enemy would enter a rectangular area formed by the two rectangular guard-rooms facing each other on opposite sides of the entrance-passage; and the same if the second gate were broken down. The third gate opened into the main street of the town, which made a sharp right-angle turn to the east. To the west and north, the third gate seems also to have led into a large open square, where the market place is undoubtedly to be found and in a section of which the

camels of visiting caravans may have been kept during the night time (1939a: 14).

The primary parallel to this gate plan was drawn from Guy's Stratum IV at Megiddo (Glueck 1939a: 15). The original construction of the solid offsets/insets wall and four-chambered gateway comprised, according to Glueck, the fortifications of the Solomonic settlement.

The second occupational period, as discerned in the 1939 season, was the result of new construction and rebuilding over the ruins of Shishak's destruction. Significant architectural changes were observed in the gate complex. The entrances to the two pairs of guard-rooms were blocked, the floor level was raised, and a mudbrick pier was constructed on each side of the inner gateway (pl. 8).

Only stratigraphic and architectural glimpses were provided for the third occupational level; it was tanta-lizingly described, as in the 1938 season, as the best preserved in the site's history. Two phases were distin-guished in the settlement's plan, which was constructed in large measure along new lines. Cultural and histori-cal synthesis predominated in the description of that period. Glueck based his synthesis on small finds (amulets, beads, buttons, nails, spearheads, fishhooks, rope fragments, etc.) and inscriptional materials. The primary data in the latter category were jar fragments with inscribed characters thought to be South Arabic, and stamped jar handles in "Phoenician-Hebrew" char-acters translated "belonging to Qawsʿanal the servant of the king" (Glueck 1939a: 19-20). The data prompted Glueck to emphasize "the intimate commercial rela-tionship between Ezion-geber: Elath and Arabia and the importance of Ezion-geber: Elath as a trade center and seaport, in addition to being an important indus-trial site" (1939a: 19). Uncertainty over the identifica-tion of Tell el-Kheleifeh is reflected in the dual desig-nation of that level as Ezion-geber III or Elath I, dated to the eighth century B.C.E.

The second season provided significant revision of the site's later stratigraphy and history. Two subse-quent levels were discerned that extended the occupa-tional history into the fourth century B.C.E. Only frag-mentary architecture has survived from the fourth period, which was constructed over the partially de-stroyed ruins of the eighth century settlement. A fifth settlement, from which no architecture has survived, was documented by red-figured and degenerate black-figured Attic ware and several small Aramaic ostraca, which Glueck dated between 500 and 300 B.C.E. The occupational horizons of Tell el-Kheleifeh, as refined in the 1939 season, dated from the tenth to the fifth century B.C.E. or later.

V. THE 1940 SEASON

The final season was conducted in the spring of 1940 on behalf of the American School in Jerusalem and the Smithsonian Institution. Though there would later be significant changes in the interpretation of several architectural features, the preliminary report on the 1940 season represents Glueck's most definitive publi-cation of the site's architecture, stratigraphy, and chro-nology (1940a: 2-18).

The final season provided significant horizontal exposure and considerable definition of the site's early architecture (pl. 45). The basic plan of the "smelter-refinery," designated Period IA, remained unchanged (pl. 3). Period IB denoted the phase in which the "flues" were plastered over, signaling, according to Glueck, a major change in the technology of refining metals. Glueck described the feature which consti-tuted the phasing:

When finally heat cracked the walls of the smelter in places, and repairs and reenforcements were neces-sary, a means of strengthening them was employed, which had hitherto been applied only to fortresses. A sloping retaining wall in all respects similar to a forti-fication glacis, was discovered during the third season of work, built against each side of the smelter. It was almost half again as wide at the bottom as the smelter walls themselves. Each row of bricks in this support-ing ramp was set about two centimeters back of the preceding row, so that by the time the top of the inward slope of the glacis reached the top of the smelter wall, only the width of the smelter wall re-mained. The outer, very steep slope of the glacis was then covered with a thick facing of strong mud-mor-tar, which effectively hid all the irregularities of the tiny steps of its successively graduated rows of bricks, and presented a surface so smooth as not to afford a toe-hold to any one desirous of ascending it. Although the glacis around the smelter can in no wise be distin-guished from a fortification glacis, it was intended not so much to keep out an enemy as to bolster up the walls of the smelter (1940a: 3).

The earliest refinery (Glueck's Period IA building) was surrounded by a casemate construction, inter-preted as a square of foundry and factory rooms. Glueck and Pinkerfeld would later represent that level as Period IC (pl. 3). During the 1940 season, however, Glueck was uncertain of the perimeters of that earliest level, allowing the possibility that an outer fortifica-tion existed that would have been beneath the later offsets/insets wall.

There is, furthermore, some reason for believing that considerably beyond the industrial square, whose outer wall is strengthened like a fortress wall with regular offsets, there was also in the very first period an outer, complex fortification system, consisting of two separate walls, with a glaçis built against each of them, and a dry moat between the two walls. All traces of it have disappeared because of a later fortification system much like it, which completely displaced it (1940a: 4).

Glueck reflected on the well-known problems of discerning phases and relationships at a site of mudbrick construction.

Both the smelter and parts of the industrial square were used and reused in later periods. Indeed, one of the main difficulties of the excavations consisted in just this fact - that wherever a later age found a good wall of a previous one, it frequently built other walls against it to form a new room. The employment of a straight stratigraphic method of excavation at Tell el-Kheleifeh, however desirable it may be generally, would have produced dire results. The problems of unravelling the puzzles of walls there, built against each other, yet frequently belonging to totally different periods, were baffling at first appearance, but usually could be solved. The frequent use of different types of bricks and different methods of brick-laying in different periods helped to distinguish one period from another. In certain parts of Tell el-Kheleifeh, walls of successive periods were built on respectively higher levels (1940a: 4).

Period II was built over the remains of Shishak's destruction, which terminated Period I, according to the excavator. That second level, as described in the 1940 preliminary publication, corresponds to the final plan later prepared by Pinkerfeld (pl. 4). The industrial complex (Pinkerfeld's IC) was surrounded in Period II by a larger fortification system, whose construction radically altered the plan of the site. Having been reduced on the northern and western sides, the casemate settlement was now located in the northwest quadrant, thereby creating a sort of inner courtyard. The new fortification system consisted of two lines of defense, the offsets/insets wall with associated four-chambered gate and a poorly preserved outer wall. The latter was constructed 3 m beyond the offsets/insets wall and was of similar construction. Glueck assumed that the distance between the walls comprised a dry moat of stamped clay and mudbrick. The stratigraphic relationship between Pinkerfeld's IC and Period II was clear. The northern and western walls of the double fortification cut through and were built over the casemate complex, also cutting through the northern row of refinery rooms. The four-chambered gate gave access to the settlement from the south.

In Periods I and II the areas enclosed within the two fortification systems were, for the most part, devoid of architecture. That changed in Period III, although the major architectural elements of the earlier levels continued (pl. 5). Glueck commented on the character of the Period III settlement:

> For the first time in its history, the place assumed the semblance of a real village, and not merely a large, fortified, industrial plant. Essentially, however, it remained an industrial settlement, with obviously a large amount of industrial work carried on also in private houses (1940a: 12).

That level was assigned to Uzziah in the eighth century B.C.E. when, according to Glueck, the site came to be known as Elath. It remained under Judaean control until the time of Ahaz, when, according to biblical tradition, the Edomites took possession. An important epigraphic find of Period III was a signet with the inscription *lytm*, "belonging to Jotham" (1940a: 13-15). Glueck allowed the possibility that Jotham was the eighth century Judean monarch (see p. 53 below).

Three phases of Edomite Period IV were identified (IV, IVA, and IVB), which Glueck dated from the end of the eighth to the end of the sixth century B.C.E. (pl. 6). Apart from Pinkerfeld's plans, published details for Period IV architecture are exceptionally sparse as are the phasing criteria. The "Qaws'anal" seal impressions were assigned to that level (pls. 74-78).

The 1940 season provided little additional data relative to the latest level (Period V). Fragmentary walls did, however, reflect construction along new lines, but a clear plan was not discernible. The Aramaic ostraca and Greek pottery provided the period's chronology, from the end of the sixth into the fourth century B.C.E. Though few details are provided relative to the ceramic repertoire, Glueck summarized his general impression: "In general, the impression obtained from the three seasons of excavations is that despite the long control exercised over Eziongeber: Elath by the Judaeans, its population, pottery and general cultural patterns fit in more with the picture of Eastern Palestine, North Arabia and Sinai, than with Western Palestine" (1940a: 18).

VI. LATER REVISIONS AND REFINEMENTS

Glueck's understanding of the site's stratigraphy, chronology, and history remained, for the most part, as presented in the 1940 preliminary report. The interpretation of certain architectural features and the overall function of the site, however, were significantly revised subsequent to that publication (Glueck 1965a: 70-87). Glueck also tempered the Tell el-Kheleifeh/ Ezion-geber identification. While he continued to interpret the site's stratigraphy on the assumption that Tell el-Kheleifeh preserved the ruins of ancient Ezion-geber, the uncertainties of the identification pervade his excavation records and later publications. He wrote, "At the present time, the mound of Tell el-Kheleifeh is the only site known on the north shore of the Gulf of Aqabah showing the occupational history necessary for either Ezion-geber or Elath or both. If Tell el-Kheleifeh is not in all finality to be identified with Ezion-geber: Elath, then it must be considered a fortified industrial, maritime, storage and caravanserai center for both (1965a: 71).

Most significant, however, were revisions relative to the interpretation of architecture in the context of metallurgical activity. These were primarily in response to Rothenberg's criticisms (1962: 44-56) concerning Glueck's consideration of the site's largest structure as a smelter or copper refinery. The two horizontal rows of apertures, found in the external and internal walls of the building, had been the most significant feature for the interpretation of the structure as a refinery. Glueck explained:

It had been our thought, which we now abandon, that the apertures served as flue-holes during Period I of this building. Through them, we opined, the strong winds from the north-northwest entered into the furnace rooms of this structure, which we called a "smelter," to furnish a natural draft to fan the flames. We had previously explored the Wadi Arabah and examined numerous copper-mining and smelting sites, many of them already visited by others, notably Fritz Frank, and had been able through surface pottery finds to place them for the first time within the framework of history. The surface sherds at these Wadi Arabah sites belonged to Iron I and early Iron II in general and especially to the 10th century period of King Solomon. We had as a result called them "King Solomon's Mines," and had attributed, as we still do, a considerable part of his wealth to his exploitation of the mineral wealth obtained there. This led to our considering the building as a smelter or copper refinery and the apertures as flue-holes (1965a: 73).

The apertures were now understood as the product of a widely-documented building technique: the strengthening of walls with wooden beams laid laterally and vertically. The interior and exterior wall surfaces were plastered with a mud coating that concealed the ends of the beams from sight. Destruction by fire, as attested in the building, would have burned away the wooden beams, leaving holes that appeared to penetrate the wall's width. Glueck observed parallels to this construction technique throughout the ancient Near East.

The nature of metallurgical activity at Tell el-Kheleifeh was accordingly revised. He abandoned the idea of full-scale smelting activity while maintaining that some measure of industrial and metallurgical activity continued throughout the various periods of occupation. As to its nature, Glueck wrote:

The small amount of slag at Tell el-Kheleifeh may be explained by the difference in metallurgical operations as carried out in the Wadi Arabah and at Tell el-Kheleifeh. At the latter place, they were devoted, we believe, to remelting the globules of copper ore obtained through several metallurgical processes in the Wadi Arabah smelting sites, in order to shape them into more easily salable ingots or to pour the molten metal into molds for manufacturing purposes. This process would have produced no slag (1965a: 75).

The structure once identified as a smelter was now viewed as a storehouse or granary.

The handmade pottery, interpreted as crucibles, was now viewed differently (Glueck 1971a: 45-56). Although Glueck considered it earlier to have been a unique tradition of the tenth and early ninth centuries B.C.E., subsequent excavations had documented its more extensive geographical and chronological limits. Glueck now judged that pottery to be the work of semi-nomadic clans who roamed the Negev and Arabah during the Iron Age.

Publications subsequent to 1940 presented some revision of the stratigraphy and chronology. The mudbrick "glaçis", the feature distinctive of Period IB, was considered an integral part of the granary's earliest construction. The building (Periods IA and B), together with the casemate fortification (Period IC), comprised the earliest occupational level. Ezion-geber I, as Glueck designated it, was tentatively attributed to the time of Solomon and its destruction to Shishak. The plan and architecture of Period II remained as presented earlier and was dated to the reign of Jehoshaphat (1 Kgs 22: 48; 2 Chr 20: 36-37). The later stratigraphy of Tell el-Kheleifeh (Periods III-V) was historically rehearsed with little significant revision.

NOTE

[1]Glueck's publications record his earliest visit to the site as being in 1937. His first visit was actually in the spring of 1934 in the company of several "explorers," including Cyrus Gordon. Gordon recalls that visit: "We noticed not far north of the shore a mound in the middle of the Araba which rather surprised us, because the winds coming down from the north are generally strong and it would have been much more reasonable to build a city on either side of the Araba. This mound is called Tell Kheleifa, later identified as Ezion Geber, the seaport of Solomon on the Red Sea, and Glueck's excavations subsequently showed that it had been built by Solomon and that the chief industry was smelting. The smelting furnaces were actually situated with their backs toward the north, whence the winds come. There are holes in the north walls to serve as flues so that the wind would come in directly. In other words, the fanning of the fire was automatically taken care of by the steady winds that sweep down the Araba. The riddle of the location was thus surprisingly but plausibly solved" (Gordon 1941: 35).

Chapter Two

The Data For Reappraisal of Glueck's Excavations

I. THE 1938-1940 EXCAVATION RECORDS

A. Photographic Documentation

The photographic record is extensive for the three seasons of excavation. An archive of positives is stored in eight large notebooks and in seven small albums. The photographs broadly encompass the following categories:

1. images of interest in the region of Tell el-Kheleifeh
2. aerial photographs (the end of each season was documented with a series of aerial photographs)
3. general views of the site in its topographical context
4. excavation photographs labeled with field provenance, and descriptive and technical architectural data
5. photographs of artifacts
6. photographs of plans, sections, and drawings.

Each image in the eight volumes is labeled with a negative-number that refers to a separate archive of negatives and duplicated positives. The seven albums of photographs, for the most part, do not have accompanying negatives, and neither collection is ordered in the above categories. Though somewhat chronological, the archive's overall organizational rationale is unclear.

The photographs are provided with brief descriptions and occasionally with technical architectural data. Some additional technical data are provided for each photograph in the 1938, 1939, and 1940 photo registers. These three volumes are largely concerned, however, with technical aspects of the photography (lighting conditions, film, exposure, etc.).

The indices to the photograph collections, which facilitate access to excavation units and architectural elements, are:

1. a photographic index to the architect's level books
2. an index to the seven small photo albums, providing access to images of architectural interest with description and some technical data
3. 1938, 1939, and 1940 photo indices to the units of excavation (generally room loci) with description, selected technical data, and references to similar features documented elsewhere in the photographic archive.

The epigraphic finds (Edomite seal impressions, a small collection of ostraca, and a Rhodian jar handle) were photographed recently by Bruce Zuckerman in an attempt to enhance the visibility of the inscriptions. That effort was successful only with the Edomite seal impressions. The ostraca have faded significantly since the time of their discovery, and the original excavation photographs remain the best record.

B. Plans and Sections

These were prepared by Jacob Pinkerfeld and redrawn for this publication by Karl Kruschen. They include the following:

1. topographical plan of Tell el-Kheleifeh and immediate environs with four-room building, offsets/insets wall, and four-chambered gate outlined as points of reference (pl. 1)
2. general plan of Tell el-Kheleifeh throughout its occupational periods (IA-V) with location of sections A-B, C-D, C'-D', E-F, G-H, and I-J (pl. 2)

3. plates containing site sections A-B, C-D, E-F, G-H, I-J, and K-L (pls. 9 and 10)
4. plans of Glueck's seven occupational levels (IA, IB, IC, II, III, IV, IVA, IVB, and V; pls. 3-6). The persistent uncertainty concerning the attribution of architectural features to the seven occupational periods and questions concerning the validity of the period sequence is reflected in Glueck's several handwritten changes in Pinkerfeld's conventions for the site's stratigraphy
5. composite plan of the building that Glueck identified as a smelter or granary in Periods IA, IB, IC, IVA, and IVB (pl. 7)
6. plan of the four-chambered gate in Period I
7. plan of the four-chambered gate in Periods I and II (pl. 8)
8. plan of the "brickyard," including the walls of Periods II, III, and IVA and Rooms 64, 64A, 74, 74A, 75, 75A, 76, 77, 78, and 93. There are no level notations.
9. reconstruction of Room 11 with technical details
10. schematic plan of Room 49 with location of eight hearths and schematic reconstruction of section A-B in this locus
11. schematic reconstruction of Room 49 "flues"
12. separate plans with isometric reconstructions of Periods I and II and Rooms 25A, 30, 39, 36A, and 49
13. isometric view of the four-room building
14. isometric reconstruction of the four-chambered gate and contiguous architecture
15. comparative study of brick construction in the four-room building for Periods I, IA, III, and IV
16. comparative study of hearths
17. comparative plan of room "shapes" in the different periods, including the following:
    a. Casemates 21 and 25 in Period IB
    b. Casemates 109 and 111 in Period IB
    c. Room 92 as attached to a Period II wall
    d. Room 15 in Period IVA (contiguous with Period IV construction)
    e. Rooms 59 and 60 in Period IVA (contiguous with architecture of Periods IB and IV)
    f. Rooms 65, 81, 130, 132, and 133 in Period II (adjoining the city wall of Period II)
    g. Rooms 47, 49, 49A, 49B, 53, and 125 in Period V
    h. a composite plan of Rooms 23, 23A, 30, 30A, and 30B in Periods IB, IV, IVA, IVB.

C. Excavation Notebooks

These include the following:
1. 1938, 1939, and 1940 Field Notes with prefaced indices of loci, artifacts, and architectural features
2. 1938 and 1940 Dictated Notes with prefaced indices of loci, artifacts, and architectural features. The 1939 Dictated Notes are missing.

D. Architect's Level Books

Five red notebooks contain Pinkerfeld's level notations with sketches and comments for the 1938 and 1940 seasons. The 1939 volume cannot be located. All notations are handwritten in German.

E. Artifact Registry

The primary artifact registry is contained in five manila folders, which record the artifacts in the following numerical sequence:

1. 1-502
2. 503-992
3. 993-5000
4. 5001-9099
5. 10,000-12,092

The following information is provided for each entry: registration number, date of find, field provenance, level of find, negative number with reference to the eight volume collection of photographs, reference to Henschel's drawings, allocation, chronology according to broad archaeological periods, general description, some technical details, and occasionally parallels with bibliographic references. Artifacts are also recorded for the three years of excavation in three blue notebooks, one for each season. Glueck registered in those volumes only a selection of the most significant finds, organized according to date of discovery. The entries generally contain only a registry number, indication of field provenance, and a brief description. References to levels or to comparative examples in the Tell el-Kheleifeh repertoire are provided occasionally. The 1938 volume records a larger selection of artifacts than the 1939 and 1940 volumes.

The entire artifact collection is also registered in a file of index cards, which present the following information: registry number, field provenance, date of find, brief description, chronological assignment, measurements, fabric, finish, decoration, reference to the various photographic collections, allocation, and occasionally a bibliographic reference. Cards frequently include a duplicated photograph, of value only for identification. Data are not provided for all of the above categories.

The artifacts currently are located in the Semitic Museum of Harvard University, the Jordan Archaeological Museum in Amman (hereafter JAM), and the Smithsonian Institution in Washington, D.C. All of the field records and the epigraphic finds are contained within the ASOR collection at the Harvard Semitic Museum. Harvard's artifact collection is also the largest of the three and constitutes a representative assemblage of the site's material culture. The Amman corpus, though small by comparison, consists largely of whole vessels. A few of the site's rarest forms, such as the "windowed" censers, are included in that collection. The smallest collection is at the Smithsonian. In light of the representative character of the Semitic Museum and Jordan Archaeological Museum collections, the pottery plates are based on those two assemblages.

Many of the small finds have been lost since the excavations. Glueck's publications and the rather poor field photographs represent the only documentation for a significant number of the artifacts (see Glueck: 1938a; 1939a; 1940a; 1965a; 1967a; 1969; 1971a; and 1971b).

F. Room File

A Room File, containing an entry for each of the excavated units, was prepared in one original and two duplicated copies. The Room File is organized in numerical sequence (room numbers) with the following information for each of the excavated units: list of the artifact finds arranged by registry number in numerical order, artifact description, level of find, reference to Henschel's drawings, and photographic references. The original Room File was annotated by Glueck and contains some additional information entered in red ink.

G. "Architectural Notes for Tell el-Kheleifeh by Jacob Pinkerfeld, 1940-1941"

Vogel prepared this 40-page summary of Tell el-Kheleifeh's architecture, intended for publication in Pinkerfeld's name, from three letters Pinkerfeld wrote to Glueck. It provides a coherent synthesis of the site's architecture and stratigraphy as finalized in consultation with Glueck. In addition to discussion of the final plans (Periods IA-V), site sections, reconstructions, and isometric projections, Pinkerfeld provided technical details on the four-room building, brickyard, hearths, brick-dimensions and laying techniques, room

shapes, the two gate complexes, and Rooms 25A, 30, 36A, 39, and 49.

H. Artifact Drawings by A. Henschel and Assistants

The drawings of selected artifacts are contained in 116 plates. They are generally of poor quality and evidence no apparent organization. Of importance, however, are Glueck's handwritten notations, which often provide data not found elsewhere concerning field provenance, assignment to occupational periods, and comparative references. The drawings also represent the only documentation for a significant number of lost objects.

I. Pottery Descriptions

Selected pottery pieces are described according to the following categories: height, diameter, color, ware, inclusions, and finish. Occasionally there is a comment on manufacturing technique. This record is of limited usefulness, given the general nature of the descriptions. The technical ceramic data need significant revision, especially for fabric.

J. Palestine Archaeological Museum Registry Cards

A record of the artifacts originally allocated to the Palestine Archaeological Museum in Jerusalem (hereafter PAM), now the Rockefeller Museum, is preserved in two sets. The following information is provided for the artifacts that comprised the collection: Kheleifeh registry number with corresponding PAM and JAM numbers, field provenance, general description, suggested dating, size, fabric, finish, decoration, and references to the photographic archives. Information is not provided for all categories.

K. Objects in the Jordan Archaeological Museum

This list is a record of artifacts transferred to the Jordan Archaeological Museum in Amman from the Palestine Archaeological Museum in Jerusalem. Each artifact is entered with its Tell el-Kheleifeh registry number and corresponding JAM and PAM numbers. A brief description accompanies each entry. There are many discrepancies between this list and the artifacts that can be located in the Jordan Archaeological Museum. I was unable to find dozens of artifacts, including significant pieces, during two visits to Amman.

L. Artifacts in the Smithsonian Institution

Like the previous entry, this record is little more than an enumeration of pieces allocated to the Smithsonian's Museum of Natural History. Under the care of Gus Van Beek, the collection is well-ordered and easily accessible.

M. Registry of Artifacts in the Smithsonian Institution

Each artifact is registered on an index card by Smithsonian registry number with a corresponding Tell el-Kheleifeh number. Each entry includes a brief description with detailed measurements. Field data are occasionally provided. This registry and the one described above provide an adequate working record for the Smithsonian collection.

N. Bead Registry

The bead registry consists of index cards for each item, although most of the beads included cannot be located. The following information is provided: registry number with corresponding allocation number, field provenance, date of discovery, level of find, comments on stratigraphic context, reference to photographic archives, composition, description, and drawing. The provenance from Tell el-Kheleifeh for a number of the beads is questionable.

O. Nelson Glueck's Bibliography on Tell el-Kheleifeh

For a bibliography of Glueck's publications on Tell el-Kheleifeh, see Vogel 1970: 382-94; 1971: 85-86; Vogel and Holtzclaw 1981: 49-50.

P. Miscellaneous Indices

1. object indices to the 1938, 1939, and 1940 Field Notes
2. object indices to the 1938 and 1940 Dictated Notes
3. square index to the 1938 Field Notes
4. room indices to the 1938 and 1940 Field Notes
5. index to room location in the grid system
6. index to the epigraphic materials with the following data: registry number, reference to the photographic archives, brief description, field provenance, period assignment , and allocation

Q. File of Correspondence

R. File of Publications Related to Tell el-Kheleifeh (several articles have been annotated by Glueck)

II. THE 1980 SURVEY OF TELL EL-KHELEIFEH

To reappraise Glueck's work, the 1938-1940 excavation records and artifact assemblage have been complemented by additional ceramic materials and site data gleaned in a 1980 survey. Accompanied by Mohammed Darwish, representative of the Jordanian Department of Antiquities, and military personnel from Aqaba, I conducted a surface survey on July 16, 1980. My objectives were threefold: to gather surface materials strewn over the site as a result of military trenching, to correlate the preserved architecture with the plan of the excavations when Glueck terminated his work in 1940, and to assess the potential for future work at the site.

Tell el-Kheleifeh is not a conspicuous site. It looks much like the many surrounding hillocks and is not easily visible from either Aqaba or Eilat. The site is some 300 m due north of a Jordanian military tower, the latter visible from both Aqaba and Eilat. Glueck's western dump, clearly visible in the aerial photographs, is approximately 6 m west of the wire fence that now demarcates the neutral zone between Israel and Jordan.

The area of extant architecture is little more than 12 m². A few of the mudbrick walls have been preserved to a height of ca. 1.5 m. The preserved architecture was carefully recorded and studied in light of Pinkerfeld's general site plan and the individual plans of Periods I-V. It is clear that the existing walls represent an architectural potpourri from the site's various periods of occupation and appear to be south-southeast of the four-room building. The excavator's northern, eastern, and western dumps provided the perimeters of identification for the fragmentary walls. Unfortunately, there are no visible remains of the site's most distinctive architectural elements (the four-room building, the casemate or offsets/insets walls or the four-chambered gateway). It was especially interesting, however, to observe two rows of horizontal transecting holes through certain walls in the northern section of preserved architecture. Glueck found such apertures, which he originally interpreted as "flues" providing an airflow into the "smelting" installations, in a number of rooms in addition to those of the four-room structure.

The mound has been disturbed at several points by military installations, the most notable an observation tower toward the southern section of the excavated area. Trenches have also been cut into the northern and western sections of the site. Those disturbances produced a wealth of finds. Our survey yielded diagnostic sherds, bone samples, whole metal objects and fragments in an advanced state of deterioration, and a representative sample of the hundreds of shells and shell fragments that cover the southwest quadrant. Two finds were of special importance: an inscribed Rhodian jar handle (pl. 84) and a bronze trefoil arrowhead. With the exception of those pieces, the survey materials are now in the Harvard Semitic Museum with the ASOR collection of Tell el-Kheleifeh artifacts. At the request of the Department of Antiquities, the inscribed jar handle and arrowhead were returned to the Jordan Archaeological Museum in Amman.

In light of Glueck's 1938-1940 pottery assemblage, the 1980 survey materials (sherds only) were fairly representative. The vessel types included bowls, cooking pots, jugs, juglets, and plates. Consistent with the excavated assemblage, Negevite pottery made up the largest corpus. The Negevite forms were extremely limited, however, and were restricted to the straight-walled vessels so characteristic of that handmade pottery. Assyrian bowls were the next largest group, followed by the typical Edomite cooking pots. The statistical ordering of the surface pottery is found in Table 1.

The surface repertoire as a whole was confined to the period between the seventh and third centuries B.C.E., although some forms might be dated as early as the eighth century B.C.E. The earlier Iron II forms, attested in the 1938-1940 collection, were not represented in the survey finds. The inscribed Rhodian jar handle (pl. 84) indicates a later horizon than that suggested by Glueck. The material remains gleaned from the survey have provided a helpful complement to the 1938-1940 artifact assemblage.

The photographic and technical recording of the extant architecture was undertaken, in large measure, to assess the potential for further work at the site. A thorough reappraisal of Glueck's excavation results can only be accomplished, in fact, with the additional data that a few carefully selected probes would provide. It is clear from the sequence of aerial photographs taken at the conclusion of each season that a few sections of the mound have survived Glueck's extensive horizontal and vertical exposure. The northern perimeter of the casemate wall and the area northwest of the four-chambered gate appear to have been un-touched. Probing in those areas could provide the independent stratigraphic and ceramic controls needed for a revision of Glueck's five occupational periods. My visit to Tell el-Kheleifeh clearly suggests the promise of continuing where Glueck left off in April 1940.

III. THE PROBLEMS OF DATA RETRIEVAL AND REAPPRAISAL

Any scholar attempting to reappraise this excavation is confronted with a host of problems, especially because Glueck conducted it more than 50 years ago. The excavation methodology and recording system Glueck utilized in the late 1930s can only be characterized as primitive compared to modern stratigraphic methods. A few specifics will emphasize the difficulties:

1. The excavation unit, for purposes of recording, falls broadly into three categories: room, street, and square. Apart from a general compass orientation, the specific location of artifacts or architectural features within the excavation unit is not recorded. In the majority of discussions, refinement is impossible apart from the confines of the five meter unit, and there are instances in which "street" features are discussed without being localized within an area of four squares. The intersection of rooms provides the only reliable refinement within the excavation unit.

2. Pinkerfeld's 1939 and 1940 level logs provide the data for little more than a "floating" stratigraphy. Although a site benchmark was established for measuring the site's topographical features, topsoil was used as the benchmark for the levels of artifacts and architectural features. The variable surface thus produced a "floating" system of level notations. Kruschen's attempts to reconstruct the surface benchmarks at key points on the mound were not successful.

3. The lack of vertical stratigraphic control is further complicated by the fact that, except the site sections of pls. 9 and 10, no sections within the excavation units were produced.

4. With only a handful of exceptions, artifacts are recorded by general description, not by registry number in Glueck's field and dictated notes. Registry information is sometimes available from the Room File, which records selected artifacts in the categories of registry number, photographic references, level, and general description. It is often impossible to match the description and registry number. Room File level notations still preclude vertical stratigraphic control.

5. The main artifact registry and the Room File contain hundreds of errors and discrepancies in data recording. Henschel's pottery drawings are frequently misnumbered and are generally of very poor quality, yet those drawings often constitute the only record

TABLE 1. SURFACE POTTERY FINDS FROM
TELL EL-KHELEIFEH, 1980

Sherds collected	Number
Negevite straight-walled vessels (cf. types on pls. 11-12)	49 (6 sherds with knob handles)
Negevite plate	1
Negevite impressed bases	2
Negevite body sherds	13
Edomite cooking pot rims (cf. types on pls. 16-18: 1-4)	16 (4 sherds with handles)
Grooved-rim jar (cf. types on pls. 20-21)	1
Grooved-rim cooking pots (cf. types on pls. 18: 5-10 and 19: 1-4)	8 (2 sherds with handles)
Assyrian bowl fragments (cf. types on pls. 25-27: 12)	4
Bowl fragments with shortened rims (cf. types on pls. 27: 15-17 and 28: 1-6)	4 (1 burnished sherd)
Carinated bowl without perforations (cf. type on pl. 29: 2)	1
Kraters with inverted and elongated rims (cf. types on pls. 22-23)	4
Inverted and thickened rim bowls with exterior groove (cf. types on pl. 34: 2, 3)	5
Inverted and thickened rim bowls without exterior groove (cf. types on pl. 35: 2-6)	3
Everted and elongated rim bowls (cf. types on pls. 35: 7-8, 11, 12; 36: 1-3, 5-7)	2
Large bowls or kraters with thickened rims	3 (1 sherd with handle and another with applied decoration)
Small bowl with slightly thickened rim	1
Flask or canteen	1 (neck and upper body fragment)
Mortarium	1
Fifth century B.C.E. Greek body sherd	1
Unidentified handles	17
Unidentified rim sherds	23
Unidentified base sherds	3
Unidentified body sherds	52
Total	215

available for the several dozen significant artifacts that cannot be located.

6. Pinkerfeld's plans correspond to stratigraphic realities only for the major fortification outlines and features of monumental architecture such as the four-room building. That is especially true for the plans presented in pls. 4-6. The criteria for the architectural composition of those "period" plans are obscure at best. Studied in the context of Glueck's field diaries and Pinkerfeld's notebooks, the plans appear to represent excavation realities more than stratigraphic ones. They do, however, undoubtedly record some measure of legitimate architectural phasing, as in the four-chambered gate, the southeastern corner of the off-sets/insets wall, and the architecture contiguous with the four-room building.

As detailed in the following chapter, the occupational periods that Glueck and Pinkerfeld discerned were, for the most part, not based on stratigraphy or ceramics but on biblical history. The Tell el-Kheleifeh-Ezion-geber - Elath identification provided the confines of interpretation. The site's archaeological data were made to conform to the historical contours of the biblical sites.

Any of the above problems would hinder a thorough reappraisal of older excavation materials. The combination is debilitating and there are yet further difficulties. Numerous pottery and architectural traditions that are well documented today were virtually unknown when Glueck was exploring the Negev and the regions of central and southern Transjordan. The Tell el-Kheleifeh records and excavated materials, like those of many early excavations, have a long and complicated history of preservation and geographical distribution. Some important records and a significant number of artifacts cannot now be located.

Those are some of the factors that have imposed limitations on the extent to which the archaeological history of Tell el-Kheleifeh can be written. The study presented in the current volume, therefore, is not intended as a final excavation report in the tradition of modern archaeological publications. Rather, it is an attempt to focus on those areas of Tell el-Kheleifeh's archaeological history and material culture that allow meaningful comment on the chronology, history, and identification of this important site. This is not the final chapter in the story of Tell el-Kheleifeh.

Chapter Three

The Identification of
Tell el-Kheleifeh

I. AN IDENTIFICATION WITH
FEW DISSENTERS

Nelson Glueck's identification of Tell el-Kheleifeh with biblical Ezion-geber has been generally accepted by the archaeological community. Aharoni's comments are representative. Discussing the growth and development of the Solomonic kingdom, he wrote:

Ezion-geber was established on the Gulf of Aqabah near Elath (I Kings 9.26, et al) as revealed by the excavations of Nelson Glueck at Tell el-Kheleifeh. This was a very strong fort surrounded by a casemate wall which was later replaced by a solid wall. Large storerooms were constructed inside which served the needs of commercial caravans and the maritime trade on the Gulf of Aqabah. This was a key point dominating the routes to South Arabia. It is no accident that the Bible should mention the riches brought in by ships operating from this port (1 Kings 10. 11, 22, et al) and the trade in precious spices and perfumes with Sheba (1979: 306, also 16, 101, 319 n. 50, 415, 434; 1982:169, 221, 245, 251).

B. Mazar and B. Rothenberg are among the dissenters concerning the Tell el-Kheleifeh: Ezion-geber identification. Mazar (1975: 46-48) identifies Tell el-Kheleifeh with biblical Abronah (Num 33: 34-36), a site that Solomon built initially as a store city on the road to Elath. Ezion-geber should be sought further to the east, according to Mazar, in the immediate vicinity of Aqaba. Rothenberg identifies Jezirat Fara'un with the ancient port of Ezion-geber (1962: 44-56; 1970: 4-29; 1972: 202-7; 1988: 5; see also Flinder 1977: 127-39 and 1989: 30-43). That site is located on an island on the western shore of the Gulf of Aqaba, some 10 km south of modern Eilat. In a survey of the region in 1967 and 1968, Rothenberg found Iron Age pottery on the island and he further suggests dating the casemate walls to the early Iron Age. The ceramic data have not been published.

The positions of Mazar and Rothenberg have not received wide acceptance. The arguments in favor of their identifications appear less susceptible to verification than those produced by Glueck in favor of the Tell el-Kheleifeh: Ezion-geber: Elath synthesis. A survey of the chronological horizons of Ezion-geber and Elath, as presented in the Hebrew Bible, will precede further discussion of the site's identification.

II. BIBLICAL REFERENCES
TO EZION-GEBER AND ELATH

The first biblical references to Ezion-geber occur in ancient Israel's wilderness traditions, found in Num 33: 35-36 and Deut 2: 8. The former refers to Ezion-geber as a place of encampment after Abronah and before the wilderness of Zin, specifically before Kadesh-barnea. The latter reference mentions the site near Elath in the southern Arabah. In the context of the command to leave the Edomites alone, the Israelites' journey is described as progressing toward the desert road of Moab, away from the Arabah road from Elath and Ezion-geber.

The site next appears, again in association with Elath, as the southernmost port city of the Solomonic empire (1 Kgs 9: 26-28; 2 Chr 8: 17). Solomon constructed a fleet of ships at Ezion-geber, located "near Elath on the shore of the Red Sea, in the land of Edom" (1 Kgs 9: 26). The stated objective of that trading venture, a joint effort with Phoenician mariners, was the gold of Ophir.

In the ninth century B.C.E., Jehoshaphat attempted unsuccessfully to continue the Arabian trade network established earlier by Solomon (1 Kgs 22: 47, 48). The reference begins with the notation that there was no king in Edom, then records the shipwreck at Ezion-geber of Jehoshaphat's newly-constructed fleet of ships. According to 1 Kgs 22: 49, Ahab's successor, Ahaziah, sought to join the trading venture but Jehoshaphat rebuffed him. 2 Chr 20: 35-37, however, records an alliance between Ahaziah and his Judean contemporary in a joint effort to construct the fleet. The alliance was the object of prophetic condemnation.

Judean control of Ezion-geber was interrupted during the reign of Jehoram (849-843 B.C.E.) when, according to 2 Kgs 8:20, Edom rebelled against Judah and set up its own king. Jehoram attempted to reassert Judean authority but was unsuccessful. That is the last biblical reference to Ezion-geber; but reference is made thereafter to Elath, the site previously mentioned in association with Ezion-geber.

Relative to the Judean/Edomite struggle for control of the region of Ezion-geber, Uzziah (Azariah) initiated a brief Judean interlude during the eighth century B.C.E. According to 2 Kgs 14: 22 and 1 Chr 26: 2, Uzziah recovered Elath from Edomite control and rebuilt the site. The Edomites, however, soon seized the opportunity to reassert their authority over the region during a time of Judean weakness and preoccupation with enemies to the north. The circumstances, favorable for Edom, occurred during the reign of Jotham's successor Ahaz (2 Kgs 16: 1-9). Jerusalem was besieged by a coalition consisting of Rezin king of Aram, and Pekah king of Israel. Though Jerusalem would be delivered and the northern coalition defeated by the intervention of Tiglath-pileser III, those events would, in large measure, conclude the Judean/Edomite struggle for control of the region (2 Kgs 16: 6).

The Massoretic Hebrew text of 2 Kgs 16: 6 may be translated, "At that time Rezin, king of Aram, recovered Elath for Aram by driving out the men of Judah. Arameans then came to Elath and have lived there to this day." The preceding verse informs the reader that "Rezin king of Aram and Pekah the son of Remaliah, king of Israel, came up to Jerusalem to wage war against Ahaz of Judah and they besieged Ahaz but were unable to bring him to battle." Verse 6 offers a number of textual problems which have produced a confused and misleading historical account.

The Massoretes, recognizing simple geographical realities and in light of 2 Kgs 14: 7, indicated that the (consonantal) word [וארמים] should be read as [וארמים] and pointed [וַאֲדוֹמִים] "and the Edomites." They had correctly recognized that the letters [ד] and [ר] had been confused. The correction, however, does not resolve the historical difficulties in the account. The text as it now stands indicates that Elath was "restored" to the distant kingdom of Aram with the clear implication that the site had once been within the Aramean sphere of influence. In light of that Massoretic correction, the second mention of [ארם] should similarly be restored to [ארם] and pointed [אֱדוֹם] "Edom."

The account is still not free from difficulty. The improbable circumstance remains that Rezin, during his siege of Jerusalem, campaigned in the extreme

south, conquered Elath, and graciously returned it to Edomite control. It is more likely that the Edomites, recognizing the opportune circumstances, regained their sovereignty over Elath and drove out the occupying forces of Judah. The leader of the Edomite campaign would have been the king of Edom and not the king of Aram. The first mention of [ארם], therefore, should also be emended to its original [אֱדוֹם]. The name Rezin should be omitted. A further confirmation of this reconstruction is provided by 2 Chr 28: 16-17, which indicates that "the Edomites came and defeated Judah and took captives." We may now suggest the following translation for 2 Kgs 16: 6: "At that time (while Ahaz was besieged in Jerusalem by Rezin and Pekah) the king of Edom restored Elath to Edom and he drove the Judeans out of Elath and Edomites came to Elath and have lived there to this day." It is clear, therefore, that the events recorded in 2 Kgs 16 resulted in Edomite sovereignty over the southern Arabah. That is the last biblical reference to Elath.

III. THE EXCAVATIONS AND THE IDENTIFICATION: A METHODOLOGICAL PROBLEM

Tell el-Kheleifeh was first identified with biblical Ezion-geber by the German explorer Fritz Frank in 1934 (1934: 243-45). That *a priori* identification has been the proverbial "Achilles heel" in the attempt to write the site's occupational history. Glueck's unreserved acceptance of the identification, at least initially, is reflected throughout his early publications. A few quotations will illustrate this important fact.

Our expedition returned to Aqabah primarily to reexamine the site of Aila and to collect sherds from Tell el-Kheleifi. Frank had previously visited the latter site and found a number of sherds which "appeared to be very old" to him. He had nevertheless correctly assumed that this site must be identified with the Solomonic port of Ezion-geber. The discovery by our expedition of the adjacent smelting sites below Mrashshash (Mrashrash) strengthened this supposition. From Frank's photograph of the sherds from Tell el-Kheleifi we were able to recognize them as belonging to Iron I-II, and thus to confirm the identification with Ezion-geber (Glueck 1937: 12; also 1935: 48).

The site of Ezion-geber has long been searched for, but it was not till a few years ago that its location near the present shore-line of the northern end of the Gulf of Aqabah could be fixed upon. A German explorer, Fritz Frank, was the first one to discover the insignificant looking little mound called Tell el-Kheleifeh situated about five hundred metres from the seashore, and about halfway between Aqabah at the east end of the head of the Gulf of Aqabah and Mrashrash at the west end. When an expedition of the American School of Oriental Research in Jerusalem visited it several years ago, it was possible to identify numerous fragments of pottery strewn over its surface as belonging to the period of King Solomon, and thus to confirm the identification of the site with Ezion-geber (Glueck 1938c: 14).

The identification of Tell el-Kheleifeh was complicated by the historical problem of the relationship between the biblical sites of Ezion-geber and Elath.

In November 1937, the School undertook soundings at Tell el-Kheleifeh in order to determine the outlines of the tell, and to see how much of it was covered by sand. Large quantities of sherds were gathered from the surface, which belonged to the Iron Age. Most of the sherds seemed to be no later than the eighth century B.C. The actual excavations have borne out the correctness of these conclusions based on surface ceramic finds. While the excavations have thus far furnished no absolute proof that Tell el-Kheleifeh is to be identified with Ezion-geber, as we have previously suggested and as was first proposed by Frank, nothing was found to invalidate the identification of Ezion-geber greatly if we know exactly where Elath was situated. Both sites—if indeed there ever were two separate sites—are to be sought in the vicinity of each other, according to the Biblical passages referring to them. If Tell el-Kheleifeh is to be identified with Ezion-geber, then the only other possibility for the site of Elath would be to identify it with Aila, several kilometres to the east of it toward 'Aqabah, and almost directly on the shore of the Gulf of 'Aqabah. Unfortunately, there are no sherds earlier than Nabataean at Aila. We and others both in the past and during the period of excavations at Tell el-Kheleifeh have made repeated visits to Aila, and carefully gone over the surfaces of the hillocks which mark ancient occupation of the site, and always with the same result, that there is not a scrap of Early Iron pottery to be found on the site. To judge from the surface finds of sherds at Aila, it has been intensively occupied from the Nabataean to the medieval Arabic period, but not before then. The possibility remains that nevertheless Early Iron and Early Bronze sherds may be found underneath the lowest accessible levels of Aila. Tell el-Kheleifeh is therefore the only demonstrably Early Iron Age site along the entire north coast of the Gulf of 'Aqabah (Glueck 1938a: 3-5).

Glueck presented his definitive synthesis of the historical problem of Tell el-Kheleifeh, Elath and Ezion-geber in a study of the site's history and topography (1938b: 2-13; 1939b: 38; 1940a: 12; 1965a: 85-86). The archaeological data of three seasons were interpreted in light of that historical synthesis. Considering the possible interpretation of 2 Chr 26:1-2 that Azariah (Uzziah) rebuilt Elath and restored it to Judah, Glueck wrote:

It is clear that the city which was lost when Edom first regained her independence from Joram of Judah was Ezion-geber. We are told, however, that it was not Ezion-geber but Elath which Uzziah restored to Judah. What then had happened to Ezion-geber during the 70-odd years that intervened between the time when Edom regained her independence from Joram of Judah and lost it again to Uzziah of Judah—figuring from the beginning of the reign of Joram to the beginning of the reign of Uzziah? There are two possible explanations which suggest themselves. The first is that Ezion-geber was utterly destroyed and left abandoned by the Edomites when they captured it from Joram's troops, while they occupied the insignificant neighboring site to the east of it, called Elath, which had fallen to them at the same time as Ezion-geber. It was then this Elath which Uzziah built or rebuilt (perhaps it too had been partly destroyed), and restored to Judah. The question rises immediately, — how could he restore Elath to Judah when, at least so far as we know, Elath had never been lost, it being Ezion-geber that had passed out of Judaean control? The alternative explanation is that when Ezion-geber was captured and destroyed by the Edomites in the time of Joram, it was abandoned for many years and there was no settlement of any moment at the head of the Gulf of 'Aqabah, with the exception of the small, straggling site of Elath, which may have been nothing more than a tiny collection of mud-brick houses somewhat to the east of it. Not being strong enough to develop into a sea-power, Edom was not able to make out of Elath what Judah had created out of Ezion-geber. Actually Edom probably no longer controlled the head of the Gulf of 'Aqabah from the time of Amaziah on, having held it in what seems to have been little more than nominal control for about 50 years. Meanwhile Ezion-geber lay a sand-covered ruin, which differed little in appearance from the sand-hillocks in the vicinity. Even the name of Ezion-geber may no longer have been heard, because two full generations had passed by since it was destroyed. In the course of time it may gradually have become identified with Elath — as belonging to Elath. When Uzziah came to the south end of the 'Arabah, he may actually have built again on the former site of Ezion-geber, which had become identified with Elath. The reasons which had impelled Solomon and Jehoshaphat, for instance, to occupy and extend Ezion-geber and to develop it into an industrial centre and a sea-port must have been as valid in Uzziah's days as in theirs. It was Ezion-geber which the Edomites had captured from Judah, and it was Ezion-geber now known as Elath which Uzziah restored to Judah. It is this alternative possibility which we believe to be the more likely one. It is possible to restore to someone only something which was previously owned. Thus in II Kings 16:6 we read that the Edomite king drove out the Judaeans from Elath and restored it to Edom. If the Ezion-geber of Solomon and Jehoshaphat and the Elath of Uzziah can be identified with each other, then the Biblical difficulties with regard to them disappear, and the archaeological ones resolve themselves into understandable relationships (1938b: 8).

Though Glueck later abandoned them, his early stratigraphic designations reflected the site's change of name. The third occupational level, assigned to Uzziah, was designated "Elath I" (Glueck 1939a: 20).

The Tell el-Kheleifeh: Ezion-geber: Elath identification provided the framework of interpretation. Tell el-Kheleifeh's archaeological data was made to conform to the historical contours of the biblical sites. From Glueck's perspective the identification was secure, even before the results of excavation were known. The strategically located site was the only candidate that evidenced an occupational history that complemented the chronological horizons of Ezion-geber and Elath, beginning in the tenth century B.C.E.

If the Ezion-geber: Elath identification is not correct, then there must be two Early Iron Age sites at the head of the Yam Suf. One of them would be Ezion-geber, being occupied from the time of the Exodus to the middle of the 9th century B.C. Its main periods of occupation would extend from the reign of Solomon to the end of the reign of Jehoshaphat, that is, from the middle of the 10th to the middle of the 9th century B.C. The second site would be Elath. It would have led an insignificant existence down to the accession of Uzziah c. 779 B.C., from which time on it flourished or suffered under various hands until about the end of the 7th century, at the latest the beginning of the 6th century B.C., when it was finally destroyed. If, however, our suggestion is correct, namely that the Elath built up and restored to Judah by Uzziah was built over the ruins of Ezion-geber, then we should expect to find at the head of Yam Suf only one Early Iron Age site, whose main occupational history extends at least from the first part of the 10th century B.C. down to approximately the end of the 7th or the beginning of the 6th century B.C. This suggestion seems to be borne out by the fact that only one Early Iron Age site has been found at the head of the Gulf of ʿAqabah, and also by

the fact that our excavations at Tell el-Kheleifeh indicate a main occupational history lasting from about the 11th century to the end of the 7th or beginning of the 6th century B.C. There is also a general agreement of the four main levels at Tell el-Kheleifeh with the main historical sequences at Ezion-geber: Elath as they are adumbrated in the pages of the Bible (Glueck 1938b: 10).

The diagnostic pottery of the earliest architecture was the Negevite ware, which Glueck considered a tenth century type unique to Tell el-Kheleifeh (1938a: 14; 1940a: 17; 1971a: 45-56). The site's architectural traditions (the four-room building, the four-chambered gate and the casemate and offsets/insets walls) could also be placed in the tenth and ninth centuries (Glueck 1939a: 14-18). Glueck's Solomonic level of the tenth century was thus supported by ceramic and architectural traditions. The Edomite cultural element, anticipated from the biblical notices, was documented by the discovery of a series of jar handles stamped with an Edomite inscription containing the theophorous name of "Qawsʿanal" (Glueck 1938a: 15-16; 1939a: 20; 1940a; 13-15; 1965a: 86-87; 1971: 225-42). In addition to the architectural traditions and ceramic repertoire, Judean presence was attested by a seal signet ring bearing the inscription "belonging to Jotham" (1940a: 13-14). Glueck attributed the reference to the Judean monarch of the eighth century, the successor of Uzziah.

The data accumulated from three seasons of excavation appeared to confirm Glueck's interpretation. Apart from the Ezion-geber of Israel's wilderness traditions (Num 33: 35-36; Deut 2: 8), the archaeology of Tell el-Kheleifeh and the history of Ezion-geber: Elath complemented each other. The missing datum was explained as follows:

In as much as Ezion-geber I is the very first settlement built upon the present site of Tell el-Kheleifeh, with all of its walls resting on virgin soil and no traces whatsoever of earlier buildings, it becomes necessary to conclude that this Ezion-geber I is not the Ezion-geber which the Israelites saw when they emerged from the Wilderness of Sinai after the sojourn there lasting forty years. The Ezion-geber they saw was probably a tiny, straggling site, with a few mud-brick huts, and a few scraggly palms, and must have been situated farther to the east, where the drinking water is less saline, and the sandstorms blown by the strong winds down the center of the ʿArabah do not occur. All traces of this earlier site of Ezion-geber have disappeared, only its name surviving in the bustling town of Ezion-geber, first built probably by Solomon in the very path of the winds blowing down the center of the ʿArabah (Glueck 1939a: 17).

Glueck revised his interpretation of several Tell el-Kheleifeh ceramic and architectural features following his last season of excavation. The revision was prompted by refinements in pottery typology and by Rothenberg's criticisms of Glueck's connecting the site with regional mining activity (1962: 44-56). Glueck's watershed study (1965a: 70-87) was entitled simply "Ezion-geber." Thereafter he tempered the identification, although his equation continued to be the basis of historical and cultural synthesis. As he asserted (1977: 713), "The fact remains, however, that Tell el-Kheleifeh is the only site thus far found on the north shore of the Gulf of Aqabah, whose pottery and other datable remains correspond with the history of Ezion-Geber and of Elath. If in the final result Tell el-Kheleifeh is not to be identified with Ezion-geber/Elath, it must then be considered an industrial and maritime satellite of the two places, a strongly fortified caravanserai and a granary city."

In light of the current reappraisal, the identification of Tell el-Kheleifeh is both an archaeological and an historical problem. The chronology of the site's pottery no longer complements the chronological horizons of biblical Ezion-geber. The pottery cannot be dated earlier than the ninth century B.C.E. and that limit is suggested only by isolated forms. The assemblage as a whole appears to date between the eighth and early sixth century B.C.E. with a presence as late as the third century B.C.E. The dates of the site's architectural traditions are too broad to provide definitive chronological refinement. Tell el-Kheleifeh, therefore, gives no clear archaeological indications, either ceramic or architectural, that is was the Ezion-geber of Israel's wilderness traditions (Num 33: 35-36). Remains are also lacking for the tenth century (1 Kgs 9: 26-28) and possibly the ninth century as well (1 Kgs 22: 47-48).

Geographical proximity is all that can be gleaned with certainty from the biblical notices on Ezion-geber and Elath. Though an historical identification of the two sites remains a possibility, as Glueck suggested in light of 2 Chr 26: 1-2, verification is lacking. One may assume the possibility or probability of the identification of Tell el-Kheleifeh, but the problem of verification precludes examination of the site in the context of Ezion-geber or Elath. Though dismissed for purposes of identification, the biblical notices pertaining to the two sites are of special importance for providing a rough chronological framework of Judean and Edomite influence and control over the region.

IV. THE PROBLEM OF IDENTIFICATION: A MISSING DATUM

As a complement to the continuing assessment of Glueck's methodology, a comment on the consequences

of his identification is appropriate. The excavator's *a priori* identification of the site constitutes the most significant methodological problem. The history of the interpretation of Tell el-Kheleifeh, its stratigraphy, ceramic and architectural traditions, and historical and cultural synthesis represents a paramount case study in the dangers of *a priori* identification. As is clear from nearly every entry in Glueck's bibliography, the biblical framework of identification became the principle of interpretation. The stratigraphic sequence, which slowly emerged through three seasons of excavation, was continually interpreted and revised in light of the biblical glimpses of Ezion-geber and Elath. The fragmentary biblical notices became a stratigraphic framework that inflexibly accommodated any revision in the archaeological data.

In light of the above, the methodological prerequisite for our reappraisal of Tell el-Kheleifeh 1937-1940 must be uncensored archaeological data. That is not to dismiss the possibility that future excavation will again suggest, and perhaps verify, the identification of Tell el-Kheleifeh with biblical Ezion-geber and/or Elath. Until such information is forthcoming, however, Tell el-Kheleifeh must be allowed to tell its own story in its own language.

The question of identification, however, could be more definitively addressed except for the lack of an essential datum. Have the site's earliest occupational levels been uncovered? Though absolute verification will remain a problem even if an earlier horizon is uncovered at Tell el-Kheleifeh, clear discernment of the site's chronological limits are essential to the problem of identification. Verification of Glueck's chronological horizons should constitute a primary objective of future fieldwork. Though Glueck extensively excavated the site and makes several references to virgin soil, the answer to the above question can still be sought at a number of points in and around the area of excavation. The northern perimeter of the earliest level, the casemate fortress, was untouched (pls. 3, 56B, and 58A). As is clear from the sequence of aerial photographs (pls. 42-45), that section was covered, beginning in the first season, by the excavation's northern dump. There are also a number of points within the excavation area where probes appear promising, such as the area to the northwest of the outer gate complex.

The 1980 surface survey was prompted by the fact that undisturbed stratigraphy had been cut by Jordanian military installations. While nothing earlier was uncovered at those points of modern trenching, the opportunity remains to investigate the possibility that earlier material may be found. Future probes may not solve the problem of identification but they could provide this essential datum. Relative to questions of cultural and historical synthesis, our reappraisal of

Tell el-Kheleifeh utilizes the biblical notices on Ezion-geber and Elath only as chronological indicators of political influence or control in the region of the southern Arabah.

Chapter Four

The Architecture

I. INTRODUCTION

The architecture of Tell el-Kheleifeh throughout its occupational history evidences a number of features that belong to Iron Age traditions. Those elements are presented here in relation to the site's two major architectural phases: the casemate fortress and the later fortified settlement, also referred to as the offsets/insets settlement. The impossibility of reconstructing Glueck's phasing of the site has been noted above. There are significant differences between Glueck's observations and our view that Tell el-Kheleifeh was occupied in two major Iron Age phases with a third, later phase of uncertain duration.

Descriptions and comparative studies are presented for the following architectural elements:

(1) the site's largest structure (the four-room building), which Glueck described as a smelter/granary (pls. 1-4, 7, 42-45, 51A, 51B);[1]

(2) the casemate fortification complex that surrounded the four-room building in the earliest occupational level (pls. 3, 55B-58A);

(3) the offsets/insets wall and associated four-chambered gateway (pls. 1, 2, 4-6, 8 and 63B-66B);

(4) the site's settlement plans before and after the construction of the offsets/insets wall.

Given the lack of refined stratigraphy with associated ceramic horizons at Tell el-Kheleifeh, studies in comparative architecture are an important methodological tool with which to reconstruct the site's chronology and history. Unfortunately, significant refinement is precluded by the broad chronological range of the architectural traditions.

II. THE FOUR-ROOM BUILDING
(PLS. 1-3, 42-45, 51A, 51B)

A. Description

Periods IA and IB, as Glueck and Pinkerfeld discerned, consisted of one monumental structure (pls. 3, 7). They theorized that the earliest level consisted solely of the large four-room building without any type of fortification. It is more likely, however, that the building never existed as an isolated architectural element but was the central edifice in the earliest occupational level, designated in our reappraisal as the "casemate fortress" (pl. 3). The structure continued throughout the site's occupational history, albeit with significant modification.

The building consisted of six rooms in its earliest phase: three roughly square units at the northern end and three larger, rectangular units extending to the south (pls. 51A, 51B). The latter were 7.40 m in length and their widths varied from ca. 2.00 to 3.00 m. The building was nearly square, measuring 13.20 m in length (N-S), with widths of 12.30 m on the north side and 13.20 m on the south side. The exterior walls were 1.20 m wide; interior walls varied between 0.95 and 1.05 m. The walls were preserved to a height of 2.70 m.

The building was built almost entirely of mudbrick (Glueck 1940f: 51-55).[2] Its bricks measured approximately 0.40 x 0.20 x 0.10 m and were laid in a construction technique that may be loosely designated as header and stretcher. The irregularities in the sizes of the bricks and the masonry style can be seen in the excavation photographs.

Two horizontal rows of "apertures" were discovered in both the exterior and interior walls of the building (pls. 52A-54B). The lower row was at an average height of 1.00 m from the bottom of the walls. The upper row was some 0.70 m higher. Most of the apertures were semicircular in section and between 0.06 and 0.10 m high. After Glueck abandoned his interpretation of the apertures as flues, he considered them evidence of a construction technique for the strengthening of walls (1965a: 73-75). Wooden beams, halved in the case of Tell el-Kheleifeh, were embedded across the widths of the walls, and thereby created a stronger bond. The semicircular holes were all that remained after the timbers were consumed in a destruction by fire.

As noted, the presence of the apertures in the site's largest building constituted an essential datum for Glueck's smelting hypothesis. But they appeared also elsewhere in the site, most notably in Room 49 (pls. 60A, 60B; see also 61A, 61B). That casemate room was given special attention in the excavation records because of the discovery of eight installations interpreted as "hearths" or "ovens," today generally referred to as *tabûns* (pls. 59A, 59B).[3] Although similar installations were found in Rooms 105, 45, 38, 36A, 25A, and 25 of the casemate system, Room 49 contained the greatest concentration. Its southern wall contained four apertures, similar to those of the four-room structure. The association of hearths and apertures in Room 49 suggests an additional function for some of the wall perforations.

Although most of the apertures can be interpreted as "burnt beam apertures," several, as described by Glueck for Rooms 3 and 49, cannot be interpreted in this way because of the regularities of their construction. Plate 52B is a detail of such an aperture, located in the south wall of Room 3. Glueck described similar features for other, primarily interior walls of the four-room building, and for Room 49. Given the climatic conditions in the southern Arabah, some of the apertures may have served for ventilation, providing a modest flow of fresh air within the mudbrick architecture. That interpretation appears especially plausible in those units that contained hearths or ovens, such as Room 49. Apart from a few photographs and brief descriptions, however, the excavation records do not provide sufficient data concerning the number and distribution of the special apertures. If the suggestion of ventilation is correct, the data are too sparse to reconstruct the system.

The substantial reinforcing wall, which constituted Glueck's Period IB, was most likely a part of the original construction (pls. 54A, 54B, 55A). That revetment, which Glueck designated as a glaçis, was composed of mudbricks, mortar, and brick fragments. Its lower thickness varied between 1.38 and 1.50 m. From preserved sections, Pinkerfeld calculated a slope of approximately 74 degrees (Architectural Notes for Tell el-Kheleifeh: 16).

B. Architectural Parallels for the Plan of Glueck's Smelter/Granary

The plan of the building reflects a common architectural tradition of the Iron Age, the four-room house (Shiloh 1973: 277-85; 1970: 180-90). It was a tradition with broad geographical and chronological limits, distributed throughout Palestine from the 11th to the beginning of the sixth century B.C.E. The functional diversity of the plan was as great as its geographical and chronological range. It was frequently found in private dwellings and monumental structures alike, in cities, villages, and fortress settlements (Cohen 1979: 61-79; Aharoni 1958: 26-38; 1967a: 1-17; Shiloh 1978: 36-51).

The assignment of the Tell el-Kheleifeh structure to the four-room house tradition is suggested here with the recognition that certain aspects of its construction and design are atypical. The absence of piers partitioning the longer rectangular units may be explained as a local variation determined by the obvious preference for mudbrick, even though stone is available in the region.[4] Its unusual size, though comparable to four-room architecture at other sites such as Hazor (Yadin 1961: pls. 44-53) may be explained by its strategic location or function. It is unfortunate that the means of access to the building was not determined. There are no indications in the excavation records that there was an entrance through the southern wall of Room 7, as would be expected in the four-room architectural tradition.

The Tell el-Kheleifeh structure, nevertheless, compared favorably in size, design, and quality of construction with the central, monumental four-room buildings at Hazor, Tell el-Hesi (Bliss 1894: 91), Tell Beit Mirsim (Albright 1943: 41-47), Tell Jemmeh (Petrie 1928: 6-7), and even Tell el-Farʿah (DeVaux 1952: pl. 10) and Tell en-Naṣbeh (McCown 1947: 206-16; especially figs. 51, 52A, 52B, 53A, 53B, 54), though the latter were somewhat smaller.

Shiloh has argued, from an architectural perspective, that storage was not a primary function of the larger buildings constructed on the four-room plan (1970: 190). Although this appeared to be true at Tell el-Kheleifeh, conclusions about function are difficult. The artifact data are exceptionally sparse for this building. A clay stopper and a few dozen Negevite sherds are the only artifacts that were saved. Extant evidence, therefore, suggests that storage was not a primary function.

Shiloh suggests that the monumental four-room buildings, including those at Tell el-Kheleifeh, functioned as citadels. The conclusion is legitimate if a citadel is defined as a stronghold or fortified place for defense or refuge. The designation should not imply specific military, political, commercial, or domestic functions. The function of each structure assigned to the four-room tradition must be determined, if possible, on the basis of its own evidence. With Shiloh's refined definition, the Tell el-Kheleifeh four-room building may be designated as a citadel. Further comment on the building's function in the context of the site's fortress and fortified settlement phases is presented below.

III. THE CASEMATE WALL
(PLS. 3, 55B-58A)

A. Description

Tell el-Kheleifeh IC, as Glueck descerned and designated it, was composed of the four-room building surrounded by a casemate wall (pl. 3). As noted, it should now be understood as the site's earliest level. The space between the architectural elements was considered to be open. As is clear from the 1939 and 1940 aerial photographs, the casemate wall was excavated on the western, southern, and eastern sides of the enclosure (pls. 2, 43-45). Pinkerfeld commented on the failure to locate the northern side of the casemate enclosure: "The northern side of the quadrant does not exist at the present time. It was destroyed and blown away by the constant north wind. In consequence of this constant direction of the wind and masses of sand carried with it, the southern part of the tell is preserved much better, as it is situated in the wind shadow" (Architectural Notes for Tell el-Kheleifeh: 18-19). It appears that the northern perimeter of the casemate wall was never excavated and was, in fact, buried beneath the excavation's northern dump (pls. 42, 56B, 58A).

Pinkerfeld described the casemate square as a *Gürtel* of rooms, measuring approximately 45 m on each preserved side (Architectural Notes for Tell el-Kheleifeh: 17). Glueck first described the casemate complex as a row of industrial workshops associated with the nearby smelting installation (1938a: 10; 1939a: 10; 1940a: 4). The architecture of Period IC was thus designated an "industrial square." A number of the casemate rooms (25, 36A, 103, 107, 109, 111, and 112) yielded several installations that Glueck interpreted as "hearths" or *tabûns*. Those installations, together with associated Negevite pottery, that Glueck identified as crucibles, appeared to support his smelting hypothesis. With subsequent revision of the site's interpretation, the *Gürtel* of rooms was recognized as a casemate fortification.

The exterior of the casemate wall was constructed with offsets and insets on the three preserved sides. Each side was constructed with three offsets and two insets, the length of each was approximately 9 m. The terminal and middle salients varied in thickness between 1.05 and 1.10 m; the recesses varied between 0.80 and 0.85 m in depth.

The interior wall of the casemate rooms was approximately 0.80 m thick on each side of the enclosure. Each of the preserved casemate perimeters, however, varied considerably in terms of room dimensions and orientation of the entrances to each of the casemate units. Though poorly preserved and briefly described, the southern row of rooms formed the entryway to the casemate fortress complex, and the entrance, or gate room, was in the center of the medial offset. The entryway, approximately 2.25 m in width, was in the southeastern corner of Room 42, and the inner courtyard was reached through the northwestern corner of this room. The outer opening of this unit was later blocked. The blocking was represented on Pinkerfeld's Period IC plan (pl. 3) and constituted an element of some confusion to both the excavator and the architect. There appears to be no other entrance to the fortress compound except that on the south side. It is not possible, however, to reach firm conclusions without the plan of the northern quadrant of the casemate wall.

The southern entryway complex probably also included Room 45, which adjoined Room 42 to the east. Room 45 measured 2.40 x 2.80 m with walls approximately 1 m thick, like those of Room 42. The inner partition walls of the remaining southern casemate rooms were approximately 0.50 m thick. The means of communication between Rooms 42 and 45 is unclear in the excavation records.

Except for the entrance complex, the doorways of the remaining southern casemate rooms were consistently located in the interior corner facing the gate. The entrances were thus in the interior eastern corner for the rooms west of the gate and in the interior western corner for those east of the gate. The dimensions of the southern casemates varied considerably.

The eastern row of casemates were of roughly similar dimensions, 4.00 x 2.10 m. The door of each unit, with the exception of the southernmost, was located in the interior southwestern corner, and thus oriented toward the gate complex. The interior partitions, separating the casemate units, were not bonded into the main walls.

The room dimensions and orientation of the entrances of the western casemates were again different. This row consisted of double rooms, that is, the discrete architectural unit appears to have been two rooms with an interior partition that was not bonded into the main parallel walls. Within each architectural unit, the room entrances were in opposite corners. The rooms that composed the larger units varied between 3.25 m and 4.30 m in length with a width of 2.00 m.

In light of the differences between the eastern, western, and southern sides of the casemate fortress, any reconstruction of the northern complex of casemate rooms would be purely conjectural. The casemate units of this earliest phase continued into later levels.

B. Chronology and Geographical Distribution of the Casemate Wall

Like the four-room house plan, the casemate wall exhibited a broad chronological span, wide geographical distribution, and functional diversity (Lapp 1976: 25-42; Aharoni 1959: 35-39). Among the earliest uses of a casemate construction were those in the MB IIC period at Shechem (Dever 1974: 31-52; figs. 2 and 4), Hazor (Yadin 1972: 61; fig. 13),[5] and Taʿanach (Lapp 1969: 17-22; figs. 10-11). Casemates were plentiful in the early Iron Age, as illustrated by Tell Beit Mirsim (Albright 1943: 12-14, 37; pls. 13-16), Beth Shemesh (Grant and Wright 1939: 23-26; fig. 1), Megiddo (Yadin 1970), Hazor (Yadin 1972: 135-40; 147-60; figs. 27; 31-37, 39, 40), and Gezer (Dever et al. 1970: 62-63). Of special interest, for reasons detailed below, are the casemate fortress fortifications found in the central Negev (Cohen 1979: 61-79).

Iron II casemates are found at numerous sites, including Samaria (Crowfoot et al. 1942: 93-107), Tell el-Qudeirat (Dothan 1965: 134-51; 1977: 697-98; Cohen 1981b: 93-107), Ramat Raḥel (Aharoni 1962a: 10-12, 59-60; figs. 10, 23), Tell el-Ful (P. Lapp 1965: 2-10; N. Lapp 1976: 36-41), Tel Mevorakh (Stern 1973: 256; 1974: 267), Khirbet el-Qom (Holladay 1971: 176), and Tel Beersheba (Aharoni 1972: 116-17; 1974a: 9-12).

Though published details are lacking, a casemate construction was uncovered at Tell Jemmeh (Van Beek 1972: 246; 1974: 139), a site of considerable interest for Tell el-Kheleifeh because there, too, were considerable Assyrian pottery and architecture. The fortification dated to the Neo-Assyrian period and continued in use until the late seventh century B.C.E. The contemporary casemate city wall excavated at Buseirah in southern Jordan should be mentioned in the same context (Bennett 1973a:1-11; 1974b: 73-76; 1974a: 1-24; 1975: 1-19; 1977: 1-10).

The casemate wall at Tell el-Kheleifeh may thus be viewed as part of an architectural tradition with a broad geographical and chronological distribution. The tradition was not unique to any cultural entity. Studied as an isolated architectural phenomenon, therefore, the casemate wall permits virtually no refinement for date or cultural affinities. It was a building tradition shared by cultures of the late second and first millennia B.C.E. and even into Roman times, as evidenced at Masada.

IV. THE OFFSETS/INSETS WALL AND ADJOINING FOUR-CHAMBERED GATE-WAY
(PLS. 1, 2, 4-6, 8, 63B-66B)

A. Description

After the destruction of the casemate fortress, the plan of Tell el-Kheleifeh was radically changed (pl. 4). The fortress was replaced by a significantly larger settlement with an offsets/insets wall and a four-chambered gateway (pls. 8, 58B, 62A-66B), features that constituted the site's fortifications throughout its later history. A large section of the earlier casemate fortress was retained, but now constituted an inner enclosure or courtyard in the northwest quadrant of the new offsets/insets plan. The northern and western perimeters of the earlier casemate wall were destroyed together with a portion of the northern wall of the four-room building.

The fortifications of this settlement were made up of two elements: a poorly preserved outer fortification wall, described by Pinkerfeld as "a thin low outside wall, whose purpose was to delay the assailant a little before he could reach the main walls" (Architectural Notes for Tell el-Kheleifeh: 26), and the offsets/insets wall with corner towers and four-chambered gateway.

The Outer Fortification Element (pls. 2, 4, 5, 62A). A 47 m length of the outer fortification element was preserved in the southeast corner of the site (square 0:23; pl. 4). Another section was preserved on the western side of the settlement, some 4 m beyond the offsets/insets wall (squares F:11, G:9, 10; pl. 4). The western segment represented a reuse of the exterior wall of the earlier casemate fortification. The two phases could be distinguished from the brick dimensions. The casemate bricks were 0.14 m thick, whereas those of the outer fortification were only 0.11 m thick. On the basis of those two sections, Pinkerfeld reconstructed the outer fortification element around the entire compound, except for the area fronting the four-chambered gateway. Its reconstructed dimensions were 70.5 m (S) x 72 m (E) x 69 m (N) x 76 m (W). The passage between the outer element and the main offsets/insets fortification was ca. 2.50-3.00 m.

The Offsets/Insets Wall (pls. 58B, 62A-63A, 67B, 68A). The main defensive element of the new settlement was a solid wall which, like the exterior of the earlier casemate wall, was characterized by salients and recesses. Each side was constructed with three offsets and two insets. The length of each varied between 9 and 12 m. The salients were gentle, protruding little more than 0.37 m. At the point of offset the width of the wall was 2.60-3.10 m; the inset thickness was 2.20-2.60 m. The dimensions of this solid wall measured 56 m

(N) x 59 m (E) x 59 m (S) x 63 m (W). A sloping revetment ca. 1.7 m thick was found in the southeast corner and reconstructed with salients and recesses around the perimeter of fortification. The total thickness of the wall, on the basis of reconstruction, varied between 3.90 and 4.80 m.

The Four-Chambered Gateway (pls. 8 and 63B-66B). The gate complex, constructed in the southern perimeter of the offsets/insets wall, was aligned on a north-south axis with the gateway (Room 42) of the earlier casemate fortress. The entrance was, therefore, on the southwestern side of the settlement. The room complex was constructed on the interior of the line of fortification. In the earliest phase of construction, the gate consisted of four rooms and three sets of "piers" (pl. 8). The plan is commonly known as a four-chambered gate.

The dimensions of the guardrooms varied: Room 100A was 4.00 x 2.30 x 4.75 x 2.30 m, Room 100B was 3.50 x 2.30 x 3.60 x 2.00 m, Room 100C was 3.50 x 2.20 x 3.75 x 2.50 m, and Room 100D was 3.30 x 2.00 x 3.40 x 2.00 m. The passageway between the southernmost of the three sets of piers was 1.70 m wide; between the middle piers it was 3.20 m wide and between the innermost set it was 3.30 m wide.

The excavators were puzzled by contiguous architecture on the eastern side. Pinkerfeld provided the following description and interpretation:

> Two narrow and oblong rooms, 86 and 88, and two very small shafts of about 1 m square, 87 and 89, were added to the proper gate-building on the east. Their purpose is not quite clear. Perhaps these were granaries accessible from the room of the whole building, or perhaps they provided, in case the first gate fell to the enemy, a path for retreat sideways for the garrison of the first guardroom, while the second gate remained closed. This could be repeated afterwards once more in the second guardroom (Architectural Notes for Tell el-Kheleifeh: 25).

Another possible interpretation is that the construction was the foundation for a stairway leading to the roof.

For reasons that are not readily apparent, both Glueck and Pinkerfeld maintained that the earliest offsets/insets fort (Period II) was devoid of architecture within the two courtyards created by the solid and casemate walls. According to Glueck, Periods III-IVB were characterized by continued building within those enclosures. It is likely, however, that the courtyards were built up, to some degree, from the earliest construction of the offsets/insets fortification. In other words, it was a fortified settlement from the beginning.

B. Comparative Architecture

The Four-Chambered Gate and Offsets/Insets Wall. Several parallels to the four-chambered gate and adjoining offsets/insets wall were known at the time of Glueck's excavations (Glueck 1939a: 14-16). Of special interest to Glueck was the gateway of similar plan excavated by Guy at Megiddo (Stratum IV) and assigned to Solomon (Lamon and Shipton 1939: fig. 86). When Glueck reported the results of the 1939 season at Tell el-Kheleifeh, he commented on the chronology of the four-chambered gate and its stratigraphic context:

> Guy's identification of the builder of Stratum IV at Megiddo with Solomon has long been generally accepted. We have already seen above that Ezion-geber I, like Stratum IV at Megiddo, was planned in advance, and built with considerable architectural and engineering skill at one time as an integrated whole. This fact, in addition to other independent archaeological evidence, makes it seem probable that the builder of Ezion-geber I was none other than the builder of Stratum IV at Megiddo and of numerous other sites throughout the length and breadth of Palestine, namely King Solomon (1939a: 15, 16).

The stratigraphy and chronology of the "Guy gate," Loud's Stratum IIIB, have been addressed by Yadin (1970: 84-89; see also 1966: 62-68; 1972: 147-64; 1973: 330), who assigned the four-chambered gate and raised level of the adjoining offsets/insets wall to Stratum IVA and who dated them to the time of Ahab in the ninth century B.C.E. Yadin's conclusions on the stratification and chronology of tenth-ninth century Megiddo have been the subject of considerable controversy (see Aharoni 1971a: 53-57; 1971b: 302-11; 1974b: 13-16; Ussishkin 1966a: 174-86; 1980: 1-18; Yadin 1973: 330). Although Ussishkin did not address specifically the chronology of the four-chambered gate, he would date this structure considerably later (1980: 1-18).

There are other parallels. Aharoni excavated two superimposed gates of four-chambered design at Tel Beersheba (Aharoni 1972: 119-22; 1973: 13-17). The earliest adjoined a casemate wall (Strata V-IV, tenth-early ninth centuries B.C.E.); the latter was constructed with an offsets/insets wall (Strata III-II, ninth-eighth centuries B.C.E.). The earlier gate was "broader and more massive and equipped with a projecting tower about 5-6 m broad" (Aharoni 1972: 119). The Strata III-II gate was 17 m wide and 14 m long with an entryway 4.20 m wide. Although in a more complex architectural context, a gate of the four-chambered plan has been uncovered at Tel Dan (Biran 1975: 276, 213-21; 1980: 168-82). This gateway was the inner element of the city's entrance complex, which also included a stone-paved square within massive outer walls. The main inner gate measured 29.5 by 17.8 m. Biran dated the complex from the end of the tenth to the beginning of the ninth century B.C.E. Aharoni reconstructed a four-chambered gate complex in the northeastern corner of the Stratum XI citadel at Tel ʿArad (1975b: 6-7 plan; see now Herzog et al. 1984: 6-8, fig. 6). According to the excavator, the fortification of the settlement was casemate in plan.

Although the offsets/insets wall was widespread in the early Iron II (Yadin 1972: 165-66, 183; Yadin et al. 1961: pl. 84: 3; Aharoni 1972: 116-17; 1973: 9), its chronological range, like that of the casemate wall, was too broad to provide significant dating refinement for Tell el-Kheleifeh's fortified settlement phase. The same may be true of the four-chambered gate plan found throughout the Iron Age, as illustrated by the examples from Megiddo IVA, Tel Beersheba V-IV (and also III-II), Tel Dan, and Tel ʿArad XI, although the last was largely reconstructed. It must be acknowledged that the examples varied significantly in size, construction techniques, masonry styles, architectural context, and adjoining fortifications. As detailed below, however, the plan of the Tel ʿArad offsets/insets settlements (Stratum X-VIII) provides the best parallel to the plan of Tell el-Kheleifeh's fortified settlement.

The Transition From a Casemate to Offsets/Insets Fortification. As we have seen, the casemate system of fortification in the Levant was found as early as the MB IIC and continued into the Roman period. The casemate wall has become for some, however, a hallmark of Solomon's defensive systems. That association is largely the product of Yadin's interpretation of the stratigraphy and architecture of tenth/ninth century Megiddo in relation to Hazor and Gezer of the same periods (for studies pertinent to Gezer, see Dever 1986: 9-34; 1982a: 19-34; 1982b; Dever et al. 1970; Dever et al. 1974; Finkelstein 1981: 136-45; Kempinski 1972: 181-86; 1976: 210-14; Kenyon 1976: 55-58; Ussishkin 1966: 174-86; 1980: 1-18; Zertal 1981: 222-28). The sequence of fortifications at Hazor and Megiddo has further suggested to some, that as a general development, the solid offsets/insets wall was the successor to the "Solomonic" casemate system. Some scholars, therefore, view the transition from casemate to solid offsets/insets construction as chronologically significant. If correct, that premise could be important for the study of Tell el-Kheleifeh because the transition between the site's two major architectural phases was marked by this change in fortification styles.

Yadin maintained that the casemate system of fortification was replaced during the reign of Rehoboam by a more formidable defensive element, the solid wall with salients and recesses (1963: 289). Thereafter, he contended, casemate walls were no longer utilized for

external fortifications but only for inner citadels or isolated fortresses whose function was primarily dwelling or storage.

One of the principal critics of that view and of Yadin's stratification of tenth/ninth century Megiddo was Aharoni (1971b: 302-11; 1982: 198-200). He maintained that the two fortification styles were in use simultaneously during the entire monarchical period and that neither enjoyed absolute preference over the other (1982: 198-200). It appears that Aharoni's observations on the sequence and significance of the casemate and offsets/insets fortification styles are correct. Although the succession may be regarded as a general development, there were numerous exceptions, such as the structures at Samaria (Kenyon 1979: 258-65), Tel Beersheba (Aharoni 1973: 34-36), Khirbet Gharra (Aharoni 1958: 36-38), Tell el-Qudeirat (Cohen 1981b: 93-104), Tel ʿArad (Aharoni 1967: 244-46), and Tell el-Ful (Lapp 1976: 36-41).

In summary, the study of Iron Age fortification systems does not provide chronological refinement for the traditions in evidence at Tell el-Kheleifeh. In fact, many of the examples of comparative architecture predated the site's pottery horizons by more than a century. This, of course, assumes that the extant pottery repertoire accurately reflects the site's chronology and that the full range of the site's occupational history has been determined.

V. THE ARCHITECTURAL PLAN OF TELL EL-KHELEIFEH

A. Introduction

The site plans of Tell el-Kheleifeh, during the casemate (pl. 3) and offsets/insets (pls. 2 and 4-6) phases, appear to be related to two well documented Iron Age architectural traditions from the region of the central Negev southward to the site of Tell el-Qudeirat: the so-called "casemate fortresses" of the central Negev and the fortified settlements as represented by Tel ʿArad, Ḥorvat ʿUza, and Tell el-Qudeirat. Although both are commonly designated by the same terms ("fort" or "fortress"), a distinction is warranted by the diversity in chronology, location, size, quality of construction, and settlement plan exhibited by the numerous examples in each category. The preferred designation here is "fortress" for the first tradition and "fortified settlement" or "offsets/insets settlement" for the second. Tell el-Kheleifeh's two main Iron Age architectural phases are compared here to the Negev fortresses and the fortified settlements to document the need for that distinction.

A typical fortress of the central Negev was a casemate wall enclosing an open courtyard (Cohen 1979:

61-79). Nearby settlements, with buildings constructed on the four-room house plan, were common. Although most of the fortresses are known only from surveys, a significant number have been excavated recently and provide good stratigraphic, ceramic, and architectural detail. Some scholars interpreted this architectural tradition as a *limes*, a fortress network demarcating political, cultural and/or commercial boundaries. Tell el-Kheleifeh's earliest occupational phase, the case-mate fortress (pl. 3), is studied here as a part of that tradition.

Tell el-Kheleifeh's offsets/insets phase, which Glueck discerned in five occupational periods (Pinkerfeld's plans II-IVB, pls. 2 and 4-6), had closer similarities to the fortified settlements of Tel 'Arad, Tell el-Qudeirat, and Horvat 'Uza than with the Negev fortress plan. The distinction between the fortress and the fortified settlements is based on the broader chronological range of the latter, their strategic location, the size and quality of their construction, and most important, the inclusion of public and domestic architecture within the perimeters of fortification.

A brief survey of the two architectural traditions illustrates the need for the distinction and provides a basis for comparison with the two major architectural phases of Tell el-Kheleifeh.

B. The Negev Fortress Tradition of Architecture

The Negev Fortresses in Recent Archaeological Research. The extensive network of Iron Age fortresses in the region of the central Negev has been well documented by recent surveys and excavations (Aharoni 1958a: 26-38; 1958b: 231-68; 1960: 97-111; 1963: 54-73; 1964d: 426-37; 1967a: 1-17; 1979b: 209-25; Cohen 1966a: 30-31; 1966b: 23-25; 1970: 6-24; 1971: 29-30; 1972a: 37; 1972b: 39-40; 1975: 171-72; 1976a: 34-50; 1976b: 53-54; 1977a: 171; 1977b: 170-71; 1979a: 61-79; Cohen and Meshel 1970: 27; 1971: 28-29; 1972: 37; Eitam 1980: 56-57; Evenari 1958: 231-68; Finkelstein 1984: 189-208; Herzog 1983: 41-59; 1984: 70-87; Glueck 1956: 17-35; 1957: 11-25; 1959a: 2-13; 1959b: 82-97; 1961: 11-18; Meshel 1973: 39-40; 1974: 273-74; 1975b: 30; 1977: 110-35; 1979a: 3-28; 1980: 70-81; Rothenberg 1967: 67-68, 86-101). The first fortresses were discovered in 1914 by Woolley and Lawrence, who designated them as military police stations constructed to ensure safe passage along the caravan routes (Woolley and Lawrence 1914-1915: 27-28, 40-43, 64-67). The surveys of Glueck and Aharoni provided a picture not of random structures but of a network of fortresses and settlements, the latter primarily agricultural, which could be classified according to plan, function, and chronology. Though there was significant variation in architectural detail, a casemate

wall surrounding a courtyard area was common to each of the fortresses. While Aharoni used the designations "fort" and "fortress" interchangeably, he distinguished four principal types (1967a: 3):

(1) forts with towers (Tell el-Qudeirat, Horvat 'Uza and Tel 'Arad);
(2) square forts without towers (Nahal Raviv, Qasr el-Ruheibeh, Beer Hafir, Har Boqer and a fort on the ridge north of Tell el-Qudeirat);
(3) oblong and round forts (Giv'at Refed, Nahal Le'ana and Yotvata);
(4) forts surrounded by polygonal enceintes (the fort above En-gedi and one at Har Hesron).

Aharoni first assigned those structures to the period between the tenth and seventh centuries B.C.E. and associated them with the Negev trade and communication network of the kingdoms of Israel and Judah (1967a: 11-13). His later revision associated dating of the fortress network with the earliest stages of Israelite occupation (Aharoni 1982: 169-72).

Although it is necessary to revise Aharoni's understanding of the central Negev fortress system and the chronology of associated ceramics, certain of his insights should be emphasized. He recognized that Tell el-Kheleifeh's two major architectural phases (casemate and offsets/insets) had affinities in plan and construction with the fortresses of the central Negev and the larger fortified settlements of Tel 'Arad, Tell el-Qudeirat, and Horvat 'Uza. Although Aharoni did not reflect the distinction in his nomenclature, he clearly differentiated between fortresses and fortified settlements.

Recent surveys and excavations have provided considerable refinement in our understanding of the architecture, pottery horizons, chronology, and geographical distribution of these fortresses. Cohen (1979: 63) suggested the following revision of Aharoni's classification:

(1) roughly oval fortresses, as illustrated by 'Ain Qudeis, 'Atar Haro'a, Horvat Haluqim, Horvat Rahba, Horvat Ketef Shivta, Nahal Horsha, and Nahal Sarpad;
(2) rectangular fortresses, including Mesad Refed, Mesad Hatira, Horvat Har Boqer, Horvat Ramat Boqer, Nahal Nafha, and Mesad Har Sa'ad;
(3) square fortresses, represented by Horvat Mesora, Horvat Ritma, Nahal Raviv, and a small fortress near 'Atar Haro'a;
(4) fortresses with towers, as illustrated by Tell el-Qudeirat and Horvat 'Uza.

Cohen, like Aharoni, distinguished between the fortified settlements of Tell el-Qudeirat (middle and upper phases) and Ḥorvat ʿUza and the casemate fortresses. His work at Tell el-Qudeirat, in fact, confirmed that the site's earliest architectural phase belonged to the category of oval fortresses (1981b: 32). Again, however, the differentiation in classification is not reflected in nomenclature. Unlike Aharoni, Cohen did not discuss Tel ʿArad in the context of those architectural traditions. Cohen commented on the date and function of the early fortress network:

> In the author's opinion, the wheel-made pottery found in the excavations and surveys of the first three fortress types clearly belongs to the 10th-century B.C. assemblage. Therefore, in all probability the fortresses were constructed during the reign of king Solomon, a vigorous and powerful ruler, whose numerous public works included the fortification of cities, the construction of store-houses, and the founding of distant trading posts. His reign was undoubtedly a period of expansion and royal planning, and the establishment of a fortress and settlement network in the Negev would have been of vital importance for the strengthening of his kingdom's southern border region. Accordingly, these fortresses served not only to guard the roads crossing the Central Negev, as suggested by Glueck and Aharoni, but also to form a strong defensive line along the southern boundary (1979: 77).

Cohen assigned the destruction of the fortress system to the campaign of Sheshonk I (biblical Shishak) into Palestine and he accepted Mazar's proposal (1957: 57-66) that some of the fortresses were named on Sheshonk's victory stele erected at Karnak.

Meshel offered another explanation for the chronology and historical background of the Negev structures (1977: 110-35; 1979: 4-28). He preferred to classify the fortresses according to size and topographical conformity (1979: 17). By assigning the wheelmade pottery to the 11th–10th centuries B.C.E., Meshel associated the architectural tradition with "one of the kings who defeated the Edomites and Amelekites." Saul or David would appear to be the likely candidates. The fortresses would thus represent the early phases of desert conquest and a "show of force" by the central authority against the local inhabitants (1977: 133). Meshel and Cohen agreed however, on the interpretation of the structures as fortresses.

Some two decades ago, Rothenberg suggested that the "fortresses" were actually settlements of the native desert inhabitants, mainly Amalekites, who settled them as early as the 13th century B.C.E. (1967: 88-97). That chronology is inconsistent, of course, with that suggested by the associated wheelmade repertoire.

The range of associated pottery types, however, has only come to light subsequent to Rothenberg's suggested chronology. Other scholars have adopted the argument that those structures were settlements and not fortresses, with the necessary refinements in chronology (Eitam 1980: 56-57; Negev 1979: 34).

Herzog rejected the basic assumption that underlies each of the above interpretations, namely, "the assumption that the Negev 'fortresses' were homogeneous in nature and that a single historical and functional interpretation can be attributed to all of them" (1983: 44). Based on comparisons between the "enclosed settlement" of Beersheba VII and the Negev "fortresses" of Ḥorvat Raḥba, Meṣad Refed, and Meṣad Ḥatira, Herzog concluded that those four sites should be dated to the same period (11th century B.C.E.) and that all should be defined as "enclosed settlements." He considered the sites to be civilian in nature and attributed their establishment to the southerly penetration of Israelite settlers. This wave of settlement was apparently the result of Philistine pressure in the Shephelah that drove the Israelite population into the arid zones to the south. Herzog provided geographical definition to the expansion (1983: 47). He distinguished between these "enclosed settlements" and the rest of the Negev "fortresses," and connected the establishment of the latter with "late geopolitical developments in the region involving royal initiative" (1983: 47).

The questions of origin and chronology were most recently addressed by I. Finkelstein (1984: 189-208). He first drew the important distinction between the Negev "fortresses" and the fortified settlements:

> Kadesh-barnea (in its final two phases), Arad Stratum VI and Ḥorvat ʿUza were, no doubt, true fortresses, built to carry out an administrative function and to defend the southern frontier of the Judean monarchy. But these differ from the other sites not only in the strength of their fortifications but in plan and interior construction as well. All those who have attempted to classify the sites have singled out these as unique, but for some reason have continued to perceive them in the same light as the other sites (1984: 193).

Based on construction, associated finds, architecture, geopolitical background, and site distribution, Finkelstein concluded that the structures represented the sedentarization of the Iron Age nomads, the impetus for which may be associated with the economic prosperity of the southern deserts in the 12th-11th centuries B.C.E. (1984: 200). Having documented the nature of this economic prosperity, Finkelstein concluded, "The desert dwellers undoubtedly participated in this intensive commerce and began to exploit the new opportunities that opened up before them, slowly lessening their dependence on pastoralism and settling in the area ecologically amenable to agriculture, namely the Negev Highlands. This process was accompanied by the absorption of typical northern elements into their material culture, such as wheel-made pottery and the four-room house" (1984: 201). The nomadic sedentarization in the Negev Highlands may have begun as early as the 12th century B.C.E., according to Finkelstein, but it reached its zenith toward the end of the 11th or early tenth century.

The Fortresses and Comparison with Tell el-Kheleifeh's Casemate Phase. The Negev fortress, as an architectural abstraction, consisted of an open courtyard surrounded by a casemate fortification. There was significant variation in the plan and size of the fortress, the size and number of casemate rooms, and the plan, position, and construction of the gateway. The architectural elements that formed the tradition, however, were consistently a casemate fortification and open courtyard. The entrance usually consisted of an open space in the line of the casemate wall. Associated architecture outside the perimeters of fortification was common, and the nearby buildings frequently exhibited the four-room house plan.

Tell el-Kheleifeh's earliest phase, the casemate fortress (pl. 3), was composed of an open courtyard surrounded by a casemate wall. Although the northern perimeter of the casemate fortification was never excavated, the plan has probably been correctly reconstructed as a square, 45 m on each side. The basic ground plan thus is comparable to the square fortresses of Naḥal Raviv, Ḥorvat Ritma, Ḥorvat Mesora, and the small fortress near ʿAtar Haroʿa.

It appears, however, that the fortress ground plan is chronologically, functionally, and typologically irrelevant in light of current data. On any reckoning, the chronology of the fortresses was too narrow to provide the refinement essential for establishing a relationship between fortress plan and date. A relationship between ground plan and function is also impossible to establish on the basis of what is presently known about the fortresses, although the problem may result from the fact that few of those structures have been excavated or published. Although they have some general validity, the classification schemes suggested by Aharoni and Cohen appear arbitrary. Rigidity in plan classification appears to be precluded by the irregular ground plans exhibited by such fortresses as Ḥorvat Ketef Shivta, Ḥorvat Raḥba, Ḥorvat Ramat Boqer, Meṣad Ḥatira, and even Ḥorvat Ḥaluqim. As suggested by those examples, topography appears to be one of the primary considerations for the plan of fortress construction.

Tell el-Kheleifeh's casemate phase may be compared with the ground plans of Naḥal Raviv, Ḥorvat Ritma, Ḥorvat Mesora, and the small fortress near ʿAtar Haroʿa. Although the Tell el-Kheleifeh fortress was significantly larger than those of similar plan, its dimensions were similar to those of other design such as ʿAin Qudeis, ʿAtar Haroʿa, Ḥorvat Raḥba, Meṣad Refed, and Meṣad Ḥatira. It is most likely that the size and quality of construction of the Tell el-Kheleifeh fortress were determined by the site's strategic location and, to some extent, the medium of construction.

A distinctive architectural element of the central Negev fortress tradition was the presence of nearby domestic architecture, often constructed on the four-room house plan. Such associated structures were seldom within the perimeters of fortification. Nearby settlements with four-room house architecture were found at the fortresses of ʿAtar Haroʿa, Ḥorvat Ḥaluqim, Ḥorvat Ramat Boqer, Ḥorvat Mesora, and Ḥorvat Ritma, for example. The absence of this architectural tradition at a number of the other settlements may be due to limited exposure. The Tell el-Kheleifeh fortress also evidenced architecture on the four-room house plan. As presented above, Glueck's smelter/granary has been assigned to that tradition. The location of the structure within the perimeters of fortification is admittedly atypical of the fortress plan.

As previously noted, the entrance to a fortress compound was generally a narrow opening that interrupted the line of casemate rooms (ʿAtar Haroʿa, Ḥorvat Ketef Shivta, Ḥorvat Har Boqer, and Ḥorvat Ramat Boqer). There was, however, some variation in design (Meṣad Ḥatira and ʿAin Qudeis), so that at Tell el-Kheleifeh, the gateway consisted of an opening through one of the southern casemate rooms (Room. 42).

The plan of Tell el-Kheleifeh's earliest occupational phase (the casemate fortress) finds good architectural parallels in the central Negev fortress plan. Tell el-Kheleifeh however, does not provide artifact data that suggest a date consistent with the Iron I date presently assigned to most of the structures in the Negev Highlands. This observation must be regarded, therefore, as a conclusion based on comparative architecture and not chronology. There remains, however, the possibility that an earlier pottery horizon remains buried within the unexcavated casemates of the northern fortification perimeter. Those problems, together with the rather scanty architectural data from contemporary sites in southern Jordan make it nearly impossible to suggest an historical, political, or cultural context or even an interpretation for the function of the casemate fortress. At most, we may speculate that it served as a caravanserai-fortress at this supremely strategic location.

C. The Fortified Settlement Tradition of Architecture

The Fortified Settlements of Tell el-Qudeirat (Kadesh-barnea), Ḥorvat ʿUza, and Tel ʿArad. Like the earlier casemate fortress phase, comparative studies are also instructive for Tell el-Kheleifeh's offsets/insets phase (Glueck's periods II-IVB; pls. 2 and 4-6). Aharoni, Cohen, Meshel, and Finkelstein have made a typological distinction between the Iron I casemate fortresses of the central Negev and those of later construction, represented by Tel ʿArad, Tell el-Qudeirat, and Ḥorvat ʿUza. Each has recognized that the fortified settlements constituted an exception to the fortress tradition in terms of geography, chronology, plan, and construction.

Tell el-Qudeirat. Following the early explorations of Woolley and Lawrence, Tell el-Qudeirat was excavated by M. Dothan, who revised and refined their study of the architecture and pottery of the main fortress phase and discerned both pre-fortress and post-fortress settlement periods (1965: 134-51). The pre-fortress period yielded only handmade pottery, which he assigned to the tenth century B.C.E. The post-fortress settlement yielded Persian material of the fifth-fourth centuries B.C.E. Dothan dated the main fortress between the ninth and seventh centuries and observed only a single building phase. The fortress had a casemate plan with eight projecting towers.

A number of unsolved problems prompted Cohen to continue excavations at the site, and he significantly refined the stratigraphy, architecture, pottery, and chronology (1981b: 93-104). Cohen discerned three fortress phases, dating between the tenth/ninth centuries and the end of the Iron Age, with scattered evidence for the Persian period. The latest fortress phase — the one studied by Woolley, Lawrence, and Dothan — was a rectangular structure (ca. 60 x 41 m) of casemate units around a courtyard. Based on epigraphic finds and wheelmade pottery, Cohen dated the settlement to the seventh-sixth centuries B.C.E. (1981b: 99-100).

The middle fortress phase had the same rectangular ground plan, but was of solid wall construction. The walls of the structure were ca. 4 m wide, dimensions reminiscent of the northern Negev settlement at Tel ʿArad. The middle fortress was also characterized by interior architecture. The wheelmade pottery found in the layer of ashes covering the beaten-earth floors dated from the eighth-seventh centuries B.C.E. (Cohen 1981b: 100).

The earliest (casemate) fortress was roughly oval in plan, although few published details are available (1981a: 32). The associated ceramic repertoire contained both wheelmade and handmade pottery.

Though the data are few, the ceramic and architectural affinities of the casemate structure suggest its assignment to the fortress tradition.

Ḥorvat ʿUza. The plan and dimensions of Ḥorvat ʿUza exhibited similarities to the latest casemate fortress at Tell el-Qudeirat (Musil 1908: 19-20; Aharoni 1958: 33-35; Cohen 1979: 74-75, fig. 11). The fort, constructed of rough-hewn limestone blocks, was rectangular in plan (ca. 53 x 41 m) and formed a casemate wall around an open courtyard. The fortification was characterized by corner and mid-wall towers, and thus was similar in plan, although smaller, to Tell el-Qudeirat. The structure was bisected into inner rectangular units by a row of casemate rooms, a feature quite atypical of the tradition. The associated ceramics dated to the eighth-sixth centuries B.C.E.

Tel ʿArad. The fortified settlements of Tel ʿArad, specifically the offsets/insets settlements of Strata X-VIII/VII (Aharoni 1981: 6-7; Herzog et al. 1984: figs. 10, 16, 21), provide good parallels to the architectural plan of Tell el-Kheleifeh's most developed offsets/insets phase.

The succession of Iron Age levels began with Stratum XII. Although the architecture was poorly preserved, Aharoni considered the fragmentary walls to have comprised a small, unfortified settlement. The Stratum XII settlement was replaced by the first in a sequence of strongly fortified citadels (Herzog et al. 1984: 6-8; fig. 6). The Stratum XI settlement was surrounded by a casemate wall that measured approximately 50 x 50 m. Similar in plan to Tell el-Qudeirat and Ḥorvat ʿUza, the fortifications included square projecting towers, one at each corner and two in between along the sides. The gate complex was located in the northeastern corner of the settlement. Aharoni reconstructed a gate plan consisting of four chambers and two towers leading into a rectangular enclosure; he largely reconstructed the plans of the four-chambered gate and the casemate fortification.

The Stratum X citadel, although of approximately the same dimensions, was rebuilt with a solid wall, 3-4 m thick (Herzog et al. 1984: 8-12; fig. 10). The fortification was constructed with gentle salients at intervals of 9 to 10 m. The slopes of the tell were strengthened by a glaçis and buttressed by a retaining wall at the lower edge of the mound. The gate complex, consisting basically of two piers, was in the eastern wall south of the Stratum XI gate. Aharoni observed the similarities between Tel ʿArad's Stratum X and the plan of Tell el-Kheleifeh's offsets/insets settlement:

It would appear that very similar innovations were introduced in the fortress at Ezion-geber, ... True, one has seen from air photographs it is most difficult to determine which of the two walls is chronologically older, but by analogy with Arad, it may be permissible to conjecture that here also the casemate wall is the earlier. In the center was placed the large administrative building, and during the course of time the entire area was filled with closely crowded rooms, although their respective phases are not easy to establish.

The new fortress was greatly expanded, especially toward the south and east, and it was now encompassed by two walls, greatly resembling those at Arad, an inner solid wall and a narrow retaining wall at the edge of the slope. Both of them are built with zigzag lines, and an earthen rampart was built up between them. The old casemate wall remained in the center of the fortress, and its rooms served as stores in addition to all of the other rooms. The gate was located close to the center of the southern side facing the sea, and it had a bipartite plan typical of that period. This obvious resemblance to Arad points to the conclusion that the two fortresses were built according to the same pattern more or less at the same time (1982: 249).

The massive offsets/insets wall was retained through Arad X-VII, and the subsequent fortifications had the appearance of a casemate plan. Aharoni's comments on the plan of the settlement's interior architecture are important for the study of Tell el-Kheleifeh's offsets/insets phase:

The plan of the citadel within the walls underwent few changes during the entire period of its existence, although it was rebuilt six times. The citadel had an open courtyard, surrounded on three sides by various buildings, among them a sanctuary. A long alley led from the gate to the courtyard, past the sanctuary on the right and a storehouse on the left. On the west side of the courtyard were mainly workshops with various installations for distilling perfume, metal working, and perhaps other crafts as well. The main living quarters in the southern part of the citadel were divided into about seven units (Amiran and Aharoni 1967: 21).

Aharoni's stratification and chronology of the "citadel" have been subjects of considerable controversy. Aharoni himself expressed several areas of uncertainty, such as the character of Strata VII and VI fortifications, the stratum to which the construction of the northern gateway should be assigned, and numerous questions concerning the construction, phasing, and function of the cult place. Questions on stratification and chronology have been raised on the basis of the pottery (Zimhoni 1985: 85-86; Mazar and Netzer 1986: 87-91), masonry styles (Yadin 1965: 180), and the paleography of the inscriptions (Cross 1979b: 75-78).

Ussishkin addressed a number of problems related to the chronology of the cult place (1988: 144-50, 153-54). The studies clearly indicate the need for a revision in Aharoni's suggested chronology for Strata X-VIII, the levels most important for the study of Tell el-Kheleifeh's fortified settlement phase. Such revision would date the settlements later than Aharoni suggested, namely, from the eighth century and later with abundant documentation for the seventh-early sixth centuries B.C.E.

Comparisons with Tell el-Kheleifeh's Offsets/Insets Phase. Unlike the fortresses of the central Negev, Tell el-Qudeirat (middle and upper phases) and Tel 'Arad (Strata XI-VII) were settlements proper, evidencing architecture within the fortification perimeters. That feature constitutes a fundamental criterion for distinguishing the two architectural traditions. Tell el-Kheleifeh's offsets/insets phase, reconstructed with interior architecture from the time of earliest construction, should be assigned to the fortified settlement tradition.

The similarities between the architectural plans of Tel 'Arad's Strata X-VIII settlements and Tell el-Kheleifeh's most developed offsets/insets phase are readily apparent. They include an element of monumental architecture in the northwest corner (although dissimilar in function), a main north-south street on the settlement's eastern side, inner-wall structures of similar plan and function, a gateway of the four-chambered plan, and the offsets/insets fortification that created similar dimensions for each of the settlements. The offsets/insets settlements of 'Arad Strata X-VIII provide good architectural parallels to the similarly fortified settlement at Tell el-Kheleifeh.

VI. SUMMARY

Tell el-Kheleifeh was occupied in two major architectural phases: the casemate fortress and the fortified settlement. It is not possible to comment on the architectural character of subsequent occupation because the remains are extremely fragmentary, although pottery and epigraphic data indicate occupation as late as the fifth to early fourth century B.C.E. Further, the excavation methodology and recording system have not preserved the data that would allow phasing within either the casemate fortress or the fortified settlement to be reconstructed.

The earliest level, the casemate fortress, consisted of a monumental four-room building surrounded by a casemate wall. There was no other architecture within the enclosure walls. As detailed above, the date of the casemate fortress cannot be determined from the artifact evidence, nor do studies in comparative architecture help. Although the ceramic indications of chronology are lacking, a casemate wall surrounding an open courtyard with associated four-room architecture combines the elements that define the central Negev fortress tradition of the early Iron Age. Examples of the latter may be described as garrisons or stations, and the same designation may be used for the earliest level at Tell el-Kheleifeh. Settlements were associated often with those structures but were consistently located outside the perimeters of fortification. Buildings frequently were constructed on the four-room plan. The similarities between Tell el-Kheleifeh's casemate fortress and the fortresses of the central Negev are striking. As emphasized, this conclusion is based on comparative architecture and not chronology.

The architectural character of Tell el-Kheleifeh changed radically with the construction of a new fortification perimeter on the offsets/insets plan. The site was now a fortified settlement similar to Tel 'Arad X–VIII and the later levels of Tell el-Qudeirat. From the earliest construction of the offsets/insets settlement, the interior spaces were, to some extent, filled with architecture. Apart from a few selected and tantalizing glimpses (see pls. 63B–66B, 68B, 70A–71B, 72B), it is not possible to determine the progression or phasing of construction within the new fortifications. It appears that the open spaces of the earlier casemate fortress, those areas between the four-room building and the casemate walls, were also built up when the new fortified settlement was constructed. The earlier fortress was now incorporated into the new settlement plan, although with considerable modification. As detailed in the following chapter, the offsets/insets settlement dated between the eighth and the early sixth century B.C.E., a chronology consistent with the similarly fortified settlements of Tel 'Arad Strata X–VIII and the later levels of Tell el-Qudeirat. With the demise of the late Iron Age settlement in the early sixth century B.C.E., no further comment on Tell el-Kheleifeh

architecture is possible. The story of subsequent occupation must be told through a handful of inscriptions and potsherds.

NOTES

[1]The structure is hereafter assigned to the architectural tradition of the "four-room" building (Shiloh 1970: 180–90), although some might prefer to assign it to the so-called "tripartite pillared plan."

[2]With the exception of an occasional lintel stone, Tell el-Kheleifeh is built of mudbrick (Glueck 1940f: 51-55).

[3]The photographic archives abound with images of such installations widely scattered over the site.

[4]Nearly 30 vertical wooden posts were uncovered during excavations. They were located primarily in the center and in the southeast corner of the mound. They were generally round palm trunks 0.15 to 0.25 m in diameter. A few were rectangular in section. Several of the posts stood on flat stones that functioned as bases. Pinkerfeld theorized that the posts served as supports to strengthen damaged ceilings. Although a number of the vertical beams were located in the center of rooms, as in Rooms 60 and 70, the available data preclude reconstruction of a plan. It is likely, however, that the vertical posts are not comparable to the stone pillars that frequently characterized four-room construction. With the exception of the central edifice of the casemate fortress, the four-room house arrangement of architectural units is not in evidence at Tell el-Kheleifeh.

[5]There is some question whether it is legitimate to interpret the architecture to the north of the Area K (Stratum 3) gate as a casemate wall. The fragmentary nature of the walls and the lack of similar architecture to the south of the gate suggest that the three units may have been components of the gate complex.

Chapter Five

The Pottery

I. THE HANDMADE POTTERY OF TELL EL-KHELEIFEH

A. The Discovery of Negevite Ware

The largest pottery corpus produced in the 1938-1940 excavations and in the 1980 survey was Negevite ware. At the time of Glueck's excavations, this hand-made tradition of pottery was largely unknown. Woolley and Lawrence had observed scattered sherds at the fortresses of Bir Birein and Kadesh-barnea and described them as "fragments of rough hand-made wares, thin-walled, of gritty clay burnt very hard in an open hearth" (Woolley and Lawrence 1914-1915: 43-67).

The pottery was rediscovered by Glueck at Tell el-Kheleifeh, who described it as "crude, handmade, friable, smoke-blackened pots, many of which were built up on a mat, and most of which have various simple types of horn or ledge-handles, or combinations of both" (Glueck 1938a: 14; 1940a: 17-18). On the problems of dating and the uniqueness of this pottery tradition, Glueck wrote: "It was difficult to believe at first, when numerous ledge-handles appeared in the excavations, that Tell el-Kheleifeh was not an Early Bronze Age site. When, however, after a comparatively large number of rooms had been opened up, and in each one of them ledge-handles had been found together with other pottery which could only be Early Iron Age, we were forced to the conclusion that the peculiar ledge-handles of Tell el-Kheleifeh belonged to a type of Early Iron Age pottery hitherto unknown in Palestine and Transjordan" (1938a: 14).

He dated the ware by associated wheelmade forms and assigned the tradition to the tenth century B.C.E. The Solomonic dating of the site's earliest occupational level was based, in part, on this pottery. Its importance for Glueck is reflected in the unfortunate fact that only Negevite sherds were saved as diagnostic for the dating of the four-room building throughout

its occupational history. It is clear, however, that wheelmade pottery was discovered in this structure. Although he provided no drawings, photographs, or technical descriptions, Glueck noted the presence of wheelmade forms in his field diaries and dictated notes.

The geographical distribution of Negevite pottery broadened with excavations and surveys in the region of the central Negev and in the Timna-Eilat area. Aharoni, for example, discovered it in a number of the Ramat Maṭred structures and assigned the tradition to the seminomadic populations of the central Negev:

This pottery was no doubt made locally by the most primitive methods, i.e. on a mat and with very bad firing. It may be conjectured that these vessels were the work of nomadic potters, who, being constantly on the move from settlement to settlement in the Negev and 'Aravah, could not make use of the more highly developed instruments of their craft, such as the potter's wheel and a permanent clay oven. These simple and cheap utensils largely satisfied the daily needs of the local population, especially as cooking pots. At the same time, a certain amount of the usual pottery of the period was imported from further north (1960: 100-101; cf. Evenari et al. 1958: 240, 243-44).

Discussing the network of forts in the Negev highlands down to the vicinity of Tell el-Qudeirat, Aharoni commented:

The overwhelming majority of the sherds found in them are not later than the eleventh or the beginning of the tenth century. Especially prominent is a primitive type of local "Negeb-ware," pots with straight sides made by hand and very uniformly fired, having flat bases which usually show cloth imprints. It would seem that this Negeb ware was made on the spot by nomadic potters who had only the most primitive of portable implements. It is widespread only in the southern Negeb from the Gulf of Elath and Kadesh-barnea to the vicinity of Yeroham in the north. From the Timna excavations it is clear that the ware has its beginning in the thirteenth-twelfth centuries and it is doubtful whether it was used after the tenth (1982: 169).

He acknowledged the possibility, however, of an earlier and later range for this tradition (1962b: 66-67).

In light of Aharoni's conclusions, Glueck revised his understanding of the function of this pottery and attributed it to the nomadic and seminomadic dwellers of the Negev, specifically the "Kenites, Rechabites, Yerahmeelites and related inhabitants of Sinai, the Negev, the Wadi Arabah and northwestern Arabia" (1971a: 46).

Recent surveys and excavations have significantly refined the chronology and distribution of Negevite pottery. It has been found at Timna, though in relatively small quantities of mostly body sherds (Rothenberg 1988: fig. 14:1-9). Some base fragments were recovered with textile impressions (Rothenberg 1988: 224-32). Rothenberg distinguishes between two classes of handmade pottery at Timna: the Negevite ware which he prefers to label "rough hand-made pottery" in light of its geographical distribution beyond the regions of the Negev, and another handmade tradition which is different in form and fabric from the Negevite pottery (1988: 94-95; 108). He dates the Negevite pottery of Timna earlier than Aharoni suggests, to the 13th century B.C.E. and perhaps even earlier, and suggests that the pottery represented a local, non-Israelite tradition that should be identified with the first settlements in the Negev mountains of the biblical Amalekites (1988: 16, n. 35). Analyzing the Timna ceramic repertoire, he writes:

> About 10% of the pottery found in the temple was of the primitive hand-made Negev ware, containing as temper fragments of slag or of "normal" pottery, and it seems to have been locally made. The makers of this pottery, who may have been Amalekite mining workers recruited in the Amalekite settlements of the Central Negev Mountains, also imitated some vessels of the "normal" wheel-made pottery used in Timna, but continued to use the same clay and slag temper whilst making their copies by hand. Also found were fragments of a primitive votive altar made of the same ware, with a snake crawling along its rim. Another new type of Negev ware was a small juglet with holes drilled through its bottom, which served perhaps as a strainer (1972: 153-54; Cf. Cohen 1981b: 102).

An early date has also been suggested by the hand-made vessel from Stratum II at Tel Masos, which

Kempinski dated to 1200/1150-1050 B.C.E. (Aharoni et al. 1974: 202, pl. 22A).

Negevite pottery is found today at numerous Iron Age sites, belonging to both the fortress and fortified settlement traditions, including the following: Ḥorvat Ḥaluqim (Cohen 1976a: 34-50), ʿAtar Haroʿa (Cohen 1970: 6–24), Ḥorvat Ritma (Meshel 1977: 110-35), Tell el-Qudeirat (Cohen 1981b: 93-104), Ḥorvat Ketef Shivta, Ḥorvat Raḥba, Naḥal Sarpad, Meṣad Refed, Meṣad Ḥatira, Ḥorvat Har Boqer, Ḥorvat Ramat Boqer, Naḥal Nafḥa, and Ḥorvat Mesora. For Meshel and Cohen on the chronology of Negevite pottery, see discussion under "The Negev Fortresses in Recent Archaeological Research" above (pp. 29-31). Despite the designation Negevite, this pottery has been found at the Jordanian site of Buseirah (Bennett 1975: fig. 67:8, 12) and at an Edomite mountain stronghold north of Petra called Baʿja (Lindner and Farajat 1987: fig. 4:8).

B. The Pottery of Tell el-Kheleifeh and Tell el-Qudeirat (Kadesh-barnea)

From the perspectives of architecture and pottery types, the site of Tell el-Qudeirat is of special interest for the study of Tell el-Kheleifeh. As we have seen, the site similarly documents the transition from casemate fortress to fortified settlement. The two sites also share pronounced similarities in pottery types and styles. Although the fabrics are notably different, the pottery of Tell el-Qudeirat, both wheel and handmade forms, offers closer parallels to Tell el-Kheleifeh than any other site. This is especially true for the Negevite tradition, which is attested for every fortress phase (Cohen 1981b: 101). Tell el-Qudeirat has, in fact, produced greater quantities of Negevite pottery than any other site.

M. Dothan excavated this pottery at Tell el-Qudeirat in his pre-fortress phase and dated it to the tenth or early ninth century B.C.E. in agreement with Glueck and Aharoni (Dothan 1965: 139). Cohen's excavations have considerably refined the site's architectural phases and associated pottery. His comments on the Negevite wares are noteworthy:

> Negev ware cannot be used for chronological purposes but rather has to be dated itself on the basis of the wheel-made pottery found together with it...B. Rothenberg's research in the Timna-Eilat area has shown that its origins may be several centuries earlier and now, since the excavations at Kadesh-barnea, it is clear that it remained in use until the end of the Iron Age. Within this rather long time span, Negev ware appears to have undergone some changes. In the earlier levels (10th century B.C.E.) at Kadesh-barnea and elsewhere, virtually the only forms are cooking-pots

and hole-mouth jars. By the time of the middle fortress (8th-7th centuries B.C.E.), however, a wide variety of forms were in use, many of them quite clearly modelled on contemporary wheel-made types. The Negev vessels found in this level at Kadesh-barnea include the common cooking-pots and hole-mouth jars, but also bowls and cups of different sizes (with and without handles) and a small chalice. The workmanship remains characteristically crude, but decorative indentation is sometimes added around the rim. As previously noted, these handmade vessels predominate among the pottery finds of the earlier two fortresses, but their representation declines, in proportion to the wheel-made ware, in the final fortress. Nevertheless, this upper level yields some interesting types, such as three oil-lamps and an incense-burner. The writer agrees that Negev ware properly should be associated with the wandering desert tribes and would further suggest that it be connected specifically with the Kenites, particularly in view of the fact that, in the Old Testament, a close relationship is posited between them and the Israelites (1981b: 102-103).

Cohen's association of Negevite pottery with the biblical Kenites, as suggested earlier by Glueck, is not demonstrable. Even the link with "wandering desert tribes" is tenuous. There is insufficient data on the social interaction or geographical proximity between Kenites and Israelites to support this ethnic identification of a ceramic tradition.

Few details have been published to date regarding a typology of Negevite pottery at Tell el-Qudeirat. Due to its fortress phasing and associated wheelmade assemblages, however, Tell el-Qudeirat is one of the few sites that offer the potential of establishing a general typological sequence of Negevite wares. Until such studies are available, however, this handmade pottery will remain a tradition with a chronology that embraced the 13th-sixth centuries B.C.E. and perhaps even later.

Tell el-Kheleifeh boasts the same range of Negevite types that are represented at Tell el-Qudeirat. The Tell el-Kheleifeh repertoire is most closely paralleled, however, by the range of types presented in the middle and latest fortress phases (eighth-sixth centuries B.C.E.). Unfortunately, only a handful of pieces from the site have yet been published. The same fact applies to the many sites that have produced this tradition of pottery. The following presentation of the Tell el-Kheleifeh assemblage includes comments on the unpublished Tell el-Qudeirat pottery and references to the published examples of this tradition.

C. Negevite Types and Parallels (pls. 11-15)

Straight-Walled Cooking Pots (pl. 11:1-6; see also unpublished nos. 251, 344, 489, 561, 626, 770, 781, 803, 928, and 929). This is the most common type in the Negevite repertoire at Tell el-Kheleifeh. These vessels frequently have two handles that may be in a variety of forms, including knobs (pl. 11:1-4), horns (pl. 12:2, 4 for an illustration of handle type), vertical (pl. 12:9, 10 for handle type), and ledge handles (pl. 11:5).
Parallels: All three fortress phases at Tell el-Qudeirat; for other sites, see Meshel 1977: fig. 8:1, 7; Cohen 1970: fig. 11:1, 7, 9; Y. Aharoni 1960: figs. 11:11, 13; 12:5, 6; Rothenberg 1972: figs. 31:1-3, 5; 35:2.

"Holemouth" Cooking Pots (pl. 12:1-4; see also unpublished nos. 553, 559, 560, 593, 905, 932 and 5018). This is a common type at Tell el-Kheleifeh attested with horn (pl. 12:2, 4), loop (pl. 12:3) and ledge (pl. 12:1) handles. A loop handle is preserved on only one example. The type derives its name from the inward stance of the vessel wall.
Parallels: All three fortress phases at Tell el-Qudeirat; for other sites, see Meshel 1977: fig. 8:2, 4; Cohen 1970; fig. 11:21; 1976a: fig. 11:1-5; Y. Aharoni 1960: fig. 11:3, 4, 7; Bennett 1975: fig. 6:8; Fritz and Kempinski 1983: pl. 161:7.

Bowls (pls. 12:5-10; 13:1-13; 14:1-10; see also unpublished nos. 90, 122, 150, 370, 373, 550, 613, 766, 787, 854, 877, 1004, 3026, 10024, and 12016). The bowls exhibit great variety in size, handle shapes and vessel profile and stance. A variety of handle types are found, including vertical (pl. 14:10), ledge (pl. 13:2, 4), bar (pl. 13:3), and knob (pl. 14:5-9) handles.
Parallels: Bar handles are the predominant type in the middle and last fortress phases of Tell el-Qudeirat. Knob handles are common on the handmade pottery of Tell el-Qudeirat and Tell el-Kheleifeh. A handle may be comprised of one to three knobs located on the extreme upper portion of the vessel's wall (pl. 14:1, 4, 5). In a few examples, the knobs decorate the entire rim (pl. 14:7-9). Handles or decorations of this type are found in the three fortress phases of Tell el-Qudeirat but are most common in the middle phase (Cohen 1981b: 101). For Negevite bowls without handles, see Meshel 1977: fig. 8:3; Cohen 1970: fig. 11:4-6, 17; Y. Aharoni 1960: fig. 11:2 and Rothenberg 1972: fig. 45:8, 10, and 11.

Small Jars or Cups Without Handles (pl. 14:11-12; also unpublished nos. 549 and 905). Parallels: See Cohen 1970 fig. 11:3; Rothenberg 1972: fig. 45:12.

Teapot (pl. 14:13; also unpublished nos. 343 and 8024). A few examples have been excavated at Tell el-Qudeirat, restricted to the earliest and middle fortress phases. See also Cohen 1970: fig. 11:11 and Y. Aharoni 1958: pl. 50:A.

Cups with Handles (pl. 15:1-5). This category is represented by only five examples. Two of the vessels have loop handles (pl. 15:3, 4) and one has a knob handle (pl. 15:1); pl. 15:2 originally had a handle. The handle type of pl. 15:5 is not distinguishable. For parallels, see Cohen 1981b: 101; 1970: fig 11:3 (with loop handle); Bennett 1975: fig. 6:12 (with knob handle).

Juglets (pl. 15:6-9; see also unpublished nos. 240, 281, 6079, and 7077). Negevite juglets are quite rare. The extant examples are of two types, both of which recall wheelmade forms: spherical or oval vessels which are clearly reminiscent of Iron II dipper juglets (cf. pl. 30:1-3, 5); and a flat-bottomed, elongated form which recalls pls. 30:9-16; 31:1-3. For parallels, see Rothenberg 1972: fig. 45:9, 13. A few examples of uncertain provenance were excavated at Tell el Qudeirat.

Chalices (pl. 15:10, 11; see also unpublished nos. 283, 589, 863, and 961). This type is represented at Tell el-Kheleifeh by only one complete vessel (pl. 15:10). Plate 15:11 is a chalice base with a denticulated ridge. The latter is a common decoration on wheelmade forms of various pottery types (pls. 29:12; 37:1-7). There are no Negevite pieces with denticulated decoration at Tell el-Qudeirat. The few wheelmade examples were restricted to the last fortress phase (seventh-sixth centuries B.C.E.). Cohen has published one Negevite chalice (1981b: 101).

The Small Vessel with Tripod Base (pl. 15:12). This appears to be unique to Tell el-Kheleifeh, though wheelmade cups with tripod bases are found in the late Iron Age Amman tomb groups.

Oil Lamps (pl. 15:13, 14; see also unpublished nos. 103, 446, 7070, and 8029). For Tell el-Qudeirat parallels, see Cohen 1981b: 101 and several unpublished examples that are restricted to the last fortress phase, seventh-sixth centuries B.C.E.

Perforated Vessels (pl. 15:15, 16; see also unpublished nos. 890 and 2496). Only two vessels of this type were excavated at Tell el-Kheleifeh (see also pl. 29 for several wheelmade examples of this type). Though unpublished, Tell el-Qudeirat has provided the only handmade parallel. Cohen has assigned this "incense burner" to the last fortress phase.

Figurine (pl. 15:17). It is uncertain whether this figurine should be classified with the Negevite assemblage. Its fabric is quite different from the typical wares of that tradition. Although evidencing the characteristic crudity of this pottery, the piece exhibits an element of decorative refinement that appears out of place.

D. Summary

Given the absence of a refined stratigraphy with associated pottery assemblages at Tell el-Kheleifeh (see chapter 4), the chronology of this site's handmade ceramics cannot be established with certainty. The Negevite forms should be dated with the wheelmade forms, to the eighth-sixth century B.C.E. (for the chronology of the wheelmade pottery, see below). This dating is also suggested by the parallels from Tell el-Qudeirat, which cluster in the middle and latest fortress phases.

There remains, however, the possibility that the Tell el-Kheleifeh corpus contains an earlier horizon of Negevite pottery that cannot be discerned typologically. Glueck's early dating of these wares was not altogether incorrect, for it surely is a characteristic pottery of the casemate fortresses of the central Negev. Refined dating for this handmade tradition will be possible only with sites like Tell el-Qudeirat, which yield a variety of forms in stratified contexts. Unfortunately, the casemate fortresses and associated structures lack the stratification of a fortified settlement like Tell el-Qudeirat. Until such data are available, the Negevite pottery is not chronologically diagnostic and must be dated contemporaneously with associated wheelmade forms.

II. THE WHEELMADE POTTERY
(PLS. 16-40)

A. Cooking Pots (pls. 16-19)

The cooking pots of Tell el-Kheleifeh fall into two categories: Edomite cooking pots and grooved rim cooking pots with necks.

1. Edomite Cooking Pots. There are two predominant cooking pot types in the Tell el-Kheleifeh repertoire: the Negevite straight-walled and holemouth vessels, generally interpreted as cooking pots; and the so-called Edomite cooking pots (pls. 16; 17; 18:1-6). The latter type shares the general form and fabric characteristics of the cooking pot class. Geographical provenance has prompted the designation of this distinctive pot as Edomite.

This form is defined by the following characteristics: a deeply grooved rim that is basically rectangular in section; typical cooking pot handles that overlap the grooved rim; and a rounded sidewall without a neck. The unthickened grooved rim and the absence of a neck are the two formal features that distinguish the Edomite cooking pot. The rim is never triangular in section as is common in other cooking pots. The two handles, which are attached just over the ridge of the rim, frequently rise up to or slightly above the level of the rim. Though most vessels are characterized by round walls, a few exhibit either a subtle or pronounced body carination (pl. 17:6, 7). A few examples exhibit atypical features such as the more vertical stance of pl. 18:3. Vessel size varies considerably within the class as is seen in the plates.

Many of the vessels have stamp impressions on the upper or lower portion of the handles. The impressions are either the Qaws'anal stamp impressions, consistently located on the upper portion of the handle; or an epigraphical or anepigraphical rectangular impression located on the lower section of the handle. The latter are very poorly preserved.

The best parallels come from the regions of central and southern Transjordan: Heshbon, (cooking pot type Ia, seventh-sixth centuries B.C.E.): Lugenbeal and Sauer 1972: pl. 5: 291, 293, 295, 296, 299, 300, 301, 303, 304; Umm el-Biyara (seventh-sixth centuries B.C.E.): Bennett 1966a: figs. 3:12, 4:8; Ghrareh (seventh-sixth centuries B.C.E.): Hart 1987a: fig. 9:7; Dhiban (Iron Age wares in a fill of the Nabataean Temple Podium): Tushingham 1972: fig. 1:18; 'Aro'er: Olavarri 1965: fig. 2:10 (with somewhat atypical grooved rim); and one example from an unspecified site in Edom, published by Glueck (1939: pl. 24:20). Although examples have not been published to date, the form is well documented at Tell el-'Umeiri. C. M. Bennett has uncovered many examples at Umm el-Biyara, Buseirah and Tawilan in late Iron Age contexts (see also En-Gedi: Mazar et al. 1966: fig. 17:6 [with infrequent inverted stance of the rim]; Ramat Raḥel: RR II. fig. 20:7; Tell Beit Mirsim: TBM I. pl. 95:9; TBM III. pl. 19:2 and 4; Tell en-Naṣbeh: TN II. pl. 48:1014 (?), 1024, 1025; 'Aro'er [Stratum II]: Biran and Cohen 1981: fig. 16:2). The 'Aro'er collection contains numerous examples of this cooking pot type.

This particular type of cooking pot clearly exhibits a regional concentration in central and southern Transjordan with scattered examples from West Bank sites. The form belongs to the late Iron Age, seventh century B.C.E. and later. While the problems in nomenclature must be acknowledged, the type is designated here as the Edomite cooking pot.

2. Grooved Rim Cooking Pots with Necks. Another class of cooking pot, though represented by considerably fewer examples than the Edomite type, is presented in pls. 18:7-10 and 19:1-4. Glueck's excavations and the 1980 survey produced some 25 sherds of this type as compared with nearly 75 examples of the Edomite cooking pot. The two features that clearly distinguish this type from the Edomite class are the presence of a neck and the rim profile. In most examples, the rim is not as deeply grooved, though it maintains a profile that is basically rectangular. Some examples, however, tend toward a triangular section (pl. 19:1, 2). Like the Edomite class, the two handles are attached just over the ridge of the rim and rise up to or slightly above the level of the rim. Although this class is represented only by sherds, the type appears to have rounded walls with no pronounced carinations. The wares of this class tend to be finer and better fired than the Edomite examples (pl. 18:8, 19:1-4; see also techni-

cal pottery data below). Unlike the Edomite pots, stamps are not found on vessels of this type. Two examples preserve a more vertical rim stance (pl. 19:3 and a fragment of unknown provenance, which has not been included in the plates).

Parallels include the following: Beersheba (Stratum II): Beer-Sheba I. pls. 60:81, 83; 70:18 (the body carination in the Beersheba examples appears to be absent in the Kheleifeh forms); Tell Beit Mirsim (Stratum A): TBM I. pl. 55:2; TBM III. pl. 19:3, 4; Tell en-Naṣbeh: TN II. pls. 47:992, 1002; 48:1014; Megiddo (Strata IV-I): Megiddo I. pl. 39:7, 8 (the typical Kheleifeh rim is more elongated), 11; Samaria (Periods II and IV): SS III. figs. 3:26; 6:31, 33, 37; 30:3; Hazor (Strata X-IV): Hazor I. pls. 55:10; 72:3; 74:23; Hazor II. pl. 99:18; Hazor III-IV. pls. 189:10 (the body carination is absent in the Kheleifeh examples); 210:20 (Kheleifeh examples have a less pronounced ridge above groove); 207:13 (Kheleifeh examples have a less pronounced ridge below groove); 248:7, 8; 255:8; Beth-Shemesh (Stratum IIa): AS IV. pl. 63:37; Gezer (Iron I): Gezer I. pl. 27:19 (vertical stance of rim comparable to pl. 19:3 but without body carination); Gezer III. pls. 22:3; 24:18 (late Iron II); Bethel: AASOR 39 (1968) pl. 65:7; Tel Masos (Stratum I): Fritz and Kempinski 1983: pl. 158:12; Dhiban (Iron Age ware in a fill of the Nabataean Temple Podium): AASOR 40 (1972) fig. 1:17, 18; Beth-zur (Stratum III): Sellers 1933: pl. 19:2; Umm el-Biyara (seventh-sixth centuries B.C.E.): Bennett 1966a: fig. 4: 7; Heshbon (seventh-sixth centuries B.C.E.): Lugenbeal and Sauer 1972: pl. 5:299; 'Aro'er: Olavarri 1965: fig. 2:8 (Kheleifeh examples without body carination); Buseirah (seventh-sixth centuries B.C.E.): Bennett 1974a: fig. 15:10.

This class of cooking pots is well-attested throughout Iron II with a cluster of good parallels in the eighth-early sixth centuries B.C.E. Its documentation is clearly earlier than the Edomite cooking pots. The latter, in fact, are fairly restricted both chronologically and geographically in comparison to the grooved-rim cooking pots with necks. This type is found as early as Hazor X and in Iron I contexts at Gezer as well. There are differences, however, between these examples and the typical vessel of this type at Tell el-Kheleifeh. The most pronounced difference is the apparent lack of a body carination in the Tell el-Kheleifeh examples.

3. Miscellaneous Cooking Pot Types. A nearly complete vessel with a different rim profile also belongs to this class (pl. 19:5). It lacks the groove that is typical of nearly every wheelmade cooking pot in the Tell el-Kheleifeh repertoire. Other descriptive and technical data are nearly identical.

For parallels to pl. 19:7, see Hazor (Stratum I): Hazor II. pls. 85:13 (note the similarity even in point of handle attachment); 252:10; Buseirah (seventh-sixth centuries B.C.E.): Bennett 1974a: pl. 16:9.

Glueck's excavations yielded a single cooking pot sherd (pl. 19:6) identical in form and fabric to a type well documented in late Iron Age contexts, especially at Ramat Raḥel and En Gedi. The type is commonly known as the "En Gedi cooking pot" since it was largely unrecognized as a distinct form prior to excavation at that site. The form is characterized by a flaring rim with groove and a subtle body carination. The clay is quite well levigated and well fired. The vessel's walls are thin and red-brown.

The type is common at En-Gedi (Mazar et al. figs. 8:14, 15; 18:1, 2, 3, 8) and is widely distributed elsewhere. See, for example, Ramat Raḥel (Stratum VA): RR I. pls. 11:24; 28:35-37; *RR II.* pls. 18:9, 10; 20:10; Meṣad Ḥashavyahu (second half of seventh-end of sixth century B.C.E.): Naveh 1962: fig. 5:2; Lachish (Stratum II): La*chish III.* pl. 93:460; *Lachish V.* pls. 47:19, 20; 49:4; 50:12; Buqeʿah Valley (late Iron Age): Stager 1975: pls. 1:14; 2:15; 3:27; 4:30; 5:1; Tel Masos (post-I, seventh century B.C.E.): Kempinski et al. 1981: pl. 11:11; Fritz and Kempinski 1983: pl. 158:8; ʿAroʿer (Stratum II): Biran and Cohen 1981: pls. 6:2; 16:1. The form is also well known in Tel ʿArad Stratum VI.

This sherd constitutes a rather unusual find at Tell el-Kheleifeh for it represents Judean pottery, both in form and fabric. The above parallels provide a sampling of contexts which date from the second half of the seventh century B.C.E. to the end of the Iron Age. The En-Gedi cooking pot is one of the diagnostic forms for Judean ceramics of the late Iron Age. It should again be emphasized that this type is represented by only one sherd at Tell el-Kheleifeh.

B. "Qawsʿanal" Jars (pls. 20-21)

A common jar form at Tell el-Kheleifeh is presented in pls. 20-21. This type will hereafter be designated the "Qawsʿanal" jar because of the frequency of this stamp impression on either the upper or lower portion of the handle (pl. 21:3, 4, 6, 7). Although not presented in the pottery plates, Kheleifeh registry numbers 241, 267, 466, 523, 524, and 528 constitute other jar fragments of this type with well-preserved "Qawsʿanal" stamp impressions.

This storage jar is defined by the following characteristics: a deeply grooved rim that recalls the rim profile and stance of the Edomite cooking pots; a thin and wide vertical handle that overlaps the grooved rim and is attached to the upper portion of the shoulder; and a sagging, bag-shaped body with rounded base. The fabric range, in general, resembles that of the inverted rim kraters (pls. 22-24).

This grooved rim jar is not a widely distributed form. Though unpublished, the best parallels come from late Iron Age contexts at Feifa. Other close paral-

lels include an incomplete vessel from a seventh-sixth century B.C.E. level at Ghrareh (Hart 1987a: fig. 9:8) and one from a late Iron Age context at Umm el-Biyara (Bennett 1966a: fig. 2:11 and also fig. 4:2-4). The latter examples are without preserved handles. The Umm el-Biyara example exhibits two of the three defining characteristics. Body profile is not preserved in this sherd. Although not published, similar jars have been found at Buseirah and Tawilan in late Iron Age contexts. See also Tell en-Naṣbeh: TN *II.* pl. 16:269 which does not, however, exhibit the deeply grooved rim.

Specific features, such as the bag-shaped body of this form, have parallels at a number of sites. See En-Gedi (Stratum V): Mazar et al. 1966: figs. 9:14 and 22:3, 4; Beersheba (Stratum II): Beer-Sheba I. pl. 57:5; Ramat Raḥel (Stratum VA): *RR II.* fig. 19:5; Samaria (Period V): *SS III.* fig. 8:1; Tell en-Naṣbeh: *TN II.* pls 14:239; 18:303; and 22:359; Tel Masos (post-I, seventh century. B.C.E.): Kempinski et al. 1981: pl. 11:16; ʿAroʿer (Stratum II): Biran and Cohen 1981: pl. 5:1. The body profile of the "Qawsʿanal" jars also recalls the distinctive late Iron holemouth jars as presented, for example, in En-Gedi (Stratum V): Mazar et al. 1966: fig. 21:8; Beersheba (Stratum II): Beer-Sheba I. pl. 58:25-28; Tell Beit Mirsim: *TBM I.* pl. 52:3-6, 9; Ramat Raḥel (Stratum V): *RR I.* fig. 29:10, 11; *RR II.* fig. 21:22, 23 and Tell en-Naṣbeh: *TN II.* pls. 24:388, 389; and 25:417. This unique jar form again emphasizes the regional character of Tell el-Kheleifeh pottery.

A similar jar form without the grooved rim is represented by a few examples (pl. 21:9, 10). Although it does not appear in the pottery plates, one whole vessel of this type was excavated by Glueck (Kheleifeh 6061, Smithsonian 388283). The jar has a rounded base without the sagging body profile. A parallel to pl. 21:9 is provided from Tell en-Naṣbeh: TN II. pl. 28:476 with recognition of the obvious differences in handle profile. Although not published to date, similar rims are known also at Tell el-ʿUmeiri. See also Hazor (Stratum VI): *Hazor II.* pl. 71:6, 7 (note the differences in handle profile and place of attachment) and *Hazor III-IV.* pl. 181:15. For general parallels to pl. 21:10, see Hazor (Stratum VI): *Hazor II.* pl. 71:5 and *Hazor III-IV.* pl. 185:14, 16, and 17.

C. Inverted Rim Kraters (pls. 22-24)

The following characteristics define the form: two or four handles; a sharply inverted rim that is flattened and basically rectangular in section; handle attachment at the uppermost point of the rim; and, occasionally, a subtle upper body carination (pl. 22:1). Three of the published sherds preserve "Qawsʿanal" stamp impressions (pls. 22:2; 23:3 and 6). There are slight variations, such as the rim and vessel wall thickness of pl. 24:5, and the unusual bar handle of pl. 24:4. The following parallels will include comments on the number of handles and data which are not characteristic of the Tell el-Kheleifeh kraters.

Parallels include: En-Gedi (Stratum V): Mazar et al. 1966: figs. 16:4 (two handles with a thicker and more triangular rim) and 16:6 (four handles with atypical upper body carination and more elongated handle); Beersheba (Stratum II): *Beer-Sheba I*. pls. 60:73-76 (two or four handles and rims that are more triangular in section); 64:8 (two handles and upper body carination); 68:14 (four handles and a more inverted rim with upper body carination); 69:13, 14 (same observations as previous citation); Tell Beit Mirsim: *TBM I*. pl. 60:2, 8 (four handles) and 60:4 (four handles and a more triangular rim); *TBM III*. pls. 20:8 (four handles and a more triangular rim) and 20:10, 16 (four and two handles respectively); Ramat Raḥel (Stratum VA): *RR II*. figs. 18:5, 6 (four handles and more triangular rims; the last example with upper body carination); 20:3 (four handles and sharper stance); Lachish: *Lachish III*. pls. 80:86 (no handles represented, more triangular rim and an upper body carination); 81:120; 82:123 (deeper form); 102:657 (rim slightly more triangular and pointed); *Lachish V*. pl. 44:13 (four handles and slightly thicker rim with lower attachment of handle); Megiddo (Strata IV-I): *Megiddo I*. pl. 27:84 (two handles, deeper with a more triangular rim); Samaria (Period II): *SS III*. figs. 3:35 (a common form in Period IV and following); 20:1 (four handles and more triangular rim); Gezer: *Gezer III*. pl. 20:21 (two handles and more triangular rim); Tell en-Naṣbeh: *TN II*. pl. 62:1426 (two handles) and 62:1427, 1429 (four and two handles respectively); Murabbaʿat: Benoit et al. 1961: pl. 6:1 (more triangular rim); ʿAroʿer (Stratum III): Biran and Cohen 1981: pl. 7:3 (four handles with upper body carination and more sharply inverted rim; see also Stratum III rim of pl. 8:3 and Stratum II rim of pl. 16:6); Heshbon (seventh-sixth centuries B.C.E.): Lugenbeal and Sauer 1972: pl. VI: 333-348, 350-352, 355, 358 (no preserved handles); Umm el-Biyara (seventh–sixth centuries B.C.E.): Bennett 1966a: fig. 3:10 (two handles and atypical bulbous rim); Ghrareh (seventh-sixth centuries B.C.E.): Hart 1988: fig. 7:11; Dhiban: *AASOR 40* (1972) fig. 17:13 (with sharply triangular rim). Although she did not publish them, Bennett found similar forms at Buseirah and Tawilan in contexts of the seventh-sixth centuries B.C.E. The form is also well documented at Tell el-ʿUmeiri. See also Holladay's discussion (1976:287) on large handled bowls, classes A and B, in which he concludes that "two or four handles are exceedingly rare before the end of the eighth century B.C.E." Our inverted rim krater type embraces both of Holladay's classes. Given his ex-

amples for each, his distinguishing criteria for the two categories are somewhat obscure.

Few of the above parallels preserve the typical features of the Tell el-Kheleifeh inverted rim krater. Heshbon and Tell el-ʿUmeiri furnish the closest parallels, though with two differences: a more triangular rim and an upper body carination that frequently is pronounced. The former is not found at Tell el-Kheleifeh and the latter is infrequent. This particular class further emphasizes the regional character of the Tell el-Kheleifeh assemblage as a whole. The En-Gedi, Beersheba, Ramat Raḥel, Lachish, Heshbon, Tell el-ʿUmeiri, ʿAroʿer (W), and Umm el-Biyara examples provide contexts that suggest a range from the late eighth-early sixth century B.C.E.

D. Assyrian Pottery and Related Forms (pls. 25-28)

Assyrian bowls in local imitation are ubiquitous at Tell el-Kheleifeh. This distinctive and well-known pottery class is the second largest assemblage at the site, after the Negevite wares. Glueck assigned this pottery to Period IV without distinguishing between IV, IVA, or IVB. Though lacking technical details, Glueck published it with the comparative data known at the time (1967b: 24-30). A handful of similar surface sherds were found in the 1980 survey.

A few of Glueck's comments are appropriate. By way of description and stratigraphic context, Glueck wrote:

> Found together with the seventh-sixth centuries B.C.E. Qausʿanal pottery with profiled rims in room 27 and 28, and particularly in room 27 at Tell el-Kheleifeh and occurring elsewhere in the same Level IV period there, are numerous examples of a distinctive, practically uniform type of small cups, many with potter's marks. The ware is usually light creamy buff, or at times light grayish or greenish buff, and is indistinguishable from that of the Qausʿanal jars. Wheel-made and wet-smoothed, these cups have a sharply carinated form, with rounded body and rounded or sometimes somewhat flattened base and high everted rim. One type has a single, pronounced, rounded or somewhat flattened loop-handle, the top of which sometimes rises above the top of the rim to which it is attached; the bottom of the loop-handle is usually attached to the top of the shoulder and the bottom of the high everted rim. Some of these cups with loop-handles have a potter's mark at the base of the handle and others at the top. Another and usually finer type of carinated cup or small bowl has no handles (1967b: 25).

He continued his description of the finer carinated cups without handles:

Found in the same context as the Qaus'anal jars and the carinated, single-handled cups with and without potters' marks are handleless, carinated cups or small bowls generally of a finer quality than the single-handled, carinated cups to which they are closely related. Wheel-made, of well baked, dark grayish brown, well levigated ware containing tiny grits, they are usually decorated with several horizontal parallel bands of dark brown paint near the outer bottom of the high, outturned rim, and at times with a band of paint on the outer surface of the top of the rim. Sometimes the bands of paint are superimposed over somewhat irregular, almost contiguous fine lines of burnishing or over more widely spaced lines of burnishing (1967b: 25).

The two basic "carinated cup" categories, as discerned by Glueck, are correct, but slight refinements are needed. Plates. 25 and 26:1-5 provide a large selection of the first class, the Assyrian cups with handles. The uniformity of the type is readily apparent. There are slight differences within the class in terms of the sharpness of the body carination and the profile of the upper body rim. Note, for example, the inward stance of the upper rim in pls. 25:17, 18 and 26:1-3. A few examples also preserve a more elongated handle. The form and fabric of this class is quite monotonous, and all examples are clearly local in origin. While attributable to this class, pl. 26:4 provides more significant variation compared to the typical carinated vessel.

A selection of the second class of Assyrian bowls, those without handles, is presented in pls. 26:6-18 and 27:1-11. As Glueck observed, these vessels are consistently finer in form and fabric than those with handles. Decoration and profile provide some variation within the class. A few examples are burnished and several, though not a majority as suggested by Glueck, are decorated with dark reddish brown bands of paint (5YR 3/2-3/4) in parallel lines on the rim portion above the body carination (pl. 27:10, 11). A notable variation in form, as illustrated in pl. 27:7 and 8, is the inward stance of the upper rim.

Also related to this type are several examples of double carinated cups with high outturned rims and rounded bases (pl. 27:12; see also Glueck 1967a: 27 and figs. 1:6; 4:2, 3 for examples published by Glueck). Most examples are decorated with dark brown (7.5 YR 3/2) and dark reddish brown (5YR 3/2-3/4) bands of paint in parallel lines from the rim to the lower carination.

The collection of Assyrian Palace ware from Tell Jemmeh, currently at the Smithsonian Institution, exhibts fabrics and refinement of form that are clearly different from the Tell el-Kheleifeh corpus. Although

a handful of sherds are questionable, the Assyrian types described above are not imported.

For parallels (imported vessels and local imitations), the largest collections of imported Assyrian bowls are known from Tell el-Far'ah: RB 58 (1951) fig. 12:1-4, 6; Tell Jemmeh, largely unpublished but see *Gerar* pls. 51:26W, 26X; 48; 65; a large unpublished corpus from Dothan; and Samaria: *SS III*. figs. 11:15, 17, 22, 23; 18:9, 10; 32:3, 5. See also Mallowan 1950: 147-83; Oats 1959: 130-46; Lines 1954: 164-67. For other examples of imported and local Assyrian bowls, see Ramat Raḥel (Stratum V): *RR I*. fig. 11:15; Heshbon: Lugenbeal and Sauer 1972: pl. 5:273 (?); see also Sauer's discussion (42-43) with parallels in northern Syria; Adoni-Nur: Harding and Tufnell 1953: fig. 21:70; Amman: Harding 1944: fig. 70:7; Umm el-Biyara (seventh-sixth centuries B.C.E.): Bennett 1966a: figs. 2:1, 3; 3:7, 8; Buseirah: Bennett 1974a: figs. 14:6; 15:2; 1975: figs. 5:16, 17; 8:6; Ghrareh (seventh-sixth centuries B.C.E.): Hart 1987a: fig. 9:3, 4; 1988: fig. 7:1, 2, 6; es-Sadeh (late Iron Age): Lindner, Farajat, and Zeitler 1988: fig. 8:4. In addition to these published examples, numerous parallels to both classes are known from Buseirah, Umm el-Biyara, and Tawilan. Very common at the three sites are the handled cups with inward stance of the upper rim. Tawilan and Buseirah have also produced numerous examples of the finer painted bowls without handles.

Kenyon assigned these wares to the latter part of the eighth century B.C.E. Noting the "regular conjunction of 'Assyrian' wares with late seventh century forms," Holladay (1976: 272) raises the question of the dating and historical attribution of this pottery and concluded that a number of these stratigraphic contexts are actually post-Assyrian in date and witness to a Babylonian influence of the late seventh and early sixth centuries B.C.E. In light of the few reliable stratigraphic contexts for imported Assyrian wares that have been published to date and the important unpublished collections from Tell Jemmeh, Buseirah, Umm el-Biyara, Tawilan, Dothan, and Shechem, Amiran's cautious assessment seems appropriate. She writes, "In all excavations it [imported Assyrian ware] appears in strata of the period following the Assyrian conquest of Samaria" (1970: 290).

Four "pointed bottle" fragments, a type commonly designated Ammonite, are attested at Tell el-Kheleifeh. Two sherds are presented in the plates (pl. 27:13, 14). The fabrics of those examples are clearly distinguishable from the site's pottery as a whole. Both pieces are burnished. Although there are possible parallels from West Bank sites (see Henschel-Simon's discussion of the type, 1944: 75-77), the best parallels come from sites in central and southern Jordan. See Buseirah: Bennett 1974a: fig. 16:6; Meqabelein: Harding 1950: pl. 16:17,

18; Nebo: Saller 1966: fig. 23:9, 10; Sahab: Harding 1948: pl. 35:31, 35, 42, 43; p. 98:31-34, 36-37; Amman: Harding 1944: pp. 71:21; 22; pls. 17:22; 18:56; Harding 1951: fig. 1:12-14; Adoni Nur: Harding and Tufnell 1953: fig. 22:94-99A; Dhiban: AASOR 36-37 (1957-1958) pls. 59:13; 77:9; AASOR 40 (1972) fig. 21:18.

The stratigraphic contexts for each parallel date to the Iron II period, not earlier than the eighth century B.C.E. Amiran suggests that the origins of this type should be sought in Assyria rather than in Ammon (1970: 291, 294-97). She writes: "The form of the vessel, and especially the absence of handles, stamp it, in our opinion, as an Assyrian product. The vessel fits well in the general assemblage of Assyrian ceramics, while among Israelite, or even Ammonite pottery, it appears foreign and unconnected with ceramic tradition, either of the past or of its own time" (1970: 296).

Plates 27:15-17 and 28:1-14 depict a class of vessels that is typologically related to the Assyrian bowls (Glueck's "carinated cups" of pls. 25 and 26:1-5). Also related is the class of vessels depicted in pls. 26:6-18 and 27:1-11, though the latter group is finer in manufacturing technique and fabric composition with some obvious typological distinctions such as the thinner and more flaring rim. Glueck correctly considered the vessels of pls. 27:15-17 and 28:1-14 to be Edomite. He also published several other types of pottery under the same designation (Glueck 1967a: 8-38), notably the Assyrian bowls (with and without handles), painted vessels of the same type, perforated vessels (with and without handles), "windowed" censers, painted bowls, and several vessel types with crenellated decoration (note especially figs. 5:2, 3 [p. 19]; 1 [p. 26]; 2 [p. 29]; 3 [p. 32]; 4 [p. 35] and 5 [p. 37]). For discussion of these vessel types, see comments for pls. 25; 26; 27:1-12; 29 and 37. Glueck also published several pieces as Edomite, though they are clearly Midianite based on form, fabric, and decoration (see figs. 1:2 [5:1] and 4:3-5).

The best parallels for the vessels of pls. 27:15-17 and 28:1-10 come from the largely unpublished sites of Buseirah and Umm el-Biyara. For the few published examples from Buseirah, see Bennett 1974a: fig. 15:4; 1975: fig. 5:8, 9, 13, and 18 (cf. also fig. 7:16 for the spouted vessel of pl. 28:14) and for those from Umm el-Biyara, see Bennett 1966a: fig. 2:10. See also the late Iron Age parallels from Ghrareh (Hart 1987a: fig. 9:5 and 1988: fig. 7:4). A number of good examples, though unpublished, are contained within the ʿAroʿer collection (see the few published vessels in Biran and Cohen 1981: fig. 15:14-19).

E. Perforated Vessels (pl. 29)

Reminiscent of the Assyrian bowls are the numerous examples of "censers" (Crowfoot 1940: 150-53),

designated "perforated cups" by Glueck (1967a: 30-33). Glueck assigned those vessels to Period IV as he did the Assyrian bowls. At a number of sites, especially in Jordan, these perforated vessels are found together with the typical Assyrian forms.

The most frequent type is presented in pl. 29:1-8. Though there is some variety, the form exhibits the following characteristics: three stump legs or conical knobs; two horizontal rows of perforations in most examples; a double body carination; and a rounded or somewhat flattened loop-handle in most examples. Occasionally a flat or concave base is attested (pl. 29:9). Plate 15:15 and 16 are Negevite vessels and may be either censers or strainers. Note the depth of the lower row of holes (cf. also Glueck 1967a: fig. 3:12).

Three "windowed" or fenestrated vessels (pl. 29:10-12) also belong to this class (see Glueck's descriptions 1967a: 31-34; figs. 2:1, 4a and b, 5a and b; 5:1, 7). In the place of perforations, these vessels have windows. Unlike the censers described above, each of these has a lid, barely preserved in pl. 29:10. The latter example is clearly reminiscent of the most common censer type with three stump legs. As drawn, the rounded profile on the left section indicates the preserved portion of the lower window.

Plate 29:11 is the crudest of the group. Its construction is, in fact, reminiscent of the handmade Negevite wares. The vessel originally had a single loop-handle which is flatter in profile than the other examples. A single small conical knob, now partially broken off, is preserved to the right of the handle. It is clear that a denticulated fringe encircled the outer bottom of the body. The blunt-edged conical teeth are much more widely spaced than the triangular, sharply pointed projections of pl. 29:12.

The finest example of a perforated vessel (pl. 29:12) is contained in the collections of the Jordan Archaeological Museum (for photograph, see Glueck 1967a: figs. 2:1; 5:1). Five rectangular windows are preserved in a convex body. The denticulated fringe, located just below the windows, is a common decoration in Glueck's Period IV pottery (pl. 37:1-7). Those fenestrated vessels, considered by some to be incense burners, have been discovered only at Tell el-Kheleifeh with one exception. One example was found in a seventh-sixth century B.C.E. context at Ghrareh (Hart 1988: fig. 7:8). Hart suggests that the lack of examples from Buseirah, Tawilan, and Umm el-Biyara indicates that the Ghrareh vessel may have been imported from Tell el-Kheleifeh (1988: 96).

Parallels to the footed vessels with perforations include the following: Nebo (Iron II): Saller 1966: figs. 15:2, 4, 5, 8; 16:1-12; 31:1-3; 32:1-9; 37:1; Buseirah: Bennett 1974a: fig. 15:1; 1975: fig. 7:18; Dhiban: AASOR 40 (1972) figs. 16:15, 16, 18; 23:7, 11; AASOR 36-37 (1957-

1958) pl. 78:2(?); Meqabelein: Harding 1950: pl. 17:9 and p. 45. For West Bank sites, see Samaria: *SS III*. fig. 26:5, 12; Megiddo (Strata V-II): *Megiddo I*. pl. 23:20, 22, 23 (the latter with one row of perforations); Hazor (XB-V): *Hazor I*. pls. 49:31; 54:18; *Hazor II*. pls. 55:43; 63:34; *Hazor III-IV*. pls. 171:16, 17; 180:13; 208:34; Lachish: *Lachish III*. pl. 90:380 and 381.

Parallels to the perforated vessels with concave or flat bases include the following: Nebo (Iron II): Saller 1966: figs. 15:6, 7; 16:13-20, 22; Megiddo (Stratum IV): *Megiddo I*. pl. 23:24 (with rounded base). Though lacking perforations, see Sahab: Harding 1948: fig. 4:23-30; pl. 35:21, 23; Adoni Nur: Harding and Tufnell 1953: fig. 21:77-81; Amman: Harding 1944: p. 70:10-13; Dhiban: *AASOR* 40 (1972) fig. 1:13; Harding 1951: fig. 1:11; Samaria: *SS III*. fig. 26:12; Hazor: (Strata VIII-VI): *Hazor I*. pl. 51:20; *Hazor II*. pl. 54:20-22; *Hazor III-IV*. pl. 182:22.

Glueck correctly assigned Period IV to the late seventh-early sixth centuries B.C.E. and acknowledged the possibility that "this late Iron II type of cup censer may also belong to the 'Assyrian' type of pottery" (1967a: 34 and n. 52; 37-38).

F. Juglets, Jugs, and Jars (pls. 30-32)

The juglets, jugs and jars of Tell el-Kheleifeh will be discussed in seven categories.

1. The most common juglet form is spherical or oval with a very narrow neck (pl. 30:1-9). Two examples exhibit a slightly more flattened body profile (pl. 30:6, 7). There is generally one handle, which is attached at a point slightly below the rim and joins the extreme upper portion of the body. Although only one vessel appears in the pottery plates (pl. 30:3), faint vertical burnishing is discerned in three examples. One spherical juglet without a handle is painted over the upper portion of the vessel and a few horizontal burnishing strokes are visible (pl. 30:5).

Parallels include the following: En-Gedi (Stratum V): Mazar et al. 1966: figs. 9:1; 10 (with ring base); 19:1, 2, 3, 4; 30:7; Beersheba (Strata III-II): Beer-Sheba I. pls. 44:6; 45:1, 3, 7, 9; 56:2, 4, 11; 62:114, 120-22 , 124, 125; 66:14-18; 67:6; 69:19; 72:19; Tell Beit Mirsim (Stratum A): TBM I. pls. 68:1-3; 69:7-18, 25; TBM II. pls. 18:10, 11, 13-15; 26:6, 7, 14, 15, 17; Lachish: *Lachish III*. pl. 88:313, 319, 333; *Lachish V*. pl. 47:28 (Stratum II); Gezer (late Iron II): *Gezer III*. pl. 19:9, 13; Hazor (Stratum V): *Hazor I*. pls. LVI:4; LXVI:9; Dhiban: *AASOR* 40 (1972) fig. 24:5. Buseirah has produced a number of the burnished, spherical juglets.

2. Elongated juglets make up the second most common type (pls. 30:10-16, 31:1-3). The body of this juglet type is basically rectangular in section with a rounded base and a neck slightly larger in diameter than that of the previous class. One handle is common, attached at the lip of the rim and frequently rising above the level of the rim. The lower handle is attached at the extreme upper portion of the body. A shoulder carination is found in a few examples (pls. 30:10-13).

Parallels for the smaller juglets include: En-Gedi (Stratum V): Mazar et al. 1966: fig. 30:13, 16, 17, 18 (latter two with spouts); Beersheba (Strata IV-II): *Beer-Sheba I*. pls. 45:8; 55:14; 56:3, 12; 62:116-18; 64:14; 74:13, 14; Tell Beit Mirsim (Stratum A): *TBM I*. pl. 69:23, 26, 27; *TBM II*. pls. 17:2, 5, 6; 18:17, 20 (with spout), 21, 24, 29; 26:1, 4, 5, 9, 12, 13, 16; Ramat Raḥel (Stratum VA): *RR I*. pl. 18:17; Lachish: *Lachish III*. pl. 88:285, 286, 294; Gezer (late Iron II): *Gezer III*. pl. 19:11, 12, 14; Hazor (Strata VI-V): *Hazor I*. pls. 56:1, 3; 61:3; 62:11; 65:12; *Hazor II*. pl. 86:9, 12; *Hazor III-IV*. pls. 184:18, 19, 20; Nebo (Iron II): Saller 1966: figs. 20:8, 15 (latter with spout); 22:18; 23:1, 2, 4; Amman: Harding 1944: p. 74:65, 66; Harding 1951: fig. 1: 21; Dhiban: *AASOR* 40 (1972) figs. 17:1, 3 (both examples with spout); 21:11; Pella: *Pella I*. pl. 126:4.

Parallels for the larger juglets include: En-Gedi (Stratum V): Mazar et al. 1966: figs. 19:8, 9; 30:14, 15; Beersheba (Stratum II): *Beer-Sheba I*. pls. 62:115; 69:20; 72:18; Tell Beit Mirsim (Stratum A): *TBM I*. pls. 68:35, 38-47 (with these examples it is difficult to distinguish between the larger and the smaller types); 69:22, 24, 28-30; *TBM II*. pls. 17:1, 3, 4; 18:16, 18, 22, 23, 26, 28; 26:10, 11; Ramat Raḥel (Stratum VA): *RR I*. pls. 18:18; 20:15; Lachish (Strata III-II): *Lachish III*. pl. 88:282 (with spout), 283, 284, 291; *Lachish V*: pls. 45:2; 47:27, 29; Hazor (Strata VIII-VA): *Hazor I*. pls. 52:14, 15; 65:11; *Hazor II*. pls. 58:7–9; 64:17; 70:2, 3, 8; 86:14, 15; 107:14; *Hazor III-IV*. pls. 180:17; 184:22, 24; 220:25, 27; Bethel (Iron II): *AASOR* 39 (1968) pls. 65:15, 16, 18; 78:1, 2; 'Aroʿer (Stratum III): Biran and Cohen 1981: pl. 7:7; Umm el-Biyara (seventh-sixth centuries B.C.E.): Bennett 1966a: figs. 2:14; 3:1; Nebo: Saller 1966: figs. 20:9; 21:6 (with spout); 22:17; 34:21; Amman: Harding 1951: fig. 1:20, 21.

3. Three larger juglets or jugs are nearly identical in form and fabric (pl. 31:4-6). These vessels are spherical in body profile with pronounced spouts. The form has one handle that overlaps the rim and is attached just below the join of the neck and body. The handles are generally flattened. Rim profiles differ slightly. The form appears to be unique to the Tell el-Kheleifeh repertoire.

4. Although represented by only a few examples, three other spouted jug types are known. A form with disc base, bulbous body, short neck and slightly pinched spout is represented in the plates by only one example (pl. 31:7). Plate 31:8 generally falls within this category. It has a disc base, a more spherical body profile than the previous example, a longer neck with everted rim and a very subtle (slightly off-centered) spout. The latter

could even be a defect in manufacturing. Plate 31:9 has a pronounced spout, lower body carination and a narrow flat base. Plate 32:1, similar to pl. 31:9, has a rounded base. The pottery records contain sketches of two elongated juglets (cf. 30:15-16 and 31:1-3) with pronounced spouts. Neither the vessels nor Henschel's drawings could be located. Apart from a single parallel to pl. 31:9 (Dhiban: *AASOR* 40 [1972] fig. 24:6), these jug types appear to be unique to Tell el-Kheleifeh.

5. The juglets, jugs, and jars in pl. 32:2-6 are the only examples of these types. Precise parallels to the vessels of this group are unknown. Plate 32:2 recalls the body profile of the spouted, spherical jugs of pl. 31:4-6.

6. A few juglets with horizontal bands of paint are presented in Henschel's drawings. Unfortunately, those pieces could not be located and the drawings are not adequate for inclusion in the plates. The juglet forms belong to classes 1, 2, and 4 above. The paint bands are dark red or dark gray and are organized in clusters of two lines (cf. pl. 27:10-12).

7. A single example of a typical Iron II burnished dipper juglet was allocated to the Smithsonian (Kheleifeh 7076; Smithsonian 388295). Among the many parallels are the following: En-Gedi (Stratum V): Mazar et al. 1966: fig. 30:1-6; Beersheba (Stratum II): Beer-Sheba I. pls. 45:10; 69:16; 72:22; Tell Beit Mirsim (Stratum A): *TBM II*. pl. 18:1, 5, 8, 9; Lachish: *Lachish III*. pl. 88:309-12, 320, 322; Hazor (Stratum V): *Hazor I*. pl. 56:5; Bethel (Iron II): *AASOR* 39 (1968) pl. 65:10, 11.

The juglets, jugs, and jars of Tell el-Kheleifeh constitute a collection with broad chronological limits, embracing the Iron II period, with some forms having even earlier antecedents. The spouted juglets, for instance, are documented in Lachish V, Beersheba IV, Megiddo VI, and Samaria VI. The forms presented here, however, are most common from the eighth-early sixth centuries B.C.E. As is clear from the comparisons, most parallels are provided by West Bank sites.

G. Decanters (pl. 32:7)

The characteristic Iron Age II decanter of the "southern" type is represented at Tell el-Kheleifeh by two whole vessels (491 and 5016), neither of which could be located but which are documented in the excavation records, and by one fragment that preserves the neck, handle, and upper body (pl. 32:7). Each of the examples exhibits the features of form and decoration that distinguish the southern type from its northern counterpart (Holladay 1976: 291-92). The body form is trapezoidal with a beaked rim, the latter constituting the diagnostic feature of the southern form. The single handle, with central, broad depression on the upper surface, is drawn from the ridged neck to the moderately carinated upper shoulder. The Kheleifeh decant-

ers are burnished from the lower extremity of the handle to the lower body carination. Plate 32:7 is preserved to only 3.5 cm below the point of handle attachment. The burnishing is poorly preserved but appears to begin just above the upper body carination and continues to the break.

Two painted decanter fragments were found at Tell el-Kheleifeh. The first, No. 11023, is a body sherd that preserves the upper body carination. The fragment is painted with alternating dark gray (7.5 R N3/0) and red (7.5 R N 5/8) lines. The second, No. 513, preserves the neck, handle, and upper body to a point 3 cm below the handle. The piece appears to lack the upper body carination. Vertical burnishing strokes are visible on the lower neck and upper shoulder to the point at which horizontal paint lines begin. Two bands of light red paint (10R 6/8) are bordered on each side by thin, weak red lines (10R 4/3). The decoration, both in form and color, recalls the Edomite painted wares (pl. 37).

Parallels include the following: En-Gedi (Stratum V): Mazar et al. 1966: figs. 9:7, 8; 20:1-5; Beersheba (Stratum II): *Beer-Sheba I*. pls. 62:100; 64:17; 74:17; Tell Beit Mirsim (Stratum A₂): *TBM I*. pl. 59:1, 2, 4, 6; *TBM III*. pl. 16:6; Ramat Raḥel (Stratum Va): *RR I*. figs. 11:26; 25:4; 28:41, 43; *RR II*. figs. 20:12; 35:4; Lachish (Strata III-II): *Lachish III*. pls. 87:264, 273-74, 276, 281; 103:665; *Lachish V*. pls. 44:17-18; 47:25; 48:12; 49:5-6 and 50:3-5, 14-16; Murrabbaʿat: Benoit et al. 1961: pl. 6:6; Beth-Shemesh (Stratum IIc): *AS IV*. pls. 45:13-16; 67:7, 8; 68:2, 6, 13, 14; Buqeʿah Valley: Stager 1975: pl. 3:24; Meṣad Ḥashavyahu (second half of seventh-end of sixth centuries B.C.E.): Naveh 1962: fig. 5:14-17; Umm el-Biyara (seventh-sixth centuries B.C.E.): Bennett 1966a: figs. 2:8; 3:6; Ghrareh (seventh-sixth centuries B.C.E.): Hart 1988: fig. 7:10; Adoni Nur: Harding and Tufnell 1953: fig. 22:102, 103; Sahab: Harding 1948: pl. 35:57; fig. 6:57; Amman: Harding 1944: p. 71:29; pl. 17:29; Buseirah: Bennett 1975: fig. 6:7.

The decanter is a vessel with broad chronological and geographical horizons. Its contexts appear to be datable between the eighth and sixth centuries B.C.E. There is also a general distinction between the "southern" and "northern" form of the decanter (Amiran 1970: 259-65; Holladay 1976: 291, 292), though the geographical perimeters are ambiguous at best. Like the En-Gedi cooking pot discussed above, the Tell el-Kheleifeh decanters are typically Judean in form and decoration.

H. Bowls (pls. 33-36:7)

The bowls of Tell el-Kheleifeh range from small to nearly krater size with wide variation in form. There are six general categories, each of which is represented by several examples with the exception of pl. 33:2.

1. There are 11 examples of small, rounded bowls with straight rim profile and low disc base (pl. 33:1).

Parallels include: En-Gedi: Mazar et al. 1966: fig. 29:13; Beersheba (Stratum II): Beer-*Sheba I*. pl. 59:41; Ramat Raḥel (Stratum V): *RR I*. figs. 11:7-9; 28:20-21; *RR II*. fig. 17:53-56; Tell Beit Mirsim: *TBM I*. pls. 65:3, 4; 67:1-6; Lachish: *Lachish III*. pl. 79:17; *Lachish V*. pl. 47:6 (Stratum II); Bethel (sixth century B.C.E.): *AASOR 39* (1968) pl. 64:10; ʿAroʿer (Stratum II): Biran and Cohen 1981: fig. 15:10; ʿAroʿer: Olavarri: 1965: fig. 1:4.

2. The collection contains a single example of a medium-sized, slightly rounded bowl with upper body carination and straight rim profile (pl. 33:2). The form has a small, irregular disc base. The quality of workmanship of this vessel stands out within the corpus.

Parallels include: En-Gedi (Stratum V): Mazar et al. 1966: figs. 15:9; 29:14; Beersheba (Stratum II): *Beer-Sheba I*. pl. 59:38; Ramat Raḥel (Stratum VA): *RR II*. fig. 17:50; Tell Beit Mirsim: *TBM I*. pls. 64:1, 7; 67:17; *TBM II*. pl. 24:6, 7, 15 (Stratum A); Lachish: *Lachish III*. pls. 79:6-8, 19; 81:95; Meṣad Ḥashavyahu: Naveh 1962: fig. 4:18; ʿAroʿer (Stratum III): Biran and Cohen 1981: fig. 7:1; Buseirah: Bennett 1975: fig. 5:12; Amman: Harding 1951: fig. 1:6, 7.

3. A common type is a medium-to large-sized deep bowl with rounded walls and slightly thickened rim (pl. 33:3-5). An exterior carination is consistently located approximately 1.5 cm. below the rim. Bases have not been preserved. One example has two loop handles and knob decorations (pl. 33:5).

Parallels include: Tell Beit Mirsim: *TBM I*. pls. 61:3; 62:14; *TBM II*. pls. 21:13 (Stratum A); 22:7; Lachish: *Lachish III*. pl. 79:45; *Lachish V*. pls. 44:1 (Stratum IV); 46:1 (Stratum III); Bethel: *AASOR 39* (1968) pl. 63:18.

4. A slightly thickened rim is also evident on three forms that exhibit a pronounced body carination (pl. 33:6-8). Unlike the previous class, these bowls are carinated in the middle of the vessel. Two of the examples exhibit a disc base (pl. 33:6, 7) and two are burnished and slipped (pl. 33:7, 8).

Parallels include: En-Gedi (Stratum V): Mazar et al. 1966: figs. 14:12; 29:5; Beersheba (Stratum II): *Beer-Sheba I*. pls. 59:54, 55, 57; 71:10; Tell Beit Mirsim (Stratum A): *TBM I*. pls. 64:9; 65:7, 8; *TBM III*. pls. 24:10, 13; 25:17-19, 22-24; Megiddo (Strata V-II range): *Megiddo I*. pls. 24:31; 28:106.

5. The "inverted rim" bowls are the most common type at Tell el-Kheleifeh, though there is significant variation within the class (pls. 33:9-15, 34; 35:1-6). The defining characteristics of these small (pl. 33:9-15) and large, deep bowls (pls. 34; 35:1-6) are the following: rounded walls and sometimes a very slight body carination; flat, disc or ring base, though the latter two are more common; and a thickened, inverted or turned-over rim which is triangular in section. Only a few

sherds are burnished or slipped. A few particulars are noteworthy. A slight body carination is present in pl. 34:2. Note also the more flattened rim profile of this example and pl. 34:3, 4. These two examples recall pl. 33:3-5 and also exhibit a slight exterior carination just below the rim. Rims frequently have a pronounced ridge in bowls of all sizes (pls. 33:9-15; 34:5-8; 35:1-5) as compared with pl. 35:6. Several bar handles are known (pl. 34:5, 6).

Parallels include: En-Gedi (Stratum V): Mazar et al. 1966: fig. 15:5 (cf. pl. 35:2, 3, 5; the Kheleifeh examples have a more inward stance of the rim); Beersheba (Strata IV-II range): *Beer Sheba I*. pls. 55:1 (cf. pl. 35:6); 70:9 (cf. pl. 35:1, 2); 72:6 (cf. pl. 34:7); 74:2 (cf. pl. 34:3); Ramat Raḥel (Stratum VA): *RR II*: fig. 17:1-3 (cf. pl. 35:2-4 for rim profile), 28 (cf. pl. 35:6); Tell Beit Mirsim: *TBM I*. pls. 61:8 (cf. pl. 34:3), 15 (cf. pl. 35:6); 62:4, 9, 18, 20 (cf. pl. 35:1); 63:1 (cf. pl. 35:1), 2 (cf. pl. 35:6), 4 (cf. pl. 35:2-5), 7, 9 (cf. pl. 33:14, 15 for rim profile only); Tell Beit Mirsim (Stratum A): *TBM III*. pls. 20:3 (cf. pl. 35:6); 21:9 (cf. pl. 33:6); 22:1 (cf. pl. 35:1); 23:2, 4, 7, 11; 26:1 (cf. pl. 33:3-5); Lachish: *Lachish III*. pl. 80:70, 72, 73, 75, 81-83, 86 (good parallels to the general characteristics of this class); *Lachish V*. pl. 44:12 (cf. pl. 35:1-6); Bethel (Iron II): *AASOR 39* (1968) pls. 62:6, 8 (cf. pl. 34:7, 8); 63:22; 64:1, 2; 80:8; Beth–Zur (Stratum III): *AASOR 38* (1968) fig. 17:11, 12; Meṣad Ḥashavyahu: Naveh 1962: fig. 4:13; ʿAroʿer (Stratum II): Biran and Cohen 1981: figs. 10:1; 15:2, 4; ʿAroʿer: Olavarri 1965: fig. 1:7; Ghrareh (seventh-sixth centuries B.C.E.): Hart 1987a: fig. 9:2 (cf. pl. 33:11-14); 1988: fig. 7:7 (cf. pl. 34:2-4; 35:1-5).

6. An everted rim profile distinguishes another common class of bowls in the repertoire (pls. 35:7-12; 36:1-7). While each of these rims generally may be characterized as everted, the rim profiles of pl. 36:1-3 and 5-7 may further be described as "inset" or "stepped." The most frequent rim profiles within this grouping include pls. 35:7, 8 and 36:1-3, 5, 6. Plates 35:9, 10 and 36:4 represent unique profiles within the corpus. Note the triangular rim of the large, deep bowl on pl. 36:7. Apart from the rim characteristics, the features that define the previous class are common in this class as well. Note, however, the unusual rounded base of pl. 35:7.

Several sites offer parallels to the general characteristics of this class. See En-Gedi (Stratum V): Mazar et al. 1966: figs. 8:6; 14:3; 15:1, 2 (the rim profile of the last example is similar to pl. 35:7, 9); Ramat Raḥel (Stratum VA): *RR II*. fig. 16:32, 33 (Cf. pl. 36:1-3, 7); Tell Beit Mirsim: *TBM I*. pls. 65:20b, 21, 24, 25; 66:3; *TBM III*. pl. 21:8, 10, 15; Bethel: *AASOR 39* (1968) pls. 63:12, 13; 64:3; Beth-Zur (Stratum III): *AASOR 38* (1968) fig. 18:4; Meṣad Ḥashavyahu: Naveh 1962, fig. 4:3, 6 (especially for the rim profile of pl. 35:9); Heshbon (seventh-sixth centuries B.C.E.): Lugenbeal and Sauer 1972: pl. 3:85, 89, 92, 97, 99; Buseirah: Bennett 1975: fig. 7:4, 9; Ghrareh (seventh-sixth centuries B.C.E.): Hart 1987a: fig. 9:1; 1988: fig. 7:3; ʿAroʿer: Olavarri 1965: fig. 2:9; Umm el-Biyara: Bennett 1966a: fig. 2:16. Although unpublished, the rim types of 36:1-3 and 5-7 are very common at Tell el-ʿUmeiri.

I. Saucers (pl. 36:8-10)

Three saucer fragments, including two nearly complete examples, are attested from Glueck's excavations. The form is characterized by a ring base, although most parallel examples have either a flat (often string-cut) or concave base, and a straight or slightly thickened rim. One example (pl. 36:10) is burnished and painted, but the painting is poorly preserved. The painting consists of a 1.5 cm thick band of red paint (7.5R 5/8) on the interior portion of the upper rim, extending slightly over the ridge. The burnishing marks extend from the lower paint band over the interior of the vessel.

Holladay (1976: 284-85) categorized these vessels as "burnished saucers." He distinguishes between saucers with "drooping" rims, as illustrated by RR II. fig. 16:14-28, and those with straight or slightly thickened rims, represented by RR II. fig. 16:1-5, 7-14, 16-19, 21, and 23-28. All examples are burnished. The Tell el-Kheleifeh forms clearly fall within the latter category.

Parallels include the following: En-Gedi (Stratum V): Mazar et al. 1966: fig. 15:3, 4 (with flat bases); Beersheba (Stratum II): Beer-Sheba I. pl. 74:3 (with flat base); Tell Beit Mirsim (Stratum A): TBM III. pl. 2:4; Ramat Raḥel (Stratum V): RR I. fig. 11:3 (with flat base) 26:1; 28:3-6 (3, 4 and 6 with flat bases); RR II. fig. 16:1-13, 17 (all Stratum VA and with flat bases); Lachish (Strata III-II): Lachish III. pl. 80:63; Lachish V. pl. 49:3 (with flat base); Bethel: AASOR 39 (1968) pl. 63:15 (base uncertain); Hazor (Strata VIII-IV): Hazor I. pls. 66:15, 29; 73:24, 28; Hazor II. pl. 48:17; Hazor III-IV. pls. 181:38; 219:6, 7; 223:9; 254:28; Beth-Zur (Stratum III): AASOR 38 (1968) fig. 17:15; Heshbon (seventh-sixth centuries B.C.E.): Lugenbeal and Sauer 1972: pl. 9:504, 515; Dhiban: AASOR 40 (1972): fig. 24:9; Sahab: Harding 1947: p. 97:1, 2 (with flat bases); Umm el-Biyara (seventh-sixth centuries B.C.E.): Bennett 1966a: fig. 2:4 (published as a cover); Buseirah: Bennett 1974a: figs. 14:1, 7, 8 (with flat bases); 15:9; Bennett 1975: fig. 6:11, 16; Nebo: Saller 1966: fig. 34:1-8.

The saucers, or "straight sided bowls," (Amiran 1970: 200, 206; pls. 64, 65) are widely distributed in contexts from the eighth century B.C.E. and later. The ring base of the Tell el-Kheleifeh examples is less common than the flat base exhibited in many of the parallels.

J. Vessels with Crenellated Decoration (pl. 37:1-7; see also 29:12)

The vessels presented here (see also Glueck 1967a: figs. 2:1-3, 6 a-c; 5:1-6) exhibit a form of decoration that is common on Edomite pottery. It is well known from the sites of Buseirah, Umm el-Biyara, ʿAroʿer (W), and Horvat Qitmit in contexts of the late Iron Age. This crenellated decoration occurs most frequently on saucers, bowls, small jars, and the so-called "windowed" censers. The pottery of Tell el-Kheleifeh contains a few dozen body sherds with this style of decoration. The Negevite vessel of pl. 15:11 contains what appears to be a crenellated decoration.

K. Painted Edomite Pottery (pl. 37:8-12; see also 28:7-9)

The Tell el-Kheleifeh collection contains several pieces of painted pottery that may be identified as Edomite. Several sherds that might be assigned to this type could not be located in the collection of the Jordan Archaeological Museum. In addition to the vessels and sherds presented in the plates, see also Glueck 1967a: figs. 4:7a, b (p. 16); 5:2 (p. 19); 1:9a (p. 26); and 5:6 (p. 37). As noted above, figs. 1:2 [5:1] and 4:3-5 are Midianite, not Edomite as suggested by the excavator. Again, the sites that provide the best parallels to the vessel types of pl. 37:8-12 and the painting on that pottery are Buseirah, Umm el-Biyara, ʿAroʿer (W), and Horvat Qitmit (for the few published pieces, see Bennett 1974a: figs. 15:3, 4, 8; 16:1, 7; 1975: figs. 5:2, 4, 8, 9, 13; 6:13, 16; see also Dornemann 1983: 65-75). One painted sherd has been published from es-Sadeh (Lindner, Farajat, and Zeitler 1988: fig. 8:10). Though unpublished, ʿAroʿer (W) offers several very close parallels to the vessel form and decoration of Pl. 37:11.

L. Lamps (pls. 38; 39:1-3)

The Tell el-Kheleifeh lamps that could be located consist generally of fragments. A representative selection from the ASOR collection is presented in the plates. Henschel's pottery plates also include working drawings of two seven-spouted lamps and three double lamps. Those pieces could not be found in the three Tell el-Kheleifeh collections, and Henschel's drawings are unsatisfactory for inclusion in the plates. There is also some question as to the site provenance of the double lamps.

The lamps belong to six categories:

1. Shallow-medium depth with rounded base and broad flange (pl. 38:1-4; see also unpublished nos. 4921 and 3018).

Parallels include: En-Gedi (Stratum V): Mazar et al. 1966: fig. 23:1, 2 (flange uncertain in the last example); Lachish: *Lachish III*. pl. 83:142, 148; Megiddo: *Megiddo I*. pls. 37:13, 14; 38:19 Strata V-II); *Megiddo II*. pls. 70:6; 72:6; 74:13; 86:16 (Strata VII-VI range); Bethel (Iron II): *AASOR* 39 (1968) pl. 65:23; Dhiban: *AASOR* 40 (1972) fig. 15:7, 8.

2. Deep lamps with rounded base and broad flange (pl. 38:5-8; see also unpublished nos. 105, 126, 207, 428, 563, 920, 1044, 2093, and 8039).

Parallels include: Beersheba (Stratum II): *Beer-Sheba I*. pl. 64:18; Megiddo (Strata IV-I): *Megiddo I*. pl. 37:10, 11, 15; Ramat Raḥel: *RR I*. pl. 28:51; Tel Masos (Strata III-II range): Fritz and Kempinski 1983: pls. 135:17, 149:9, 10; 157:17; Umm el-Biyara (seventh-sixth centuries B.C.E.): Bennett 1966a: fig. 2:12, 13.

3. Medium-deep lamps with rounded base and slight flange (pls. 38:9; 39:1).

Parallels include: Lachish: *Lachish III*. pl. 83:141; 143, 147; Megiddo: *Megiddo II*. pls. 62:1-4; 66:9, 11, 12; 70:7; 79:7-9; 86:13, 14; Dhiban: *AASOR* 40 (1972) figs. 15:4-6, 14; 20:1, 12; 23:19.

4. Shallow-medium depth with slight base and broad flanges (pl. 39:2).

Parallels inlcude: Beersheba (Strata III and II): *Beer-Sheba I*. pls. 56:7; 63:135; 64:19; Lachish (Stratum IV): *Lachish V*. pl. 44:8; Megiddo (Stratum V): *Megiddo I*. pl. 38:18; Tell Beit Mirsim (Stratum A₂): *TBM I*. pl. 70:1-3; *TBM III*. pl. 15:5; Ramat Raḥel (Stratum V): *RR I*. pl. 11:35; Meṣad Ḥashavyahu (eighth-seventh centuries B.C.E.): Naveh 1962: pl. 5:19; Dhiban: *AASOR* 40 (1972) figs. 15:10; 20:4-7.

5. Broad and very shallow lamps with broad flange and less pronounced spout (pl. 39:3; see also unpublished no. 7091). Precise parallels to this form are rare.

6. Three seven-spouted lamps and lamp fragments, including one handmade example. None of these could be located for technical drawing. The handmade lamp (no. 102) has a crude base and five preserved spouts. No. 5086, as sketched by Henschel, has a chalice base 6 cm high. The lamp is intact, preserving all seven spouts.

Parallels include: Lachish: Lach*ish III*. pl. 90:359; Megiddo (Stratum III): *Megiddo I*. pl. 37:16: Tell Beit Mirsim: *TBM I*. pl. 23:3; Tell en-Naṣbeh: *TN II*. pl. 71:1625; Hazor (Strata V-IV): *Hazor I*. pl. 71:25; Samaria: *SS III*. pl. 27:5 (with two preserved spouts); Murrabbaʿat: Benoit et al. 1961: pl. VI:3.

Absent from the Tell el-Kheleifeh assemblage are the high-based lamps that are among the hallmarks of late Iron Age pottery in Judah. See, for example, En-Gedi (Stratum V): Mazar et al. 1966: figs. 23:5-9; 32:8-9; Beersheba (Stratum II): Beer-Sheba I. pls. 63:133, 134, 136; 64:21; Lachish (Stratum II): *Lachish V*. pls. 48:2-4;

49:8; 50:6; Ramat Raḥel (Stratum V): *RR I*. pls. 11:32-34, 36-88; 27:5, 8; 28:50.

M. Miscellaneous Forms

Vessels with "handled" bases (pl. 39:4, 5). Several "handled" base fragments are attested. Two are presented in the plates (pl. 39:4, 5). Three "handles" can be reconstructed for each example. Given the regional character of the Tell el-Kheleifeh assemblage, specifics in terms of reconstructed vessel form are nearly impossible. Parallel base fragments suggest assignment to a krater or large bowl category.

Although similar bases are documented earlier (Fritz and Kempinski 1983: pl. 150:2), eighth century B.C.E. contexts and later are provided by Buseirah: Bennett 1975: fig. 8:2; Dhiban: *AASOR* 40 (1972) figs. 22:11; 13:24, 26; Lachish: *Lachish III*. pl. 81:118; Megiddo (Strata IV-III): *Megiddo I*. pls. 17:84; 25:65 and Tell en-Naṣbeh: *TN II*. pl. 63:1441.

Funnels (pl. 39:6). Two complete funnels were uncovered in Glueck's excavations (nos. 12056 and 3097), the last example is presented in pl. 39:6. The rim profile recalls that of the Assyrian bowls and is quite closely paralleled by a number of teapot and bowl forms (pl. 28:10-12). Each vessel has a single, slightly elongated, loop handle. The fabrics are generally reminiscent of the "Qawsʿanal" jars (pls. 20-21). Ware descriptions and technological studies were not possible on those pieces, which were allocated to the Jordan Archaeological Museum.

There are no precise parallels to this form (cf. *Lachish III*. pl. 89:375 [specifics are difficult with this poor drawing]; *Gezer I*. pl. 28:17 [no handles, different rim profile]; Beersheba [Stratum II]: *Beer-Sheba I*. pl. 63:130; [comparable only in belonging to the same class]: Tell en–Naṣbeh: *TN II*. pl. 77:1775-77 [no handles; different rim profile]).

Flasks or Canteens (pl. 40:1-5; see also unpublished nos. 552, 597, 4025, and 6062). For the only close parallel to the forms presented in the plates, see Saller 1966: figs. 20:14, 14a; 23:25, 26.

III. A COMMENT ON THE EDOMITE POTTERY OF TELL EL-KHELEIFEH

When Glueck excavated at Tell el-Kheleifeh and conducted his pioneering surveys in the Negev and southern Transjordan, the material culture of the Edomites was almost unknown. Apart from the biblical references to those people and their land, relatively little was even known of their political and cultural history. While significant strides have been made since Glueck's work, many years, perhaps even decades, of research and exploration will be necessary before an authoritative history of Edom can be written.

At present, there are still areas of great uncertainty, such as Edomite origins, the early political and cultural history of the people, the geographical boundaries of Edom at any given time in its history, and the nature of the relationship between the later Edomites and the Nabataeans. These are only a few of the problems. Edomite material culture is still quite unknown and the lack includes Edomite script and language in addition to pottery traditions. Nevertheless, there has been a significant increase in the archaeological data from the regions that were under Edomite political, commercial, or cultural influence. We now know considerably more than Glueck did about the archaeological history of the Edomites, their material culture, and their land (see Bartlett 1969; 1972; 1977; 1979; 1989; Bennett 1966a; 1971a; 1973a; 1974a; 1975; 1977; 1982a; 1983; 1984; Biran and Cohen 1981; Dayton 1972; Dornemann 1982; 1983; Hadidi 1982; 1987; Hart 1986; 1987a; 1987b; 1988; Hart and Falkner 1985; Herr 1980; Jobling 1981; 1982; 1983; 1984; Lindner and Farajat 1987; Lindner, Farajat, and Zeitler 1988; MacDonald 1980; 1982a; 1982b; 1983; 1984; 1988; MacDonald, Rollefson, and Roller 1982; MacDonald, Rollefson, and Banning 1983; Mazar 1985; Oakshott 1983; Sauer 1985; 1986; Sawyer and Clines 1983). A number of sites that have produced Edomite pottery and other material culture are largely unpublished to date, such as Buseirah, Tawilan, Umm el-Biyara, Ghrareh, es-Sadeh, Hasevah, and several others in the eastern and western Negev.

Throughout this chapter, the term Edomite has been applied to several types of pottery from Tell el-Kheleifeh (see discussion for pls. 16; 17; 18:1-6; 20; 21:1-8; 28:15-17; 28 and 37). We have noted in the final chapter of this volume that caution must be exercised with regard to this identification. It is uncertain whether one can speak of this ceramic assemblage as an ethnic pottery tradition. In light of what is presently known, that identification appears appropriate. The Edomite pottery of Tell el-Kheleifeh, however, must continue to be examined in light of newly published material and fresh data from the field.

IV. TELL EL-KHELEIFEH AND HORVAT QITMIT

A few comments on the recent excavations at Horvat Qitmit are appropriate. Qitmit is a small site in the eastern Negev that dates to the last decades of the Iron II period. I. Beit-Arieh uncovered a small shrine there and identified it as Edomite based on its pottery, epigraphic finds, and the iconography of numerous figurines (Beit-Arieh 1984; 1986b; 1988; Beit-Arieh and Beck 1987). The site also yielded many cult objects, including zoomorphic and anthropomorphic figurines, cult stands, and incense burners. The excavator suggested that the presence of an Edomite shrine in the eastern Negev may indicate Edomite occupation of that region at a time when Judah was weakened by the conflict with Babylon.

Beit-Arieh has identified three categories of pottery at Horvat Qitmit: domestic Judahite forms of the late seventh and early sixth centuries B.C.E.; Edomite pottery (decorated and plain); and "vessels of types common in Eretz Israel and Transjordan" but which he associates primarily with Edomite sites (1987: 18). Several eastern Negev sites have produced small quantities of Edomite painted pottery, including Tel Malhata, Tel 'Ira, Tel Masos, 'Aro'er (W), Tel Sera', Tel Haror, Tell el-Qudeirat, and Tell Jemmeh. All that material dates to the late seventh and early sixth centuries B.C.E.

Tell el-Kheleifeh produced a significant horizon of pottery that has been identified as Edomite (Glueck 1967a: 8-38 and 1971a: 45-46),and, although the pottery of Horvat Qitmit has not yet been published, it is clear from the available data that there are numerous parallels to the Tell el-Kheleifeh repertoire (see, for example, Beit-Arieh 1989: figs. 12:13, 15; 14:1, 2, 6, 7, 8, 10, 13, and 15). The late Iron Age assemblage of Horvat Qitmit will be very important for the continued study of Tell el-Kheleifeh.

V. SUMMARY

The Tell el-Kheleifeh records do not contain a compendium of the pottery assemblages that Glueck associated with each of the occupational periods. Given the excavation methodology and recording system and the resulting lack of horizontal and vertical controls, that information cannot be retrieved. Glueck, however, published a representative selection of his Period IV pottery types (Glueck 1967a), but whether it represents a discrete horizon remains unanswerable. In light of the work with the records reported here, it is even impossible to completely isolate the pottery that should be associated with the two major architectural phases (casemate fortress and fortified settlement), though Glueck's period IV corpus should probably be assigned to the latter.

Reexamination of Tell el-Kheleifeh's pottery has produced significant revision in the site's chronological horizons. The earliest pottery is represented by six Midianite sherds (Glueck 1967a: fig. 1:2 [5:1] and 4:3-5). The five body sherds and one sherd that preserves a small section of a rim are identified as Midianite based on their fabrics and geometric motifs. They should be dated between the 13th and the 12th century B.C.E. (Rothenberg 1988: 93-94, figs. 4-13; Rothenberg and

Glass 1981: 85-114; 1983: 65-124). Because the Tell el-Kheleifeh records do not provide a reliable field provenance for those pieces, little can be said about their significance. At any rate, it is clear that six sherds, without a reliable stratigraphic context, do not document an occupational horizon.

While acknowledging the presence of forms that can be dated earlier, most of the pottery dates between the eighth and early sixth centuries B.C.E. We must also allow the possibility, though not yet clearly documented, that selected forms could have continued later than the traditional end of the Iron Age and perhaps well into the fifth century B.C.E. Glueck's Period V yielded several ostraca and some pottery that document an occupation as late as the fourth century B.C.E. As noted above, however, the architecture of that level was very poorly preserved. A stamped amphora handle, found on the surface during the 1980 survey, dates as late as the third century B.C.E. Like the Midianite sherds, however, this piece cannot be considered significant in terms of the site's occupational history.

Without rehearsing the specific types that are paralleled, the pottery of Tell el-Kheleifeh has its closest affinities with the horizons of En-Gedi V (late seventh-early sixth centuries B.C.E.), Ramat Raḥel VA (late seventh-early sixth centuries B.C.E.), Tel Beersheba II (eighth century B.C.E.), Lachish III-II (eighth-early sixth centuries B.C.E.), Gezer VI-V (eighth-early sixth centuries B.C.E.), Beth-Zur III (late Iron Age), Meṣad Ḥashavyahu (second half of the seventh-end of the sixth century B.C.E.), Buqeʿah Valley (seventh-early sixth centuries B.C.E.), Tel Masos (post I; seventh century B.C.E.), Tell el-Farʿah (S), Niveau I (middle of the eighth-early sixth centuries B.C.E.), Beth-shemesh IIC (late Iron Age), Tell Beit Mirsim A2 (eighth-seventh centuries B.C.E.), ʿAroʿer (W) III-II (eighth-seventh centuries B.C.E.), Tel ʿArad VII and VI (late Iron Age), Hazor VI-III (eighth-seventh centuries B.C.E.), Samaria Pottery Periods V-VIII (eighth-seventh centuries. B.C.E.), Tell el-Qudeirat's middle and latest fortress phases (eighth-early sixth centuries B.C.E.), Heshbon (seventh-sixth centuries B.C.E.), Dhiban, and Pella (late Iron Age contexts). Numerous parallels come from the largely unpublished sites of Umm el-Biyara and Tawilan. C. M. Bennett has published a selection of pottery from Buseirah (seventh-sixth centuries B.C.E.) which offers a number of good parallels. Edomite pottery of the late Iron Age, with some good parallels to Tell el-Kheleifeh forms, has recently been discovered at Ghrareh, es-Sadeh and Feifa. The Jordanian tomb groups of Amman (Adoni Nur, Meqabelein and Sahab) parallel many Tell el-Kheleifeh forms. Although their chronology is debated, a date between the eighth and early sixth centuries B.C.E. would be very close.

The above contexts clearly define the chronological limits of the pottery corpus as a whole. A few of the Tell el-Kheleifeh forms are known from earlier contexts such as Hazor X-VII and Tel Masos II-I. However, those pottery types are not unique to the earlier contexts but are well known in post-eighth century B.C.E. levels as well.

In light of what is currently known about the typology and chronology of the Negevite wares, the handmade assemblage of Tell el-Kheleifeh should be dated in accordance with the chronology of the wheelmade pottery. The Negevite wares of Tell el-Kheleifeh and Tell el-Qudeirat are most closely paralleled in the latter's middle and last fortress phases (eighth-early sixth centuries B.C.E.).

Chapter Six

The Tell el-Kheleifeh Inscriptions

ROBERT A. DIVITO

I. INTRODUCTION

With the exception of an inscribed Rhodian jar handle discovered in the 1980 survey, the small but varied collection of inscriptions found at Tell el-Kheleifeh has already been published by Glueck in several articles appearing between 1938 and 1971. Although the considerable interest their publication generated was linked initially to the identification of the site with biblical Ezion-geber, today the significance of the corpus lies in its contribution to the history of the ancient Near East more generally and to the field of paleography. Short lists of personal names, seal impressions, and fragmentary receipts make up the bulk of the Tell el-Kheleifeh collection. Yet, in spite of their restricted content, they offer scholars invaluable information on the scope of local, national, and international forces that came to bear on one of the few archaeological sites to have been excavated in southern Transjordan. And, as is evident from the contributions of numerous scholars who have participated over the years in the decipherment of the collection, the inscriptions provide crucial data for understanding the development and evolution of the scripts of several ancient Semitic peoples, ranging from Phoenicia to the Arabian peninsula.[1]

The collection, now housed in Amman, Cambridge, Mass., and Washington, D.C., consists of one signet, 22 identical seal impressions, two jar inscriptions, nine ostraca, and two inscribed sherds, in addition to the Rhodian jar handle. The inscriptions themselves are inked, incised, or impressed. While some pieces are well preserved, others are at best only partially legible. Time has been particularly harsh on the ostraca. In most cases, their ink has faded to such an extent that the original photographs, taken only with the aid of filters, are far superior to the results of more recent photographic efforts. Accordingly, only the original photographs have been selected for inclusion in this volume.

Table 2 is a catalogue of the epigraphic material by registry number,[2] with each item's current repository and field registry description.

The varied inscriptions contained in the corpus obviously yield important data for reconstructing the occupational history of Tell el-Kheleifeh. Nevertheless, since the primary importance of the corpus currently lies in its contribution to West Semitic paleography, that discipline provides the focus for the following analysis. Such a focus is perhaps even more desirable in light of the recent finds at Ḥorvat ʿUza and Qitmit (Beit-Arieh and Cresson 1985: 96-101; Beit-Arieh and Beck 1987), which have brought to light several Edomite inscriptions. The latter are written in a script exhibiting peculiarities directly comparable to roughly contemporaneous inscriptions found at Tell el-Kheleifeh, and as such are likely to fuel a debate that has gradually taken shape concerning the status of such "peculiarities" in general. Do such features—in Edomite as well as in the scripts of neighboring Moab and Ammon—constitute a distinctive "national script" tradition (Cross 1973: 13; 1975a: 10-14; Herr 1980: 31-33), or do they reveal merely an adaptation of the script of larger, more powerful neighbors by those who possessed "a lesser measure of cultural independence" (Naveh 1982: 100-12)? Given the paucity of inscriptions written in the script employed by the ancient Edomites prior to their adoption of Aramaic in the late sixth century B.C.E., the question has no easy answer. What is clear, though, is the desirability of a fresh, systematic paleographical examination of the Tell el-Kheleifeh inscriptions critical to the discussion.

In addition to the inscriptions that are treated here as representative of the ancient Edomite script, the Tell el-Kheleifeh collection contains inscriptions representing several other script traditions, including Aramaic, Phoenician, South Semitic, and Greek. Of these, the Aramaic and Phoenician scripts are generally well documented; nevertheless, a dearth of early fourth-century B.C.E. Aramaic and Phoenician inscriptions

TABLE 2. CATALOGUE OF INSCRIPTIONS
FROM TELL EL-KHELEIFEH

Reg. No.	Repository	Description	Period
146	ASOR	Seal impression	Iron II
215*	ASOR	Seal impression	Iron II
241*	ASOR	Seal impression	Iron II
243	ASOR	Seal impression	Iron II
267	ASOR	Seal impression	Iron II
278*	ASOR	Seal impression	Iron II
381	Smiths., No. 388,192	Seal impression	Iron II
463*	JAM, No. 2866	Seal impression	Iron II
464*	ASOR	Seal impression	Iron II
466	JAM, No. 2806	Seal impression	Iron II
467*	ASOR	Seal impression	Iron II
528*	ASOR	Seal impression	Iron II
724*	JAM, No. 2862	Seal impression	Iron II
742	ASOR	Seal impression	Iron II
822	ASOR	Seal impression	Iron II
1014	ASOR	Seal impression	Iron II
2092	ASOR	Seal impression	Iron II
2096*	Smiths., No. 388,245	Seal impression	Iron II
2098*	ASOR	Seal impression	Iron II
6049	ASOR	Seal impression	Iron II
9098	ASOR	Seal impression	Iron II
20, 271		Seal impression	Iron II
7022*	Smiths., No. 388,291	Signet	Iron II
374*	ASOR	Jar graffito	Iron II
469*	JAM, No. 2838	Jar inscription	Iron II
2069*	Smiths., No. 388, 240	Ostracon	Persian
2070*	ASOR	Ostracon	Persian
2071*	ASOR	Ostracon	Persian
6043*	Smiths., No. 388,277	Ostracon	Iron II
7094*	Smiths., No. 388,299	Ostracon	Persian
8058*	ASOR	Inscribed sherd	Persian
8096*	ASOR	Ostracon	Persian
9027*	ASOR	Inscribed sherd	Iron II
10,007*	ASOR	Ostracon	Persian
3059A,B*	ASOR	Sherds with potter's mark?	Persian
Unreg-istered*	ASOR	Rhodian jar handle	Hellenistic

*Pieces shown in the plates are marked with an asterisk.

gives the material of the Persian period presented here particular paleographical significance. Even the single occurrence of a letter can be useful to the paeographer in determining or confirming a letter form's evolution and this, in turn, makes possible the refinement of typologies indespensable to the dating of inscriptional material generally.

Following are the inscriptions contained in the Tell el-Kheleifeh collection together with their analysis.

II. THE INSCRIPTIONS

A. Signet (Reg. No. 7022)

Room 63A; 8x11x5 mm; (pl. 79):

lytm   "belonging to Yatom (Yātōm)

One of the most widely discussed pieces to have come from Tell el-Kheleifeh is this seal, enclosed in a copper casing, that bears the clear retrograde inscription *lytm*. The inscription is incised above a beautifully carved horned ram, apparently in stride, and before which is carved another figure, yet to be firmly identified. Suggestions for the latter have ranged from the figure of a man (Glueck 1940a: 13), to a portable bellows (Avigad 1961: 18-22), an ingot of copper (de Vaux 1966: 153-54), and, most recently, a scarab-beetle (Galling 1967: 133-34). As Galling notes (1967: 131-32), the design of the holder, consisting of two bronze volutes, makes it highly unlikely that it could be worn as a ring. Most likely it simply hung from a chain.

The orthography of the inscription would seem to rule out Albright's oft-quoted contention that the seal's owner be identified as Jotham (*ywtm*), son of Uzziah (Glueck 1940a: 15, n. 9). The lack of a patronymic, especially on a seal such as this one where most of the available space is occupied by a carved figure, is not uncommon; therefore, its absence does not support the notion that its owner is a well-known personage (Galling 1967: 132). Also, *Yātōm*, "orphan," makes a perfectly acceptable West Semitic name (Noth 1980: 231), having been found in the Elephantine papyri (Cowley 1923: no. 33:4 and *passim*; note also Aramaic *Yatma* in no. 11:1) and probably on a Phoenician seal of the fifth century B.C.E. (Hestrin and Dayagi-Mendels 1979: 162, no. 128).

Given both the conservative tendency of formal scripts in general and the limited basis for comparison that an inscription of only four letters can afford, it is difficult to assign a precise date to the seal. The *mem* and the *taw* are the most interesting letters paleographically, distinguishing the script from both Hebrew and Aramaic and suggesting an approximate date. The large-headed *mem*, first noted as diagnosti-

cally significant by Rosenthal (1942: 8-9) and more recently by Naveh (1982: 102), is quite similar to examples in the Moabite series, especially those that are less squat and in which the leg does not curve sharply to the left. The head itself consists of a "double-L" (often found in Hebrew and Moabite); but, as noted by Herr (1978: 163), the foot of the right "L" is incomplete. The *taw* appears as an inverted Roman cross, whose closest parallel is that of the *bᶜlntn* seal. Herr (1978: 158) identified the latter as probably Moabite and dated to the seventh century B.C.E., perhaps the second half. If we allow, then, for the peculiarities of the *mem* and the *taw* in the Yatom seal and the conservatism of its script, a date in the first half of the seventh century B.C.E. would seem suitable.[3]

B. Seal Impressions

Reg. Nos. 146 (Q:ll),[4] 215 (O:12), 241 (Rm. 27), 243 (Rm. 27), 267 (Rm. 34), 278 (Rm. 27), 381 (Rm. 49), 463 (Rm. 27), 464 (Rm. 27), 466 (Rm. 27), 467 (Rm. 27), 528 (Rm. 25A), 724 (Rm. 28), 742 (Rm. 30), 822 (P:12), 1014 (Rm. 45), 2092 (Rm. 50), 2096 (Rm. 50), 2098 (Rm. 49), 6049 (?), 9098 (Rm. 25A), 20,271 (?)

Horizontal axis approximately 11 mm.; (pls. 74-78):

lqwsᶜnl   "belonging to Qawsᶜanal,
ᶜbd hmlk   servant of the king."

The inscription is divided between two registers, separated by a double horizontal line, and fills the entire impression. Evidently all of the impressions, which appear for the most part on jar handles (though reg. no. 146 belongs to a seventh or early sixth-century cooking pot), were produced by a single seal. Any observable differences in letter form are simply a function of the poor condition of the impressions, which would be difficult to read on account of their size even if they were in pristine condition. Photographs are often misleading, because the angle and nature of the light-source play such a critical role in their composition. In any case, although not even one of the *qwsᶜnl* seal impressions preserves the complete inscription without damage or loss of letters (in some cases, only enough remains to assign the impression to the *qwsᶜnl* group), the composite reading is virtually certain. It is, in fact, the original reading of Glueck in 1938 (1938a: 17).

As the title "servant of the king" makes explicit, Qawsᶜanal was a high-ranking functionary of the king. His name contains as its theophoric element the well-known Edomite deity Qaws, or Qôs, familiar now from a growing number of personal names, particularly in the second half of the first millennium B.C.E. (Beit-Arieh and Beck 1987; Geraty 1972; Naveh 1973;

1979). See below also reg. no. 6043. The element *ʿnl* remains without solution. Attempts to read *ʿānā-lī* "has answered me," first proposed by Maisler (Glueck 1938b: 13, n. 45), are precluded by the orthography.[5] However, as Milik (1958: 240) first noted, the same name evidently occurs in Greek transcription, *Kōsanelou*, in an inscription from Alexandria dating to 134 B.C.E. (*CIG* 3: 4682:8). Also, Aharoni (1975b: 28) has proposed reading *[qw]sʿnl* in a damaged context at ʿArad (ostracon 12:3). Although Aharoni's reading is hardly conclusive, it, along with Milik's Greek name, supports the identification of *ʿnl* as an item belonging to the lexicon of the Edomite onomasticon.

In addition to the evidence for Edomite linguistic affiliation which the Canaanite prefixed article h- provides, the impressions are particularly valuable paleographically. The date and provenance of the impressions, the occurrence of an Edomite personal name, and the script's peculiarities—together suggest we have here an example of the formal script employed in ancient Edom. In spite of the generally poor condition of the impressions, the large number of specimens available makes it possible for the most part to determine the details of particular letter forms, with doubt remaining only about the letter *dalet*.

In reg. no. 241, where *dalet* is almost completely preserved, as well as in the more poorly preserved specimens of reg. nos. 463, 724, 215, and 146, *dalet* appears as a triangle whose shaft on the right has broken through to the top rather than to the bottom, as expected in Hebrew at least after the mid-eighth century B.C.E. To date, very few examples of lapidary *dalet* are attested in either Edomite or Moabite. Tailless, triangular *dalet*s are found both in the Meshaʿ stele and in the eighth–seventh-century Moabite seal *lkmššdq* (Galling 1941: 186, no. 92; Herr 1978: 157, no. 5 and fig. 75); but in the sixth-century Moabite seal of Meshaʿ (son of) ʿAdiʾel the *dalet* has the breakthrough at the top (Hestrin and Dayagi-Mendels 1979: 146, no. 116). Because the *mem* of the latter had not been engraved in the negative (mirror-writing), and as a result appears inverted in impressions with the shaft on the left, Hestrin and Dayagi-Mendels comment: "The seal was carved by an unskilled craftsman; the letters *mem* and *dalet* are inverted." However, except for the inversion of the letter *mem*, the engraving had certainly been executed with skill; and the failure to engrave in retrograde script does not in any case account for the breakthrough of *dalet*'s shaft to the top. Another explanation than that of inversion is required.

The only clear example of a formal lapidary *dalet* on an Edomite seal is the Buseirah seal no. 368, dated to the second half of the eighth century B.C.E. by Puech (1977: 12-13), or the first half of the seventh by Herr (1978: 163). Here, too, the shaft of *dalet* breaks through

on the top and not on the bottom. While Herr regards this as a probable engraver's error, Puech notes the Qawsʿanal parallel and muses about a single scribal school being the source of the two seals (13 and n. 9). Another example of an inverted *dalet* is the controverted Diringer seal no. 64 (1934: 220), *lmnḥmt ʾšt gdmlk*, which Israel (1979: 175-76) classified as Edomite in origin. These instances of inverted *dalet* suggest that the Qawsʿanal *dalet* does not represent a simple engraving error but a regional characteristic of the formal lapidary Edomite (and possibly Moabite) script, as already suggested by Israel. (Indeed, this may show the influence of South Semitic scripts, whose own tradition of *dalet* manifests the "breakthrough" of the shaft on the top and at the bottom.) The same form may well be behind the cursive *dalet* found in the recently discovered Ḥorvat ʿUza ostracon (line 4), where the letter's identification has apparently been questioned because of the same unexpected breakthrough of the shaft on the top (Beit-Arieh and Cresson 1985: 98, fig. 2, pl. 12: 2). Note, however, the cursive *dalet* of ostracon reg. no. 6043 and that of the mid-seventh-century Umm el-Biyara ostracon, where the breakthrough is at the bottom and the head is partially open (Bennett 1966: 398-99 and pl. 22a).

Some paleographical comment on the other letter forms found in the Qawsʿanal impressions is required.

Lamed, of little paleographical significance, appears to be essentially the form found on the Yatom seal with a rounded baseline. (The appearance of a flat baseline in reg. no. 528, for example, is probably due to the deterioration of the impressions.)

The *qop* (reg. nos. 241, 278, 381, 463, 467, 528, 2096) appears to represent an old lapidary tradition in which a circular head, formed by two semicircles, is bisected by a vertical shaft. Here, however, the top is open and the two strokes meet only at, or perhaps slightly below, the top of the shaft. The angularity of the head gives *qop* a slightly conical appearance reminiscent of the Umm el-Biyara seal from the first half of the seventh century (Bennett 1966: 399-401 and pl. 22b) as well as of the incised inscription recently unearthed in the Edomite shrine at Qitmit (Beit-Arieh and Beck 1987: 19). The heads of the latter however, are closed. Compare, too, the Qawsʿanal *qop* with the cursive *qop* in reg. no. 6043, below, with its horizontal "S"-top, a development of the Aramaic cursive and argillary scripts of the seventh century B.C.E. (Cross 1975a: 17).

The *waw* (reg. nos. 278, 528, 2098, 20, 271) is essentially that of the Umm el-Biyara seal—an inverted "h," familiar in Aramaic (cf. reg. nos. 374 and 6043 below for a more cursive treatment with a shallow head), rather than the hamza-*waw* of Hebrew.

The Qawsʿanal *samek* is archaic: three horizontal bars, possibly bisected by a vertical shaft. The shaft itself protrudes slightly above the top bar and well below the lower bar, similar again to the *samek* found in the Umm el-Biyara seal. The same form seems to be present in the incised Qitmit inscription. Note that the bars lack the tick that developed in the eighth-century Hebrew seal script. The closest Moabite parallel is that of the eighth–seventh-century Moabite seal *lkmšᶜm* (Hestrin and Dayagi-Mendels 1979: 17, no. 2; dated ca. 700 B.C.E., according to Herr 1978: 156). Among Aramaic seals the closest parallels disappear in the eighth century B.C.E. (Herr 1978: 57).

In contrast to the seal from Buseirah, no. 368, and, more interestingly, the cursive of reg. no. 6043, the slightly squared *ᶜayin* here is open at the top, as in the jar graffito reg. no. 374. In Moabite, open *ᶜayin*'s appear in two sixth-century seals (Hestrin and Dayagi-Mendels 1979: 145-46, nos. 115 and 116), while in Ammonite seals open forms of *ᶜayin* appear late in the seventh century, probably under the influence of Aramaic (Herr 1980: 23). In Hebrew, of course, the closed forms perdure.

The head of *nun* in the Qawsᶜanal impressions (reg. nos. 146, 463, 464, 528) appears to consist of a small "L," or check mark, whose foot enters the leftward curving shaft on the left slightly below the top (thus producing a small right shoulder). Essentially the same form of *nun* is found in the Hebrew seal script of the eighth and seventh centuries B.C.E., while in Moabite more squat examples with larger heads appear in the seals of the sixth.

Due to their poor state of preservation, details of the *bet* on individual impressions are often unclear or apparently contradictory. The head is, however, closed (cf. reg. nos. 146, 215, 241, 528, 724, 2096, 2098), and appears to have a somewhat pointed nose. The basically upright shaft extends well below the head, with the foot dipping below the horizontal about 45 degrees. The form is essentially that of the *bᶜlntn* seal, (Herr 1978: 158, no. 8), probably Moabite, or the incised inscription from Qitmit.

In the *lmlklbᶜ* seal from Buseirah, no. 368, the *he* has three horizontal bars extending from the shaft. The only instance of *he* from Tell el-Kheleifeh is this one, where, quite unexpectedly, it seems to be a two-bar form, with no extension of the top bar to the right of the shaft. While the two-bar *he* occurs in Ammonite seals exclusively (Herr 1980: 21-22), Moabite, like Hebrew, exhibits to date only the three-bar types. In the incised inscription from Qitmit, the *he*, unfortunately damaged by a break in the inscription, appears to be of the three-bar type.

Mem (reg. nos. 241, 463, 528) has a large head, approximately half the height of the letter, composed of a "double-L." As noted above in connection with the Yatom seal, this large head has diagnostic significance

for both Moabite and Edomite (for corresponding Moabite forms, see Avigad 1970: pl. 30, nos. 6 and 7). With Hebrew and Moabite, the shaft here curves sharply to the left at its bottom.

Kap (e.g., reg. nos. 463 and 528) has the classical V-shaped bars, meeting slightly below the top of the shaft on the left. The latter curves to the left at the bottom.

In general, a date for these impressions in the late seventh, or perhaps the early sixth century, would appear about right. The open *qop*, for example, would seem to indicate a date after the *qwsgbr* seal, ascribed to the first half of the seventh century B.C.E.; the open *ᶜayin* suggests the late seventh century into the sixth (as in the Ammonite seal series; Herr 1980: 22-23). Note that the *samek* is quite archaic here, tolerating a date in the late seventh century perhaps, but certainly not one too far into the sixth, as the more advanced letters might suggest.

C. Inked Ostracon (Reg. No. 6043)

Room 70; 83x140 mm; (pl. 82):

1. rᵓl
2. bdq[ws]
3. šlm
4. qwsb[nh]
5. pgᶜqws
6. nᶜm
7. škk
8. rpᵓ
9. pgᶜqws
10. qwsny

Today the writing on the dark inside surface of this ostracon from an eighth–sixth-century cooking pot is barely discernible to the naked eye. Only traces of the bottom lines—and not distinct letter forms—are visible. Consequently, any analysis is dependent on the original photographs taken by Schweig, using colored filters, and those made in 1966 by Raymond. They show that the ostracon contains at least ten lines of an ink inscription, only the beginnings of which are now legible. Together they comprise a list of names, a number of which may be identified by the theophoric element Qaws, or Qôs. As the reading presented here is substantially that of Glueck (1941: 3-6; 1971: 226-29; see also, Albright 1941: 11-15; Rosenthal 1942: 8-9; Naveh 1966: 27-30), my comments may be restricted to a few points of interpretation and to some of the significant paleographical features of the script.

Line 1: *rᵓl*, if correctly read, may be the same name as biblical *Rĕᵓūᵓēl* (Exod 2:18; an Edomite, Gen 36:4). The pointed nose of *reš*'s head, perhaps slightly opened at the top, can be distinguished from the more rounded nose of the *dalet* in line 2, and would be identical to the *reš* of line 8. Note in the Umm el-Biyara ostracon (Bennett 1966: 398-99, and pl. 22a), dated to the mid-seventh century, the *reš* (line 1) is definitely open and has a pointed nose, though the stance is more tilted to the left. See also the apparently open *reš* on the late seventh-early sixth-century B.C.E. ostracon from Ḥorvat ʿUza (Beit-Arieh and Cresson 1985: 99-100). ʿAyin, drawn in two strokes and slightly squarish, is closed (cf. lines 5, 6, and 9), as it is in the Umm el-Biyara ostracon (line 2), in contrast to open ʿayin found in the Ḥorvat ʿUza ostracon. The manner of writing ʾalep is less clear. It has been compared to the characteristic form at Lachish. I suggest that a more typically Aramaic ductus is in evidence here: neither of the bars on the right crosses the shaft, while the bar on the left is drawn separately. This is also the form that Cross has recognized on the Ammonite Heshbon IV ostracon, dated to the end of the seventh or to the beginning of the sixth century B.C.E. (1975a: 14-15, fig. 2). Perhaps it is this form which lies behind the rather clumsy ʾalep, if indeed it is ʾalep, in line 8.

Line 2: *bdq[ws]*, "in the hand (= protection) of Qaws," makes a suitable Edomite name. The large head of *bet* appears to be slightly open at the top (perhaps open as well in line 4) in contrast to the Qawsʿanal *bet*. On the Ḥorvat ʿUza ostracon it is also open. Note that at Tell el-Kheleifeh the baseline is still distinct from the vertical shaft. *Qop* still seems to be the best reading for the third letter, the extreme leftward stance found again in line 4. (The peculiarity of the form may be due, in part, to the irregularity of the writing surface.) In lines 5, 9, and 10 the stances are more upright. In all cases, however, the head seems to have developed (from an older type where the head is drawn in two semi-circles; cf. the Qawsʿanal impressions) into the "S"-shaped head familiar in the seventh- and sixth-century Aramaic cursive and argillary scripts.

Line 3: The reading is uncontested. For possible vocalizations of the name *šlm*, see biblical *Šallūm*, 2 Kgs 15:10, or *Šillēm*, Gen 46:24. The *šin*, in the form of a "double-check W," is similar to that of the Umm el-Biyara ostracon (line 1), where the downstroke of the right "v" dips below the upstroke of the first. The *mem* (also line 6) is perhaps only a slightly more advanced form of the lapidary Qawsʿanal *mem*, while lagging behind that of the Umm el-Biyara ostracon typologically: a large head, composed of a "double-L" (quite similar to that found on the ostracon from Ḥorvat ʿUza), and an oblique shaft turning to the left for a baseline. On the Umm el-Biyara ostracon large-headed *mem* has only a vestigial right shoulder due to the fact that the shaft starts its downstroke only slightly above the foot of the right "L."

Line 4: Albright's (1941: 13-14) restoration, based on the second-century B.C.E. Greek transcription *Kosbanos*, "Qôs has made," is reasonable (for the name, see Geraty 1972: 96). The *waw* (also lines 5, 9, and especially 10) is clearly in the tradition of the inverted "h," seen already in the Qawsʿanal impressions and found also at Ḥorvat ʿUza (line 5), alongside more developed forms (line 3) where the head appears to be straightening out. In the *samek* (also lines 9 and 10) the three horizontal bars of the archaic form, found, for example, in the Qawsʿanal impressions, have given way to a zigzag head, of a type first attested in Aramaic at the end of the eighth century B.C.E. in the Nimrud ostracon but quickly replaced in the seventh by a simplified "z" (Naveh 1970: fig. 2). The graffito from Buseirah, no. 583, dated by Puech to ca. 700 B.C.E., or even in the seventh century, appears to illustrate an early stage in the process of the bars' breakdown (1977: 14-15 and pl. 5); the form here is rather advanced, though probably not as developed as the form found at Ḥorvat ʿUza.

Line 5: The *samek* is uncertain, but the traces in the photograph would fit an otherwise reasonable restoration of the theophoric element *Qaws-* (cf. biblical *Pagʿīʾēl*, Num 1:13), suggested by Albright (1941: 13).

Line 6: The ʿayin may be slightly open at the top because of the nearly straight right-hand stroke; if it were the remains of *dalet*'s shaft, the stance would be reversed from that of *dalet* in line 2. Only the head of the *nun* is visible to me, but *Naʿam* would make an acceptable name (cf. 1 Chr 4:15) or name-element (Noth 1980: 117, n. 2; Benz 1972: 362).

Line 7: The *kap* is reminiscent of Ammonite cursive: a triangular bar on the top left of a graceful, slightly oblique shaft (Cross 1975a: 16 and fig. 2). While the Qawsʿanal *kap* represents the more classic lapidary form, note a *kap* similar to this one on the inscribed sherd from Buseirah, no. 157, dated by Puech from the end of the eighth to the beginning of the sixth centuries B.C.E. (1977: 11 and pl. 4a). The *šin* is problematic (cf. line 3), but still seems the best reading. The name, apparently derived from a root *škk* or *śkk*, remains unexplained.[6]

Line 8: It is difficult to tell, but *reš*, with a large head and pointed nose, may be slightly open at the top. The letter read by Milik (Bennett 1966: 99) as *reš* in the Umm el-Biyara ostracon, dated to the mid-seventh century, also has a pointed nose and is definitely open, as is *reš* in the Ḥorvat ʿUza ostracon. By contrast, in ostracon no. 816 from Buseirah the head of *reš* (with a pointed nose) is closed (Puech 1977: 17 and pl. 5b), as it is on the jar graffito reg. no. 374 from Tell el-Kheleifeh. The name *rpʾ* is, of course, known from the Bible, cf. 1 Chr 8:2 (*Rāpāʾ*) and Num 13:9 (*Rāpûʾ*)

Line 9: The reading is plausible, if not probable, but the shafts of what have been read in the series of zigzag traces following *qop* as the heads of *waw* and *samek*, respectively, are barely visible. Also, I am not certain what is to be ascribed to the head of the presumed *waw* in the traces following *qop*.

Line 10: While not evident in the photographs, there are traces of another letter, albeit unclear, after the letter usually identified as *yod*. If the latter is indeed *yod* and final, it indicates the name is a hypocoristicon.

Glueck (1971: 228) assigns to this particular sherd a ceramic date no earlier than the end of the seventh century B.C.E. and no later than the end of the sixth, with a likelihood that it belongs to the first half of the sixth century. On paleographical grounds such a date, at the end of the seventh to the beginning of the sixth century B.C.E., is certainly possible. However, the "mixed" character of the script must be taken into account (Naveh 1966: 28-30; 1970: 66-68; 1982: 104-11). For example, as has long been recognized, a number of letters or features strongly suggest Aramaic elements: perhaps *ʾalep*; the opening of *bet*, *dalet*, and *reš*; *gimel*; *waw*; *samek*; and *qop*. Yet while the *ʾalep* and the "S-top" *qop* fit comfortably into the second half of the seventh century and into the sixth, the other letters (with the exception of *gimel* and *waw*) do not represent a contemporary Aramaic cursive. In reg. no. 6043 the heads of *bet*, *dalet*, and *reš* are only slightly open, and the squarish-looking *ʿayin* is still closed (in line 6 probably a closed form is intended). The *samek*, of a type attested in Aramaic in the Nimrud ostracon at the end of the eighth century B.C.E., was already out of fashion in the seventh. And perhaps more importantly, the large-headed *mem* illustrates essentially the characteristic Edomite-Moabite form seen already in the more conservative lapidary of the Qawsʿanal impressions, even as the *kap* finds its best parallels (apart from the Buseirah sherd) in the Ammonite series stemming from Deir ʿAllā.

Given the extremely small number of cursive Edomite inscriptions available for comparison and their poor state of preservation, dating on purely paleographical grounds is, of course, precarious. Crucial to the analysis are the ostracon from Buseirah, no. 816, dated by its script to the seventh century, or even towards 700 B.C.E. (Puech 1977: 17); the ostracon from Umm el-Biyara, ascribed by its associated pottery to the mid-seventh century (Bennett 1966: 398); and, most recently, the ostracon from Ḥorvat ʿUza, unearthed with several Hebrew ostraca in an Israelite stratum datable to the end of the seventh–beginning of the sixth century B.C.E. (Beit-Arieh and Cresson 1985: 96). On purely typological grounds, the script of the Tell el-Kheleifeh ostracon would seem to lag slightly behind the cursives of Umm el-Biyara and Ḥorvat ʿUza, while

appearing slightly advanced over comparable forms found at Buseirah. For example, in contrast to closed *bet* and *reš* at Buseirah, the Tell el-Kheleifeh ostracon no. 6043 shows at least tentative steps toward opening those letters, as well as the head of *dalet*. Note that on the Umm el-Biyara ostracon, *dalet*, *reš*, and probably *bet* are open; *bet* and *reš*, definitely open at Ḥorvat ʿUza. *ʿAyin* in no. 6043, however, is still closed, as it is at Buseirah and Umm el-Biyara. Since it has opened at Ḥorvat ʿUza (also, open *ʿayin* in the Qawsʿanal impressions and the graffito reg. no. 374), it becomes difficult to assign a date for the Tell el-Kheleifeh ostracon much later than the end of the seventh century B.C.E.

As the comparison with contemporary Aramaic has already suggested, the large-headed *mem*, less advanced than its counterpart on the Umm el-Biyara ostracon, and perhaps *samek* (cf. Ḥorvat ʿUza), both point to the same conclusion. However, a *terminus a quo* for the Kheleifeh ostracon is more difficult to fix, even if typological considerations place it after Buseirah, which is dated on the basis of its script, and before Umm el-Biyara, dated on the basis of associated pottery. The latter suggests a date at least slightly earlier than the mid-seventh century B.C.E. Nevertheless, the Tell el-Kheleifeh *ʾalep*, with a ductus more typically Aramaic, seems to preclude so early a date, since this particular *ʾalep* is first found in Aramaic on the Assur ostracon, which on historical grounds is also assigned a mid-seventh-century B.C.E. date (Naveh 1970: 15). Outside of the Aramaic series, its closest parallel is the Ammonite *ʾalep*, drawn in the same manner, found on the Heshbon IV ostracon dated by Cross to the end of the seventh–beginning of the sixth century B.C.E. (1975a: 14). (Note, too, the similarity of *kap* on this ostracon to reg. no. 6043.) In addition, it will be recalled that Glueck (1971: 228) was reluctant to assign a ceramic date to this particular sherd any earlier than the end of the seventh century B.C.E. Consequently, any attempt made here to date the ostracon more precisely in the seventh or sixth century B.C.E. can only be regarded as a provisional effort, until refinements come in the typology on which its dating has been based. With that caution, a general assignment to the second half of the seventh century B.C.E., perhaps even toward the century's end, cannot be far wrong.

D. Jar Graffito (Reg. No. 374)

Room 49; Jug height, 158 mm; (pl. 80:A):

lʿmyrw   "belonging to ʿAmîrû"

A small, round-bottomed jug contains the six-letter graffito, which had been incised after baking (Glueck 1971: 234-35). Though the friable surface is filled with numerous holes and breaks, real uncertainty surrounds only the reading of the fourth letter. Here there is a large break in the center of the right diagonal—worse now than when Glueck noted it. If the outer diagonal on the left is secondary as Glueck believed it to be, *yod* remains the preferred reading.

Chief interest lies again in the script, which appears to be another example of the lapidary Edomite. As in the Qaws'anal impressions, the somewhat more rounded 'ayin found here is definitely open (cf. the closed 'ayin of reg. no. 6043 above). *Mem* has the large head characteristic of the inscriptions examined thus far, here more than half the height of the letter. As in the cursive, the shaft is oblique and bends into a slightly dipping baseline. However, the head is made up of two slightly concave verticals, apparently introduced as a simplification of the expected "double-L."[7] *Reš*, with a long shaft (bent to accommodate writing on a spherical surface), has a closed head, and *waw* is the expected upside-down "h."

As late as 1971, Glueck felt the last letter could also be read as a *nun*, yielding the name 'Amîrān. Yet since one expects the same tendency to be operative in the shaft of *nun* as in the shaft of *mem*, the lack of any curvature to the left in the shaft argues for the reading *waw*, as above (cf. the Qaws'anal *nun*). In any case, it is difficult to draw chronological conclusions from letter forms in this graffito, given the lack of genuinely comparable material and the relatively few letters upon which to draw. We expect a late seventh- to early sixth-century B.C.E. date to be about right, to accommodate the open, rounded 'ayin and the closed *reš*.[8]

E. Inscribed Sherd (Reg. No. 8058)

Room 110; 39x26 mm; (pl. 83:B):

1. ʾrš̌
2. r ...?

On a small sherd, which Glueck attributed to Period V (fifth–fourth centuries B.C.E.), are the remains of at least a two-line inscription, containing the Phoenician name ʾrš̌ (Benz 1972: 68, 276). The script is also Phoenician, as already noted in a communication from Cross reported by Glueck (1971: 235-36). While there is some uncertainty about reading the ʾalep after *šin*, the first three letters in line 1 are certain. In the second line I am unable to explain the incisions following and to the upper left of a probable *reš* (Glueck 1971: 235).

The shaft of the ʾalep is long, tilted only slightly to the left, with the large head centered upon it and the cross lines converging to its left. It finds its best parallels in mid-fifth-century B.C.E. forms (viz., Tabnit, ʾEšmun'azor), prior to ʾalep's increased counterclock-

wise rotation, evident already in the ʾEšmun'azor Inscription (Peckham 1968: 87; Mullen 1974: 25-30). *Reš* (line 1) has a pointed nose and long vertical shaft, but its chronological horizon is too broad to help in dating. *Šin* is more helpful in this regard, and finds its closest parallels again in the fifth century B.C.E. The older three-prong *šin* with an angular base has here developed into a more rounded form, with the center line dropped into the middle of the base (the rounded form having developed in the last half of the sixth century B.C.E., as in the Saqqarah papyrus; Peckham 1968: 99-100, 170). Note that it has not developed the flat baseline characteristic of some of the ʾEšmun'azor *šins*, nor is there any "breakthrough" of the right arm below the baseline, as already in the ʾEšmun'azor Inscription. Thus, the ʾalep and *šin* together suggest a mid-fifth, or more generally, a fifth-century B.C.E. date for the inscription.

F. Ostracon (Reg. No. 2069)

Room 50; 90x63 mm; (pl. 81:A):
Obverse

1.	qrplgs ṭpyʾn[?	"Tax-gatherer: jars, X...
2.	ḥmr ṭpyʾn 2 [	Wine, jars, 2
3.	ḥmr [1+ ?	Wine, 1+ (?)

Ostracon reg. no. 2069, found together with ostracon reg. nos. 2070 and 2071, bears the clearest ink inscription of all the Tell el-Kheleifeh ostraca. Though apparently the beginning of the inscription and the beginning of each of the three lines on the obverse are intact, the left side of each line has been broken off, and the original ostracon may well have contained even more lines of writing. Due to the breakage and what appears to be a smearing of the ink, the numeral presumed to be at the end of line 1 is not clear. The end of the third line is broken off as well, but what remains following the word *ḥmr* suggests that another numeral may be read, perhaps a vertical stroke representing the unit "1." In what remains of the inscription, only the letter *samek* in line 1 is unclear. Although a vein on the surface of the clay is partly to blame, one gets the impression that the scribe first began to write the following *ṭet* and then corrected himself. Regardless of the merits of this suggestion, the intended form seems to be the "double-hook" *samek* current in the fourth century B.C.E.: a smaller hook raised above the line and forming the head from which emerges a larger, rounded hook (Naveh 1970: 48).

The explanation of *qrplgs* in line 1 as the transliteration into Aramaic of Greek *karpologos*, along with its interpretation, "tax-gatherer (in kind)," had been suggested by Albright when the ostracon was first published by Glueck (1940b: 8-9, n. 12; also, Geraty 1975: 57, n. 13; Cross 1981: 68). The use here of an item of Greek technical vocabulary offers clear evidence of the intrusion of Greek loanwords already in the Persian period. From the mention of a "tax-gatherer" and the listing of jars of wine, one may infer that this ostracon contains a receipt for taxes paid in kind (Glueck 1940a: 16). For *ṭĕpîʾān*, see Mishnaic *ṭāpî* (Jastrow 1967: 1:546), and Albright's comments on this suggestion by Youtie (Glueck 1940b: 8).

The script displays the extreme cursive of the late fifth- and early fourth-century B.C.E. Aramaic and has been compared to that of an Aramaic ostracon of that date from ʿArad by Aharoni and Amiran (1964: 142). Since 1964 additional ostraca from ʿArad have come to light, as well as the mid-fourth-century Aramaic ostraca from Beersheva, published by Naveh (1973: 79-82, pls. 35-38; 1979: 182-98, pls. 24-31), and these have considerably enlarged the previously small corpus of Aramaic ostraca from the fourth century. Were the *samek* in reg. no. 2069 clearly of the "double-hook" variety suggested, we would have unambiguous grounds for a more precise date in the early fourth century. Notable in our ostracon is the absence of the distinction developed during the fourth century between medial and final forms, or "semi-ligatures" (*lamed, mem, pe*) (Naveh 1970: 46). *Lamed*, for example, represents a form that disappears after the mid-fourth century but which is standard in the fifth, a small tail at the end of the base having already begun to emerge at the end of the fifth. The *ʾalep* also has typological significance. Its short leg on the left of the downstroke has yet to develop into the crescent shape that emerges in the late fifth century, and the fifth-century *ʾalep* represented on this ostracon disappears for the most part in the second half of the fourth century. Thus, aside from the *qop* and perhaps *reš*'s stance, the script of reg. no. 2069 could easily fit into the fifth century, or in view of a late fifth-century form such as the *ḥet* (with its horizontal bar drawn in a separate stroke below the top of the downstrokes), more precisely into the late fifth century B.C.E. However, the short-legged *qop* suggests a slightly later date in the early fourth century, as the downstroke is generally short relative to the main shaft until the very end of the fifth century (Birnbaum 1971: 2: nos. 144-47). Indeed, the "open" form exhibited here bears a close resemblance to specimens from the late fourth-century (e.g., Ostracon Sachau 62: 2) and later (Naveh 1970: fig. 9, no. 3; Geraty 1972: pls. 9-10). The topline issues in an almost vertical downstroke, forming, as it were, a new leg equal to the shaft. Note also the marked leftward tilt of all three examples of *reš* in this ostracon, a trait more characteristic of late fourth-century forms. (The short left leg of *gimel* seems to be a peculiarity of this ostracon, without any typological significance.) In any

case, since the letter forms other than *qop* and *reš* may extend down into the fourth century, an early fourth-century B.C.E. date has the most likelihood.

There are traces of writing on the reverse of ostracon reg. no. 2069, in which a couple of faint letters may be identifiable. Practically speaking, nothing of the original inscription (a continuation of the obverse?) remains.

G. Ostracon (Reg. No. 2071)

Room 50; 57 x 34 mm; (pl. 81:C):

1.	šlmn ʿbd	Šalman, the servant...]
2.	lḥy ʿb[d]	Luḥay, the serva[nt...]
3.	bʿlyt[n]	Baʿlyatō[n...]
4.	ʾšbʿ/[l]	ʾEšbaʿ/[l...]

From the same period as reg. no. 2069 comes ostracon reg. no. 2071, bearing a four-line inscription in Aramaic script. There are some indications that the ostracon is a palimpsest (Glueck 1940b: 5), and the sherd is now broken at the left with the loss of at least a few letters. The fourth line may have been added secondarily by another hand.

This is a list of the names of four persons, the first two of which are followed by the qualification ʿbd, "servant (of PN?)." The reading itself is relatively untroubled. As Glueck (1940b: 7) suggested, the remains after the *yod* in the third line probably represent the top of the shaft and the right arm of *taw*, to be completed with the restoration of a *nun*, yielding the well-known Phoenician name *bʿlytn* (Benz 1972: 328-29). What may be traces of an earlier writing have cast doubt on reading *šin* in the fourth line (Glueck 1971: 232, n. 43); nevertheless, the reading *ʾšbʿ*, or the full name *ʾšbʿ[l]*, remains the most satisfactory solution.[9] Note that Luḥay (Arabic diminutive qutayl pattern) in line 2 is also found, in a compound name, on ostracon reg. no. 2070 (obverse), *šlmlḥy* (Ryckmans 1934: 1: 120; Benz 1972: 338). For Šalman note 2 Kgs 17:3, Hos 10:14, and Glueck's (1940b: 6, n. 5) references to extra-biblical attestations. The apparently diverse ethnic origins of the names (viz., Phoenician *bʿlytn*, South Semitic *lḥy*, etc.) is striking.

The script of ostracon reg. no. 2071 again falls generally within the fifth, probably the late fifth, to early fourth century B.C.E. As in the case of reg. no. 2069, the letter forms display none of the telltale signs of an exclusively fourth-century hand, such as the appearance of developing semi-ligatures. The *ʾalep*, again without the crescent-shaped leg, could fit easily into the fifth century, its lower limit perhaps extending down to the mid-fourth century. *Ḥet* is somewhat faded, but appears to be the same type as in reg. no. 2069 with the horizontal bar slightly below the top of the downstrokes. *Lamed* is drawn with a gracefully curving shaft that descends into a foot lowered well below horizontal and tapered at its tip (see line 3). At the tip of the foot a small tick downward (lines 2 and 3), still rare at the end of the fifth century, is perhaps indicative of an early fourth-century hand, but the foot, regrettably, is faded. Only the *bet* in line 4, which appears to come from a second hand, with its rightward declining shaft and foot upturned horizontally to the left into a kind of baseline, seems more suitable in the early fourth century than in the fifth. Therefore, given the general similarity of the script to that of reg. no. 2069 as well as the common find spot of reg. nos. 2069, 2070, and 2071, we are inclined to an early fourth-century B.C.E. date within the broader chronological horizon already suggested (Naveh 1970: 44).

H. Ostracon (Reg. No. 7094)

Room 81; 34 x 33 mm; (pl. 83:A):

bršl*m*   *bar šillēm*, "Baršillēm"

Indicative of the same general period as the script of ostraca reg. nos. 2069 and 2071 is the script of this Aramaic ostracon, containing the single name or patronymic *bršlm* (Glueck 1971: 233-34). The sherd is broken on the left (and on the right?), leaving only the right downstroke of a presumed *mem*, the head having originally curved up to the top of the downstroke. This is the most likely solution, since the reading *waw* (Glueck 1940b: 10) has little to recommend it from a paleographical point of view. The orthography suggests the vocalization *šillēm* rather than *šallūm* (cf. Cowley 1923: no. 22, col. 1:20, 3:1, 5:3; contra Glueck 1971: 234).

Ostracon reg. no. 7094 is probably to be dated to the early fourth century B.C.E. While the *bet* is standard in the fifth century and disappears by and large after the mid-fourth century, the *lamed* is characteristic of the fourth-century cursive script.

I. Ostracon (Reg. No. 10,007)

Room 94; 79 x 61 mm; (pl. 83:C):

Ostracon reg. no. 10, 007 is one of several illegible or nearly illegible ostraca that Glueck (1971: 237) discovered amidst the debris of Level V, dated to the fifth–fourth centuries B.C.E. He suggested its faint traces represented a late cursive Edomite script, reading in the second, barely legible line, *hm*[*r*], "wine." Cross, however, recognized that the traces display not a late Edomite cursive, but an Aramaic cursive probably of the fourth century (F. M. Cross, personal communication, spring 1980): the *het*, in particular, displays a good fifth–fourth century Aramaic form. Cross has suggested reading the following:

1. zzn kspʾ   "the sum of X *zūz'*s:
2. ḥny   Ḥōnî (PN)."

The two *zayin*s in line 1 are admittedly quite uncertain (note also the defective orthography), and the *nun* and the *yod* (of the "triple movement" type?) (Cross 1979a: 143) are not entirely clear. Though the measure, or type of coinage, ordinarily follows the word *ksp*, the reverse is also found: viz., 8 *šql ksp* (Jean and Hoftijzer 1965: 124). Ostracon reg. no. 10,007 would then represent something like a fragmentary receipt. Another reading, in a similar vein, is also possible:

1. *ttn* kspʾ[10]   "You will give the sum...
2. ḥ(ntn) k(rn) [ ][11]   Wheat: X kor."

In this interpretation what is taken for *zayin* in line 1 represents the right downstroke of *taw*.[12] In the second line, the reading of a *kap*, essentially the same form as that found in the first line (cf. Papyrus Luparensis, Cross 1979: 137, fig. 1), avoids the difficulty of seeing *nun* in this period with a developed right shoulder. Considerable reservation, of course, attends either reading.

The script would seem to place the ostracon in the fourth century B.C.E., perhaps in the early fourth, since the "N-shaped" *het* is largely replaced in the extreme cursive by the mid-fourth century, to judge by the Aramaic ostraca of that date found at Beersheva (Naveh 1973; 1979). *Kap* has a narrow head, with a downstroke curving slightly from the right to the left; in the second half of the century the downstroke tends to be either vertical or to incline slightly to the right. *Samek* is a particularly useful chronological index in view of its rapid development in this period. In reg. no. 10,007 it has advanced well beyond the "double-hook" form, the upper left hook having been lost and simplified into a vertical downstroke, while the right downstroke curves to the left at its bottom (thus almost "closing" the letter). It is a form that has already emerged in the Aramaic ostraca of the early fourth century discovered at ʿArad (Tadmor 1973: nos. 159-162). *Pe* is short, its shaft curling to the left at the bottom. Note also the somewhat unusual ʾ*alep* (if this is indeed a letter and not a numeral), with the long horizontal left leg, thickening at its extremity.

J. Ostracon (Reg. No. 2070)

Room 50; 59 x 50 mm; (pl. 81:B):

Obverse:	Reverse:
1. ʿ*bd*m*s*[.]	1. psʾ
2. ʿ*bd*ʾ*šmn*	2. *knšy*
3. ʾ*bšlm*	3. bd*ḥrn*
4. *šlmlḥy*	
5. *šmrb*ʿ*l*	

This ostracon, written in a cursive Phoenician script (Naveh 1966: 27), was found with ostraca reg. nos. 2069 and 2071. The obverse and the reverse each contain a list of personal names, though apparently each list is from a different hand. The names are, for the most part, clearly of a Phoenician type. Owing to apparent smudging and to the fading of the ink on the badly pitted surfaces, the first line on the obverse and the last line on the reverse are particularly difficult, and the readings offered here can only be provisional.

On the obverse the traces suggest the possibility of reading *ʿbd* in the first line, as in the second, followed by *mem* and perhaps *samek* (cf. line 1, reverse). If so, the latter's form, approximately a figure "2" resting atop what looks like the shaft of a *lamed*, would reflect the simplification and merger of the three horizontal bars of the classical *samek*, a development seen already at the beginning of the sixth century B.C.E. (Peckham 1968: 161).[13] Unfortunately what follows this to complete the name is also unclear.[14]

The rest of the names on the obverse present little problem. The reading *ʿAbdʾešmun*, "servant of ʾEšmun" (Benz 1972: 150, 278), is virtually certain, despite the badly faded *nun* and only traces remaining of the head of *mem*. In the third line the vocalization *ʾAbīšillēm*, "my Father has requited" (Benz 1972: 257, 417; Stamm 1965: 420) is probably to be preferred to alternative vocalizations (cf. 1 Kgs 15:2; 2 Sam 3:3), but the vocalization of the fourth name, *šlmlḥy* (*Šalōm-laḥay, Šillēm-laḥay*?), with the *lḥy*-element found in reg. no. 2071, can only be conjectured (Benz 1972: 418). Finally, in the fifth line the *mem* is unclear due simply to the effacement of its shaft; otherwise, the reading *Šamōrbaʿl*, first suggested by Cross (Glueck 1971: 230, n. 38; see also, Benz 1972: 421), fits nicely.

On the reverse the surface is even more pitted and irregular, and it is, in fact, a defect in the surface of the sherd that accounts for what looks like the horizontal foot of a *bet* in the first letter of line 1. *Pe* with a long shaft is the preferred reading, though the name *psʾ* (a hypocoristic?) is otherwise unattested.[15] The second line offers no problem: the name, as Naveh (1966: 28) noted, occurs frequently enough in the Punic onomasticon in the variant forms *knš*, *knšʾ knšy*, *knšyt* (f.), and *knšm* (Benz 1972: 333). At the end of the third line the ink has been badly smudged, making the second element of the name almost illegible. For this line Cross (personal communication, spring 1980) has suggested the reading *bdḥrn*, taking the checked downstroke after the *dalet* as *ḥet*'s right vertical shaft, for a form similar to that of the obverse (line 4). The upper horizontal has been effaced, but the left vertical may still be traced underneath the smudged portion of the name, along with a large *reš* (the oblique shaft is tilted to the right at the top) and a *nun*.[16] *Bōd-Ḥōrōn*, "in

the hand of Horon," is not otherwise known in the Phoenician onomasticon, but compare *ʿbdḥwrn* (Benz 1972: 309).

Since the number of inscriptions in the cursive Phoenician script of the Persian period, especially in the fourth century B.C.E., is small, the Tell el-Kheleifeh material makes an important contribution. The letter forms on reg. no. 2070 fall generally into the cursive series of the latest Elephantine ostraca but typologically are earlier than those of the mid-fourth-century jar inscriptions from Shiqmona, indicating, as Cross suggested (1968: 229), an early fourth-century date. This accords with the same general date given to ostraca reg. nos. 2069 and 2071.

The head of *bet* (lines 2, 3, 5; line 3, reverse) is only vestigial, and the letter as a whole (except perhaps in line 2) is generally open, or not tightly curled. The latter trait, according to Cross (1968: 230), is rare before the fourth century B.C.E. On the obverse (line 2), *dalet* is apparently of the one-stroke type, while on the reverse (line 3) its head is vestigial.

The *ḥet* appears to be of a type transitional between that of the Saqqarah *ḥet* and that of the more advanced Mit-Rahineh ostracon, which Cross (1968: 230, n. 25) put in the late fourth century. It certainly is not as developed as the latest Elephantine forms consisting of three vertical or curved strokes. The left shaft is drawn down from left to right, and from it, below the top, the short topmost cross line juts upward to the right. From its tip the old center line then is drawn down parallel to the left shaft, while the bottom line has been reduced to another short upward stroke jutting out from the middle vertical, before dropping immediately down into the right shaft.

The foot of *yod* on the obverse (line 4) is obscured by the shaft of *lamed* below, but would seem to be the same form as that on the reverse of the ostracon (line 2). The top line and shaft are drawn in a continuous arc, which moves up to the right from the left before curving down to the right, making a 90 degree angle. The middle stroke has yet to break free of the shaft, a sporadic development in the Elephantine cursive but standard in the late fourth century (Cross 1968: 230).

Kap (line 2, reverse) is a narrow form with a slightly curving shaft and a short single-stroke head drawn into a shaft below its top (cf. the medial form found in the jar inscriptions from Shiqmona), characteristic of the late fifth and early fourth centuries.

The *lamed* still has a base, in contrast to the medial Shiqmona forms; but the foot is quite short (e.g., line 2) and appears to be drawn independently of the tapered shaft in an inverted curve from left to right — somewhat advanced typologically over the fifth-century forms (cf. Elephantine). Note the length of the "dropline" from the foot in the second example of *lamed* in line 4.

As Cross (1968: 230) noted, a virtually identical *mem* is to be found in the Shiqmona jar inscriptions, in the Tell el-Kheleifeh ostracon having almost assumed an "x-form." The latter is the prototype of the earliest neo-Punic *mem*s.

Nun has yet to develop into the straight line, tilted to the right, attested already at Elephantine and regular in the fourth century.

All the *'ayin*s are open on the Tell el-Kheleifeh ostracon, a fifth-century development found occasionally in the Elephantine ostraca.

K. Ostraca (Reg. Nos. 3059A, 3059B)

Room 50; 59 x 39 mm and 45 x 31 mm, respectively; (pl. 84:A, B):

The two sherds were catalogued as ostraca, but it is not clear that they ever bore actual inscriptions. One of them, 3059A, bears an ink marking in the form of an upside-down "h" and to its right, on the broken edge, the traces of another mark, or letter. Given the fact that the sherds were discovered in a fifth–fourth-century context, the inverted "h" looks more like a rather formal Aramaic *dalet* than anything else. The markings, however, may simply represent potter's marks.

L. Ostracon (Reg. No. 8096)

Room 125; 38 x 27 mm; (pl. 83:E):
Illegible

M. Inscribed Sherd (Reg. No. 9027)

Room 91; 53 x 38 mm; (pl. 83:D):

This small sherd, catalogued as belonging to Iron II, was found amidst surface debris, and bears the partial remains of two incised letters, or marks, at its top. They have not been identified (Glueck 1971: 236).

N. Jar Inscription (Reg. No. 469)

Room 40; (pl. 80:B):

These fragments of a large sixth-century jar, found at Tell el-Kheleifeh in a context that Glueck dated to the seventh–sixth centuries B.C.E. (his Level IV), bear two characters, incised after baking, perhaps in an ancient South Semitic script (Glueck 1938a: 16; 1967: 23-24; 1971: 236-37). While they have been the subject of considerable discussion, the two characters have yet to be satisfactorily identified or explained. On the one hand, Ryckmans (1939: 247-49, pl. 6) has interpreted the two characters as composite Minaean signs, or monograms: the character on the right as composed of a *lamed* over a *bet* (less likely a *samek*) and the one on the left, a *ḥet* above a reverse *yod* (less likely, an *'ayin*). The monograms represent, then, the first two letters of both the name and the epithet of the jar's maker, or something of the sort. Boneschi (1961: 213-23), on the other hand, interprets the monograms differently, reading: *sl-ḥd* (*sāll*/*sall-ḥādd*), "vin pur, piquant"—a reference to the contents of the jar. Albright (1952: 43-44), for his part, regards the characters as proto-Dedanite and in no case Minaean.

O. Rhodian Jar Handle

Surface; 42 x 14 mm; (pl. 84:C):

ʾepì Xeno*phan*eu[s]   "In (the term of) Xenophanes,
ʾArtamitíou   (in the month of) Artamitios."

The reading of the stamp is that of V. R. Grace (personal communication, 28 Dec. 1982).[17]

The date is specified by year and month, the year by the name of the eponym, at Rhodes probably the annual priest of Helios, who gave his name to the year. Grace suggests a date close to 200 B.C.E. for the term of Xenophanes.

III. NOTES

[1] The analysis presented here was carried out for the most part in the fall of 1984 and in the spring of 1985; a more or less complete manuscript was first submitted in July 1985. Since then the ostracon in a cursive Edomite script recently unearthed at Ḥorvat 'Uza has been published (Beit-Arieh and Cresson 1985). The latest draft of this manuscript has been updated and expanded to take it into account, as well the one unfortunately fragmentary inscription published from the Edomite shrine at Qitmit (Beit-Arieh and Beck 1987).

[2] Although with this final publication of Kheleifeh it might be desirable to forgo the designation of items in the collection by registry number, I have chosen not to do so—in spite of the awkwardness—to avoid the confusion that would inevitably result. With the exception of the Rhodian jar handle, all the pieces presented here are well known in numerous publications by their registry numbers and it would be artificial to introduce a new numbering system now.

[3] Herr 1978: 163 remarks: "The first half of the 7th or the M7th should be about right...." Naveh 1982: 104 dates it to the late eighth century.

[4] For reasons that are unclear, Glueck localized certain excavated materials by reference to the grid system rather than according to the room number.

[5] Note for that reason Milik 1958: 239 attempted to read *'nl* as a dialectical form of pan-semitic *'ml*, thus "Qaus est efficace".

[6]See Noth 1980: 178, for biblical *śokyāh* (1 Chr 8:10), who refers the name to Yahweh's role as protector: "umzaunt hat Jahwe." Note that the text of 1 Chr 8:10 is in dispute.

[7]Harding's drawing in Glueck 1938b: 9, fig. 2 is in this instance correct. What is drawn as a broken line in Albright's rendering from a photograph in Glueck 1938a: 17, fig. 7 represents a discoloration in the surface rather than an incision.

[8]The Ammonite series may offer an analogy here once again. Cf. Cross 1975a: 12-16, fig. 2.

[9]For abbreviated *ʾšbʿ* , see perhaps 1 Chr 4:21 (MT: *ʾašbēaʿ*); for *ʾšbʿl*, 1Chr 8:39. Benz 1972: 277-78.

[10]For *ksp* as the object of this verb, see Cowley 1923: no. 1:7; 5:7; passim.

[11]For these abbreviations, see Naveh 1979: no. 1 and n. 5: no. 3 and n. 11.

[12]For *ttn* in the Aramaic of the Persian Period, see Segert 1975: 280.

[13]For examples of the various types of mergers the crossbars of the classical *samek* went through, see the script charts for *CIS* 111, the Saqqarah Papyrus, and *CIS* 86B in Peckham 1968: pls. 8, 10, and 1.

[14]For a partially preserved name *ʿbdms....* in the Phoenician onomasticon, see Benz 1972: 447. I have played with the idea of reading the first line *ʿbdmsṭ*, hardly an improvement semantically! On this reading *samek* is a cursive form found in the Elephantine ostraca, approximately an upside-down figure "2" (viz. no. 7, pl. 10 in Peckham 1968: 111), typologically advanced over that of the reverse. The *ṭet* would only be partially preserved and, in fact, contiguous to the *samek*, producing the present confusion of forms.

[15]The element "ps" occurs in the Phoenician name *PSNʿM*: Benz 1972: 392. At Ugarit see the unexplained name *pss/pṡṡ*: Gröndahl 1967: 312.

[16]Glueck 1971: 230-31, n. 41 had suggested *Bōdrummōn*, but the checked head of "*reš*" on this reading would be difficult to justify paleographically.

[17]In a letter to G. Pratico, December 28, 1982.

Chapter Seven

The Metal Objects from Tell el-Kheleifeh

FRANK L. KOUCKY AND NATHAN R. MILLER

I. INTRODUCTION

The climatic conditions at Tell el-Kheleifeh are not conducive to the preservation of metal objects. The region, with sandy soils, has a warm climate marked by seasonal wet and dry changes and is close to the sea. These factors combine to allow deep corrosion of the metal objects.

In addition to excavating numerous metal objects, Glueck and his assistants collected each day green fragments from the surface of the tell. They deposited the fragments into cigarette boxes and labeled the containers with general information about field provenance. The green surface fragments proved to be a mixture of bits of corroded copper, copperalloys, ore fragments, slag fragments, and green glass fragments. While the nature of the original objects can not be identified for any of the fragments, they do suggest that metal, ore, and slag were abundant at the site. The numerous small fragments of ore and slag give added support to the contention that metal working was done at the site.

After cleaning the objects, we hoped to analyze them by X-ray fluorescence analysis (XRF) but we had to abandon that attempt because the alteration layers on the samples gave variable results. To obtain analytical data we had to section and polish the samples and study them with reflected light under the microscope. Miller, in an unpublished thesis (1982), described and photographed all the metal objects and analyzed many of them chemically. Miller's study discusses the dangers of analyzing corroded metal objects and describes the nature of the corrosion products that have developed on these materials.

II. THE OBJECTS

A. Slags

Six large fragments of slag are included in the metal object collection from the site and nearly a hundred small pieces are in the surface collections. All the large fragments were studied in polished section and two were analyzed chemically. The slags are quite variable in porosity. They have altered to a green surface color but internally are a brown-black. All of the samples are rich in copper prills. At most metal-working sites of the Iron Age, the copper content of the slags is below 2 percent. These slags contain about 10 percent copper and it is this high copper content that causes the green surface alteration. It is not known if the samples are typical of the slags of the site or if they were collected because of their green color. If they are typical it would suggest poor metallurgical techniques.

The slags contain a high iron to silica ratio, which suggests that the smelting was done at temperatures near 1200 degrees C at the wustite-fayalite eutectic. Their surface features suggest a low viscosity slag such as would form from a high iron slag. They are similar to the B-type slags of Cyprus (see Koucky and Steinberg 1989). The high aluminum and calcium content of the slags suggest that minor Ca-pyroxene and feldspar might form. Polished sections of the slag show the predominance of only two phases, wustite and fayalite. To make a slag of this type the original ore must have been fluxed with an iron oxide.

B. Copper Ore Specimens

Four large fragments and numerous small pieces of copper ore are among the metal specimens. All have altered to a green color externally but internally they exhibit a fine-grained sandstone matrix with two types of cement. One type is cemented by a soft black chalcocite (Cu_2S) and the other is cemented with green fibrous acanthite and malachite. Since no known sources occur near the area, the copper-rich ore specimens must have been carried to the site. The ores are similar to those in the Timna region.

C. The Copper and Copper-Alloy Objects

The most abundant copper objects at the site are fragments of rods, pins, and needles. None are thicker than a pencil: all are of variable lengths, the longest approximately 12 cm. Since they are all fragments, they could be pieces of nails, fibula pins, fragments of fishhooks, or simply raw stock from which other objects were manufactured. It is probable that rod-shaped copper was manufactured at the site for fabrication into other objects. No molds were found at the site but the copper rods could be made without molding the copper.

D. Nails

The best preserved metal objects are the nails. Unfortunately nails do not vary enough over time to be of value for dating. The longest nail (pl. 73: 2) is 10 cm long and weighs 23. 23 grams. Several nail heads have widths of 2.7 cm, suggesting that they could have been nearly double the size of the nail shown on the plate. Most nail heads are circular with nearly round stems. The nails may have been preserved in wooden fragments, which provided a local reducing environment that prevented the intense corrosion found on the other metal objects. Most of the nails are of pure copper, but a few have trace amounts of tin and other metals, suggesting that waste bronze had been added to batches of copper during their manufacture. Thirteen definite nails are included in the objects, but many of the fragments classified as rod fragments could be pieces of nails. Pure copper resists marine erosion and it is not unlikely that nails were manufactured at the site for boat repairs.

E. Fishhooks

Bent and sharpened hooks are fairly common in the collection of metal objects. Twelve definite examples and many possible fragments have been identified. Several are bent back at the point to form a barb and a few are flattened at the point end into a barb shape. The alteration on the shanks of three of the hooks show the pattern of wrapped twine (pl. 73: 8). None of the hooks is complete and so the original length of the shank is not known. The hooks vary in size, most range from 1.5 to 2 cm, and the largest has a curved diameter of about 2.5 cm.. Most of the hooks were formed by bending a thin pure copper rod. Only one bronze hook (no. 11077) is in the collection. The iron objects from the site are in very poor condition. It is possible that several of the fragments were small iron hooks, but such hooks would rapidly corrode in sea water and it is probable that copper hooks were preferred.

F. Fibulae

About ten fibulae and fibulae fragments are included in the metal object collection (Table 3). The length of most of the fibulae is between 7 and 8 cm (only one is larger, no. 7054, at 8.8 cm), but they were all bent to use a bow pin 4.5 to 5 cm long. All the preserved clasp ends are of the coiled wire spring type with a bronze pin. The best formed fibulae are bronze (with about 10 percent tin), but the collection contains several pure copper fibulae (nos. 73, 408, 6057, and 11084). All the fibulae are similar to late Iron II-Persian types.

TABLE 3. COMPARISONS TO FIBULAE FOUND AT TELL EL-KHELEIFEH			
Kheleifeh #	Length (cm)	Comparisons	
1068	7.5	Megiddo I	78:4 (M-1487)
		Megiddo I	78:19 (M-4530)
		Lachish III	58:19 (1480)
10094	6.5	Lachish III	56:37 (562)
10077	5.0		
6057	5.0	Lachish III	58:15 (562)
1000	3.0		
9000	5.5	Lachish III	58:15 (562)
9010	3.1	Hazor III-IV	CCXXI: Vb B 2919-1 (Fe)
		Megiddo I	78:21 (M-1141)
		Lachish III	58:21 (7109)
11084	3.7	Lachish III	Type 2c
	(fragment)		
7054	4.5	Lachish III	58:22
		Megiddo I 78:20	

G. Rings and Links

The collection includes rings formed from bent rods. The largest is 2.5 cm in diameter. None are large enough to use as ankle or arm bracelets and their thick shape would make them uncomfortable as finger rings. Eight small links (each about 1 cm) are attached together in a chain (pl. 73: 13).

H. Copper Foil Objects

Several pieces of folded thin copper foil and numerous small foil fragments are found in the collection. They are completely corroded and are extremely brittle. They give little hint as to the original object.

I. Metal Weights

In the field Glueck labeled about five small bronze discs as weights. Those bronze pellets (pl. 73: 22, 23) are similar in size and shape to the weights found at Lachish (cf. Lachish III. 51: 7-14). All the weights from

Lachish were inscribed on one side. Unfortunately the pellets found at Tell el-Keleifeh are deeply corroded and no inscriptions remain.

J. Fork Tridents

Four rod fragments were shaped into a form that could belong to a fork or trident (pl. 73: 15). They are between 7 and 9 cm long and appear to indicate that the fork trident was 4 to 5 cm wide. That is much smaller than the trident found in the tomb at Lachish (Lachish III. 56: 38). The fragments complement the fishhooks to suggest that fishing on the Gulf's coral reefs was important to the site's economy.

K. Arrowheads

The collection contains five fragments of copper-alloy trefoil arrowheads (nos. 275, 300, 21-D-11, 21-D-13; one found during the 1980 survey, and one probable iron trefoil arrowhead, no. 7038). In addition there is one semi-bodkin type point (no. 142) of copper alloy, which is more rectangular than square in section. Analyses of the trefoil arrowheads at other locations suggest that they are commonly made of a lead-rich bronze (cf. Lachish IV. pl. 60: 53 and unpublished Tell el-Hesi arrowheads). It has been suggested that the lead-rich bronze alloy was used because it was more fluid than the iron versions and would better cast the thin fins of this type of arrowhead. The arrowheads from Tell el-Kheleifeh are also of the lead-rich bronze alloy, but it should be noted that arrowhead no. 300 is a normal 10 percent tin bronze with no lead.

Trefoil arrowheads with short internal sockets are known from many sites. The following table provides parallels to the Tell el-Kheleifeh repertoire:

TABLE 4. PARALLELS TO THE TELL EL-KHELEIFEH REPERTOIRE

Site	Reference		Number
Megiddo	Megiddo I	88:12	M-2312
Megiddo	Megiddo I	88:13	M-1597
Lachish	Lachish III	60:53	
Lachish	Lachish IV	36:16	
Hazor	Hazor III-IV	110:3	
Tell el-Hesi	Nos. 419 and 426		
(unpublished)	No. 371		

L. Blades

The collection contains only one bronze knife blade (no. 301). It is 12 cm long and 2.5 cm wide and its shank was probably mounted in wood without rivets. Many of the iron-rich lumps, when cracked open, indicate an original iron object with a blade shape. None of these could be cleaned to learn the blade shape, but it is not unlikely that most knives used at the site were iron.

III. TABLES

TABLE 5. METAL OBJECTS FROM TELL EL-KHELEIFEH

Object		Tell el-Kheleifeh #	
1. Nail	x1 *	2076	
2. Nail	x1	4063	
3. Nail	x1.5	1051	
4. Nail	xxl	1052	
5. Nail	x2	90086	(section)
6. Nail	x1.5	48	(section)
7. Hook	x1.7	21-d-15	
8. Hook	x2	11077	
9. Hook	x1	9029	
10. Hook	x1	9081	
11. Trefoil Arrowhead	x2	275	
12. Trefoil Arrow	x1.5	300	(end view)
13. Chain links	x3	29	
14. Gaff	x2	442	
15. Trident	x1	365	
16. Fibula	x1.5	5071a	
17. Fibula	x1.5	11084	
18. Fibula	x1	9000	
19. Ring	x2	2081	
20. Fibula	x1.5	7093	
21. Ring	x2	349	
22. Weight	x2	21-D-7	
23. Weight	x2	21-D-36	

* Second column designations represent magnification (pl. 73)

TABLE 6. X-RAY FLUORESCENCE ANALYSIS (UNCORRECTED)

Object	Cu	Fe	Pb	Trace	Alloy-type
Nails					
973	+95%	~1%	—	As, Sr, Zr	Copper
8099	+95	~1%	~2%	Ag, Sn	Copper
52	+95	~1		Sr, Ni, Pb	Copper
Fibulae					
408	+95	~1%		Zn, Ni, Sr	Copper
73	+95	~1		Zn, As, Sr	Copper
6075	+95	~1	~2	2% Zn, Ni	Copper
10094	~90	~1		10% Sn, Ni	Bronze
11084	+95	~1		———	Copper
Hook					
100072	+95	~1		Zn, Pb	Copper
Arrowhead					
275	~50		~25%	20% Sn, Ag	Pb-bronze
Miscellaneous					
11082	+95	~1	~1	1% As, Sr	Copper

TABLE 7. ELECTRON PROBE ANALYSES OF OBJECTS (WEIGHT PERCENT)

Object	Cu	Fe	Sn	Pb	Ca	Alloy
Nails						
90086	99.04%	0.26%				Copper
2076	100.00					Copper
Fibulae						
10000	92.36		7.64			Bronze
10094	90.53		9.45			Bronze
Ring						
21-D-16	90.05	1.51	9.95			Bronze
349	5.38	1.51	26.72	27.72	42.22	?
Fishhook						
402	64.48					Copper
11077	64.75		36.24			Bronze
Trefoil Arrowhead						
275	48.48		17.42	25.90		Pb-bronze
300	90.94		9.02			Bronze
Miscellaneous Object						
11083b	21.66		74.28			?
364	81.51		18.49			Bronze
111	60.41		2.33	31.25		Pb-bronze

Silver Coin					
21-D-9 (altered)	Ag-69.95	Br-15.71	Cl-8.76	Al-4.12	Si-1.45

Chapter Eight

Summary

I. THE ARCHITECTURE AND POTTERY OF TELL EL-KHELEIFEH

A. The Casemate Fortress and Fortified Settlement

Tell el-Kheleifeh was occupied in two major architectural phases: the casemate fortress and the fortified settlement. Plate 3, representing Glueck's Period IC, shows the casemate fortress phase, the site's earliest level. Plate 4 (Glueck's Period II) reveals the skeletal architectural components of the later fortified settlement phase (the offsets/insets wall and four-chambered gate). Plates 5 and 6 (Glueck's Periods III-IVB) depict the gradual building that occurred within the perimeters of the offsets/insets fortification. As emphasized, however, the earliest phase of this second level was surely not composed of vast empty spaces within the new fortifications. It was undoubtedly characterized by some building within the compound. The plans of pls. 5 and 6 preserve walls that should be assigned to those interior spaces from the time of the settlement's earliest construction. Unfortunately, Glueck's excavation methodology and recording system preclude refinement in the phasing of this settlement.

The fragmentary architecture of Glueck's Period V suggests a third architectural phase or, at the very least, a postscript to the history of the site. The slight archaeological evidence and the inadequate recording of the architecture and artifacts of this level preclude more than general observations. Phoenician and Aramaic ostraca of the fifth-early fourth century B.C.E., together with a handful of fifth century B.C.E. Greek body sherds, constitute the most reliable dating criteria for this post-Iron Age level. There are also a few sixth-fifth century B.C.E. storage vessel sherds depicted in the excavation photographs that probably belong to this level. Unfortunately, the sherds were assigned to the Amman collection and could not be located for drawing and inclusion in the plates. The repertoire of

forms that document this level of occupation is, however, very limited.

B. The Pottery

The pottery of Tell el-Kheleifeh falls broadly into two categories: the handmade Negevite wares and the wheelmade forms. Within the latter category are the Midianite, Edomite, and local Assyrian assemblages. A typology of Negevite pottery has not yet been established, and as a result those forms must be dated on the basis of associated wheelmade vessels. While the presence of forms that can be dated earlier must be acknowledged, most of the wheelmade pottery dates between the eighth and early sixth centuries B.C.E. and has close affinities with sites on both sides of the Jordan River. The ceramic parallels are most notable from Tell el-Qudeirat, ʿAroʿer (W), Ḥorvat Qitmit, Heshbon, Buseirah, Umm el-Biyara, Tawilan, Ghrareh, and the Jordanian tomb groups. Tell el-Kheleifeh's handmade wares find their closest parallels from Tell el-Qudeirat and certain of the central Negev fortresses.

II. THE CHRONOLOGY OF THE CASEMATE FORTRESS AND THE FORTIFIED SETTLEMENT

The wheelmade pottery clearly suggests the late Iron Age for the occupation of Tell el-Kheleifeh, although it is not possible to isolate the pottery assemblages associated with the two major architectural phases. Do the site's architectural traditions suggest a similar date? Unfortunately, significant dating refinement is precluded by the broad chronological horizons of several of the architectural traditions. That is especially true of the casemate and offsets/insets walls, the four-chambered gate, and the four-room house traditions. An eighth-early sixth century B.C.E. date is suggested, however, by the plan of Tell el-Kheleifeh's offsets/insets phase. This plan has been assigned to the fortified settlement tradition represented by Ḥorvat 'Uza, Tell el-Qudeirat (middle and upper phases), and Tel 'Arad X-VIII. Each of those settlements dates between the eighth and the early sixth centuries B.C.E. The fortified settlements of Tel 'Arad X-VIII offer very close parallels to the fortified settlement at Tell el-Kheleifeh. While the plan of Tell el-Qudeirat's middle and upper phases is not as close, the pottery assemblages of those two phases offer numerous parallels to the wheelmade and handmade forms at Tell el-Kheleifeh.

Do these horizons encompass the construction and occupation of the casemate fortress phase as well? That question must remain unanswered without additional data. We have assigned the architecture of that level to the casemate fortress tradition of the central Negev, but have emphasized repeatedly that this conclusion is based on comparative architecture and not on chronology. It is clear that dating of Tell el-Kheleifeh's pottery to the late Iron Age is not consistent with the current dating of the central Negev fortresses to the tenth century B.C.E. or earlier.

Two obvious questions are raised by the disparity between the suggested chronology of the casemate fortress tradition and the late Iron Age date of Tell el-Kheleifeh's wheelmade pottery. Have the central Negev fortresses been dated correctly? Should Tell el-Kheleifeh's earliest architectural phase be assigned to that tradition? If both questions are answered affirmatively, the absence of an Iron I pottery horizon must be explained. There is surely the possibility that Glueck did not thoroughly expose and accurately document the site's earliest architecture. That emphasizes the importance of probing the northern perimeter of the earliest fortress buried beneath the excavation's dump. It is significant that Glueck saved only Negevite pottery to document the earliest phase of the four-room building that comprised the central edifice in the casemate fortress. As noted elsewhere, Glueck simply did not save other pottery types, although it is clear from the excavation records that the assemblage included wheelmade forms.

It is unfortunate that a typological sequence of Negevite pottery has not yet been established. We have dated Tell el-Kheleifeh's handmade corpus to the eighth-early sixth centuries B.C.E., in accordance with the wheelmade pottery, but have acknowledged the possibility that certain of the Negevite forms might date earlier.

There is, of course, the possibility that either or both of the above questions should be answered negatively. Until the wheelmade pottery of the central Negev fortresses is published, it is impossible to evaluate the Iron I date of this architectural tradition.

III. A COMMENT ON TELL EL-KHELEIFEH'S POLITICAL AND CULTURAL HISTORY

It should be noted, as a general impression, that Tell el-Kheleifeh's architectural traditions suggest stronger affinities with sites to the west of the Jordan River than with those of Transjordan. That may be explained to some degree by the fact that the western region has been more extensively explored and excavated than the regions to the east and southeast, especially northwestern Arabia.

The pottery of Tell el-Kheleifeh does not confirm that impression. The wheelmade forms have numerous parallels from the Amman tomb groups, Heshbon, Buseirah, Tawilan, Umm el-Biyara, and Ghrareh (Edomite cooking pots, inverted rim kraters, painted wares, and Assyrian types). Further publication of those sites and others will undoubtedly continue to document the ceramic similarities between Tell el-Kheleifeh and the regions of central and southern Transjordan.

The handmade and certain wheelmade forms have clear affinities with sites west of the Jordan River and the Arabah, most notably Tell el-Qudeirat, 'Aro'er, Ramat Raḥel, Lachish, Beersheba, En-Gedi, and Tel 'Arad. With the exception of a handful of sherds, the similarities are in form and not fabric. The Tell el-Kheleifeh horizon cannot be characterized as Judean pottery.

Mudbrick walls and pottery speak softly of culture but are virtually silent about political history. The anepigraphic evidence of archaeology allows us to glimpse the material traits of racial, religious, or social groups, although interpretations must always be speculative. Writing a site's political history demands written sources, which most often become available once a secure or at least probable historical identification is established. Such is not the case with Tell el-Kheleifeh, and the meager inscriptional materials are not the fabric of political history.

The problems are particularly acute for the site's casemate fortress phase, which cannot even be anchored in time. A casemate wall and a four-room building are hardly definitive indications of either politics or a specific cultural group. If future research on Tell el-Kheleifeh and the central Negev fortresses provides a clear affirmation to our two earlier questions, much will be written on the site's political and cultural history. Until then, however, for the earliest architectural phase we are limited to archaeological history.

The political history and cultural affinities of the fortified settlement are similarly difficult to interpret, although there are some tantalizing glimpses. The archaeological evidence clearly reflects the regional or cultural influences expected from the biblical notices. That does not assume the Tell el-Kheleifeh: Ezion-Geber identification, but only accepts as historically accurate the biblical picture of Israelite/Edomite struggle for control of the region.

Edomite influence is clearly reflected in the ceramic traditions (pls. 16, 17, 18:1-4, 20, 21, 28:7-9, 37) and epigraphic evidence (pls. 74-78). Judean influence or, perhaps better, colonial presence is suggested by the settlement's basic architectural definition, as closely paralleled by Tel ʿArad and Tell el-Qudeirat. Cultural affinities to the west and northwest are further indicated by the pottery (most clearly in pls. 11-15, 18:7-10, 19:6, 31: 7 and 36:8-10) and, although limited, by the epigraphic evidence (see chapter 6). The well documented Assyrian influence in the eastern and western regions is reflected in the pottery (pls. 25-29), but not in the architectural traditions.

The cultural indications provided by the anepigraphic evidence of the fortified settlement are surely more instructive than those of the casemate fortress. The data cannot, however, be translated into political history with any measure of confidence. For instance, does the presence of Edomite pottery indicate control or influence of politics or commerce? The designation of this ceramic tradition as Edomite is largely the product of its geographical distribution and it is uncertain whether one can even speak of it as an ethnic pottery tradition. Similar questions may be asked for each of the site's pottery and architectural traditions. Given the available data, the political and cultural history of Tell el-Kheleifeh cannot be written with any confidence.

IV. IN MEMORY OF NELSON GLUECK

It is appropriate to conclude with a comment on the pioneering figure in whose memory this reappraisal is conducted. Revision is inevitable and is not to be confused with criticism. The refinements of excavation methodology and ceramic typology in contemporary archaeology give the attempts of the late 1930s the appearance of prehistory. Those who are unwilling to concede that time will do the same to the archaeology of today delude themselves. Nelson Glueck remains the paradigm — the focal point of interaction — for the archaeology and historical geography of the Negev and Transjordan. He was the true pioneer, one who has gone before us into the wilderness, preparing the way for others to follow.

Bibliography

Aharoni, M.

1981 The Pottery of Strata 12-11 of the Iron Age Citadel at Arad. *EI* 15: 181-204.

Aharoni, M., and Aharoni, Y.

1976 The Stratification of Judahite Sites in the 8th and 7th Centuries B.C.E. *BASOR* 224: 73-90.

Aharoni, Y.

1958 The Negeb of Judah. *IEJ* 8: 26-38.

1959 The Date of Casement Walls in Judah and Israel and Their Purpose. *BASOR* 154: 35-39.

1962a *Excavations at Ramat Raḥel, I, Seasons 1959 and 1960*. Serie archaeologica 2. Rome: Centro di studi semitici, University of Rome.

1962b The Iron Age Pottery of the Timnaʿ and ʿAmran Area. Pp. 66-67 in Beno Rothenberg, Ancient Copper Industries in the Western Arabah. *PEQ* 94: 5-71.

1964 *Excavations at Ramat Raḥel. Seasons 1961 and 1962*. Serie archaelogica 6. Rome: Centro di studi semitici, University of Rome.

1965 The Citadel of Ramat Raḥel. *Archaeology* 18: 15-25.

1967a Forerunners of the Limes: Iron Age Fortresses in the Negev. *IEJ* 17: 1-17.

1967b Excavations at Tel Arad: Preliminary Report on the Second Season, 1963. *IEJ* 17: 233-49.

1967c The Negeb. Pp. 385-403 in *Archaeology and Old Testament Study*, ed. D. W. Thomas. Oxford: Clarendon.

1968 Arad: Its Inscriptions and Temple. *BA* 31: 2-32.

1970 Three Hebrew Ostraca from Arad. *BASOR* 197: 16-42.

1971a The Stratification of Israelite Megiddo. *EI* 10: 53-57.

1971b The Stratification of Israelite Megiddo. *JNES* 31: 302-11.

1972 Excavations at Tel Beer-Sheba. *BA* 35: 111-27.

1973 *Beer-sheba I: Excavations at Tel Beer-Sheba 1969-1971 Seasons*. Publications of the Institute of Archaeology 2. Tel Aviv: Institute of Archaeology, University of Tel Aviv.

1974a Excavations at Tel Beer-Sheba. *TA* 1: 34-42.

1974b The Building Activities of David and Solomon. *IEJ* 24: 13-16.

1975a Arad. The Upper Mound. Pp. 82-89 in *EAEHL*, ed. M. Avi-Yonah. Jerusalem: Israel Exploration Society.

1975b *Arad Inscriptions. Judean Desert Studies*. Jerusalem: Israel Exploration Society.

1975c *Investigations at Lachish, the Sanctuary and the Residency (Lachish V)*. Publications of the Institute of Archaeology 4. Tel Aviv: Institute of Archaeology, University of Tel Aviv.

1975d The "Nehemiah" Ostracon from Arad. *EI* 12: 72-76.

1976 Nothing Early and Nothing Late: Re-Writing Israel's Conquest. *BA* 39: 55-76.

1979 *The Land of the Bible: A Historical Geography*. Philadelphia: Westminster.

1981 *Arad Inscriptions*. Jerusalem: Israel Exploration Society.

1982 *The Archaeology of the Land of Israel*. Philadelphia: Westminster.

Aharoni, Y., and Amiran, R.

1958 A New Scheme for the Sub-Division of the Iron Age in Palestine. *IEJ* 8: 171-84.

1964a Excavations at Tel Arad: Preliminary Report on the First Season, 1962. *IEJ* 14: 131-47.

1964b Arad: A Biblical City in Southern Palestine. *Archaeology* 17: 43-53.

Aharoni, Y.; Evanari, M.; Shanan, L.; and Tadmor, N. H.

1960 The Ancient Desert Agriculture of the Negev V. An Israelite Agricultural Settlement at Ramat Maṭred. *IEJ* 10: 23-36, 97-111.

Aharoni, Y.; Fritz, V.; and Kempinski, A.

1974   Excavations at Tel Masos (Khirbet El-Meshâsh), Preliminary Report on the First Season, 1972. *TA* 2: 64-74.

1975   Excavations at Tel Masos (Khirbet Meshâsh), Preliminary Report on the Second Season, 1974. *TA* 2: 97-124.

Albright, W. F.

1932   *The Excavation of Tell Beit Mirsim, Vol. I. The Pottery of the First Three Campaigns.* AASOR 12. New Haven: ASOR.

1941   Ostracon No. 6043 from Ezion-Geber. *BASOR* 82: 11-15.

1943   *The Excavation of Tell Beit Mirsim, Vol. III. The Iron Age.* AASOR 21-22. New Haven: ASOR.

1952   The Chaldaean Inscriptions in Proto-Arabic Script. *BASOR* 128: 39-45.

Amiran, R.

1959   A Late Assyrian Stone Bowl from Tell el-Qitaf in the Bet-She'an Valley. *'Atiqot* 2 (English Series):129-32.

1970   *Ancient Pottery of the Holy Land; from Its Beginnings in the Neolithic Period to the End of the Iron Age.* New Brunswick, N. J.: Rutgers University.

Amiran, R., and Aharoni, Y.

1967   *Ancient Arad.* Jerusalem: Israel Museum Catalogue 32.

Amiran, R., and Dunayevsky, I.

1958   The Assyrian Open-Court Building and Its Palestinian Derivatives. *BASOR* 149: 25-32.

Avigad, N.

1961   The Jotham Seal from Elath. *BASOR* 163: 18-22.

1970   Ammonite and Moabite Seals. Pp. 284-95 in *Near Eastern Archaeology in the Twentieth Century,* ed. J. A. Sanders. Garden City: Doubleday.

Bartlett, J. R.

1969   The Land of Seir and the Brotherhood of Edom. *JTS* 20: 1-20.

1972   The Rise and Fall of the Kingdom of Edom. *PEQ* 104: 26-37.

1977   The Brotherhood of Edom. *JSOT* 4: 2-27.

1979   From Edomites to Nabataeans: A Study in Continuity. *PEQ* 111: 53-66.

1982   Edom and the Fall of Jerusalem, 587 B.C. *PEQ* 114: 13-24.

1989   *Edom and the Edomites.* JSOT Supplement Series 77. Sheffield, England: JSOT.

Bawden, G.

1983   Painted Pottery of Tayma and Problems of Cultural Chronology in Northwest Arabia. Pp. 37-52 in *Midian, Moab and Edom,* eds. J. F. A. Sawyer and D. J. A. Clines. JSOT Supplement Series 24. Sheffield, England: JSOT.

Beck, P.

1982   The Drawings from Ḥorvat Teiman (Kuntillet 'Ajrud). *TA* 9: 3-68.

1987   The Sculptures. Pp. 23-28 in *Edomite Shrine: Discoveries from Qitmit in the Negev,* ed. I. Beit-Arieh. Jerusalem: Israel Museum Catalogue 277.

Beebe, H. K.

1968   Ancient Palestinian Dwellings. *BA* 31: 38-58.

Beit-Arieh, I.

1984   H. Qitmit. *HA* 45: 42.

1986a Ḥorvat 'Uzza - A Border Fortress in the Eastern Negev. *Qadmoniot* 19.1-2: 31-40.

1986b An Edomite Temple at Ḥorvat Qitmit. *Qadmoniot* 19.3-4: 72-79.

1988   New Light on the Edomites. *BAR* 14: 28-41.

1989   New Data on the Relationship Between Judah and Edom Toward the End of the Iron Age. Pp. 125-131 in *Recent Excavations in Israel. Studies in Iron Age Archaeology.* AASOR 49, eds. S. Gitin and W. G. Dever. Winona Lake, IN: Eisenbrauns.

Beit-Arieh, I., and Beck, P.

1987   *Edomite Shrine: Discoveries from Qitmit in the Negev.* Jerusalem: Israel Museum Catalogue 277.

Beit-Arieh, I., and Cresson, B.

1985   An Edomite Ostracon from Ḥorvat 'Uza. *TA* 12: 96-101.

Bennett, C. M.

1966a Fouilles d'Umm el Biyara: Rapport Préliminaire. *RB* 73: 372-403.

1966b Notes and News: Umm el-Biyara. *PEQ* 98: 123-26.

1971a An Archaeological Survey of Biblical Edom. *Perspective* 12: 35-44.

1971b A Brief Note on Excavations at Tawilan, Jordan 1968-70. *Levant* 3: V-VIII.

1972a Buseira. *RB* 79: 426-30.

1972b Notes and News: Buseirah. *PEQ* 104: 3-4.

1973a Excavations at Buseirah, Southern Jordan, 1971: A Preliminary Report. *Levant* 5: 1-11.

1973b The Third Season of Excavations at Buseirah. *ADAJ* 18: 85.

1974a Excavations at Buseirah, Southern Jordan, 1972: Preliminary Report. *Levant* 6: 1-24.

1974b Buseira. *RB* 81: 73-76.

1975 Excavations at Buseirah, Southern Jordan, 1973: Third Preliminary Report. *Levant* 7: 1-19.

1977 Excavations at Buseirah, Southern Jordan, 1974: Fourth Preliminary Report. *Levant* 9: 1-10.

1978 Some Reflections on Neo-Assyrian Influence in Transjordan. Pp. 165-71 in *Archaeology in the Levant: Essays for Kathleen Kenyon*, eds. R. Moorey and P. Parr. Warminster, England: Aris & Phillips.

1982a Excavations at Tawilan in Southern Jordan, 1982. *LA* 32: 482-87.

1982b Neo-Assyrian Influence in Transjordan. Pp. 181-87 in *Studies in the History of Archaeology of Jordan I*, ed. A. Hadidi. Amman: Department of Antiquities of Jordan.

1983 Excavations at Buseirah (Biblical Bozrah). Pp. 9-17 in *Midian, Moab and Edom*, eds. J. F. A. Sawyer and D. J. A. Clines. JSOT Supplement Series 24. Sheffield, England: JSOT.

1984 Excavations at Tawilan in Southern Jordan, 1982. *Levant* 16: 1-23.

Benoit, P.; Milik, J. T.; and de Vaux, R.

1961 Les Grottes de Murabbaʿât. Discoveries in the Judaean Desert, Vol. II. Oxford: Clarendon.

Benz, F. L.

1972 *Personal Names in the Phoenician and Punic Inscriptions*. Rome: Biblical Institute.

Bikai, P. M.

1978 The Late Phoenician Pottery Complex and Chronology. *BASOR* 229: 47-56.

Biran, A.

1980 Two Discoveries at Tel Dan. *IEJ* 30: 89-98.

Biran, A., and Cohen, R.

1981 Aroer in the Negev. *EI* 15: 250-273.

Birnbaum, S.

1971 *The Hebrew Scripts*. Leiden: E. J. Brill.

Boneschi, P.

1961 Les monogrammes Sud-Arabes de la grande jarre de Tell el-Heleyfeh (Ezion-Geber). *Rivista degli studi orientali* 36: 213-23.

Boraas, R. S., and Geraty, L. T.

1974 The Fourth Campaign at Tell Hesbân (1974): A Preliminary Report. *AUSS* 14: 1-15.

1978 The Fifth Campaign at Tell Hesbân (1976): A Preliminary Report. *AUSS* 16: 1-17.

Branigan, K.

1966 The Four-Room Buildings of Tell en-Nasbeh. *IEJ* 16: 206-8.

CIG

1828- *Corpus inscriptionum graecarum*. Paris:
1877 Académie des inscriptions et belles-lettres.

CIS

1881- *Corpus inscriptionum semiticarum*. Paris: Académie des inscriptions et belles-lettres.

Clark, V. A.

1983 The Iron IIC/Persian Pottery From Rujm Al-Henu. *ADAJ* 27: 143-63.

Cohen, R.

1966a Sede Boqer Area. *HA* 17: 30-31.

1966b Sede Boqer Area. *HA* 18-19: 23-25.

1970 ʾAtar Haroʿa. *ʿAtiqot* 6 (Hebrew Series): 6-24.

1971 Ketef Shivta. *HA* 39: 29-30.

1972a Mesad Har Boqer. *HA* 40: 37.

1972b Surveys in the Negev. *HA* 41-42: 39-40.

1975 H. Rahba. *IEJ* 25: 171-72.

1976a Excavations at Horvat Haluqim. *ʿAtiqot* 11 (English Series): 34-50.

1976b H. Ketef Shivta. *HA* 49-50: 53-54.

1976c Kadesh-Barnea, 1976. *IEJ* 26: 201-2.

1977a ʿEin Qudeis. *IEJ* 27: 171.

1977b H. Mesora. *IEJ* 27: 170-71.

1979 The Iron Age Fortresses in the Central Negev. *BASOR* 236: 61-79.

1981a Did I Excavate Kadesh-Barnea? *BAR* 7: 21-33.

1981b Excavations at Kadesh-barnea, 1976-1978. *BA* 44: 93-104.

1985 The Fortresses King Solomon Built To Protect His Southern Frontier. *BAR* 11: 56-70.

1986 Solomon's Negev Defense Line Contained Three Fewer Fortresses. *BAR* 12: 40-45.

Cohen, R., and Meshel, Z.

1970 Mesudat Refed and Mesudat Hatira. *HA* 37: 27.

1971 Kh. Ritma. *HA* 39: 28-29.

1972 Mesad Har Boqer. *HA* 40: 37.

Cowley, A.

1923　*Aramaic Papyri of the Fifth Century B.C.* Oxford: Clarendon.

Cross, F. M.

1961　The Development of the Jewish Scripts. Pp. 133-202 in *The Bible and the Ancient Near East,* ed. G. E. Wright. Garden City, New York: Doubleday.

1968　Jar Inscriptions from Shiqmona. *IEJ* 18: 226-33.

1969　Epigraphic Notes on the Amman Citadel Inscription. *BASOR* 193: 13-19.

1973　Notes on the Ammonite Inscription from Tell Sīrān. *BASOR* 212: 12-15.

1975a　Ammonite Ostraca from Heshbon: Heshbon Ostraca IV-VIII. *AUSS* 13: 1-20.

1975b　El-Buqeiʿa. Pp. 267-70 in *EAEHL,* ed. M. Avi-Yonah. Jerusalem: Israel Exploration Society.

1979a　The Development of the Jewish Scripts. Pp. 133-202 in *The Bible and the Ancient Near East,* ed. G. E. Wright. Winona Lake: Eisenbrauns.

1979b　Two Offering Dishes with Phoenician Inscriptions from the Sanctuary of ʿArad. *BASOR* 235: 75-78.

1981　An Aramaic Ostracon of the Third Century B.C.E. from Excavations in Jerusalem. *EI* 15: 67-69.

Cross, F. M., and Milik, J. T.

1956　Explorations in the Judaean Buqêʿah. *BASOR* 142: 5-17.

Crowfoot, G. M.

1940　Some Censer Types from Palestine, Israelite Period. *PEQ*: 72: 150-53.

Crowfoot, J. W.

1934　An Expedition to Baluʿah. *PEQ*: 66: 76-84.

Crowfoot, J. W.; Crowfoot, G. M.; and Kenyon, K. M.

1957　*Samaria-Sebaste III. The Objects from Samaria.* London: Palestine Exploration Fund.

Crowfoot, J. W.; Kenyon, K.; and Sukenik, E. L.

1942　*Samaria-Sebaste I. The Buildings at Samaria.* London: Palestine Exploration Fund.

Dajani, R. W.

1966a　Four Iron Age Tombs from Irbed. *ADAJ* 11: 88-101.

1966b　An Iron Age Tomb from Amman (Jabal el-Jofeh al-Sharqi) *ADAJ* 11: 41-47.

Dayton, J. E.

1972　Midianite and Edomite Pottery. *PSAA* 5: 25-38.

Dever, W. G.

1974　The MB IIC Stratification in the Northwest Gate Area at Shechem. *BASOR* 216: 31-52.

1982　The Late Bronze, Iron Age, and Hellenistic Defenses of Gezer. *JJS* 33: 19-34.

1984　Gezer Revisited: New Excavations of the Solomonic and Assyrian Period Defenses. *BA* 47: 206-18.

1985　Solomonic and Assyrian Period "Palaces" at Gezer. *IEJ* 35: 217-30.

1986　Late Bronze Age and Solomonic Defences at Gezer: New Evidence. *BASOR* 262: 9-34.

Dever, W. G.; Lance, H. D.; and Wright, G. E.

1970　*Gezer I: Preliminary Report of the 1964-66 Seasons.* Jerusalem: Hebrew Union College Biblical and Archaeological School in Jerusalem.

Dever, W. G.; Lance, H. D.; Bullard, G.; Cole, D.; Furshpan, A.; Holladay, J.; Seger, J.; and Wright, R.

1971　Further Excavations at Gezer, 1967-1971. *BA* 34: 94-132.

Dever, W. G.; Lance, H. D.; Bullard, G.; Cole, D.; and Seger, J.

1974　*Gezer II: Report of the 1967-70 Seasons in Fields I and II.* Jerusalem: Hebrew Union College/Nelson Glueck School of Biblical Archaeology.

Diringer, D.

1934　*Le iscrizioni antico-ebraiche palestinesi.* Firenze: Felice Le Monnier.

Dornemann, R. H.

1982　The Beginning of the Iron Age in Transjordan. Pp. 135-40 in *Studies in the History and Archaeology of Jordan I,* ed. A. Hadidi. Amman: Department of Antiquities of Jordan.

1983　*The Archaeology of the Transjordan in the Bronze and Iron Ages.* Milwaukee: Milwaukee Public Museum.

Dothan, M.

1965　The Fortress at Kadesh-Barnea. *IEJ* 15: 134-51.

1977　Kadesh Barnea. Pp. 697-98 in *EAEHL* eds. M. Avi-Yonah and E. Stern. Jerusalem: Israel Exploration Society.

Eitam, D.

1980 The "Fortresses" of the Negev Uplands - Settlement Sites. *Qadmoniot* 13.3-4: 56-57.

Finkelstein, I.

1984 The Iron Age "Fortresses" of the Negev Highlands: Sedentarization of the Nomads. *TA* 11: 189-209.

1985 The Iron Age "Fortresses" in the Negev - Sedentarization of Desert Nomads. *EI* 18: 366-379.

1986 The Iron Age Sites in the Negev Highlands - Military Fortresses or Nomads Settling Down. *BAR* 12: 46-53.

1988 *The Archaeology of the Israelite Settlement.* Jerusalem: Israel Exploration Society.

Flinder, A.

1977 The Island of Jezirat Faraᶜun. *IJNAUE* 6: 127-39.

1989 Is This Solomon's Seaport? *BAR* 15: 30-43.

Frank, F.

1934 Aus der ᶜArabah, I: Tell el-Chlēfi. *ZDPV* 57: 243-45.

Franken, H. J.

1969 *Excavations at Tell Deir ᶜAlla I: A Stratigraphical and Analytical Study of the Early Iron Age Pottery.* Leiden: E. J. Brill.

1976 The Problem of Identification in Biblical Archaeology. *PEQ* 108: 3-11.

Fritz, V., and Kempinski, A.

1983 *Ergebnisse der Ausgrabungen auf der Hirbet el-Msâs (Tel Masos) 1972-1975.* Wiesbaden: Otto Harrassowitz.

Galling, K.

1941 Beschriftete Bildsiegel des ersten Jahrtausends v. Chr. vornehmlich aus Syrien und Palästina. Ein Beitrag zur Geschichte der phönikischen Kunst. *ZDPV* 64: 121-202.

1967 Das Siegel des Jotham von Tell el-Ḥlēfi. *ZDPV* 83: 131-34.

Geraty, L. T.

1972 Third Century B.C. Ostraca from Khirbet el-Kôm. Unpublished Dissertation, Harvard University.

1975 The Khirbet el-Kôm Bilingual Ostracon. *BASOR* 220: 55-61.

1985 The Andrews University Madaba Plains Project: A Preliminary Report on the First Season at Tell el-ᶜUmeiri. *AUSS* 23: 85-110.

Geraty, L. T.; Herr, L. G.; and La Bianca, S.

1987 The Madaba Plains Project: A Preliminary Report on the First Season at Tell el-ᶜUmeiri and Vicinity. *ADAJ* 31: 187-99.

Geraty, L. T; Herr, L. G.; La Bianca, S.; Battenfield, J. R.; Christopherson, G. L.; Clark, D. R.; Cole, J. A.; Michèle Daviau, P.; Hubbard, L. E.; Lawlor, J. I.; Low, R.; and Younker, R. W.

1989 Madaba Plains Project: The 1987 Season at Tell el-ᶜUmeiri and Vicinity. *ADAJ* 33: 145-75.

Gitin, S.

1990 *Gezer III. A Ceramic Typology of the Late Iron II, Persian and Hellenistic Periods at Tell Gezer.* Jerusalem: Nelson Glueck School of Biblical Archaeology, Hebrew Union College.

Glueck, N.

1934 Explorations in Eastern Palestine, I. Pp. 1-113 in *AASOR* 14. New Haven: ASOR.

1935 *Explorations in Eastern Palestine, II.* AASOR 15. New Haven: ASOR.

1937 Explorations in Eastern Palestine, III. *BASOR* 65: 8-29.

1938a The First Campaign at Tell el-Kheleifeh (Ezion-Geber). *BASOR* 71: 3-17.

1938b The Topography and History of Ezion-Geber and Elath. *BASOR* 72: 2-13.

1938c Ezion-Geber: Solomon's Naval Base on the Red Sea. *BA* 1: 13-16.

1938d Solomon's Seaport: Ezion-Geber. *Asia* 38: 591-95.

1939a The Second Campaign at Tell el-Kheleifeh (Ezion-Geber: Elath). *BASOR* 75: 8-22.

1939b Ezion-Geber: Elath, the Gateway to Arabia. *BA* 2: 37-41.

1939c Gateway to Arabia: Ezion-Geber. *Asia* 39: 528-32.

1939d King Solomon's Seaport of Ezion-Geber on the Gulf of Aqabah. *ILN* (Aug. 5, 1939): 246-47.

1939e *Explorations in Eastern Palestine, III.* AASOR 18-19. New Haven: ASOR.

1940a The Third Season of Excavation at Tell el-Kheleifeh. *BASOR* 79: 2-18.

1940b Ostraca from Elath. *BASOR* 80: 3-10.

1940c *The Other Side of the Jordan.* New Haven: ASOR.

1940d The Pittsburgh of Old Palestine. *Scientific American* (Jan., 1940): 22-24.

1940e Ezion-geber: Singapore of Solomon. *Asia* 40: 663-69.

1940f Ezion-Geber: Elath-City of Bricks with Straw. *BA* 3: 51-55.

1941 Ostraca from Elath. *BASOR* 82: 3-11.

1951 *Explorations in Eastern Palestine, IV*. AASOR 25-28. New Haven: ASOR.

1956 The Fourth Season of Exploration in the Negeb. *BASOR* 142: 17-35.

1957 The Fifth Season of Exploration in the Negev. *BASOR* 145: 11-25.

1959a An Aerial Reconnaissance of the Negev. *BASOR* 155: 2-13.

1959b The Negev. *BA* 22: 82-97.

1960 *Rivers in the Desert*. New York: Farrar, Straus, and Giroux.

1961 The Archaeological History of the Negev. *HUCA* 32: 11-18.

1965a Ezion-geber. *BA* 28: 70-87.

1965b Further Explorations in the Negev. *BASOR* 179: 6-29.

1967a Some Edomite Pottery from Tell el-Kheleifeh, Parts I and II. *BASOR* 188: 8-38.

1967b Transjordan. Pp. 428-453 in *Archaeology and Old Testament Study*, ed. D. W. Thomas. Oxford: Clarendon.

1969 Some Ezion-Geber: Elath Iron II Pottery. *EI* 9: 51-59.

1971a Iron II Kenite and Edomite Pottery. *Perspective* 12: 45-46.

1971b Incense Altars. *EI* 10: 120-25.

1971c Tell el-Kheleifeh Inscriptions. Pp. 225-42 in *Near Eastern Studies in Honor of William Foxwell Albright*, ed. H. Goedicke. Baltimore: Johns Hopkins.

1977 Tell el-Kheleifeh. Pp. 713-17 in *EAEHL*, eds. M. Avi-Yonah and E. Stern. Jerusalem: Israel Exploration Society.

Gophna, R.

1964 Iron Age Sites Between Beer-sheba and Tell el-Farʿah. *Yediot* 28: 236-46.

Gordon, C.

1941 *The Living Past*. New York: John Day.

Grant, E., and Wright, G. E.

1938 *Ain Shems Excavations (Palestine), Part IV (Pottery)*. Biblical and Kindred Studies 7. Haverford, PA: Haverford College.

1939 *Ain Shems Excavations (Palestine), Part V (Text)*. Biblical and Kindred Studies 8. Haverford, PA: Haverford College.

Gregori, B.

1986 "Three Entrance" City Gates of the Middle Bronze Age in Syria and Palestine. *Levant* 18: 83-102.

Gröndahl, F.

1967 *Die Personennamen der Texte aus Ugarit*. Roma: Pontificium Institutum Biblicum.

Hadidi, A.

1987 An Ammonite Tomb at Amman. *Levant* 19: 101-20.

Hadidi, A., ed.

1982 *Studies in the History and Archaeology of Jordan I*. Amman: Department of Antiquities of Jordan.

1987 *Studies in the History and Archaeology of Jordan III*. Amman: Department of Antiquities of Jordan.

Harding, G. L.

1944 Two Iron Age Tombs from ʿAmman. *QDAP* 11: 67-74.

1948 An Iron-Age Tomb at Sahab. *QDAP* 13: 92-102.

1950 An Iron-Age Tomb at Meqabelein. *QDAP* 14: 44-48.

1951 Two Iron-Age Tombs in Amman. *ADAJ* 1: 37-40.

Harding, G. L., and Tufnell, O.

1953 The Tomb of Adoni Nur in Amman. *PEFA* 6: 48-72.

Hart, S.

1986 Some Preliminary Thoughts on Settlement in Southern Edom. *Levant* 18: 51-58.

1987a Five Soundings in Southern Jordan. *Levant* 19: 33-47.

1987b The Edom Survey Project 1984-85: The Iron Age. Pp. 287-90 in *Studies in the History and Archaeology of Jordan III*, ed. A. Hadidi. Amman: Department of Antiquities of Jordan.

1988 Excavations at Ghrareh, 1986: Preliminary Report. *Levant* 20: 89-99.

Hart, S., and Falkner, R. K.

1985 Preliminary Report on a Survey in Edom, 1984. *ADAJ* 29: 255-77.

Henschel-Simon, E.

1944 A Note on the Pottery of the ʿAmman Tombs. *QDAP* 11: 75-80.

Herr, L. G.

1978 *The Scripts of Ancient Northwest Semitic Seals*. Harvard Semitic Museum, Harvard Semitic Monograph Series 18. Missoula: Scholars.

1980   The Formal Scripts of Iron Age Transjordan. *BASOR* 238: 21-34.
1988   Tripartite Pillared Buildings and the Market Place in Iron Age Palestine. *BASOR* 272: 47-67.

Herzog, Z.
1983   Enclosed Settlements in the Negeb and the Wilderness of Beer-sheba. *BASOR* 250: 41-49.
1987   The Stratigraphy of Israelite Arad: A Rejoinder. *BASOR* 267: 77-79.

Herzog, Z.; Aharoni, M.; Rainey, A.; and Moshkovitz, S.
1984   The Israelite Fortress at Arad. *BASOR* 254: 1-34.

Hestrin, R., and Dayagi-Mendels, M.
1979   *Inscribed Seals.* Jerusalem: Israel Museum.

Hestrin, R., and Stern, E.
1973   Two "Assyrian" Bowls from Israel. *IEJ* 23: 152-55.

Holladay, J. S.
1971   Khirbet el-Qôm. *IEJ* 21: 175-77.
1976   Of Sherds and Strata: Contributions toward an Understanding of the Archaeology of the Divided Monarchy. Pp. 253-293 in *Magnalia Dei: The Mighty Acts of God*, eds. F. M. Cross; W. E. Lemke; and P. D. Miller. Garden City: Doubleday.

Ibach, R.
1987   *Archaeological Survey of the Hesban Region. Hesban 5.* Berrien Springs: Andrews University.

Ibrahim, M.
1972   Excavations at Sahab, 1972. *ADAJ* 17: 23-36.
1974   Second Season of Excavations at Sahab, 1973 (Preliminary Report). *ADAJ* 19: 55-61.
1975   Third Season of Excavations at Sahab, 1975 (Preliminary Report). *ADAJ* 20: 69-82.

Israel, F.
1979   Miscellanea Idumea. *Rivista biblica* 27: 171-203.

Jastrow, M.
1967   *A Dictionary of the Targumim, the Talmud Babli and Yerushalmi and the Midrashic Literature.* Brooklyn: P. Shalom.

Jean, C.-F., and Hoftijzer, J.
1965   *Dictionnaire des inscriptions sémitiques de l'ouest.* Leiden: E. J. Brill.

Jobling, W. J.
1981   Preliminary Report on the Archaeological Survey Between Maʿan and ʿAqaba, January to February 1980. *ADAJ* 25: 105-12.
1982   The ʿAqaba-Maʿan Archaeological and Epigraphic Survey, 1982 Season. *LA* 32: 467-70.
1983   The 1982 Archaeological and Epigraphic Survey of the ʿAqaba-Maʿan Area of Southern Jordan. *ADAJ* 27: 185-96.
1984   The Fifth Season of the ʿAqaba-Maʿan Survey, 1984. *ADAJ* 28: 191-202.

Kelso, J.
1968   *The Excavation of Bethel (1934-1960).* AASOR 39. Cambridge: ASOR.

Kempinski, A., and Fritz, V.
1977   Excavations at Tel Masos (Khirbet el-Meshâsh), Preliminary Report on the Third Season, 1975. *TA* 4: 136-58.

Kempinski, A.; Zimchoni, D.; Gilboa, E.; and Rösel, N.
1981   Excavations at Tel Masos: 1972, 1974, 1975. *EI* 15: 154-80.

Kenyon, K.
1964   Megiddo, Hazor, Samaria and Chronology. *BIA* 4: 143-56.
1971   *Royal Cities of the Old Testament.* New York: Schocken.
1976   The Date of the Destruction of Iron Age Beer-Sheba. *PEQ* 108: 63-64.
1978   *The Bible and Recent Archaeology.* Atlanta: John Knox (rev. ed. 1987. London: British Museum.
1979   *Archaeology in the Holy Land.* New York: W.W. Norton.

Kochavi, M.
1969   Excavations at Tel Esdar. *ʿAtiqot* 5 (Hebrew Series): 14-98.

Koucky, F., and Steinberg, A.
1989   Metallurgical Studies: Ancient Mining and Mineral Dressing in Cyprus. Pp. 275-327 in *American Expedition to Idalion Cyprus 1973-1980*, eds. L. Stager and A. Walker. (Oriental Institute Communications 24). Chicago: University of Chicago.

Lamon, R. S., and Shipton, G. M.

1939   *Megiddo I. Seasons of 1925-34, Strata I-V*. Chicago: University of Chicago.

Lapp, N. L.

1976   Casement Walls in Palestine and the Late Iron II Casement at Tell el-Fûl (Gibeah). *BASOR* 223: 25-42.

Lapp, P.

1965   Tell el-Fûl. *BA* 28: 2-10.
1969   The 1968 Excavations at Tell Ta'annek. *BASOR* 195: 2-49.

Lindner M., and Farajat, S.

1987   An Edomite Mountain Stronghold North of Petra (Ba'ja III). *ADAJ* 31: 175-85.

Lindner, M.; Farajat, S.; and Zeitler, J. P.

1988   Es-Sadeh: An Important Edomite-Nabataean Site in Southern Jordan (Preliminary Report). *ADAJ* 32: 75-99.

Lindsay, J.

1976   The Babylonian Kings and Edom, 605-550 B.C. *PEQ* 108: 23-39.

Lines, J.

1954   Late Assyrian Pottery from Nimrud. *Iraq* 16: 164-67.

Loud, G.

1948   *Megiddo II. Seasons of 1935-39*. Chicago: University of Chicago.

Lugenbeal, E. N., and Sauer, J. A.

1972   Seventh-Sixth Century B.C. Pottery from Area B at Heshbon. *AUSS* 10: 21-69.

Macalister, R. A. S.

1912   *The Excavation of Gezer. Vols. I-III*. London: Palestine Exploration Fund.

MacDonald, B.

1980   The Wadi El Ḥasā Survey 1979: A Preliminary Report. *ADAJ* 24: 169-83.
1982a   The Wadi el-Ḥasā Archaeological Survey 1982. *LA* 32: 472-79.
1982b   The Wâdī el-Ḥasā Survey 1979 and Previous Archaeological Work in Southern Jordan. *BASOR* 245: 35-52.

1983   The Late Bronze and Iron Age Sites of the Wadi el-Ḥasā Survey 1979. Pp. 18-28 in *Midian, Moab, and Edom*, eds. J. F. A. Sawyer and D. J. A. Clines. JSOT Supplement Series 24. Sheffield, England: JSOT.
1984   The Wadi el-Ḥasā Archaeological Survey. Pp. 113-28 in *The Answers Lie Below*, ed. H. O. Thompson. Landham, MD: University Press of America.
1988   *The Wadi el-Ḥasā Archaeological Survey 1979-1983, West-Central Jordan*. Waterloo, Ontario: Wilfred Laurier University.

MacDonald, B.; Rollefson, G. O.; and Roller, D. W.

1982   The Wadi el-Ḥasā Survey 1981. *ADAJ* 26: 117-31.

MacDonald, B.; Rollefson, G. O.; Banning, E. B.; Byrd, B.; and D'Annibale, C.

1983   The Wadi El Ḥasā Archaeological Survey 1982: A Preliminary Report. *ADAJ* 27: 311-23.

Mackenzie, D.

1911   *The Excavations at Ain Shems, 1911. PEFA* 1: 41-94.
1913   *Excavations at Ain Shems (Beth-Shemesh)*. London: Palestine Exploration Fund.

Malamat, A.

1968   The Last Kings of Judah and the Fall of Jerusalem. *IEJ* 18: 137-56.
1975   The Twilight of Judah in the Egyptian-Babylonian Maelstrom. *VTS* 28: 123-45.

Mallowan, M. E. L.

1950   The Excavations at Nimrud (Kalhu), 1949-1950. *Iraq* 12: 147-83.

Mazar, A., and Netzer, E.

1986   On the Israelite Fortress at Arad. *BASOR* 263: 87-91.

Mazar, B.

1957   The Campaign of Pharaoh Shishak to Palestine. *VTS* 4: 57-66.
1975   Ezion-Geber and Ebronah. *EI* 12: 46-48.

Mazar, B.; Dothan, T.; and Dunayevsky, I.

1966   En-Gedi: The First and Second Seasons of Excavations, 1961-1962. 'Atiqot English Series 5. Jerusalem.

Mazar, E.

1985 Edomite Pottery at the End of the Iron Age. *IEJ* 35: 253-69.

McCown, C. C.

1945 The Long-Room House at Tell en-Naṣbeh. *BASOR* 98: 2-15.

McCown, C. C., et al.

1947 *Tell en-Naṣbeh I: Archaeological and Historical Results*. New Haven: ASOR.

McLeod, B. H.

1962 The Metallurgy of King Solomon's Copper Smelters. Pp. 68-71 in Beno Rothenberg, Ancient Copper Industries in the Western Arabah. PEQ 94: 5-71.

McNicoll, A.; Smith, R. H.; and Hennessy, B.

1982 *Pella in Jordan I: An Interim Report on the Joint University of Sydney and the College of Wooster Excavations at Pella 1979-1981* (2 vols.). Canberra: Australian National Gallery.

Meshel, Z.

1973 Survey in the Negev. *HA* 45: 39-40.
1975a On the Problem of Tell el-Kheleifeh, Elath and Ezion-Geber. *EI* 12: 49-56.
1975b Har Ha-Negev Survey. *HA* 54-55: 30.
1977 Ḥorvat Ritma - An Iron Age Fortress in the Negev Highlands. *TA* 4: 110-35.
1978a *Kuntillet ʿAjrud. An Israelite Religious Centre in Northern Sinai.* Jerusalem: Israel Museum Catalogue 175.
1978b Kuntillet ʿAjrud. An Israelite Religious Center in Northern Sinai. *Expedition* 20/4: 50-54.
1979 Who Built The "Israelite Fortresses" in the Negev Uplands. *Cathedra* 11: 3-28.

Meshel, Z., and Cohen, R.

1980 Refed and Ḥatira: Two Iron Age Fortresses in the Northern Negev. *TA* 7: 70-81.

Meshel, Z., and Sass, B.

1974 Yotvata. *IEJ* 24: 273-74.

Meyers, C.

1976 Kadesh Barnea: Judah's Last Outpost. *BA* 39: 148-51.

Milik, J. T.

1958 Nouvelles inscriptions Nabatéene. *Syria* 35: 227-51.

Miller, J. M.

1979a Archaeological Survey of Central Moab: 1978. *BASOR* 234: 43-52.
1979b Archaeological Survey South of Wadi Mujib: Glueck's Sites Revisited. *ADAJ* 23: 79-92.
1982 Recent Archaeological Developments Relevant to Ancient Moab. Pp. 169-73 in *Studies in the History and Archaeology of Jordan I*, ed. A. Hadidi. Amman: Department of Antiquities of Jordan.

Miller, N.

1982 Corrosion Analysis and Interpretation of the Copper and Copper-Alloy Artifacts from Tell el-Kheleifeh. Unpublished Senior Thesis, College of Wooster.

Mullen, E.

1974 A New Royal Sidonian Inscription. *BASOR* 216: 25-30.

Myers, J. M.

1971 Edom and Judah in the Sixth-Fifth Centuries B.C. Pp. 377-92 in *Near Eastern Studies in Honor of William Foxwell Albright*, ed. H. Goedicke. Baltimore: Johns Hopkins.

Naveh, J.

1962 The Excavations at Meṣad Ḥashavyahu, Preliminary Report. *IEJ* 12: 89-113.
1966 The Scripts of Two Ostraca from Elath. *BASOR* 183: 27-30.
1970 *The Development of the Aramaic Script.* Jerusalem: Ahva.
1973 The Aramaic Ostraca. Pp. 79-82 in *Beer-sheba I: Excavations at Tell Beer-Sheba (1969-1971 Seasons)*, ed. Y. Aharoni. Tel Aviv: Institute of Archaeology, University of Tel Aviv.
1979 The Aramaic Ostraca from Tel Beer-Sheba (Seasons 1971-1976). *TA* 6: 182-98, pls. 24-31.
1982 *Early History of the Alphabet.* Jerusalem: Magnes.

Negev, A.

1979 Water in the Desert and the Nature of the Iron Age Fortresses in the Negev Uplands. *Cathedra* 11: 29-36.

Noth, M.

1980 *Die israelitischen Personennamen im Rahmen der gemeinsemitischen Namengebung.* Hildesheim: Georg Olms.

Nylander, C.

1977 A Note on the Stonecutting and Masonry of Tel Arad. *IEJ* 17: 56-59.

Oakeshott, M. F.
1983 The Edomite Pottery. Pp. 53-63 in *Midian, Moab and Edom*, eds. J. F. A. Sawyer and D. J. A. Clines. JSOT Supplement Series 24. Sheffield, England: JSOT.

Oates, J.
1959 Late Assyrian Pottery from Fort Shalmaneser. *Iraq* 21: 130-46.

Oded, B.
1970 Observations on Methods of Assyrian Rule in Transjordania after the Palestinian Campaign of Tiglath-Pileser III. *JNES* 29: 177-86.

O'Dwyer Shea, M.
1983 The Small Cuboid Incense-Burner of the Ancient Near East. *Levant* 15: 76-109.

Olavarri, E.
1965 Sondages à 'Arô'er sur l'Arnon. *RB* 72: 77-94.
1969 Fouilles à 'Arô'er sur l'Arnon. *RB* 76: 230-59.

Parr, P. J.
1978 Pottery, People and Politics. Pp. 203-9 in *Archaeology in the Levant: Essays for Kathleen Kenyon*, eds. R. Moorey and P. Parr. Warminster, England: Aris & Phillips.
1982 Contacts Between North West Arabia and Jordan in the Late Bronze and Iron Ages. Pp. 127-33 in *Studies in the History and Archaeology of Jordan I*, ed. A. Hadidi. Amman: Department of Antiquities of Jordan.

Peckham, J. B.
1968 *The Development of the Late Phoenician Scripts.* Cambridge: Harvard University.

Petrie, F.
1928 *Gerar.* London: British School of Archaeology in Egypt.

Platt, E. E.
1978 Bone Pendants. *BA* 41: 23-28.

Pratico, G.
1985 Nelson Glueck's 1938-1940 Excavations at Tell el-Kheleifeh: A Reappraisal. *BASOR* 259: 1-32.
1986 Where is Ezion-Geber? A Reappraisal of the Site Archaeologist Nelson Glueck Identified as King Solomon's Red Sea Port. *BAR* 12: 24-35.

Puech, E.
1977 Documents épigraphiques de Buseirah. *Levant* 9: 11-20.

Reisner, G.; Fisher, C. S.; and Lyon, D. G.
1924 *Harvard Excavations at Samaria.* Cambridge: Harvard University.

Rosenthal, F.
1942 The Script of Ostracon No. 6043 from Ezion-Geber. *BASOR* 85: 8-9.

Rothenberg, B.
1962 Ancient Copper Industries in the Western Arabah. *PEQ* 94: 5-71.
1967a Excavations at Timna, 1964-66. *BMH* 19: 53-70.
1967b Archaeological Sites in the Southern Arabah and the Eilat Mountains. Pp. 283-331 in *The Eilat Survey*, vol II, ed. Z. Ron. Eilat Regional Council, Yatvata.
1970 An Archaeological Survey of South Sinai. *PEQ* 102: 4-29.
1972 *Timna, Valley of the Biblical Copper Mines.* London: Thames & Hudson.
1988 *The Egyptian Mining Temple at Timna.* London: Institute for Archaeo-Metallurgical Studies.

Rothenberg, B., and Glass, J.
1981 Midianite Pottery. *EI* 15: 85-114.
1983 The Midianite Pottery. Pp. 65-124 in *Midian, Moab and Edom*, eds. J. F. A. Sawyer and D. J. A. Clines. JSOT Supplement Series 24. Sheffield, England: JSOT.

Ryckmans, G.
1934 *Les noms propres sud-sémitiques.* Louvain: Bureaux du Muséon.
1939 Un fragment de jarre avec caractères minéens a Tell el-Kheleyfeh. *RB* 48: 247-49.

Saller, S. J.
1966 Iron Age Tombs at Nebo, Jordan. *LA* 16: 165-298.

Sauer, J. A.
1982 Prospects for Archaeology in Jordan & Syria. *BA* 45: 73-84.
1985 Ammon, Moab and Edom. Pp. 206-14 in *Biblical Archaeology Today*, ed. A. Biran. Jerusalem: Israel Exploration Society.
1986 Transjordan in the Bronze and Iron Ages: A Critique of Glueck's Synthesis. *BASOR* 263: 1-26.

Sawyer, J. F. A., and Clines, D. J. A.

1983   *Midian, Moab and Edom: The History and Archaeology of Late Bronze and Iron Age Jordan and
North-West Arabia.* JSOT Supplement Series
24. Sheffield, England: JSOT.

Schmidt, N.

1910   Kadesh Barnea. *JBL* 29: 61-76.

Segert, S.

1975   *Altaramäische   Grammatik.*   Leipzig:
Enzyklopädie.

Sellers, O.

1933   *The Citadel of Beth-Zur.* Philadelphia: Westminster.

Sellers, O.; Funk, R.; McKenzie, J.; Lapp, P.; and Lapp,
N.

1968   *The 1957 Excavation at Beth-Zur.* AASOR 38.
New Haven: ASOR.

Sheffer, A.

1976   Comparative Analysis of a "Negev Ware"
Textile Impression from Tel Masos. *TA* 3: 81-
88.

Shiloh, Y.

1970   The Four-Room House — Its Situation and
Function in the Israelite City. *IEJ* 20: 180-90.

1973   The Four-Room House - The Israelite Type
House? *EI* 11: 277-85.

1978   Elements in the Development of Town Planning in the Israelite City. *IEJ* 28: 36-51.

1980   Solomon's Gate at Megiddo As Recorded By
Its Excavator, R. Lamon, Chicago. *Levant* 12:
69-76.

1987   The Casemate Wall, the Four Room House,
and Early Planning in the Israelite City. *BASOR*
268: 3-15.

Stager, L. E.

1975   Ancient Agriculture in the Judaean Desert: A
Case Study of the Buqê^cah Valley in the Iron
Age. Unpublished Ph.D dissertation, Harvard
University.

Stamm, J. J.

1965   Hebraische Ersatznamen. *AS* 16: 413-24.

Stern, E.

1973   Tel Meborach. *IEJ* 23: 256-57.

1974   Tel Mevorakh (Tel Meborach). *IEJ* 24: 266-68.

Tadmor, M.

1973   *Inscriptions Reveal.* Jerusalem: Israel Museum.

Thompson, H. O.

1972a   Cosmetic Palettes. *Levant* 4: 148-50.

1972b   The 1972 Excavation of Khirbet Al-Hajjar.
ADAJ 17: 47-72.

1973   The Excavation of Tell Siran (1972). *ADAJ* 18:
5-14.

1977   The Ammonite Remains at Khirbet al-Hajjar.
BASOR 227: 27-34.

1983   The Tell Siran Bottle: An Additional Note.
BASOR 249: 87-89.

1984   Madaba-An Iron Age Tomb. Pp. 147-83 in *The
Answers Lie Below,* ed. H. O. Thompson.
Lanham, MD: University Press of America.

Tufnell, O., et al.

1953a   *Lachish III: The Iron Age (Text).* London: Oxford
University.

1953b   *Lachish III: The Iron Age (Plates).* London: Oxford University.

1958a   *Lachish IV: The Bronze Age (Text).* London:
Oxford University.

1958b   *Lachish IV: The Bronze Age (Plates).* London:
Oxford University.

Tushingham, A. D.

1954   Excavations at Dibon in Moab, 1952-53. *BASOR*
133: 6-26.

1972   *The Excavations at Dibon (Dhībân) in Moab. The
Third Campaign 1952-53.* AASOR 40. Cambridge: ASOR.

Ussishkin, D.

1966a   King Solomon's Palace and Building 1723 in
Megiddo. *IEJ* 16: 174-86.

1966b   Building IV in Hamath and the Temples of
Solomon and Tell Tayanat. *IEJ* 16: 104-10.

1973   King Solomon's Palaces. *BA* 36: 78-105.

1978   Excavations at Tel Lachish - 1973-1977, Preliminary Report. *TA* 5: 1-97.

1980   Was the "Solomonic" City Gate at Megiddo
Built by King Solomon? *BASOR* 239: 1-18.

1988   The Date of the Judaean Shrine at Arad. *IEJ* 38:
142-57.

Van Beek, G. W.

1972   Tel Gamma. *IEJ* 22: 245-46.

1974   Tel Gamma. *IEJ* 24: 138-39.

1983   Digging Up Tell Jemmeh. *Archaeology* 36.1: 12-
19.

de Vaux, R.

1952 La quatrième campagne de fouilles à Tell el-Fârᶜah, près Naplouse. *RB* 59: 551-83.

1966 Archéologie palestinienne. *RB* 73: 153-54.

Vogel, E. K.

1970 Bibliography of Nelson Glueck. Pp. 382-94 in *Near Eastern Archaeology in the Twentieth Century*, ed. J. A. Sanders. Garden City: Doubleday.

1971 Bibliography of Holy Land Sites. *HUCA* 42: 1-96.

Vogel, E. K., and Holtzclaw, B.

1981 Bibliography of Holy Land Sites, Part II. *HUCA* 52: 1-92.

Wampler, J. C.

1947 *Tell en-Naṣbeh: The Pottery*, Vol. II. Berkeley and New Haven: Palestine Institute of Pacific School of Religion and ASOR.

Weippert, M.

1982 Remarks on the History of Settlement in Southern Jordan during the Early Iron Age. Pp. 153-62 in *Studies in the History and Archaeology of Jordan I*, ed. A. Hadidi. Amman: Department of Antiquities of Jordan.

Winnett, F. V.

1952 Excavations at Dibon in Moab, 1950-51. *BASOR* 125: 7-20.

Winnett, F. V., and Reed, W. L.

1964 *The Excavations at Dibon (Dhîbân) in Moab.* AASOR 36-37. New Haven: ASOR.

Woolley, C. L., and Lawrence, T. E.

1914-
1915 *The Wilderness of Zin.* PEFA 3: 2-132.

Wright, G. E.

1950 The Discoveries at Megiddo, 1935-39. *BA* 13: 28-46.

1955a Review of O. Tufnell, *Lachish III: The Iron Age. JNES* 14: 188-89.

1955b Review of O. Tufnell, *Lachish III: The Iron Age. VT* 5: 97-105.

1959a Samaria. *BA* 22: 67-78.

1959b Israelite Samaria and Iron Age Chronology. *BASOR* 155: 13-29.

1961 The Archaeology of Palestine. Pp. 73-112 in *The Bible and the Ancient Near East*, ed. G. E. Wright. Garden City: Doubleday.

1962 Archaeological Fills and Strata. *BA* 25: 34-40.

Yadin, Y.

1958a Excavations at Hazor, 1957. Preliminary Communiqué. *IEJ* 8: 1-14.

1958b Solomon's City Wall and Gate at Gezer. *IEJ* 8: 80-86.

1960 New Light on Solomon's Megiddo. *BA* 23: 62-68.

1965 A Note on the Stratigraphy of Arad. *IEJ* 15: 180.

1970 Megiddo of the Kings of Israel. *BA* 33: 66-96.

1972 *Hazor.* London: British Academy.

1973 A Note on the Stratigraphy of Israelite Megiddo. *JNES* 32: 330.

1975 *Hazor: The Rediscovery of the Great Citadel of the Bible.* New York: Random House.

1976 Beer-sheba: The High Place Destroyed by King Josiah. *BASOR* 222: 5-17.

1980 A Rejoinder. *BASOR* 239: 19-23.

Yadin, Y.; Aharoni, Y.; Amiran, R.; Dothan, T.; Dunayevsky, I.; and Perrot, J.

1958 *Hazor I: An Account of the First Season of Excavations, 1955.* Jerusalem: Magnes.

1960 *Hazor II: An Account of the Second Season of Excavations, 1956.* Jerusalem: Magnes.

1961 *Hazor III-IV: An Account of the Third and Fourth Seasons of Excavations, 1957-1958. The Plates.* Jerusalem: Magnes.

Yassine, K., ed.

1988 *Archaeology of Jordan: Essays and Reports.* Amman: University of Jordan.

Zimhoni, O.

1985 The Iron Age Pottery of Tel ᶜEton and its Relation to the Lachish, Tell Beit Mirsim and Arad Assemblages. *TA* 12: 63-90.

Technical Pottery Data

PAMELA VANDIVER, AND GARY D. PRATICO

PLATE NO. 11

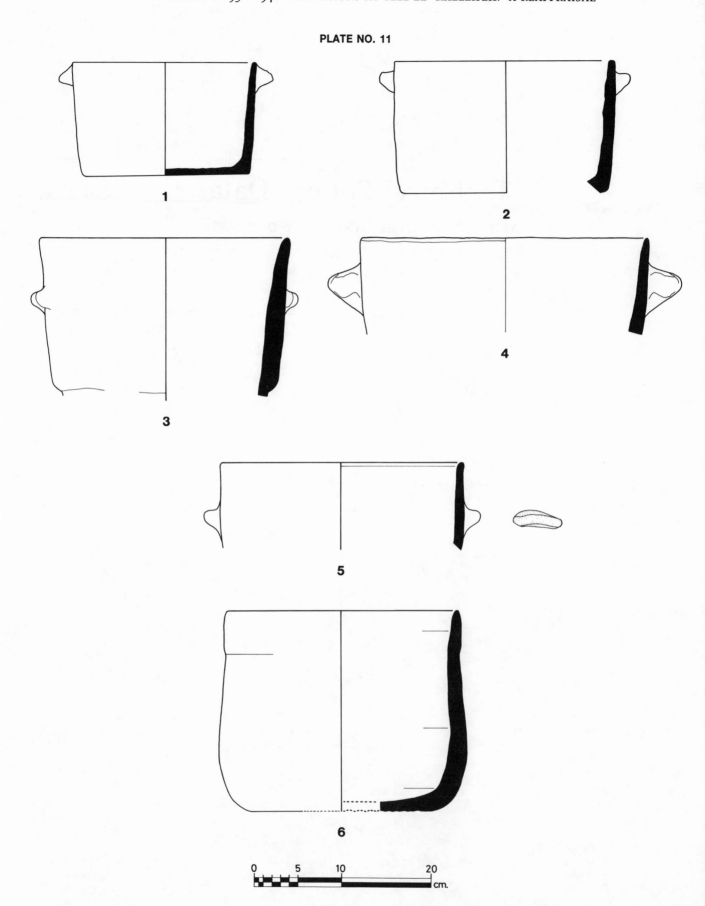

1

2

3

4

5

6

PLATE NO. 11

PL#:	Reg.#:	Date:	Prov:	Level:	Photo:	All:	Munsell References:
11:1		6-6-38				JAM	
11:2	929	6-6-38	Rm. 44	-50 cm		JAM	
11:3			L:12	Surface		ASOR	ext. 5 YR 6/3, int. 5 YR 6/4, sec. 2.5 YR 6/6
11:4	359	4-7-38	Rm. 35	-25 cm	562:2	ASOR	ext. 5 YR 7/2, int. 5 YR 7/3
11:5	827	4-20-38	P:12		564:6	ASOR	ext. 2.5 YR 6/6, int. 10 R 6/6, sec. 5 YR 7/1
11:6	781	4-20-38	Rm. 18		514:4	ASOR	ext. 5 YR 7/3, int. 5 YR 7/4, sec. 5 YR 7/3

PL#:	Description:	Body Comp. and Texture:
11:1	Negevite cooking pot, lip and base fragment; lug handle; flat base; vertical wall.	
11:2	Large Negevite cooking pot, lip and body fragment; lug handle; vertical wall.	
11:3	Large Negevite cooking pot, lip and body fragment; horizontal lug handle.	Fine textured ferrugenous clay; heavily tempered (30%); inclusions: Fe_3O_4, $CaCo_3$, lime, minor slate, burned out organic particles; minor HCl reaction.
11:4	Large Negevite cooking pot, lip and body fragment; lug handle, vertical wall.	Coarse; red and white inclusions.
11:5	Large size Negevite cooking pot, wall fragment with lug handle.	Type of clay not specified; some temper; inclusions: Fe_2O_3, minor qtz, Fe_3O_4, burned out organic particles; medium HCl reaction.
11:6	Large Negevite cooking pot; circular mat-impressed base; bottom thinner than wall.	Type of clay not specified; inclusions: minor Fe_2O_3/Fe_3O_4, $CaCo_3$, qtz, some burned out organic particles; strong HCl reaction.

PL#:	Method of Mfg:	Surf. Decor:	Firing:	State of Pres:
11:1				
11:2				
11:3	Handbuilt; lip smoothed by rotating pot; double lug handle well smoothed into body; bottom formed into molds; poorly aligned inclusions.	Surface exterior wiped in many directions with tool or rag.	Incompletely oxidized body; (MOHS 3 or 3→).	Interior surface worn and spalling, some exterior and interior weathering and carbon smudging.
11:4	Handbuilt.	None.	Oxidation.	Good.
11:5	Handbuilt; horizontal lug handle well worked into body.	Surface marks from wiping.	Mixed oxidation state, interior cross section grey, exterior red; (MOHS 3→).	Good.
11:6	Handbuilt; base is formed from several lumps of clay pressed side by side into a circular mat; inclusions aligned in wall.	Interior wiped on diagonal in both directions; exterior wall has diagonal indentations going from lower right to upper left impressed into shoulder of pot.	Mixed oxidation state, brown interior of wall; (MOHS 3→)	

PLATE NO. 12

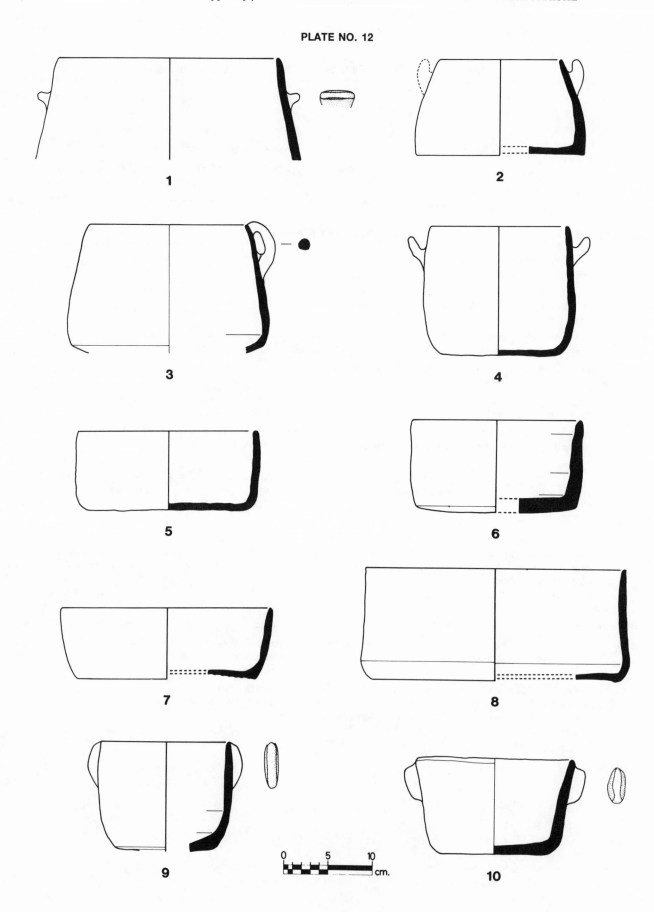

PLATE NO. 12

PL#:	Reg.#:	Date:	Prov:	Level:	Photo:	All:	Munsell References:
12:1	829	4-20-38	Q:11		564:1	ASOR	ext. 7.5 YR 8/4, int. 7.5 YR 7/4, sec. 5 YR 6/3
12:2	12,017	4-24-40	Rm. 36	-8 cm	1495:3, 1497:3	ASOR	ext. 5 YR 4/1, int. 5 YR 5/1, sec. 5 YR 6/2
12:3	560	4-16-38	Rm. 19		5:12:5, 606:2, 1614:2	ASOR	ext. 5 YR 4/1, int. 10 R 6/6, sec. 10 R 6/3
12:4	561	4-16-38	Rm. 19		512:2, 606:3	JAM	
12:5	3026	4-25-39	Rm. 50	-50 cm	629:4	JAM	
12:6	551	4-15-38	Rm. 35A	-2 m	516:6	ASOR	ext. 5 YR 6/3, int. 5 YR 6/4, sec. 5 YR 6/1
12:7	12,068	5-5-40	Rm. 25A		1498:1	ASOR	ext. 5 YR 7/4, int. 5 YR 7/2, sec. 5 YR 7/6
12:8	5028	5-12-39	Rm. 49A		629:1	ASOR	ext. 5 YR 6/1, int. 5 YR 6/1, sec. 5 YR 7/2
12:9	471	4-12-38	Rm. 23	-1.10 m	559:4	ASOR	ext. 5 YR 6/3, int. 7.5 YR 6/4, sec. 5 YR 6/4
12:10	626	4-18-38	Rm. 35A		517:7	ASOR	ext. 5 YR 7/3, int. 5 YR 6/3, sec. 5 YR 5/2

PL#:	Description:	Body Comp. and Texture:
12:1	Large Negevite cooking pot, lip and body fragment; horizontal lug handle.	Medium texture; black and white inclusions.
12:2	Squat Negevite cooking pot, lip and base fragment, flat base.	Fine textured ferrugenous clay; lightly tempered (10-30%); average particle size (1-2 mm); inclusions: qtz/spar, sand temper, minor shale and organic burnout.
12:3	Medium-size Negevite cooking pot, lip and base fragment; rounded base, vertical loop handle with drying cracks at top and bottom.	Fine textured ferrugenous clay; lightly tempered (10-30%); inclusions 0.1-5 mm: major Fe_2O_3, minor qtz, Fe_3O_4, organic burnout equiaxed and fibrous; no HCl reaction.
12:4	Medium-size Negevite cooking pot, lip and base fragment; flat base; horn handle.	
12:5	Medium-size Negevite bowl, lip and base fragment; vertical wall.	
12:6	Medium-size Negevite bowl, lip and base fragment; flat, thick base; vertical wall.	Coarse texture; black and white inclusions.
12:7	Medium-size Negevite bowl, lip and base fragment; low walls; mat impressed base.	Type of clay not specified; heavily tempered body; coarse particle size (up to 4 mm); inclusions: qtz, $CaCO_3$, Fe_2O_3, Fe_3O_4; strong HCl reaction.
12:8	Medium-size Negevite bowl, lip and base fragment; mat impressed base.	Fine textured ferrugenous clay; lightly tempered body (10-30%); particle size 0.1-5 mm; inclusions: major Fe_2O_3, qtz, hematite surrounded with ring of Fe_3O_4; no HCl reaction.
12:9	Medium-size Negevite bowl, lip and base fragment; vertical lug handle.	Type of clay not specified; fine to coarse particle size (.5 mm to 2-4 mm); inclusions: qtz, $CaCO_3$, minor Fe_3O_4; some HCl reaction.
12:10	Medium-size Negevite bowl, lip and base fragment; vertical lobed handle; vertical wall.	Medium to coarse; black and white inclusions, some fibrous vegetal temper which has burned out.

PL#:	Method of Mfg:	Surf. Decor:	Firing:	State of Pres:
12:1	Handbuilt.	None.	Reduction.	Worn.
12:2	Handbuilt on base support; horizontally wiped surfaces.		Body and surfaces tan with grey patches on exterior.	Good.
12:3	Handbuilt; handle not well worked into body; inclusions aligned in wall.	Interior and exterior surfaces wiped horizontally from upper left to lower right.	Interior central body layer grey, surface layers reddish brown, blackened exterior; MOHS 3→).	Good, sand and organic residue adheres to one side near lip.
12:4				
12:5				
12:6	Handbuilt with coiled basket or mat impression in base.	None.	Low; mostly reduction.	Worn.
12:7	Handbuilt on circular mat; pot not placed concentrically on mat; flat, thin base; base has cracks on bottom surface; base formed from several lumps of clay pressed side-by-side into mat.	Wiped with long strokes parallel to base.	Mixed oxidation state, surface more oxidized than interior; grey exterior and brown interior on one side; light reddish brown (exterior) to darker brown (interior) on other side of pot; two cracks in base completely through the bottom could be result of firing a very thin-bottomed vessel; (MOHS 4).	Good.
12:8	Handbuilt on circular mat; base formed from several lumps of clay pressed side-by-side into mat; base thinner than walls.	Surface wiped with short strokes.	Mixed oxidation state; interior of cross-section red, exterior grey; (MOHS 4→).	Good.
12:9	Handbuilt; rounded base formed in mold of unknown material; vertical lug handle well worked into body.	Exterior surface wiped from lower left to upper right.	Mixed oxidation state; interior reduced, exterior oxidized brown; (MOHS 4).	Good, interior surface weathered.
12:10	Slab built, in sections.	None.	Reduction and oxidation mixed.	Good, cracking of base from forming and drying.

PLATE NO. 13

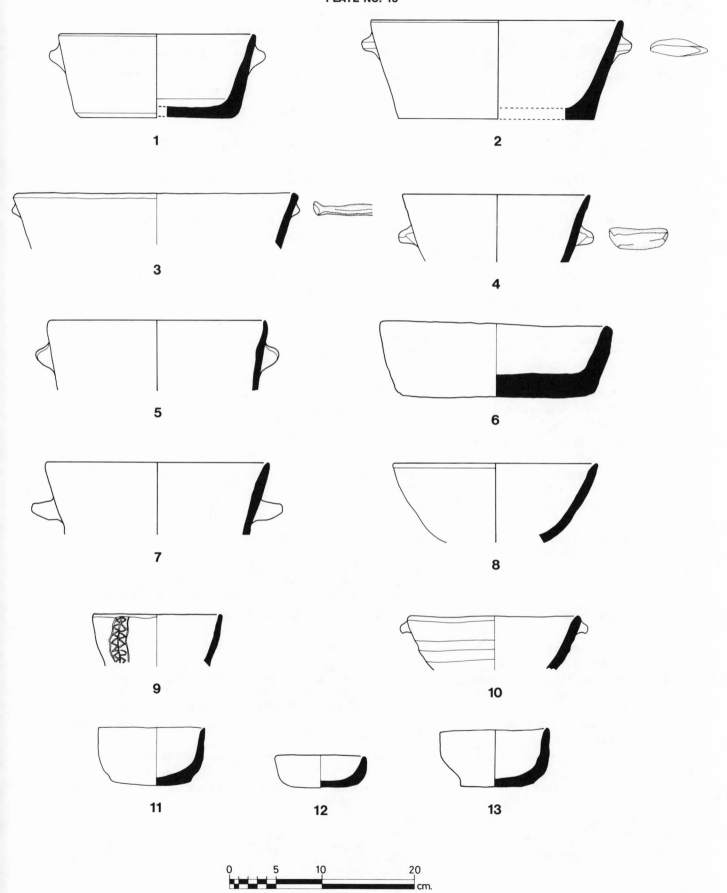

PLATE NO. 13

PL#:	Reg.#:	Date:	Prov:	Level:	Photo:	All:	Munsell References:
13:1	619	4-18-38	Rm. 35A		514:3	ASOR	ext. 5 YR 7/3, int. 5 YR 7/2, sec. 5 YR 6/1
13:2	565	4-18-38	0:9		514:2	ASOR	ext. 5 YR 7/1, int. 5 YR 6/1, sec. 5 YR 6/1
13:3	735	4-18-38	Rm. 19	-1.50 m		ASOR	ext. 10 YR 7/2, int. 2.5 Y 7/2
13:4	606	4-18-38	Rm. 35A		565:7	ASOR	ext. 7.5 YR 5/2, int. 5 YR 4/1, sec. 5YR 5/1
13:5	6002	3-12-40	Rm. 48	Debris	1453:3	JAM	
13:6	90	3-26-38	0:9	Surface	5:168, 1629:1	ASOR	ext. 5 YR 6/1, int. 2.5 YR 5/2, sec. 5 YR 6/1
13:7	11,020	4-16-40	Rm. 19		1465:1,2	ASOR	ext. 2.5 YR 6/2, int. 2.5 YR 6/4, sec. 2.5 YR 6/2
13:8	913	6-6-38	Rm. 17A		711	ASOR	ext. 10 YR 5/6, int. 7.5 YR 5/6
13:9	10,092	4-14-40	Rm. 39		1475:2	ASOR	ext. 5 YR 7/2, int. 2.5 YR 6/4
13:10	492	4-14-38	Rm. 17			ASOR	ext. 2.5 YR 6/6, int. 2.5 YR 6/6
13:11	284	4-4-38	Rm. 30		516:7,8	ASOR	ext. 5 YR, int. 5 YR 7/3, sec. 5 YR 7/3
13:12	1015	4-15-39	Rm. 25	-1.60 m	633:7	ASOR	ext. 7.5 YR 7/2, int. 7.5 YR 7/2, sec. 7.5 YR 7/2
13:13				Debris		ASOR	ext. 5 YR 7/3, int. 5 YR 7/3, sec. 5 YR 7/3

PL#:	Description:	Body Comp. and Texture:
13:1	Medium-size Negevite bowl, lip and base fragment; lug handle, mat impressed base.	Type of clay not specified; heavily tempered; inclusions: qtz, minor $CaCO_3$, Fe_2O_3; medium HCl reaction.
13:2	Medium-size Negevite bowl, lip and base fragment.	Fine textured ferrugenous clay; lightly tempered (10-30%); average particle size (1-2 mm); inclusions: qtz/spar, sand temper, minor shale and organic burnout.
13:3	Large Negevite bowl, lip and body fragment; horizontal lug handle.	Coarse texture; black and white inclusions; fibrous vegetal temper.
13:4	Negevite bowl, lip and body fragment with horn handles.	Clay heavily tempered; large particle size (up to 6 mm); inclusions: major Fe_2O_3 and Fe_3O_4, minor qtz/spar, some equiaxed organic burnout.
13:5	Medium-size Negevite bowl, lip and body fragment; lug handle.	
13:6	Medium-size Negevite bowl, lip and base fragment; thick, flat base; low wall.	Very coarse; black and white inclusions.
13:7	Negevite bowl, lip and body fragment; three upturned lug handles.	Type of clay not specified; heavily tempered; large particle size (up to 7 mm); inclusions: major Fe_2O_3 and Fe_3O_4 (up to 3 mm), minor qtz/spar, fairly large scale fibrous organic temper (0.5 x 3 - 7 mm), some equiaxed organic burnout.
13:8	Negevite bowl, lip and body fragment.	Type of clay not specified; inclusions: Fe_2O_3, Fe_3O_4, qtz, minor organic burnout; no HCl reaction.
13:9	Small Negevite bowl, lip and body fragment.	Medium to fine texture; a few black inclusions.
13:10	Small Negevite bowl, lip and body fragment; uneven horizontal, knobbed handle.	Fine textured ferrugenous clay; heavily tempered (~30%); inclusions: $CaCO_3$, Fe_3O_4, mica, sherd temper, other rock, fibrous organic burnout and minor equiaxed burnout; HCl reaction, strong reaction rings around Fe_3O_4.
13:11	Small Negevite bowl, lip and base fragment.	Type of clay not specified; inclusions: major qtz, $CaCO_3$, minor Fe_3O_4, organic temper; strong HCl reaction.
13:12	Small Negevite bowl with flat base.	Fine textured ferrugenous clay; lightly tempered (10-30%); fine particle size; inclusions: minor qtz, $CaCO_3$, mica; medium HCl reaction.
13:13	Small Negevite bowl.	Type of clay not specified; inclusions: major qtz, $CaCO_3$, minor Fe_3O_4, organic temper; strong HCl reaction.

PL#:	Method of Mfg:	Surf. Decor:	Firing:	State of Pres:
13:1	Handbuilt on circular mat; base formed from several lumps of clay pressed side-by-side into mat; base thinner than walls; horizontal lug handle well worked into wall.	Diagonal wiping marks on interior in both directions.	Reduced body and surface; brown body; in cross section interior grey and reduced; surface partially oxidized to brown; low degree of vitrification; (MOHS 3).	Good, some surface encrustation on exterior.
13:2	Probably turned.		Body and surfaces tan; (MOHS 3).	Accretions on interior and exterior surfaces.
13:3	Handbuilt; exterior rib marks.	None.	Mixed, mostly reduced.	Worn.
13:4	Handbuilt; uneven rim.		Dark grey core with brownish red oxidized surface.	Surface worn.
13:5				
13:6	Handbuilt in slabs.	None.	Low, reduced.	Poor, interior cracked.
13:7	Handbuilt; uneven rim; lugs individually formed.	Wipe marks parallel to rim.	Dark grey core with brownish red oxidized surface.	Interior surface worn.
13:8	Handbuilt; poor alignment of inclusions.	Wiping marks parallel to base; stamp seal on exterior 20 mm from lip; 2 incomplete incised lines on exterior.	Mixed oxidation state; interior grey core with red surfaces; (MOHS 4).	Good.
13:9	Handbuilt.	Vertical incised pattern.	Oxidation.	Good.
13:10	Handbuilt; pinched and smoothed by wiping; alignment of pores and Fe_3O_4 inclusions show body extended in upward motion and smoothed in horizontal direction; handle formed as lump or short coil with 2 knobs pinched out then smoothed by wiping.	Body and handle smoothed by wiping.	Brown body with grey rings around organic burnout; (MOHS 3).	Good, inner surface somewhat worn.
13:11	Rough exterior; flat base; walls and base are same thickness.	Exterior surface wiped in many directions, most slightly inclined to horizontal.	Brownish grey body and surface; (MOHS 3→).	Good.
13:12	Handbuilt; flat base; bottom pinched; finger imprint in center of underside of base; walls and bottom same thickness.	Surface is heavily textured by short pieces of chaff.	Brownish grey body and surface.	Good.
13:13	Rough exterior; flat base; walls and base unusually thick for this size vessel.	Exterior surface wiped in many directions.	Brownish grey body and surface; (MOHS 3-3→).	Good.

PLATE NO. 14

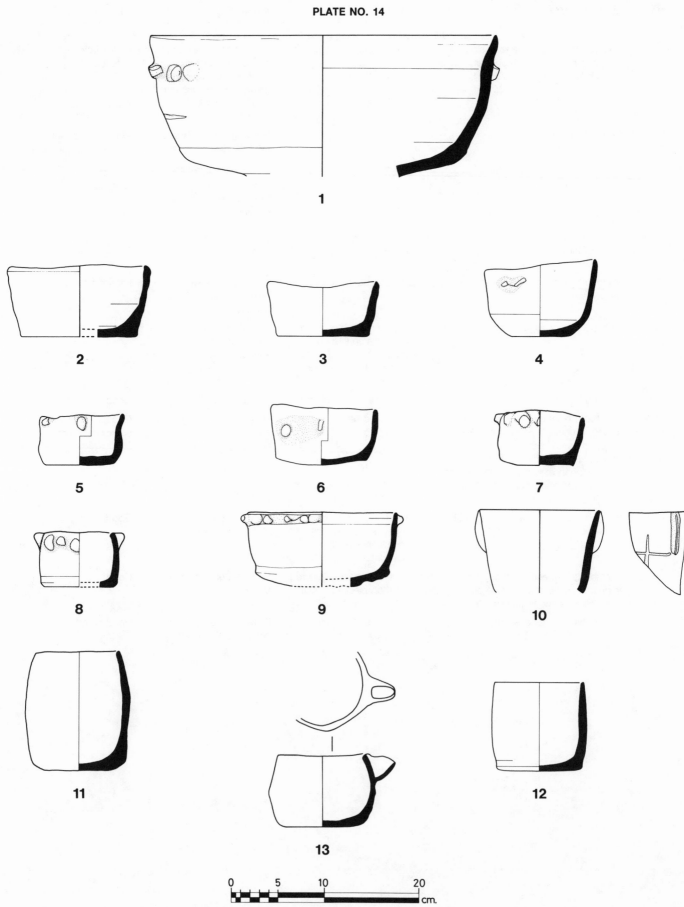

PLATE NO. 14

PL#:	Reg.#:	Date:	Prov:	Level:	Photo:	All:	Munsell References:
14:1	613	4-18-38	Rm. 35A		514:1	ASOR	ext. 7.5 YR 6/2, int. 2.5 YR 6/4, sec. 10 R 6/3
14:2	8075	3-31-40	Rm. 107		1451:10	ASOR	ext. 5 YR 7/3, 5 YR 7/4, sec. 7.5 YR 7/4
14:3	3051	4-26-39	Rm. 49B	-1.90 m	633:6	ASOR	ext. 5 YR 7/4, int. 5 YR 7/4, sec. 5 YR 7/3
14:4	4006	4-30-39	Rm. 49B		633	ASOR	ext. 5 YR 7/2, int. 5 YR 7/3, sec. 5 YR 6/3
14:5				Debris			ext. 5 YR 7/2, int. 5 YR 7/3, sec. 5 YR 6/3
14:6	12,014	4-24-40	Rm. 36	-8 cm	1453:11	ASOR	ext. 5 YR 7/3, int. 10 YR 4/1
14:7	391	4-9-38	Rm. 58	Surface	534:6, 632:6	ASOR	ext. 5 YR 6/2, int. 5 YR 5/1, sec. 2.5 YR N4/
14:8	7060						
14:9	587	4-18-38	P:17		530:5, 626:1	ASOR	ext. 7.5 YR 7/2, int. 7.5 YR 6/4
14:10	204	3-31-38	Rm. 18	-50 cm	605:14	ASOR	
14:11	11,003	4-15-40	Rm. 33			ASOR	ext. 7.5 YR 6/4, int. 5 YR 6/4, sec. 5 YR 6/1
14:12	344	4-7-38	Rm. 41	-1 m	1453:5	ASOR	ext. 5 YR 7/4, int. 10 YR 8/3, sec. 5 YR 5/1
14:13	343	4-7-38	Rm. 15	-1.30 m	540:5, 613:7	ASOR	ext. 5 YR 7/4, int. 2.5 YR 6/4

PL#:	Description:	Body Comp. and Texture:
14:1	Large Negevite bowl, lip and base fragment; double lug handle, slightly everted rim.	Fine textured ferrugenous clay; lightly tempered (10-30%); particle size 0.1-5 mm; inclusions: Fe_2O_3, Fe_3O_4, minor qtz, $CaCO_3$, organic burnout equiaxed and fibrous; medium HCl reaction.
14:2	Small Negevite bowl, lip and base fragment; flat base.	Fine textured ferrugenous clay; heavily tempered (~30%); coarse particle size; inclusions: $CaCO_3$, qtz, Fe_3O_4, mica, incompletely burned out organic material, minor eqiaxed burnout; strong HCl reaction, reaction ring around Fe_3O_4.
14:3	Small Negevite bowl, lip and base fragment; flat base.	Type of clay not specified; inclusions: major Fe_2O_3 (earthy Fe_2O_3 and consolidated Fe_2O_3), qtz, minor Fe_3O_4; no HCl reaction.
14:4	Small Negevite bowl, lip and base fragment; rounded base; horizontal knob-lug handle.	Type of clay not specified; inclusions: qtz, $CaCO_3$, Fe_3O_4; no HCl reaction.
14:5	Small Negevite bowl with flat base.	Type of clay not specified; inclusions: major Fe_2O_3, minor Fe_3O_4, qtz; no HCl reaction.
14:6	Small Negevite bowl, fragmentary (2/3 extant); double lug handle.	Fine textured ferrugenous clay; heavily tempered body (~30%); inclusions: qtz/spar and lime, fibrous burnout, minor equiaxed organic burnout.
14:7	Small Negevite bowl with flat base.	Type of clay not specified; inclusions: Fe_2O_3, Fe_3O_4, qtz; no HCl reaction.
14:8	Small Negevite bowl, lip and base fragment; row of lugs at lip.	Fine textured ferrugenous clay; lightly tempered (10-30%); average particle size (1-2 mm); inclusions: qtz/spar, sand temper, minor shale and organic burnout.
14:9	Small Negevite bowl, lip and base fragment; knob decoration around rim.	Medium texture; black and white inclusions.
14:10	Small Negevite bowl, lip and body fragment; vertical lug handle.	Fine textured ferrugenous clay; lightly tempered (10-30%); average particle size (1-2 mm); inclusions: qtz/spar, sand temper, minor shale and organic burnout.
14:11	Small Negevite vessel, lip and base fragment; thick, flat base and vertical walls.	Coarse texture; black and brown inclusions; a few white inclusions.
14:12	Small Negevite vessel, lip and base fragment; vertical walls; flat base.	Fine textured ferrugenous clay; heavily tempered (30-50% volume fraction); inclusions: minor lime and qtz/spar, $CaCO_3$, Fe_3O_4, mica; very porous, strong HCl reaction.
14:13	Small Negevite vessel, lip and base fragment; spouted; flat base.	Coarse texture; red, white and black inclusions; some vegetal temper, both fibrous and rounded seedlike burned out impressions.

PL#:	Method of Mfg:	Surf. Decor:	Firing:	State of Pres:
14:1	Handbuilt; rounded base formed in molds; lip formed by rotation; base tends to be thinner than wall; inclusions well aligned in wall.	Both interior and exterior have been raised and scraped in many directions, vertically, horizontally and diagonally.	Mixed oxidation state; interior oxidized brown and exterior grey; (MOHS 4).	Carbon blackened exterior.
14:2	Handbuilt; uneven wall thickness (5-12 mm); wall pinched and scraped; base shows very little evidence of working; inclusions and pores in random orientation.	On interior and exterior are scrape marks from shaping or smoothing tool 1-2 cm long in random orientation, on exterior with diagonal direction preferred, on interior preferred direction is parallel to base; thumb imprint near lip on exterior, and finger print on interior.	Reduced body and surface; grey color, low firing temperature; (MOHS 4)	Good, some surface encrustation on exterior.
14:3	Handbuilt; inclusions aligned parallel to wall.	Horizontal marks from wiping.	Mixed oxidation; interior of cross-section red, exterior grey; one side of pot is more reduced than other side; (MOHS 3).	Good, some weathering on interior at bottom.
14:4	Handbuilt; walls and base same thickness; horizontal placement of knobbed lug handle.	Wiping marks in vertical direction.	Brownish grey body and surface; (MOHS 4).	Good.
14:5	Handbuilt; inclusions aligned parallel to wall.	Horizontal wiping marks.	Mixed oxidation; (MOHS 3).	Good.
14:6	Handbuilt.	Surfaces wiped.	Grey body with yellow surfaces (possible salt addition).	Good.
14:7	Handbuilt.	Horizontal wiping marks.	Mixed oxidation; (MOHS 3→).	Good.
14:8	Handbuilt; base formed in molds.		Body and surfaces tan; (MOHS 3).	Good.
14:9	Medium texture; black and white inclusions.	None.	Oxidized.	Good.
14:10	Handbuilt on base support.	Incised X near base of handle.	Tan body and surfaces; (MOHS 3).	Surfaces worn.
14:11	Hand formed, finger impressions on interior.	None.	Nearly neutral.	Worn.
14:12	Handbuilt; thick sidewalls (10 mm); thin base (4 mm); poor alignment of chaff and inclusions.	Interior has white coating ($CaCO_3$).	Mixed oxidation state; body has regions with 2 layers, one red and the other black; (MOHS 3-4).	Worn surfaces.
14:13	Hand formed.	None.	Low oxidation.	Broken with lime encrustation on part of surface.

PLATE NO. 15

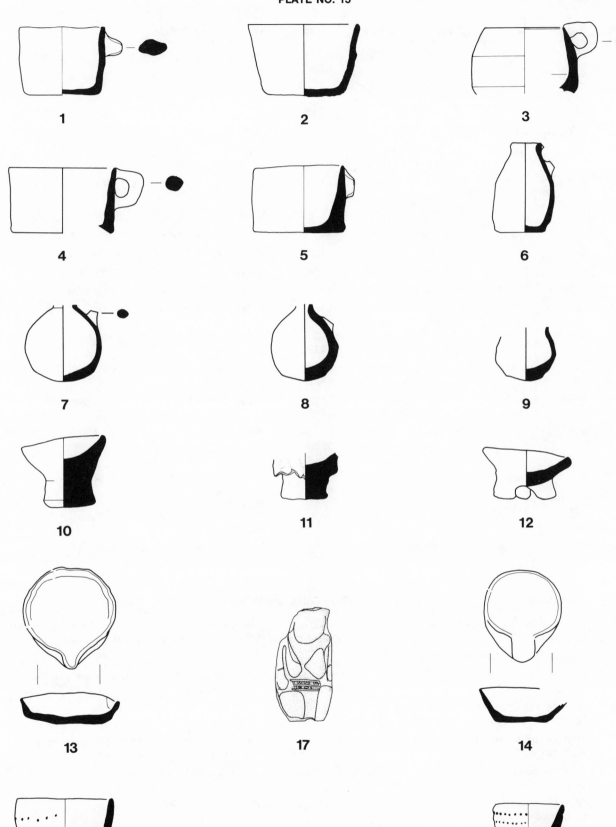

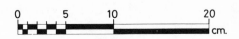

PLATE NO. 15

PL#:	Reg.#:	Date:	Prov:	Level:	Photo:	All:	Munsell References:
15:1	257	4-3-38	P:9	Surface	540:4, 626:2, 1619:2	ASOR	ext. 5 YR 4/1, int. 5 YR 5/1, sec. 5 YR 5/2
15:2	150	3-29-38	N:11	-50 cm	540:3, 629:3	JAM	
15:3	12,023e	4-27-40	Rm. 38			ASOR	
15:4	438	4-11-38	Rm. 22A	-70 cm	534:2, 613:6	JAM	
15:5	854	4-20-38	L:12	-1 m	513:4, 517:4	ASOR	ext. 7.5 YR 5/2, int. 5 YR 5/3, sec. 5 YR 5/1
15:6	5098	3-12-40	Rm. 48		1450:2	ASOR	ext. 5 YR 6/4, int. 5 YR 7/6
15:7	10,029	4-9-40	Rm. 25A	-32 cm	1450:14	ASOR	ext. 2.5 YR 6/4, int. 5 YR 6/4, sec. 5 YR 5/4
15:8	8002	3-25-40	Rm. 113	-91 cm	1450:7	ASOR	ext. 2.5 YR 5/2, sec. 2.5 YR N3/
15:9	6020	3-13-40	Rm. 43	-66 cm	1454:10	ASOR	ext. 2.5 YR 8/2, int. 2.5 YR 8/2
15:10	7092	3-24-40	Rm. 112	-97 cm	1453:6	ASOR	ext. 7.5 YR 7/4, int. 5 YR 6/3, sec. 5 YR 5/1
15:11	56	3-23-38	L:9	-1 m	530:3, 534:7, 613:4, 1432:2	ASOR	ext. 5 YR 7/4, int. 5 YR 7/3, sec. 5 YR 7/6
15:12	2015	4-20-39	Rm. 40	-1.50 m	620:4, 1423:3	ASOR	ext. 5 YR 7/2, int. 5 YR 6/2, sec. 5 YR 5/1
15:13	6081	3-17-40	Rm. 73		1452:7, 1452a:7	ASOR	ext. 5 YR 5/1, int. 5 YR 6/1, sec. 5 YR 5/1
15:14	446	4-11-38	Rm. 10	-60 cm	531:5, 532:4, 638:1	ASOR	ext. 5 YR 6/2, int. 7.5 YR 7/2, sec. 7.5 YR 6/2
15:15	890	4-23-38	Rm. 34	-1.70 cm	540:1, 643:4	ASOR	ext. 7.5 YR 6/4, int. 7.5 YR 6/4, sec. 7.5 YR 6/4
15:16	249 b	4-3-38	Rm. 27	-1 m		ASOR	ext. 5 YR 6/2, int. 5 YR 6/2
15:17	9044	4-6-40	Rm. 43		1492:1, 1493:2, 1494:1	ASOR	

PL#:	Description:	Body Comp. and Texture:
15:1	Negevite cup, lip and base fragment; lug handle; flat base.	Fine textured ferrugenous clay; lightly tempered (10-30%); inclusions: minor Fe_3O_4, Fe_2O_3, $CaCO_3$, qtz/spar and lime; medium HCl reaction.
15:2	Negevite cup, lip and base fragment; flat base.	
15:3	Negevite cup, lip and body fragment; loop handle.	Type of clay not specified; heavily tempered; inclusions: sherd temper, qtz, mica, $CaCO_3$, minor Fe_2O_3; strong HCl reaction.
15:4	Negevite cup, lip and body fragment; loop handle.	
15:5	Negevite cup, lip and base fragment; flat base; knob handle.	Type of clay not specified; heavily tempered; inclusions: qtz, Fe_3O_4, $CaCO_3$, platey particles; medium HCl reaction.
15:6	Small Negevite juglet, lip and base fragment; flat base; vestiges of body to lip handle.	Medium texture; some red and white inclusions.
15:7	Small Negevite juglet, body and base fragment; thick rounded base.	Medium texture; black, red and white inclusions.
15:8	Small Negevite juglet, body and base fragment; thick rounded base.	Medium texture; black, red and white inclusions.
15:9	Small Negevite juglet; lip missing.	Calcareous clay; texture and composition not identified.

15:10	Small Negevite chalice, complete; pedestal base.	Type of clay not specified; heavily tempered; inclusions: qtz, Fe_3O_4, organic burnout; no HCl reaction.
15:11	Small Negevite chalice, base and body fragment; pedestal base.	Fine textured ferrugenous clay; heavily tempered (~30%); inclusions: $CaCo_3$, lime, minor slate, organic; strong HCl reaction.
15:12	Small Negevite footed vessel; three legs; complete.	
15:13	Small, shallow Negevite lamp.	Type of clay not specified; inclusions: Fe_2O_3, Fe_3O_4, qtz, burned out organic material; no HCl reaction.
15:14	Small Negevite lamp.	Type of clay not specified; inclusions: Fe_2O_3, Fe_3O_4, qtz, burned out organic material, other white particles; no HCl reaction.
15:15	Negevite perforated vessel, two-thirds complete; thick ring base; most of rim missing; three rows of perforations around body.	Coarse texture; black with some white inclusions.
15:16	Negevite perforated vessel; most of rim missing; very thick base; three rows of perforations, many incomplete, around upper body.	Coarse texture; red, black and white inclusions.
15:17	Negevite figurine fragment.	Coarse texture; black and white inclusions.

PL#:	Method of Manufacture:	Surface Decor:
15:1	Handbuilt; thin walls (4-6 mm); inclusions well aligned with walls; some pinch marks; rounded lug handle well worked into body.	Interior and exterior wiped parallel to base in long strokes; a few strokes diagonal from left to upper right; asphalt-like coating interior and exterior now mostly worn away.
15:2		
15:3	Handbuilt; wall smoothed; some pinching; loop handle well joined to body and lip; thick base (17 mm); walls (6 mm).	Interior wiped and smoothed at slight inclination from lower left to upper right; exterior wiping in small short strokes in random direction.
15:4		
15:5	Handbuilt; wall worked on both sides as platey inclusions are parallel to wall near surface and not well aligned on interior; thin flat base (4 mm), wall (10 mm); rounded knob handle (20 x 20 mm).	Surface smoothed in short strokes nearly parallel to base.
15:6	Handbuilt with finger impressions.	None.
15:7	Thrown.	None.
15:8	Handbuilt.	
15:9	Possibly thrown, rotation involved in formation; base formed by pinching; finger print on interior at base.	
15:10	Crudely hand formed, punched out of a lump of clay; base narrowed by squeezing in hand.	Interior wiped in random directions.
15:11	Hand formed; pedestal base with 8 protruding lumps where cup joins pedestal; flat bottom.	Surface wiped, residue on interior of cup.
15:12	Handbuilt, finger imprints on both surfaces.	
15:13	Handbuilt.	Horizontal wiping marks.
15:14	Handbuilt; inclusions aligned parallel to walls; thin wall (3-4 mm); rough bottom surface.	Surface wiped parallel to base.
15:15	Handbuilt.	None.
15:16	Handbuilt with rows of holes pierced from the exterior.	None.
15:17	Handbuilt.	None.

PL#	Firing:	State of Pres:
15:1	Mixed oxidation state; black and grey reduced body becomes reddish near thick handle; (MOHS 3).	Good.
15:2		
15:3	Reduced body and surface; grey color; (MOHS 2➤).	Some surface encrustation high in CaCO₃ on top of black coating.
15:4		
15:5	Reduced body and surface; grey in color; (MOHS 3).	Good, exterior smudged, carbon residue wipes off when rubbed.
15:6	Oxidized mostly with a reduced area on one side.	Good.
15:7	Oxidized with one reduced black flash mark from firing.	Good.
15:8	Oxidized.	Good.
15:9	Mixed oxidation state; light grey;(MOHS 3-4).	Good.
15:10	Variables; one side black, the other side red; probably a waster; black part of base cracked and blown out during initial stages of firing; unusually thick piece (60 mm) and was probably fired too rapidly to allow gases to evolve at the surface; (MOHS 4)	Good, residue.
15:11	Oxidized; (MOHS 4).	Surfaces worn; residue of sand and possibly organic material on interior.
15:12	Grey body with brown and grey surfaces.	Good.
15:13	Light reduction; (MOHS 4).	Good.
15:14	Grey body; light reduction; (MOHS 4).	Good.
15:15	Medium; neutral to reducing atmosphere.	Worn surface.
15:16	Low in mixed atmosphere.	Poor.
15:17	Low firing in oxidation atmosphere.	Poor.

PLATE NO. 16

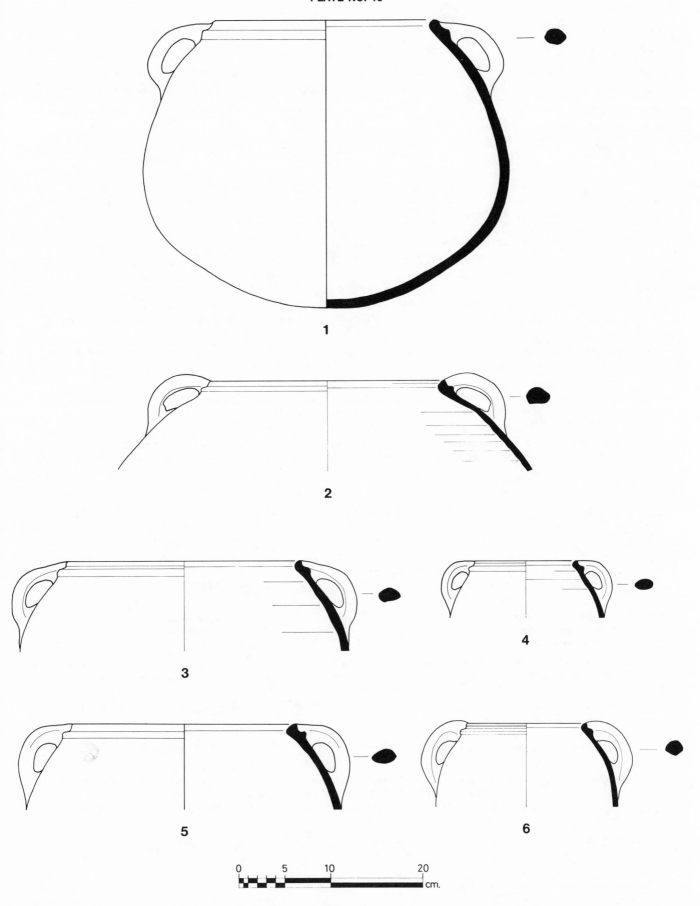

PLATE NO. 16

PL#:	Reg.#:	Date:	Prov:	Level:	Photo:	All:	Munsell References:
16:1						JAM	
16:2	819	4-20-38	Rm. 21	-30 cm	641:3	ASOR	ext. 7.5 YR 5/2, int. 5 YR 6/4, sec. 2.5 YR 6/6
16:3			Rm. 28	1.20 m			ext. 7.5 YR 8/4, int. 5 YR 7/4, sec. 5 YR 7/6
16:4	508 c						ext. 5 YR 7/4, int. 5 YR 5/1, sec. 5 YR 5/1
16:5	2061	4-23-39	Rm. 49	-1 m	602:8	ASOR	ext. 5 YR 7/6, int. 5 YR 7/6, sec. 5 YR 7/4
16:6	10,006	4-8-40	Rm. 25A		1464:11	ASOR	ext. 2.5 YR 5/2, int. 7.5 YR 6/4, sec. 5 YR 7/4

PL#:	Description:	Body Comp. and Texture:
16:1	Edomite cooking pot, lip and base fragment; ovoid shape; 2 handles; rounded base; closed-form vessel.	
16:2	Edomite cooking pot, lip and handle fragment; ovoid shape; 2 handles.	Fine textured ferrugenous clay; heavily tempered (30-50% volume fraction); coarse particles (1-3 mm); inclusions: qtz/spar, Fe_2O_3, equiaxed burned out particles, unidentified platey inclusions; no HCl reaction.
16:3	Edomite cooking pot, lip and handle fragment; ovoid shape; 2 handles.	Fine textured ferrugenous clay; heavily tempered; coarse particles; inclusions: qtz/spar, Fe_2O_3, Fe_3O_4, equiaxed burned out particles, platey inclusions; no HCl reaction.
16:4	Edomite cooking pot; closed-form vessel, lip and handle fragment; ovoid shape.	Fine textured ferrugenous clay; lightly tempered (10-20%); inclusions: qtz/spar ($\leq$0.5 mm), Fe_2O_3 rare (1-2 mm); no HCl reaction.
16:5	Edomite cooking pot, lip and handle fragment; ovoid shape; 2 handles; closed-form vessel.	Fine textured ferrugenous clay; heavily tempered (30-50%); coarse particled inclusions: qtz/spar/limestone ($\leq$1.0 mm), Fe_2O_3 ($\leq$2.0 mm); equiaxed and fibrous organic burnout; weak HCl reaction.
16:6	Edomite cooking pot, lip and handle fragment; ovoid shape; 2 handles; closed-form vessel.	Fine textured ferrugenous clay; heavily tempered (30-50%); coarse particles (1-3 mm); inclusions: qtz/spar, Fe_2O_3, equiaxed burned out particles, platey inclusions; no HCl reaction.

PL#:	Method of Mfg:	Surf. Decor:	Firing:	State of Pres:
16:1				
16:2	Probably slow turned, lip turned quite rapidly; marks on interior only; rolled lip; pulled handles reinforced with clay where joined to body; inclusions aligned with wall.	Incised "x" on surface to right of handle.	Oxidized body with grey reduced surface; low degree of vitrification; (MOHS 3).	Exterior surface worn.
16:3	Possibly turned; marks on interior only; rolled lip; handles reinforced; inclusions poorly aligned.		Oxidized with exterior light grey reduction; low degree of vitrification; (MOHS 3).	Both surfaces worn.
16:4	Lip shaped by rapid turning; pulled handle joined with extra clay.		Heavily reduced body and surfaces; medium degree of vitrification; (MOHS 4).	Accretions on exterior.
16:5	Formed with some form of turning, as circumferential marks present; crooked handles; lip formed by turning and handles reinforced with clay where they join body.		Mixed oxidation state; interior splotches of red and grey, exterior also has patches; low degree of vitrification; (MOHS 3-3-►).	Both surfaces worn; exterior surface has accretions.
16:6	Probably turned; lip not rolled; pulled handle; inclusions aligned; handle crooked; handles reinforced with clay where they join body.	One rectangular stamp applied horizontally at base of handle.	Oxidized body with reduced outer surfaces; low degree of vitrification; (MOHS 3).	Interior and exterior surfaces worn.

PLATE NO. 17

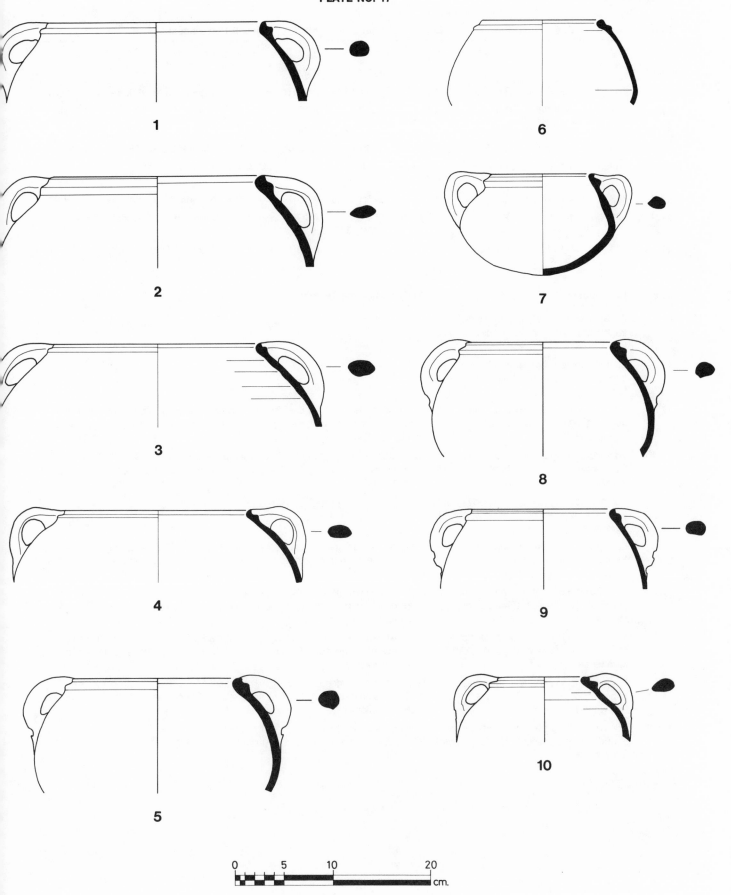

1

2

3

4

5

6

7

8

9

10

0 5 10 20 cm.

PLATE NO. 17

PL#:	Reg.#:	Date:	Prov:	Level:	Photo:	All:	Munsell References:
17:1						JAM	
17:2						JAM	
17:3	10,005	4-8-40	Rm. 25A	Debris	1464:15	ASOR	ext. 10 YR 5/1, int. 2.5 YR 6/6, sec. 2.5 YR 6/6
17:4	677	4-18-38	Rm. 42	-1 m	600:7	ASOR	ext. 5 YR 5/3, int. 2.5 YR 6/8, sec. 2.5 YR 6/6
17:5						JAM	
17:6	5034 b	5-12-39	Rm. 33	-2 m	596:11	ASOR	ext. 2.5 YR 6/4, int. 2.5 YR 6/6, sec. 2.5 YR 6/8
17:7	8092	4-2-40	Rm. 125	+114 to +107	1497:5	ASOR	ext. 5 YR 6/3, int. 5 YR 7/3
17:8	783	4-20-38	Rm. 20		641:1	ASOR	ext. 2.5 YR 5/6, int. 2.5 YR 6/8, sec. 2.5 YR 6/6
17:9	221	4-2-38	0:12	-50 cm	554:2, 600:1, 715	ASOR	ext. 10 YR 4/1, int. 5 YR 5/4, sec. 2.5 YR 5/6
17:10	477	4-13-38	Rm. 27	-1 m		ASOR	ext. 5 YR 6/1, int. 5 YR 7/6, sec. 2.5 6/8

PL#:	Description:	Body Comp. and Texture:
17:1	Edomite cooking pot, lip and handle fragment; ovoid shape; 2 handles; closed-form vessel.	
17:2	Edomite cooking pot, lip and handle fragment; ovoid shape; 2 handles; closed-form vessel.	
17:3	Edomite cooking pot, lip and handle fragment; ovoid shape; 2 handles; closed-form vessel.	Fine textured ferrugenous clay; heavily tempered (30-50%); coarse particles (1-3 mm); inclusions: qtz/spar, Fe_2O_3, equiaxed burned out particles, platey inclusions; no HCl reaction.
17:4	Edomite cooking pot, lip and handle fragment; ovoid shape; 2 handles, closed-form vessel.	Fine textured ferrugenous clay; heavily tempered (30-50%); coarse particles (1-3 mm); inclusions: qtz/spar, Fe_2O_3, equiaxed burned out particles, platey inclusions; no HCl reaction.
17:5	Edomite cooking pot, lip and body fragment; ovoid shape; 2 handles; closed-form vessel.	
17:6	Edomite cooking pot, lip and body fragment; ovoid shape; closed-form vessel.	Fine textured ferrugenous clay; lightly tempered (ca. 10%); inclusions: qtz/spar (≤0.5 mm), equiaxed limestone, organic burnout, short fibrous burnout; weak HCl reaction.
17:7	Edomite cooking pot, lip and handle fragment; ovoid shape; 2 handles; closed-form vessel.	Fine textured ferrugenous clay; heavily tempered (30-50%); coarse particles; inclusions: qtz/spar, Fe_2O_3, equiaxed burned out organic, platey inclusions; no HCl reaction.
17:8	Edomite cooking pot, lip and handle fragment; ovoid shape; 2 handles; closed-form vessel.	Fine textured ferrugenous clay; heavily tempered (30-50%); coarse particles (1-3 mm); inclusions: qtz/spar, Fe_2O_3, equiaxed burned out particles, platey inclusions; no HCl reaction.
17:9	Edomite cooking pot, lip and handle fragment; ovoid shape; 2 handles; closed-form vessel.	Fine textured ferrugenous clay; heavily tempered (30-50%); coarse particles (1-3 mm); inclusions: qtz/spar, Fe_2O_3, equiaxed burned out particles, platey inclusions; no HCl reaction.
17:10	Edomite cooking pot, lip and handle fragment; ovoid shape; 2 handles; closed-form vessel.	Fine textured ferrugenous clay; lightly tempered (ca. 10%); inclusions: qtz/spar (≤0.5 mm), equiaxed limestone, organic burnout, short fibrous burnout; weak HCl reaction.

PL#:	Method of Mfg:	Surf. Decor:	Firing:	State of Pres:
17:1				
17:2				
17:3	Probably turned; lip not rolled; pulled handle; inclusions aligned; handles crooked; handle base attaches to left of top join.	One rectangular stamp applied horizontally at base of handle.	Oxidized body with reduced outer surfaces; low degree of vitrification; (MOHS 3).	Interior and exterior surfaces worn.
17:4	Probably turned; lip not rolled; pulled handle; inclusions aligned; handles crooked; handle base attached to left of top join.	One rectangular stamp applied horizontally at base of handle.	Oxidized body with reduced outer surfaces; low degree of vitrification; (MOHS 3).	Interior and exterior surfaces worn.
17:5				
17:6	Probably thrown; fine surface with circumferential ridges 1.0 mm apart and larger ridges 7-10 mm apart; exterior wiped.		Oxidized red body and surfaces; medium degree of vitrification; (MOHS 4).	Exterior surface worn.
17:7	Lip turned, base appears to be molded and joined with upper body at noticeable line, below which the surface is smooth and above which surface is rough; handles reinforced with clay where they join body.		Body oxidized with grey reduced exterior surface; low degree of vitrification; (MOHS 3).	Worn outer surface.
17:8	Probably turned; lip not rolled; pulled handle; inclusions aligned; handles crooked; handle base attached to left of top join.	One rectangular stamp applied horizontally at base of handle.	Oxidized body with reduced outer surfaces; low degree of vitrification; (MOHS 3).	Interior and exterior surfaces worn.
17:9	Probably turned; lip not rolled; pulled handle; handles reinforced with clay where they join body; inclusions aligned.	Two rectangular stamps applied horizontally at base of handle.	Oxidized body with reduced outer surfaces and slight inner surface reduction; low degree of vitrification; (MOHS 3).	Exterior surface worn.
17:10	Probably thrown; fine surface with circumferential ridges 1.0 mm apart and larger ridges 7-10 mm apart.	Horizontal incised line at base of handle.	Oxidized red body and interior surface; exterior surface grey; medium degree of vitrification; (MOHS 4-4 ➤).	Exterior surface worn.

PLATE NO. 18

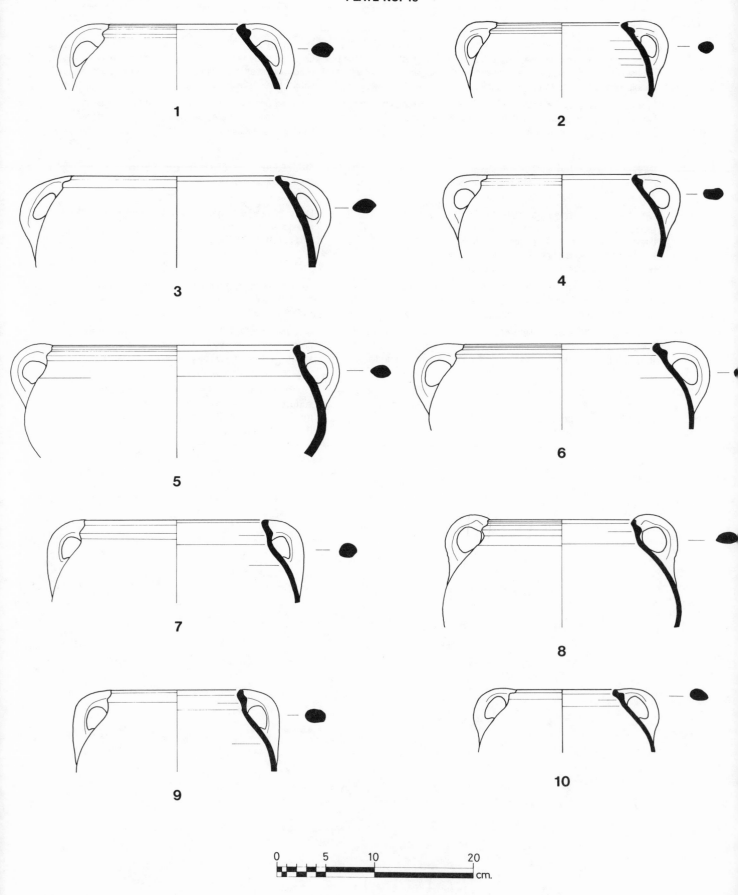

PLATE NO. 18

PL#:	Reg.#:	Date:	Prov:	Level:	Photo:	All:	Munsell References:
18:1	243	4-3-38	Rm. 27	-1.50 m.	555:4, 746	ASOR	ext. 10 YR 8/3, int. 2.5 Y 8/2, sec. 7.5 YR 8/4
18:2	714	4-18-38	Rm. 34	-1 m	556:4, 558:3	ASOR	ext. 7.5 6/4, int. 7.5 YR 7/4
18:3	242	4-3-38	Rm. 27	-1.50 m		ASOR	ext. 5 YR 7/4, int. 5 YR 7/4, sec. 5 YR 7/4
18:4	146	3-29-38	Q:11	-50 cm	555:6, 735	ASOR	ext. 7.5 YR 7/4, int. 7.5 YR 7/6, sec. 7.5 YR 7/4
18:5	12,022	4-27-40	Rm. 36		1479:2	ASOR	ext. 5 YR 7/4, int. 5 YR 6/2, sec. 2.5 YR 6/6
18:6						JAM	
18:7	12,023	4-27-40	Rm. 38			ASOR	
18:8	6091	3-18-40	Rm. 105		1479:6	ASOR	ext. 10 YR 5/1, int. 7.5 YR 7/4, sec. 7.5 YR N5
18:9						JAM	
18:10	5099	3-12-40	Rm. 76	Debris	1464	ASOR	ext. 10 YR 5/2, int. 7.5 YR 6/4, sec. 7.5 YR 5/

PL#:	Description:	Body Comp. and Texture:
18:1	Edomite cooking pot, lip and handle fragment; ovoid shape; 2 handles; closed-form vessel.	Fine textured calcareous clay; lightly tempered ($\leq$10%); fine particle size ($\leq$1.0 mm); inclusions: qtz/spar, limestone, equiaxed organic burnout; weak HCl reaction.
18:2	Edomite cooking pot, lip and handle fragment; ovoid shape; 2 handles; closed-form vessel.	Fine textured ferrugenous clay; lightly tempered (10-20%); inclusions: qtz/spar ($\leq$0.5 mm), minor limestone; weak HCl reaction.
18:3	Edomite cooking pot, lip and handle fragment; ovoid shape; 2 handles; closed-form vessel.	Medium texture; red and some white inclusions.
18:4	Edomite cooking pot, lip and handle fragment; ovoid shape; 2 handles; closed-form vessel.	Fine textured ferrugenous clay; lightly tempered (ca. 10%); inclusions: limestone ($\leq$0.5 mm), equiaxed organic burnout, short fibrous burnout; weak HCl reaction.
18:5	Edomite cooking pot, lip and handle fragment; ovoid shape; 2 handles; closed-form vessel.	Fine textured ferrugenous clay; somewhat tempered (10-30%); coarse particles (1-2 mm); inclusions: qtz/spar, Fe_2O_3, equiaxed burned out particles, platey inclusions; no HCl reaction.
18:6	Edomite cooking pot, lip and handle fragment; ovoid shape; 2 handles; closed-form vessel.	
18:7	Cooking pot, lip and handle fragment; ovoid shape; 2 handles; closed-form vessel.	Fine textured ferrugenous clay; heavily tempered (30-50%); coarse particles; inclusions: qtz/spar, Fe_2O_3, equiaxed burned out organic, platey inclusions; no HCl reaction.
18:8	Cooking pot, lip and handle fragment; ovoid shape; 2 handles; closed-form vessel.	Fine textured ferrugenous clay; lightly tempered (10-20%); fine particles; inclusions: qtz/spar ($\leq$0.5 mm), two kinds of organic burnout, Fe_3O_4; weak HCl reaction.
18:9	Cooking pot, lip and handle fragment: ovoid shape; 2 handles; closed-form vessel.	
18:10	Cooking pot, lip and handle fragment; ovoid shape; 2 handles; closed-form vessel.	Fine textured ferrugenous clay; lightly tempered (10-20%); fine particles; inclusions: qtz ($\leq$0.5 mm), two kinds of organic burnout; weak HCl reaction.

PL#:	Method of Mfg:	Surf. Decor:	Firing:	State of Pres:
18:1	Upper surface and lip formed by rapid rotation; handles reinforced with clay where they join body.	Oval stamp seal at top of handle with arrow shape at left of seal, vertical incised line at base of handle.	Oxidation; yellowish brown body and surfaces; low degree of vitrification; (MOHS 3-3➤).	Exterior surfaces worn.
18:2	Lip and upper body shaped by rapid turning; pulled handle tapers to bottom, joined with extra clay at base.	Handle stamped with round seal at top of handle, horizontal incised line at base of handle which may be unintentional.	Somewhat oxidized; light brown body and surfaces; medium degree of vitrification; (MOHS 4).	Good.
18:3	Thrown with pulled handles and turned over rim.	None.	Medium firing in oxidation with exterior postfire blackening.	Worn.
18:4	Upper surface and lip formed by rapid rotation; handles crooked; handle joined with excess clay left of bottom join.	Horizontal incised line at base of handle and oval stamp seal at top of handle.		Exterior surface worn.
18:5	Thrown, fine circumferential marks on interior and exterior; lip not rolled; handles reinforced with clay where they join body.		Oxidized but has two layers; intermediate brown and exterior red; exterior has black flashing mark from stacking during firing.	Good.
18:6				
18:7	Probably turned; lip not rolled over; handles reinforced with clay where they join body.	Incised cross to left of handle.	Body oxidized with grey reduced exterior surface; low degree of vitrification; (MOHS 3).	Worn outer surface.
18:8	Thrown on flat wheel; handles reinforced with clay where they join body.	Two incised horizontal lines at base of handle near left side.	Heavily reduced body and exterior surface; inner surface oxidized; (MOHS 4).	Good.
18:9				
18:10	Lip and upper body shaped by rapid turning; lip not turned over; pulled handles joined with extra clay.	Incised horizontal line at base of handle.	Heavily reduced body and surfaces; medium degree of vitrification; (MOHS 4-4➤).	Good, exterior surface somewhat worn.

PLATE NO. 19

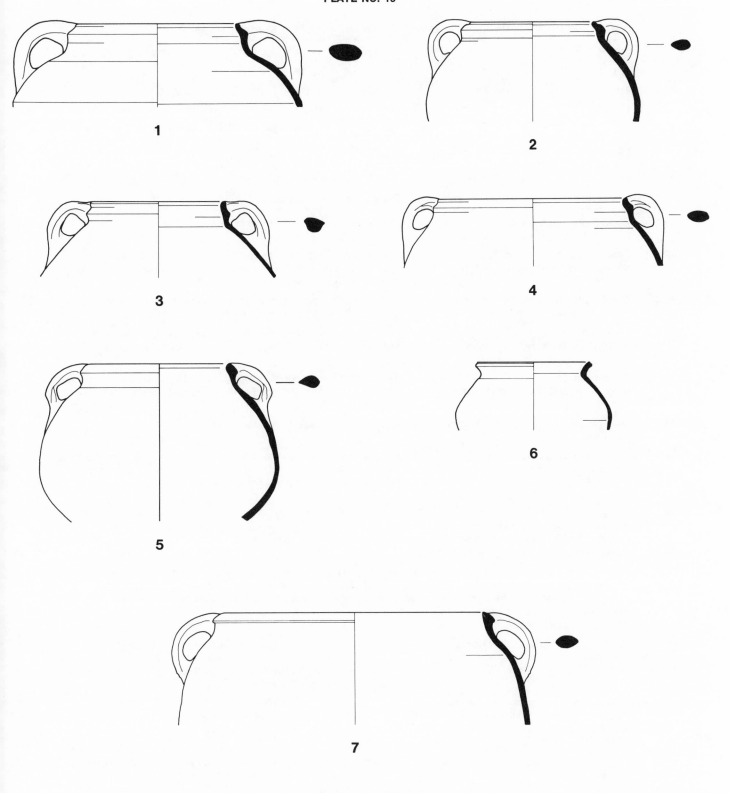

PLATE NO. 19

PL#:	Reg.#:	Date:	Prov:	Level:	Photo:	All:	Munsell References:
19:1	918	6-6-38	Rm. 17A		652:4	ASOR	ext. 5 YR 5/1, int. 2.5 YR 6/6, sec. 10 YR 4/1
19:2	12,015	4-24-40	Rm. 94		1497:7	ASOR	
19:3	915	6-6-38	Rm. 24		602:5	ASOR	ext. 5 YR 6/4, int. 5 YR 6/4
19:4	10,035		Rm. 25A	Debris	1497:1	ASOR	ext. 7.5 YR N4/, int. 5 YR 5/3, sec. 5 YR 5/1
19:5	599	4-18-38	Rm. 25	-2 m	523:1	ASOR	ext. 2.5 YR 5/4, int. 2.5 YR 6/6, sec. 2.5 YR 6/6
19:6	981	4-12-39	Rm. 38		595:2	ASOR	ext. 2.5 YR 4/2, int. 2.5 YR 5/6, sec. 5 YR 5/3
19:7	809	4-20-38	R:12	-30 cm		ASOR	ext. 5 YR 6/4, int. 2.5 YR 6/6, sec. 2.5 YR 6/6

PL#:	Description:	Body Comp. and Texture:
19:1	Cooking pot, lip and handle fragment; ovoid shape; 2 handles; closed-form vessel.	Medium texture; black and white inclusions.
19:2	Cooking pot; lip and handle fragment; ovoid shape; 2 handles; closed-form vessel.	Fine textured ferrugenous clay; lightly tempered (ca. 10%); inclusions: qtz/spar ($\leq$0.5 mm), equiaxed limestone, organic burnout, short fibrous burnout; weak HCl reaction.
19:3	Cooking pot, lip and handle fragment; ovoid shape; 2 handles; closed-form vessel.	Fine textured ferrugenous clay; lightly tempered (10-20%); inclusions: qtz/spar ($\leq$0.5 mm), minor limestone; weak HCl reaction.
19:4	Cooking pot, lip and handle fragment; ovoid shape; 2 handles; closed-form vessel.	Fine textured ferrugenous clay; lightly tempered (10-20%); fine particles; inclusions: qtz/spar ($\leq$0.5 mm), two kinds of organic burnout; no HCl reaction.
19:5	Cooking pot, lip and handle fragment; ovoid shape; 2 handles; closed-form vessel.	Fine textured ferrugenous clay; heavily tempered (30-50%); coarse particles (1-3 mm); inclusions: qtz/spar, Fe_2O_3, equiaxed burned out particles, platey inclusions; no HCl reaction.
19:6	Small cooking pot, lip and body fragment; flaring rim.	Fine texture; some black and white inclusions.
19:7	Cooking pot, lip and handle fragment; ovoid shape; 2 handles; closed-form vessel.	Fine textured ferrugenous clay; heavily tempered (20-30%); coarse particles; inclusions: qtz/spar, lime ($\leq$4.0 mm), Fe_2O_3 ($\leq$3.0 mm), equiaxed organic burnout ($\leq$5.0 mm), no platey particles; weak HCl reaction.

PL#:	Method of Mfg:	Surf. Decor:	Firing:	State of Pres:
19:1	Probably thrown with pulled handles; thickened rim.	None.	Reduced.	Good, exterior smudged black.
19:2	Upper surface and lip formed by rapid rotation; vertical wipe marks on interior of lower body and wipe marks around lower handle attachment; handles reinforced with clay where they join body.	Horizontal incised line at base of handle and perhaps a diagonal in center of handle.	Reddish brown body and surface; medium degree of vitrification; (MOHS 4-4→)	Exterior surface accretions, otherwise good.
19:3	Lip and upper body shaped by rapid turning; pulled crooked handles attached at base to left of top join.		Somewhat oxidized; light brown body and surfaces; medium degree of vitrification; (MOHS 4).	Good.
19:4	Lip and upper body probably shaped by rapid turning; pulled handles joined with excess clay.		Heavily reduced body and surfaces; medium degree of vitrification; (MOHS 3).	Exterior surface worn.
19:5	Probably turned; lip not rolled; pulled handles; handles poorly made; inclusions aligned.		Oxidized body with reduced outer surface; low degree of vitrification; (MOHS 3).	Interior and exterior surfaces worn.
19:6	Thrown.	Exterior red-slipped and burnished; horizontal bands of decoration at intervals.	Oxidation.	Good.
19:7	Upper surface wiped by turning rapidly.	Three horizontal incised lines at base of handle.	Oxidized; (MOHS 4).	Heavily worn, especially exterior surface; lime spalling.

PLATE NO. 20

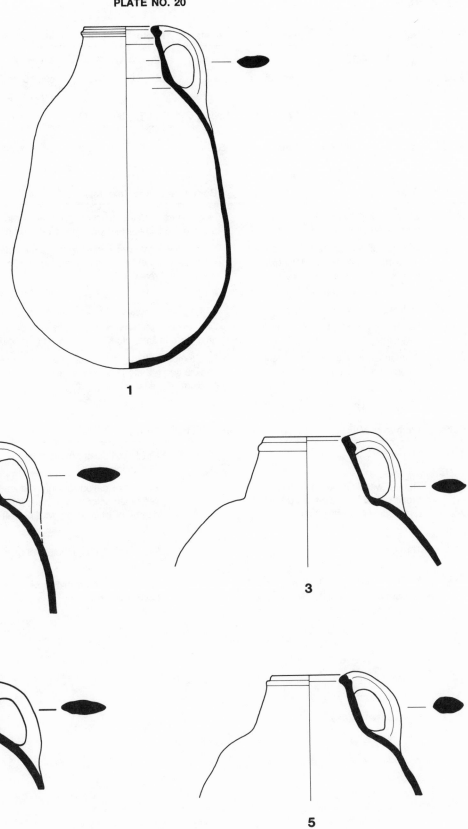

PLATE NO. 20

PL#:	Reg.#:	Date:	Prov:	Level:	Photo:	All:	Munsell References:
20:1	10,087	4-13-40	Rm. 125		1251, 1701	ASOR	ext. 5 YR 7/2, int. 10 YR 7/3, sec. 2.5 YR 6/4
20:2	12,059	5-1-40	Rm. 46		668, 686	ASOR	ext. 10 YR 7/3, int. 2.5 Y 8/4, sec. 2.5 Y 8/4
20:3						JAM	ext. 10 YR 7/3, int. 2.5 Y 8/2, sec. 5 Y 8/2
20:4	528	4-15-38	Rm. 25A	Debris	511:2, 739, 740	ASOR	ext. 2.5 Y 7/2, int. 5 Y 8/3, sec. 5 Y 8/2
20:5	726	4-18-38	Rm. 36	-50 cm		ASOR	ext. 5 Y 7/2, int. 7.5 YR 6/4, sec. 7.5 YR 6/4

PL#:	Description:	Body Comp. and Texture:
20:1	Storage jar, 1 lip and 2 small body fragments; strap handle.	Fine textured calcareous clay; lightly tempered (≤10%); fine particle size; inclusions: qtz/spar and lime, other with yellow reaction ring; medium HCl reaction.
20:2	Storage jar, lip and body fragment with no identification marks on handle; compound lip; strap handle.	Fine textured calcareous clay; lightly tempered (≤10%); fine particle size (most ≤1.0 mm, rare ≤ 3 mm); inclusions: qtz/spar and lime, other with yellow reaction ring; medium HCl reaction.
20:3	Storage jar, lip and body fragment; strap handle.	
20:4	Storage jar, lip and 2 small body fragments; strap handle.	Fine textured calcareous clay; lightly tempered (≤10%); fine particle size; inclusions: qtz/spar and lime, other with yellow ring; medium HCl reaction.
20:5	Storage jar, lip and body fragment; compound lip; strap handle.	Fine tempered ferrugenous clay; medium tempered body (10-20%); mostly medium particle size (~2 mm); inclusions: qtz/spar and lime, Fe_2O_3 and some organic; medium HCl reaction.

PL#:	Method of Mfg:	Surf. Decor:	Firing:	State of Pres:
20:1	Thrown.		Fired in oxidation; medium degree of vitrification; (MOHS 4).	Worn surfaces.
20:2	Thrown with thin wall (4-8 mm); broad pulled handle attached to lip and body with excess clay.		Fired in oxidation to slight reduction; yellow tan color to light grey; medium degree of vitrification; (MOHS 3-4).	Good.
20:3				
20:4	Thrown.		Fired in oxidation; medium degree of vitrification; (MOHS 4).	Accretions on interior surface.
20:5	Thrown; handle pulled, joined at tip and bottom with excess clay; particles in body well aligned.		Slightly reduced body; greyish brown; (MOHS 3-3 ➤).	Good, but accretions on exterior surface.

PLATE NO. 21

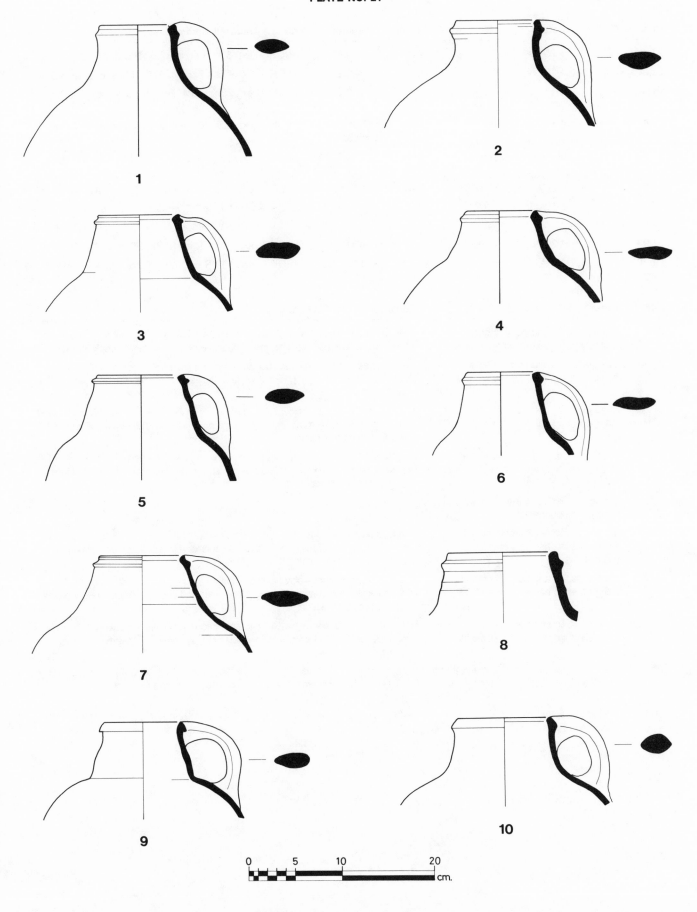

PLATE NO. 21

PL#:	Reg.#:	Date:	Prov:	Level:	Photo:	All:	Munsell References:
21:1	3002	4-25-39	Rm. 33	-2 m	620:1	ASOR	ext. 5 YR 6/4, int. 2.5 YR 5/6, sec. 2.5 YR 5/6
21:2	777	4-20-38	Rm. 18		678:2	ASOR	ext. 2.5 Y 7/2, int. 5 YR 5/3, sec. 5 YR 5/3
21:3	464	4-12-38	Rm. 27	-2 m	556:2, 558:4, 734	ASOR	ext. 7.5 YR 6/4, int. 2.5 Y 7/2, sec. 5 Y 7/1
21:4	467	4-12-38	Rm. 27	-2 m	556:6, 558:6, 773	ASOR	ext. 2.5 Y 8/2, int. 2.5 Y 7/2, sec. 10 YR 7/1
21:5	463	4-12-38	Rm. 27	-2 m	552:2, 743, 744	JAM	ext. 10 YR 7/3, int. 2.5 Y 8/2, sec. 5 Y 8/2
21:6	215	4-2-38	O:12	-50 cm		ASOR	ext. 10 YR 7/1, int. 10 YR 7/1, sec. 10 YR 7/2
21:7	465	4-12-38	Rm. 27	-2 m		ASOR	ext. 10 YR 7/2, int. 2.5 Y 7/2, sec. 10 YR 7/4
21:8			Rm. 47				ext. 5 YR 6/4, int. 5 YR 5/4, sec. 5 YR 5/1
21:9	753	4-20-38	Street 26		600:6	ASOR	ext. 5 Y 6/1, int 10 YR 6/2, sec. 10 YR 5/1
21:10	9054	4-6-40	Rm. 33	-10 cm	1464:1	ASOR	ext. 10 YR 5/1, int. 5 YR 6/1, sec. 2.5 YR 5/

PL#:	Description:	Body Comp. and Texture:
21:1	Storage jar, lip and body fragment; incised strap handle; compound rim.	Fine textured ferrugenous clay; medium tempered body (20-30%); fine particle size (≤0.5 mm); inclusions: qtz/spar and lime, some organic burnout; weak HCl reaction.
21:2	Storage jar, lip and body fragment; compound lip; strap handle.	Fine textured ferrugenous clay; heavily tempered (30-50%); coarse particle size; inclusions: Fe_2O_3, Fe_3O_4, platey white particles, qtz/spar and lime, organic; weak HCl reaction.
21:3	Storage jar, lip and body fragment; stamped strap handle; compound lip.	Fine textured calcareous clay; lightly tempered (≤10%); fine particle size (most ≤1.0 mm, rare inclusion ≤3 mm); inclusions: qtz/spar and lime, other with yellow reaction ring; medium HCl reaction.
21:4	Storage jar, lip and body fragment; stamped strap handle; compound lip.	Fine textured calcareous clay; lightly tempered (≤10%); fine particle size (most ≤1.0 mm, rare inclusion ≤3 mm): inclusions: qtz/spar and lime, other with yellow reaction ring; medium HCl reaction.
21:5	Storage jar, lip and body fragment; strap handle; compound lip.	
21:6	Storage jar, lip and body fragment; stamped strap handle; compound lip.	Fine textured calcareous clay; lightly tempered (≤10%); fine particle size (most ≤1.0 mm, rare inclusion ≤3 mm); inclusions: qtz/spar and lime, other with yellow reaction ring; medium HCl reaction.
21:7	Storage jar, lip and body fragment; stamped strap handle; compound lip.	Fine textured calcareous clay; lightly tempered (≤10%); fine particle size (most ≤1.0 mm, rare inclusion ≤3 mm); inclusions: qtz/spar and lime, other with yellow reaction ring; medium HCl reaction.
21:8	Storage jar, lip and neck fragment; compound lip; no identifying marks.	Fine textured ferrugenous clay; lightly tempered (≤10%); fine particle size (most ≤10 mm, rare inclusion ≤3 mm); inclusions: qtz/spar and lime; other with yellow reaction ring; medium HCl reaction.
21:9	Storage jar, lip and body fragment; 2 seal impressions and incised lines on strap handle.	Fine textured ferrugenous clay; medium tempered body (10-20%); fine particle size (≤1.0 mm) with some exceptions; inclusions: qtz/spar and lime, rare organic burnout; weak HCl reaction.
21:10	Storage jar, lip and body fragment; incised strap handle and simple rim.	Fine textured ferrugenous clay; medium tempered body (10-20%); fine particle size (≤1.0 mm) with some exceptions; inclusions: qtz/spar and lime, rare organic burnout; weak HCl reaction.

PL#:	Method of Mfg:	Surf. Decor:	Firing:	State of Pres:
21:1	Thrown; broad pulled handle; 5-6 mm wall thickness.	Vertical line incised from upper to lower portion of handle; line 70 mm long.	Fired in oxidation; red with residual dark core as a layer on interior; (MOHS 4).	Good.
21:2	Thrown; broad pulled handle; thick wall up to 13 mm.		Fired in slight reduction; greyish brown body and surfaces; (MOHS 4).	Good.
21:3	Thrown with thin wall (6-10 mm); broad pulled handle attached to lip and body with excess clay.	Stamp impression at base of handle.	Fired in oxidation to slight reduction; yellow tan color to light grey; medium degree of vitrification; (MOHS 3→4); no defects.	Good, surface accretions.
21:4	Thrown with thin wall (6-10 mm); broad pulled handle attached to lip and body with excess clay.	Stamp impression at top of handle, 2 horizontal incised lines at base of handle.	Fired in oxidation to slight reduction; yellow tan color to light grey; medium degree of vitrification; (MOHS 3→4); no defects.	Good, surface accretions.
21:5				
21:6	Thrown with thin wall (6-10 mm); broad pulled handle attached to lip and body with excess clay, appears to be joined with an upper section near neck-body transition.	Stamp impression at base of handle.	Fired in oxidation to slight reduction; yellow tan color to light grey; medium degree of vitrification; (MOHS 3→4); no defects.	Good, surface accretions.
21:7	Thrown with thin wall (6-10 mm); broad pulled handle attached to lip and body with excess clay.	Stamp impression at base of handle.	Fired in oxidation to slight reduction; yellow tan color to light grey; medium degree of vitrification; (MOHS 3→4); no defects.	Good, surface accretions.
21:8	Thrown.		Fired in oxidation; (MOHS 4).	Worn inner surface.
21:9	Thrown; lip rim rolled over and not smoothed.	Handle has seal at base and at top, oval seal horizontal on top and vertical at base; incised lines beneath each seal on a diagonal.	Fired in reduction; black body and surface; (MOHS 4).	Good.
21:10	Thrown; broad pulled handle.	Handle incised with 2 designs, probably post firing; one incised line at base of handle.	Fired in reduction; black body with reddish surface; (MOHS 4).	Interior surface worn and pitted.

PLATE NO. 22

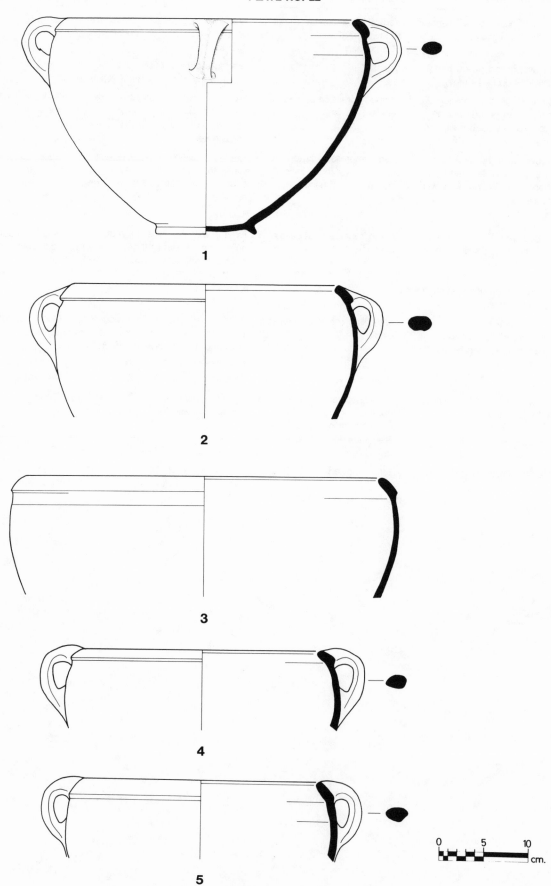

1

2

3

4

5

PLATE NO. 22

PL#:	Reg.#:	Date:	Prov:	Level:	Photo:	All:	Munsell References:
22:1	6012	3-12-40	Rm. 46		1399, 1496:1	ASOR	ext. 5 Y 7/2, int. 10 YR 7/3, sec. 10 YR 6/2
22:2	2098	4-25-39	Rm. 49			ASOR	ext. 7.5 YR 6/4, int. 7.5 YR 7/4, sec. 5 YR 8/4
22:3	594	4-18-38	Rm. 33	Surface	595:18	ASOR	ext 5 Y 7/2, int. 7.5 YR 6/4
22:4	278	4-4-38	Rm. 27	-2 m	554:3, 600:15, 745	ASOR	
22:5			Q-12-13	0.1 m			ext. 7.5 YR 7/4, int. 7.5 YR 7/4, sec. 2.5 YR 6/6

PL#:	Description:	Body Comp. and Texture:
22:1	Krater, lip and handle fragment; ovoid shape; closed form.	Fine textured calcareous clay; lightly tempered ($\leq$10%); fine particle size ($\leq$1.0 mm); inclusions: qtz/spar, limestone, equiaxed organic burnout; weak HCl reaction.
22:2	Krater, lip and handle fragment; ovoid shape; stamped handle; closed-form.	Fine textured ferrugenous clay; lightly tempered (10-20%); fine particles ($\leq$1.0 mm, rare particle $\leq$2.0 mm); inclusions: qtz/spar, lime, Fe_2O_3, equiaxed organic burnout; negligible to weak organic HCl reaction.
22:3	Krater, lip and body fragment; ovoid shape; stamped handle; closed-form.	Fine textured ferrugenous clay; lightly tempered (10-20%); fine particles ($\leq$1.0 mm, rare particle $\leq$2.0 mm); inclusions: qtz/spar, lime, Fe_2O_3, equiaxed organic burnout; negligible to weak organic HCl reaction.
22:4	Krater, lip and handle fragment; ovoid shape; stamped handle; closed-form.	Fine textured ferrugenous clay; lightly tempered (10-20%); fine particles ($\leq$1.0 mm, rare particle $\leq$2.0 mm); inclusions: qtz/spar, lime, Fe_2O_3, equiaxed organic burnout; negligible to weak organic HCl reaction.
22:5	Krater, lip and handle fragment; ovoid shape; stamped handle; closed-form.	Fine textured ferrugenous clay; lightly tempered (10-20%); fine particles ($\leq$1.0 mm, rare particle $\leq$2.0 mm); inclusions: qtz/spar, lime, Fe_2O_3, equiaxed organic burnout; negligible to weak organic HCl reaction.

PL#:	Method of Mfg:	Surf. Decor:	Firing:	State of Pres:
22:1	Upper surface and lip formed by rapid rotation.	Stamp seal at top of handle.	Oxidation; yellowish brown body and surfaces; low degree of vitrification; (MOHS 3-3→).	Worn surfaces.
22:2	Upper surface and lip formed by rapid rotation.	Oval stamp placed horizontally at top of handle.	Fired in oxidation; brownish red body and surfaces.	Good; accretion on interior.
22:3	Upper surface and lip formed by rapid rotation.	Oval stamp placed horizontally at top of handle.	Fired in oxidation; brownish red body and surfaces.	Good.
22:4	Upper surface and lip formed by rapid rotation.	Oval stamp placed diagonally at top of handle.	Fired in oxidation; brownish red body and surfaces.	Good; accretion on interior.
22:5	Upper surface and lip formed by rapid rotation.	Oval stamp placed horizontally at top of handle.	Fired in oxidation; brownish red body and surfaces.	Good; accretion on interior.

PLATE NO. 23

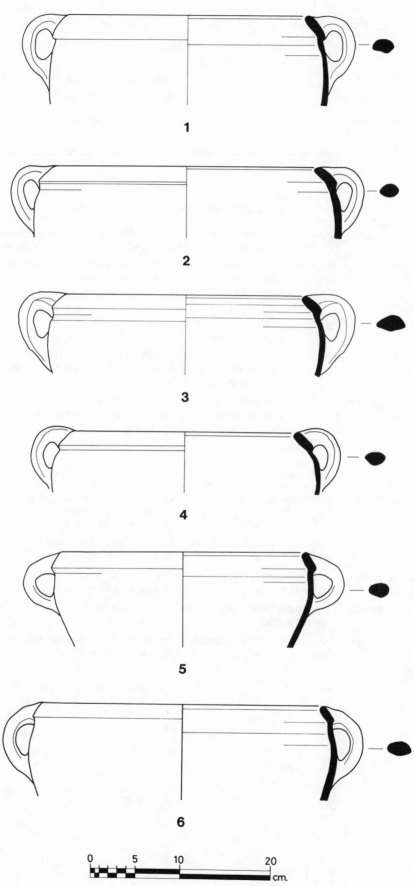

PLATE NO. 23

PL#:	Reg.#:	Date:	Prov:	Level:	Photo:	All:	Munsell References:
23:1	434	4-10-38	Rm. 39	Surface	596:7	ASOR	ext. 2.5 Y 8/2, int. 2.5 Y 8/2, sec. 5 Y 7/1
23:2							
23:3	2092	4-25-39	Rm. 50	-15 cm	751	ASOR	ext. 10 YR 7/2, int. 10 YR 8/2, sec. 5 YR 7/4
23:4		3-24-38	K2	10 cm		ASOR	ext. 2.5 Y 8/2, int. 10 YR 8/3, sec. 10 YR 7/3
23:5	783	4-20-38	Rm. 20		641:1	ASOR	ext. 5 Y 7/2, int. 5 Y 7/2, sec. 5 Y 7/2
23:6	822	4-20-38	P:12		555:3, 736	ASOR	ext. 5 Y 7/2, int. 5 Y 7/2, sec. 5 Y 7/2

PL#:	Description:	Body Comp. and Texture:
23:1	Krater, lip and handle fragment; ovoid shape; stamped handle; closed-form.	Fine textured calcareous clay; lightly tempered ($\leq$10%); fine particle size ($\leq$1.0 mm); inclusions: qtz/spar, limestone, equiaxed organic burnout; weak HCl reaction.
23:2	Krater, lip and handle fragment; ovoid shape; stamped handle; closed-form.	Fine textured ferrugenous clay; lightly tempered (10-20%); fine particles ($\leq$1.0 mm, rare particle $\leq$2.0 mm); inclusions: qtz/spar, lime, Fe_2O_3, equiaxed organic burnout; negligible to weak HCl reaction.
23:3	Krater, lip and handle fragment; closed-form; ovoid shape; stamped handle.	Fine textured ferrugenous clay; lightly tempered (10-20%); fine particles ($\leq$ 1 mm, rare particle $\leq$2.0 mm); inclusions: qtz/spar, lime, Fe_2O_3, equiaxed organic burnout; negligible to weak organic HCl reaction.
23:4	Krater, lip and handle fragment; ovoid shape; closed-form.	Fine textured ferrugenous clay; lightly tempered ($\leq$10%); fine particles ($\leq$0.5 mm); inclusions: qtz/spar, equiaxed burned out particles and fine elongated pores from organic burnout; no HCl reaction.
23:5	Krater, lip and handle fragment; closed-form.	Fine textured ferrugenous clay; lightly tempered; fine particles; inclusions: qtz/spar, Fe_2O_3, equiaxed organic burnout.
23:6	Krater, lip and handle fragment; ovoid shape; stamped handle; closed-form.	Fine textured calcareous clay; lightly tempered ($\leq$10%); fine particle size ($\leq$1.0 mm); inclusions: qtz/spar, limestone, equiaxed organic burnout; weak HCl reaction.

PL#:	Method of Mfg:	Surf. Decor:	Firing:	State of Pres:
23:1	Upper surface and lip formed by rapid rotation.	Stamp seal at top of handle.	Oxidation; yellowish brown body and surface; low degree of vitrification; (MOHS 3-3 ➤).	Good.
23:2	Upper surface and lip formed by rapid rotation.	Oval stamp placed horizontally at top of handle.	Fired in oxidation; brownish red body and surfaces.	Heavily worn surfaces.
23:3	Upper surface and lip formed by rapid rotation.	Oval stamp placed vertically at top of handle.	Fired in oxidation; brownish red body and surfaces.	Stained surfaces.
23:4	Lip probably shaped by rapid turning; handles reinforced with clay where they join body.		Heavily reduced body and surfaces; medium degree of vitrification; (MOHS 4).	Worn exterior surface.
23:5	Upper surface and lip formed by rapid rotation.			Heavily worn surfaces.
23:6	Upper surface and lip formed by rapid rotation.	Stamp seal at top of handle.	Oxidation; yellowish brown body and surfaces; low degree of vitrification; (MOHS 3-3 ➤).	Good.

PLATE NO. 24

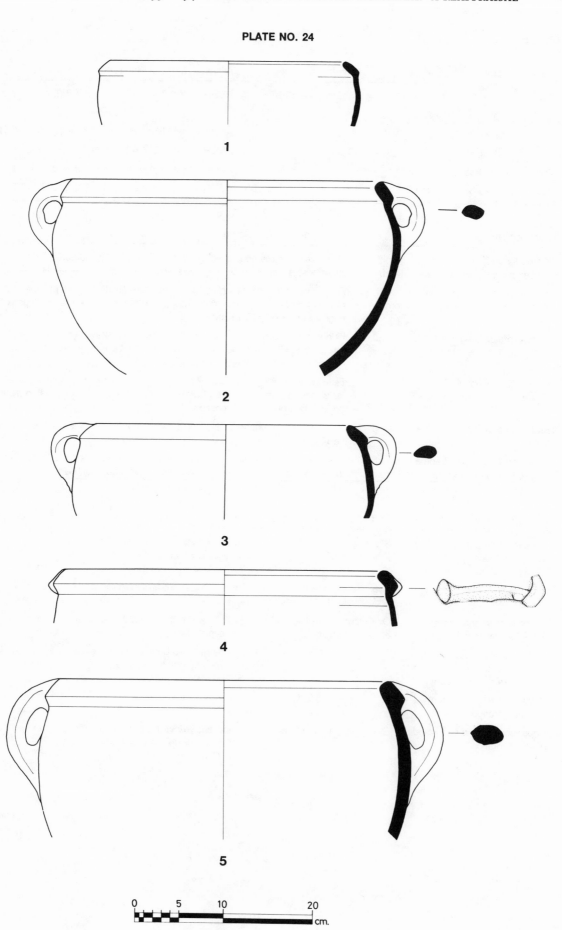

PLATE NO. 24

PL#:	Reg.#:	Date:	Prov:	Level:	Photo:	All:	Munsell References:
24:1	306	4-4-38	Rm. 27	-2 m	595:9-10	ASOR	ext. 5 YR 6/6, int. 5 YR 6/6
24:2	904	6-6-38	Rm. 35A	-60 cm	524:2, 646:1	ASOR	
24:3	11,090	4-22-40	Rm. 125		1464:17	ASOR	ext. 7.5 YR 7/4, int. 5 YR 7/4, sec. 5 YR 7/4
24:4	4016	5-1-39	Rm. 42	-1.20 m		ASOR	
24:5	659	5-1-40			1481:2	ASOR	

PL#:	Description:	Body Comp. and Texture:
24:1	Krater, rim and body fragment; rounded.	Medium texture; white and red inclusions.
24:2	Krater, lip, handle and body fragment.	Ferrugenous clay; particle size < 3 mm; inclusions: qtz/spar and lime, Fe_2O_3, Fe_3O_4, equiaxed organic burnout.
24:3	Krater, lip and handle fragment; ovoid shape; stamped handle; closed-form.	Fine textured ferrugenous clay; lightly tempered (10-20%); fine particles (≤1.0 mm, rare particle ≤2.0 mm); inclusions: qtz/spar, lime, Fe_2O_3, equiaxed organic burnout; negligible to weak organic HCl reaction.
24:4	Krater, lip fragment	
24:5	Krater, lip and body fragment; stamped handle.	Ferrugenous clay; particle size < 4 mm; inclusions: unidentified platey particles, Fe_2O_3, Fe_3O_4, qtz/spar/lime, fibrous organic burnout.

PL#:	Method of Mfg:	Surf. Decor:	Firing:	State of Pres:
24:1	Thrown.	None.	Medium firing in oxidation.	Good.
24:2	Handbuilt body with wheel-turned lip.	Groove beneath lip inset.	Brownish red interior and surfaces.	Good, accretion on interior.
24:3	Upper surface and lip formed by rapid rotation.	Oval stamp placed horizontally at top of handle.	Fired in oxidation; brownish red body and surfaces.	Worn surfaces.
24:4	Probably wheel thrown.		Grey interior; reduced with red surface layers on interior and exterior; (MOHS 3).	Worn surfaces.
24:5		Stamped oval seal on diagonal above handle.	Red oxidized body with grey surface layer and outer surface; (MOHS 3-3→).	Worn surfaces.

PLATE NO. 25

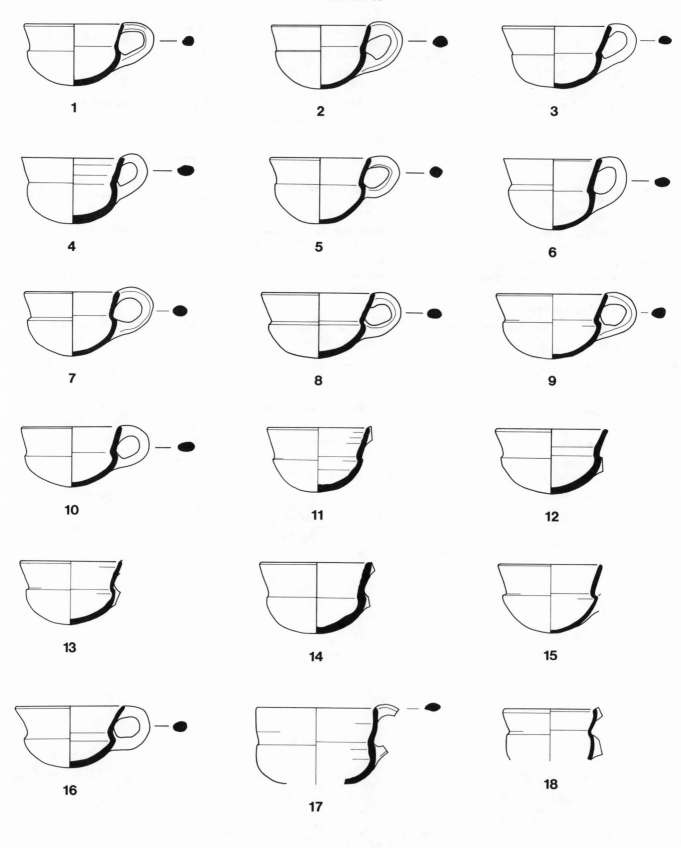

PLATE NO. 25

PL#:	Reg.#:	Date:	Prov:	Level:	Photo:	All:	Munsell References:
25:1	962	4-11-39	Rm. 49	-1.60 m	610:8	ASOR	
25:2	329	4-6-38	Rm. 37	-1 m	613:3	ASOR	ext. 5 YR 5/1, int. 5 YR 6/2, sec. 5 YR 5/1
25:3	2026	4-21-39	Rm. 40	-1 m	611:4	ASOR	ext. 2.5 Y 8/2, int. 5 Y 8/2, sec. 5 Y 8/2
25:4	5044	5-12-39	Rm. 27	-1 m	610:4	JAM	
25:5	6011	3-13-40	Rm. 46		1456:3	ASOR	ext. 7.5 YR 8/2, int. 5 YR 7/4, sec. 5 YR 7/4
25:6	8087	4-1-40	Rm. 125		1453:7	JAM	
25:7	924	6-6-38	Rm. 27		637:2	JAM	
25:8	923	6-6-38	Rm. 27		591:1	ASOR	2.5 Y 8/2, int. 2.5 Y 8/2, sec. 2.5 Y 8/2
25:9	462	4-12-38	Rm. 27	-2 m	536:4, 537:2, 538:3, 589:4	ASOR	ext. 2.5 Y 8/2, int. 10 YR 7/3, sec. 10 YR 7/1
25:10	460	4-12-38	Rm. 27	-2 m	536:2, 537:3, 538:4, 589:3	JAM	
25:11	925	6-6-38	Rm. 27		589:6	ASOR	ext. 2.5 Y 8/2, int. 2.5 Y 8/2, sec. 10 YR 7/3
25:12	461	4-12-38	Rm 27	-2 m	610:6	ASOR	ext. 7.5 YR 6/4, int. 7.5 YR 6/2, sec. 7.5 YR 6/4
25:13	459		Rm. 27	-2 m		ASOR	ext. 5 YR 7/2, int. 5 YR 7/2, sec. 5 YR 7/4
25:14	457	4-12-38	Rm. 27	-2 m		ASOR	ext. 10 YR 8/3, int. 7.5 YR 7/4, sec. 7.5 7/4
25:15						JAM	
25:16	926	6-6-38	Rm. 27		591:3	ASOR	ext. 10 YR 7/2, int. 2.5 Y 7/2, sec. 5 Y 8/1
25:17	3053	4-26-39	Rm. 49A	-1.40 m	610:3	ASOR	ext. 7.5 YR 6/2, int. 10 YR 6/2, sec. 10 YR 5/1
25:18	8073	3-31-40	Rm. 105	Debris	1456:4	ASOR	ext. 5 YR 6/2, int. 5 YR 6/2, sec. 5 YR 5/1

PL#:	Description:	Body Comp. and Texture:
25:1	Cup, lip, handle and base fragment; rounded base; carinated; strap handle.	Medium texture; some white, red and black inclusions.
25:2	Cup, lip and body fragment; rounded, hand-trimmed base; carinated; strap handle.	Fine textured ferrugenous clay; medium amount of temper (10-30%); particle size small (≤1.0 mm, occasional 1-3 mm); inclusions: qtz/spar and lime, Fe_2O_3, equiaxed burnout up to 3 mm.
25:3	Cup, handle and body fragment; rounded base; strap handle.	Fine textured calcareous clay; lightly tempered (10-20%); fine particle size (≤1.0 mm); inclusions: qtz/spar, lime, fine fibrous organic burnout, minor Fe_2O_3, medium HCl reaction.
25:4	Cup, lip and body fragment; rounded base; strap handle.	
25:5	Cup, lip and body fragment; rounded, hand-trimmed base; carinated; strap handle.	Fine textured ferrugenous clay; medium amount of temper (10-30%); fine particle size (≤1.0 mm, occasional 1-3 mm); inclusions: qtz/spar and lime, Fe_2O_3; equiaxed burnout up to 3 mm.
25:6	Cup, lip and body fragment; carinated; rounded base; strap handle.	
25:7	Cup, lip and body fragment; carinated; rounded base; strap handle.	
25:8	Cup, lip and body fragment; carinated; rounded base; strap handle.	Medium texture; black and white inclusions; some burned out vegetal material.
25:9	Cup, lip and body fragment; carinated; rounded base; strap handle.	Fine textured calcareous clay; lightly tempered (10-20%); fine particle size (≤1.0 mm); inclusions: qtz/spar, lime, fine fibrous organic burnout, minor Fe_2O_3; very weak HCl reaction.
25:10	Cup, lip and body fragment; carinated; rounded base; strap handle.	

25:11	Cup, lip and body fragment; carinated; rounded base; vestige of handle at rim.	Fine textured calcareous clay; lightly tempered (10-20%); fine particle size ($\leq$1.0 mm); inclusions: qtz/spar, lime, fine fibrous organic burnout, minor Fe_2O_3; weak HCl reaction.
25:12	Cup, lip and body fragment; hand-trimmed rounded base; carinated; vestige of handle below carination.	Fine textured ferrugenous clay; medium amount of temper (10-30%); fine particle size ($\leq$1.0 mm, occasional 1-3 mm); inclusions: qtz/spar and lime, Fe_2O_3, equiaxed burnout up to 3 mm.
25:13	Cup, lip and body fragment; hand-trimmed, rounded base; carinated; vestige of handle at carination.	Fine textured ferrugenous clay; medium amount of temper (10-30%); fine particle size ($\leq$1.0 mm, occasional 1-3 mm); inclusions: qtz/spar and lime, Fe_2O_3, equiaxed burnout up to 3 mm.
25:14	Cup, lip and body fragment; carinated; rounded base; vestiges of handle at rim and carination.	Fine textured calcareous clay; lightly tempered (10-20%); fine particle size ($\leq$1.0 mm); inclusions: qtz/spar, lime, fine fibrous organic burnout, minor Fe_2O_3; very weak HCl reaction.
25:15	Cup, lip and body fragment; carinated; rounded base.	
25:16	Cup, handle and body fragments; carinated; rounded base; strap handle.	Fine textured calcareous clay; lightly tempered (10-20%); fine particle size ($\leq$1.0 mm); inclusions: qtz/spar, lime, fine fibrous organic burnout, minor Fe_2O_3; medium HCl reaction.
25:17	Cup, lip and body fragment; hand-trimmed base; carinated; handle broken and partially missing.	Fine textured ferrugenous clay; medium amount of temper (10-30%); fine particle size ($\leq$1.0 mm, occasional 1-3 mm); inclusions: qtz/spar and lime, Fe_2O_3; equiaxed burnout up to 3 mm.
25:18	Cup, lip and body fragment; carinated; vestiges of handle at rim and body.	Fine textured ferrugenous clay; medium amount of temper (10-30%); fine particle size ($\leq$1.0 mm), pores larger (1-3 mm); inclusions: qtz/spar and lime ($\leq$1.0 mm); equiaxed burnout ($\leq$3 mm).

PL#:	Method of Manufacture:
25:1	Thrown; exterior trimmed.
25:2	Thrown, with hand trimmed base; handles pulled and attached with excess clay at base and lip.
25:3	Thrown; fine circumferential marks < 1.0 mm apart and deeper impressions, 7-10 mm apart; pulled handle joined at lip and at widest part of body with excess clay at base but not top; the base has facets from hand trimming.
25:4	
25:5	Thrown; hand-trimmed base; handles pulled and attached with excess clay at base and lip.
25:6	
25:7	
25:8	Thrown; exterior trimmed and wiped.
25:9	Thrown; fine circumferential marks < 1.0 mm apart and deeper impressions 7-10 mm apart; pulled handle joined at lip and at widest part of body with excess clay at base but not at top; the base has facets from hand-trimming.
25:10	
25:11	Thrown; fine circumferential marks 1.0 mm apart and deeper impressions 7-10 mm apart; pulled handle joined at lip and at widest part of body with excess clay at base but not at top; the base has facets from hand-trimming.
25:12	Thrown; hand-trimmed base, handles pulled and attached with excess clay at base and lip.
25:13	Thrown; hand-trimmed base; handle pulled and attached with excess clay at base and lip.
25:14	Thrown; fine circumferential marks <1.0 mm apart and deeper impressions 7-10 mm apart; pulled handle joined at lip and at widest part of body with excess clay at base but not at top; the base has facets from hand-trimming.
25:15	
25:16	Thrown; fine circumferential marks < 1.0 mm apart and deeper imressions, 7-10 mm apart; pulled handle joined at lip and widest part of body with excess clay at base but not at top; the base has facets from hand-trimming.
25:17	Thrown: hand-trimmed base; handles pulled and attached with excess clay at base and lip.
25:18	Thrown.

PL#	Surf. Decor:	Firing:	State of Pres:
25:1	None.	Oxidized body.	Exterior worn; some fire blackening.
25:2		Reduction fired to grey color; (MOHS 3-4).	Good.
25:3	Indented circumferential groove between body and lip.	Surfaces and interior light yellowish brown; medium degree of vitrification; (MOHS 4); no defects.	Good, no wear.
25:4			
25:5		Oxidation fired; (MOHS 3-4).	Good.
25:6			
25:7			
25:8	None.	Medium in oxidation.	Worn.
25:9	Indented and circumferential groove between body and lip.	Surfaces and interior light yellowish brown; medium degree of vitrification; (MOHS 4); no defects.	Good, no wear.
25:10			
25:11	Indented circumferential groove between body and lip.	Surfaces and interior light yellowish brown; medium degree of vitrification; (MOHS 4); no defects.	Good, no wear.
25:12		Oxidation fired; (MOHS 3-4).	Good.
25:13		Oxidation fired; (MOHS 3-4).	Good.
25:14	Indented and circumferential groove between body and lip.	Surfaces and interior light yellowish brown; medium degree of vitrification; (MOHS 4); no defects.	Good, no wear.
25:15			
25:16	Indented circumferential groove between body and lip; "v" mark incised to left of base of handle.	Surfaces and interior light yellowish brown; medium degree of vitrification; (MOHS 4); no defects.	Good, no wear.
25:17		Reduction fired to grey color, (MOHS 3-4).	Good.
25:18		Reduction fired light grey to black body and surfaces; (MOHS 3-4).	Good.

PLATE NO. 26

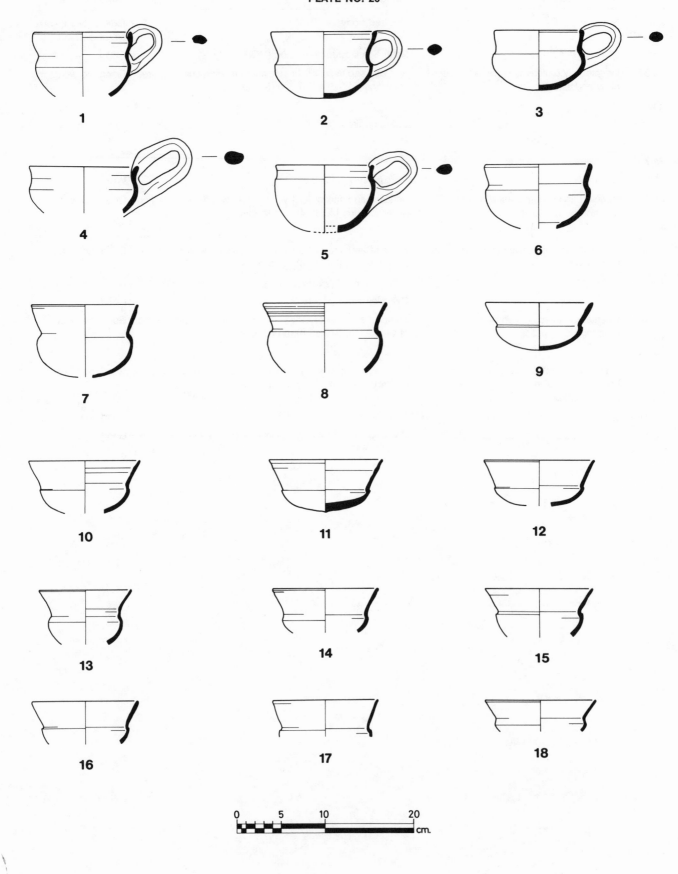

PLATE NO. 26

PL#:	Reg.#:	Date:	Prov:	Level:	Photo:	All:	Munsell References:
26:1	832	4-20-38	Q:11		602:1	ASOR	ext. 5 YR 5/2, int. 5 YR 6/4, sec. 5 YR 5/1
26:2	196	3-31-38	Rm. 24B	-1 m	591:5	ASOR	ext. 5 Y 8/1, int. 5 Y 8/2, sec. 5 Y 8/1
26:3	184	3-31-38	Rm. 24A	-1.50 m	591:4	ASOR	ext. 2.5 Y 8/2, int. 2.5 Y 8/2, sec. 2.5 Y 8/2
26:4	985	4-12-39		-1.50 m	602:12	ASOR	ext. 5 Y 8/2, int. 5 Y 7/1, sec. 10 YR 7/3
26:5	218	4-2-38	P:11	-50 cm	1456:2	ASOR	ext. 5 Y 8/2, int. 2.5 Y 7/2, sec. 5 Y 7/1
26:6	12,045	4-30-40	Rm. 36		1456:5	ASOR	ext. 2.5 Y 7/2, int. 2.5 Y 8/2, sec. 2.5 Y 7/2
26:7	853	4-20-38	L:12	-1 m		ASOR	ext. 5 YR 7/4, int 5 YR 7/6, sec. 5 YR 7/4
26:8	82	3-24-38	Q:11	-55 cm		ASOR	ext. 5 YR 6/2, int. 5 YR 6/2, sec. 5 YR 5/1
26:9	4003	4-30-39	Rm. 49A	-1.38 m	621:2	JAM	
26:10	5043	5-12-39	Rm. 35		644:18	ASOR	ext. 7.5 YR 7/4, int. 5 YR 6/4, sec. 5 YR 4/1
26:11	8070	3-31-40	Rm. 105		1456:7	ASOR	ext. 5 YR 6/2, int. 5 YR 7/2, sec. 5 YR 5/1
26:12	186	3-31-38	Rm. 24A	-1.50 m	529:2, 644:12	ASOR	ext. 2.5 YR 6/6, int. 2.5 YR 6/4, sec. 5 YR 6/1
26:13	10,042	4-9-40	Rm. 69	Debris	1456:9	ASOR	ext. 10 R 5/3, int. 10 R 5/4, sec. 10 R 5/6
26:14	4050	5-5-39	Rm. 49A	-1.38 m	644:26	ASOR	ext. 5 YR 6/3, int. 5 YR 6/6, sec. 5 YR 5/1
26:15	9051	4-6-40	Rm. 46		1456:16	ASOR	ext. 5 YR 6/2, int. 5 YR 6/2, sec. 5 YR 6/1
26:16						JAM	
26:17						JAM	
26:18	795	4-20-38	Rm. 21		601:2	ASOR	ext. 5 YR 4/1, int. 5 YR 4/1, sec. 5 YR 5/1

PL#:	Description:	Body Comp. and Texture:
26:1	Cup, lip and body fragment; carinated; strap handle.	Fine textured ferrugenous clay; medium amount of temper (10-30%); fine particle size (≤ 1.0 mm with occasional 1-3 mm); inclusions: qtz/spar and lime, Fe_2O_3, equiaxed burnout up to 3 mm.
26:2	Cup, handle and body fragment; carinated; rounded base; strap handle.	Fine textured calcareous clay; lightly tempered (10-20%); fine particle size (≤ 1.0 mm); inclusions: qtz/spar, lime, fine fibrous organic burnout, minor Fe_2O_3; very weak HCl reaction.
26:3	Cup, handle and body fragment; carinated; rounded base; strap handle.	Fine textured calcareous clay; lightly tempered (10-20%); fine particle size (≤ 1.0 mm); inclusions: qtz/spar, lime, fine fibrous organic burnout, minor Fe_2O_3; very weak HCl reaction.
26:4	Cup, handle and body fragment; carinated; strap handle.	Fine textured calcareous clay; lightly tempered (10-20%); fine particle size (≤ 1.0 mm); inclusions: qtz/spar, lime, fine fibrous organic burnout, minor Fe_2O_3; very weak HCl reaction.
26:5	Cup, handle and body fragment; carinated; rounded base; strap handle.	Fine textured calcareous clay; lightly tempered (10-20%); fine particle size (≤ 1.0 mm); inclusions: qtz/spar, lime, fine fibrous organic burnout, minor Fe_2O_3; very weak HCl reaction.
26:6	Cup, lip and body fragment; carinated; rounded base.	Fine textured calcareous clay; lightly tempered (10-20%); fine particle size (≤ 1.0 mm); inclusions: qtz/spar, lime, fine fibrous organic burnout, minor Fe_2O_3; weak HCl reaction.
26:7	Cup, lip and body fragment; rounded base, wheel-turned base; carinated.	Fine textured ferrugenous clay; medium amount of temper (10-30%); fine particle size (≤ 1.0 mm), pores larger (1-3 mm); inclusions: qtz/spar and lime (≤ 1.0 mm), equiaxed burnout (≤ 3 mm).
26:8	Cup, lip and body fragment; carinated.	Fine textured ferrugenous clay; medium temper (10-30%); fine particle size (≤ 1.0 mm), pores larger (1-3 mm); inclusions: qtz/spar and lime, equiaxed burnout.
26:9	Cup, lip and body fragment; carinated; rounded base.	
26:10	Cup, lip and body fragment; carinated.	Fine textured ferrugenous clay; medium amount of temper (10-30%); fine particle size (≤ 1.0 mm), pores larger (1-3 mm); inclusions: qtz/spar and lime (≤ 1.0 mm), equiaxed burnout (≤ 3 mm).

26:11   Cup, lip and body fragment; wheel-turned base; carinated. | Fine textured ferrugenous clay; medium amount of temper (10-30%); fine particle size (≤1.0 mm), pores larger (1-3 mm); inclusions: qtz/spar and lime (≤1.0 mm), equiaxed burnout (≤3.0 mm).

26:12   Cup, lip and body fragment; wheel-turned, rounded base; carinated. | Fine textured ferrugenous clay; medium amount of temper (10-30%); fine particle size (≤1.0 mm), pores larger (1-3 mm); inclusions: qtz/spar and lime (≤1.0 mm), equiaxed burnout (≤3 mm).

26:13   Cup, lip and body fragment; burnished lip; carinated. | Fine textured ferrugenous clay; lightly tempered body (10-20%); fine particle size (≤1.0 mm) and large equiaxed burnout particles (≤4.0 mm); inclusions: qtz/spar and lime; weak HCl reaction.

26:14   Cup, lip and body fragment; carinated. | Fine textured ferrugenous clay; medium amount of temper (10-30%); fine particle size (≤1.0 mm), pores larger (1-3 mm); inclusions: qtz/spar and lime (≤1.0 mm), equiaxed organic burnout (≤3 mm).

26:15   Cup, lip and body fragment; carinated. | Fine textured ferrugenous clay; medium amount of temper (10-30%); fine particle size (≤1.0 mm), pores larger (1-3 mm); inclusions: qtz/spar and lime (≤1.0 mm), equiaxed organic burnout (≤3 mm).

26:16   Cup, lip and body fragment; carinated.

26:17   Cup, lip and body fragment; carinated.

26:18   Cup, lip and body fragment; burnished lip; carinated. | Fine textured ferrugenous clay; lightly tempered body (10-20%); fine particle size (≤1.0 mm) and large equiaxed burnout particles (≤4.0 mm); inclusions: qtz/spar and lime; weak HCl reaction.

PL#:	Method of Manufacture:
26:1	Thrown; hand-trimmed base; handles pulled and attached with excess clay at bottom and lip.
26:2	Thrown; fine circumferential marks < 1.0 mm apart and deeper impressions 7-10 mm apart; pulled handle joined at lip and at widest part of body with excess clay at bottom but not at top; the base has facets from hand-trimming.
26:3	Thrown; fine circumferential marks 1.0 mm apart and deeper impressions 7-10 mm apart; pulled handle joined at lip and at widest part of body with excess clay at bottom but not at top; the base has facets from hand-trimming; elongated handle placed at a diagonal to body.
26:4	Thrown; fine circumferential marks 1.0 mm apart and deeper impressions 7-10 mm apart; pulled handle joined at lip and at widest part of body with excess clay at bottom but not at top; the base has facets from hand-trimming; elongated handle placed at a diagonal to body.
26:5	Thrown; fine circumferential marks 1.0 mm apart and deeper impressions 7-10 mm apart; pulled handle joined at lip and at widest part of body with excess clay at bottom but not at top; the base has facets from hand-trimming; elongated handles placed at a diagonal to body.
26:6	Thrown; fine circumferential marks 1.0 mm apart and deeper impressions 7-10 mm apart; pulled handle joined at lip and at widest part of body with excess clay on bottom but not at top; the base has facets from hand-trimming.
26:7	Thrown; wheel-turned base, 3-10 mm wall thickness.
26:8	Thrown; wheel-turned base; 3-10 mm wall thickness.
26:9	
26:10	Thrown; wheel-turned base; 3-10 mm wall thickness.
26:11	Thrown; wheel-turned base; 3-10 mm wall thickness.
26:12	Thrown; wheel-turned base; 3-10 mm wall thickness.
26:13	Thrown; circumferential throwing marks; 4-9 mm wall thickness; lip burnished by turning on wheel when leather hard and compressing surface; trimmed on wheel.
26:14	Thrown; wheel-turned base; 3-10 mm wall thickness.
26:15	Thrown; wheel-turned base; 3-10 mm wall thickness.
26:16	
26:17	
26:18	Thrown; circumferential throwing marks; 4-9 mm wall thickness; lip burnished by turning on wheel when leather hard and compressing surface; base wheel-trimmed.

PL#	Surf. Decor:	Firing:	State of Pres:
26:1		Reduction fired to grey in color; (MOHS 3-4).	Good.
26:2	Indented and circumferential groove between body and lip.	Surfaces and interior light yellowish brown; medium degree of vitrification; (MOHS 4); no defects.	Good, no wear.
26:3	Indented circumferential groove between body and lip.	Surfaces and interior light yellowish brown; medium degree of vitrification; (MOHS 3); no defects.	Good, no wear.
26:4	Indented circumferential groove between body and lip.	Surfaces and interior light yellowish brown; medium degree of vitrification; (MOHS 4); no defects.	Good, no wear.
26:5	Indented circumferential groove between body and lip.	Surfaces and interior light yellowish brown; medium degree of vitrification; (MOHS 4); no defects.	Good, no wear.
26:6	Indented circumferential groove between body and lip.	Surfaces and interior light yellowish brown; medium degree of vitrification; (MOHS 4); no defects.	Good, no wear.
26:7		Reduction fired light grey to black body and surfaces; (MOHS 3-4).	Good.
26:8		Reduction fired light grey to black body surfaces; (MOHS 3-4).	Good.
26:9			
26:10		Reduction fired light grey to black body and surfaces; (MOHS 3-4).	Good.
26:11		Reduction fired light grey to black body and surfaces; (MOHS 3-4).	Good.
26:12		Reduction fired light grey to black body and surfaces; (MOHS 3-4).	Good.
26:13	Lip burnished in linear circumferential pattern.	Red oxidized on interior surface and body; grey on exterior.	Good.
26:14		Reduction fired light grey to black body surfaces; (MOHS 3-4).	Good.
26:15		Reduction fired light grey to black body surfaces; (MOHS 3-4).	Good.
26:16			
26:17			
26:18	Lip burnished in linear circumferential pattern; 2 mm hole drilled in lip.	Grey to black interiors and surfaces.	Good.

PLATE NO. 27

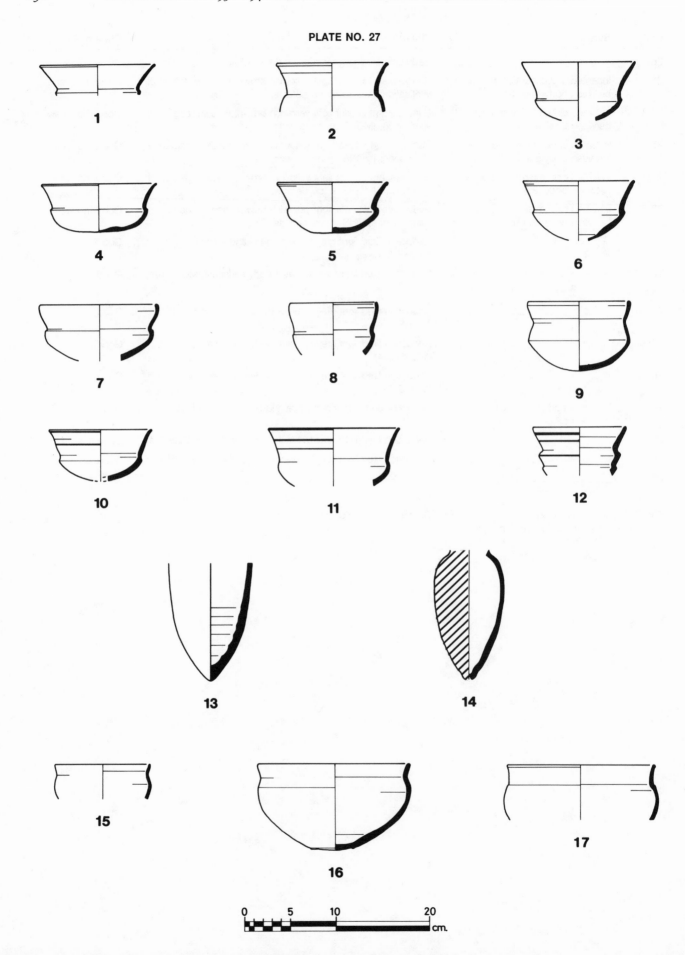

PLATE NO. 27

PL#:	Reg.#:	Date:	Prov:	Level:	Photo:	All:	Munsell References:
27:1	779	4-20-38	Rm. 18		644:13	ASOR	ext. 5 YR 6/1, int. 5 YR 5/1, sec. 5 YR 5/1
27:2	10,049	4-9-40	Rm. 36		1456:11	ASOR	ext. 10 R 5/3, int. 2.5 YR 6/4, sec. 2.5 YR 5/2
27:3	187	3-31-38	Rm. 24A	-1.50 m		ASOR	ext. 2.5 YR 6/6, int. 2.5 YR 5/2, sec. 5 YR 5/1
27:4	3049	4-26-39	Rm. 49A	-2 m	621:5	ASOR	ext. 5 YR 6/4, int. 5 YR 6/4, sec. 5 YR 6/3
27:5	4004						ext. 5 YR 6/4, int. 5 YR 6/6, sec. 5 YR 6/2
27:6	478	4-13-38	Rm. 27	-1 m		ASOR	ext. 2.5 YR 6/4, int. 2.5 YR 6/6, sec. 5 YR 6/1
27:7	183	3-31-38	Rm. 24A	-1.50 m	1456:12	ASOR	ext. 2.5 YR 5/6, int. 2.5 YR 5/8, sec. 5 YR 5/1
27:8			P:10				ext. 5 YR 5/1, int. 5 YR 5/1, sec. 5 YR 4/1
27:9	624	4-18-38	Rm. 35A	-2 m	592:1, 610:1	ASOR	ext. 5 YR 8/3, int. 5 YR 7/4, sec. 5 YR 7/4
27:10	5026	5-10-39	Rm. 37			JAM	
27:11	5043	5-12-39	Rm. 35		644:18	JAM	
27:12	951	4-10-39	Rm. 60	-1 m	621:1, 1465:19	JAM	
27:13	984	4-12-39	Rm. 60		594:6, 1466:10	JAM	
27:14	259	4-4-38	Rm. 28	-2 m	541:1, 594:5, 1463:5, 1619:7	ASOR	ext. 5 YR 6/4, int. 7.5 YR 6/4, sec. 10 R 6/1
27:15	372	4-8-38	Rm. 46	-80 cm	601:5	ASOR	ext. 5 YR 6/4, int. 7.5 YR 6/4, sec. 10 R 6/1
27:16	7030	3-22-40	Rm. 109		1451:8	ASOR	
27:17						JAM	

PL#:	Description:	Body Comp. and Texture:
27:1	Cup, lip and body fragment; burnished lip; carinated.	Fine textured ferrugenous clay; lightly tempered body (10-20%); fine particle size (≤1.0 mm) and large equiaxed burnout particles (≤4.0 mm); inclusions: qtz/spar and lime; weak HCl reaction.
27:2	Cup, lip and body fragment; burnished lip.	Fine textured ferrugenous clay; lightly tempered body (10-20%); fine particle size (≤1.0 mm) and large equiaxed burnout particles (≤4.0 mm); inclusions: qtz/spar and lime; weak HCl reaction.
27:3	Cup, lip and body fragment; rounded, wheel-turned base; carinated.	Fine textured ferrugenous clay; medium amount of temper (10-30%); fine particle size (≤1.0 mm), pores larger (1-3 mm); inclusions: qtz/spar and lime (≤1.0 mm), equiaxed organic burnout (≤3.0 mm).
27:4	Cup, lip and body fragment; wheel-turned, indented base; carinated.	Fine textured ferrugenous clay; lightly tempered (≤10%); fine particle size (≤0.5 mm); inclusions: qtz/spar, lime, equiaxed organic burnout; weak HCl reaction.
27:5	Cup, lip and body fragment; wheel-turned, indented base; carinated.	Fine textured ferrugenous clay; lightly tempered (≤10%); fine particle size (≤0.5 mm); inclusions: qtz/spar, lime, equiaxed organic burnout; weak HCl reaction.
27:6	Cup, lip and body fragment; rounded, hand trimmed base; carinated.	Fine textured ferrugenous clay; heavily tempered (30-50%); fine particle size; organic burnout, fibrous type; equiaxed burnout; inclusions: qtz/spar, lime (≤1.0 mm); weak HCl reaction.
27:7	Cup, lip and body fragment; rounded, base; carinated.	Fine textured ferrugenous clay; heavily tempered (30-50%); fine particle size; organic burnout, fibrous type; equiaxed burnout; inclusions: qtz/spar, lime up to 1 mm; weak HCl reaction.
27:8	Cup, lip and body fragment; carinated.	Fine textured ferrugenous clay; medium size inclusions (~30%).
27:9	Cup, lip and body fragment; rounded, hand-trimmed base; carinated.	Fine textured ferrugenous clay; heavily tempered (30-50%); fine particle size; organic burnout, fibrous type; equiaxed burnout; inclusions: qtz/spar, lime up to 1 mm; weak HCl reaction.
27:10	Cup, lip and body fragment; carinated; horizontal painted bands.	

27:11   Cup, lip and body fragment; carinated;
        horizontal painted bands.

27:12   Cup, lip and body fragment; double
        carination; horizontal painted bands.

27:13   Juglet, body fragment; pointed base.

27:14   Juglet, body fragment; pointed base;   Fine texture; very few black and white inclusions.
        burnished.

27:15   Cup, lip and body fragment; carinated.   Medium texture; fine black and white inclusions.

27:16   Small bowl; lip, body and base fragment;   Fine texture; few black and white inclusions.
        flaring rim; carinated.

27:17   Small bowl, lip and body fragment; rounded
        upper body.

PL#:	Method of Mfg:	Surf. Decor:	Firing:	State of Pres:
27:1	Thrown; circumferential throwing marks; 4-9 mm wall thickness; lip burnished by turning on wheel when leather hard and compressing surface.	Lip burnished in linear circumferential pattern.	Grey to black interiors and surfaces.	Good.
27:2	Thrown; circumferential throwing marks; 4-9 mm wall thickness; lip burnished by turning on wheel when leather hard and compressing suface.	Lip burnished in linear circumferential pattern.	Grey to black interiors and surfaces.	Good.
27:3	Thrown; wheel-turned base, 3-10 mm wall thickness.		Reduction fired light grey to black body and surfaces; (MOHS 3-4).	Good.
27:4	Thrown; circumferential throwing marks; 4-6 mm wall thickness; base wheel-trimmed and center indented.		Body lightly reduced to greyish brown with orange brown surface; low degree of vitrification; (MOHS 3→).	Good.
27:5	Thrown; circumferential throwing marks; 4-6 mm wall thickness; base wheel-trimmed and center indented.		Body lightly reduced to greyish brown with orange brown surface; low degree of vitrification; (MOHS 3→).	Good.
27:6	Thrown; fine circumferential marks 1.0 mm apart and deeper finger impressions 5-10 mm apart; 3-10 mm wall thickness; base hand-trimmed.		Interior reduced black layer with red exterior; medium degree of vitrification; (MOHS 4).	Good.
27:7	Thrown; fine circumferential marks 1 mm apart and deeper finger impressions 5-10 mm apart; 3-10 mm wall thickness; base hand-trimmed.		Interior reduced black layer with red exterior; medium degree of vitrification; (MOHS 4).	Good.
27:8	Thrown.		Reduced.	Good.
27:9	Thrown; fine circumferential marks 1.0 mm apart and deeper finger impressions 5-10 mm apart; 3-10 mm wall thickness; base hand-trimmed.		Interior reduced black layer; black exterior surface; medium degree of vitrification; (MOHS 4).	Good.
27:10				
27:11				
27:12				
27:13				
27:14	Thrown; exterior trimmed and slipped.	Brown slip, burnished on wheel.	Oxidation.	Good.
27:15	Thrown.	None.	Interior reduced; red; oxidized surface layer and exterior.	Good.
27:16	Thrown; exterior trimmed and wiped.	None.	Medium firing in oxidation; inner core still black from early reduction of firing.	Good.
27:17				

PLATE NO. 28

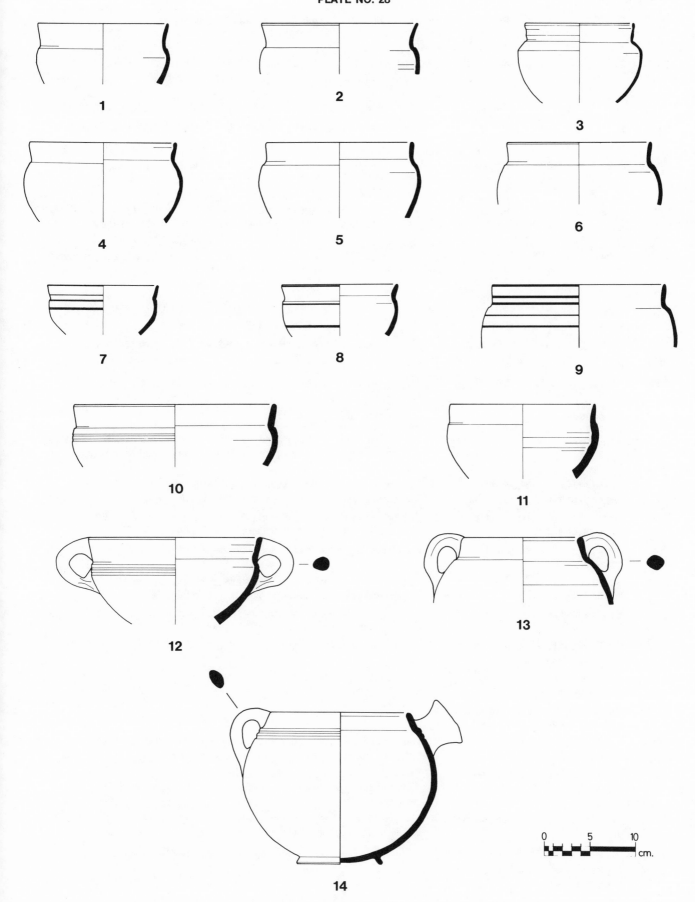

PLATE NO. 28

PL#:	Reg.#:	Date:	Prov:	Level:	Photo:	All:	Munsell References:
28:1			Rm. 49A	-2.20 m			
28:2	217	4-2-38	N:12	Surface	552:3, 593:14, 1465:5	ASOR	ext. 10 YR 7/3, int. 7.5 YR 7/4, sec. 7.5 YR 6/4; 4 painted lines: 7.5 YR 5/2
28:3	290	4-4-38	Rm. 36	-50 cm	590:10	ASOR	ext. 5 YR 6/3, int. 5 YR 5/3, sec. 5 YR 5/1
28:4	790	4-20-38	Rm. 21		590:17	ASOR	ext. 10 YR 8/3, int. 2.5 Y 8/2, sec. 10 YR 8/4
28:5	859	4-20-38	Rm. 15		593:4	ASOR	ext. 7.5 YR 6/2, int. 2.5 YR 6/6, sec. 2.5 YR 6/6
28:6	312	4-6-38	Rm. 42	-1 m	549:5, 645:5, 1462:1	ASOR	ext. 5 YR 6/4, int. 2.5 YR 6/8, sec. 10 YR 5/1
28:7	1083	4-19-39	Rm. 60	-1 m	593:9, 1465:21	ASOR	ext. 10 YR 5/3, int. 10 YR 5/1, sec. 10 YR 5/1; 3 painted lines: 10 YR 4/1, 2 painted lines: 7.5 YR 5/2
28:8	3004	4-25-39	Rm. 33	-2 m	601:22	ASOR	ext. 5 Y 8/2, int. 2.5 Y 8/2, sec. 2.5 Y 8/2; painted lines: 5 Y 6/1.
28:9						JAM	
28:10			Rm. 27	-2 m		JAM	ext. 5 YR 7/6, int. 7.5 YR 7/4, sec. 5 YR 7/4
28:11	4014	5-1-39	Rm. 49A		601:13	ASOR	ext. 5 Y 8/3, int. 5 Y 7/2, sec. 5 Y 8/1
28:12	4077	5-7-39	Rm. 40	-1 m	619:3	ASOR	ext. 5 Y 8/2, int. 5 Y 8/2, sec. 5 Y 7/1
28:13						JAM	
28:14	5095	3-12-40	Rm. 46		1496:2	JAM	

PL#:	Description:	Body Comp. and Texture:
28:1	Bowl, lip and body fragment; carinated.	Fine textured calcareous clay; lightly tempered (10-20%); fine particle size (≤1.0 mm); inclusions: qtz/spar, lime, fine fibrous organic burnout, minor Fe_2O_3; weak HCl reaction.
28:2	Small painted bowl, body and lip fragment; carinated.	Ferrugenous clay; heavily tempered (~30%); medium particle size (≤3.0 mm); inclusions: qtz/spar, lime only, equiaxed organic burnout, Fe_2O_3.
28:3	Small painted bowl, body and lip fragment; carinated.	Ferrugenous clay; heavily tempered (~30%); medium particle size (≤3.0 mm); inclusions: qtz/spar, lime only, equiaxed organic burnout, Fe_2O_3.
28:4	Small painted bowl, body and lip fragment.	Calcareous clay; lightly tempered; fine particle size (≤1.0 mm).
28:5	Small painted bowl, body and lip fragment.	Ferrugenous clay; heavily tempered (~30%); fine inclusion size (≤2.0 mm); inclusions: Fe_2O_3, qtz/spar/lime, fibrous organic burnout.
28:6	Small painted bowl, body and lip fragment.	Ferrugenous clay; heavily tempered (~30%); fine particle size (≤2.0 mm); inclusions: Fe_2O_3, qtz/spar/lime, fibrous organic burnout.
28:7	Small painted bowl, lip and body fragment; carinated.	Fine texture; few white inclusions.
28:8	Small painted bowl, body and lip fragment, carinated.	Calcareous clay; lightly tempered; fine particle size (<1.0 mm).
28:9	Medium-size bowl, lip and body fragment; carinated; horizontal painted bands.	
28:10	Medium-size bowl, body and lip fragment; carinated.	Ferrugenous clay; heavily tempered (~30%); medium particle size (<3.0 mm); inclusions: qtz/spar, lime, equiaxed organic burnout, Fe_2O_3.
28:11	Small bowl, lip and body fragment; carinated.	Fine textured calcareous clay; lightly tempered (10-20%); fine particle size (≤1.0 mm); inclusions: qtz/spar, lime, fine fibrous organic burnout, minor Fe_2O_3; very weak HCl reaction.
28:12	Bowl, lip and body fragment; carinated, strap handle.	Ferrugenous clay; heavily tempered (~30%); medium particle size (<3.0 mm); inclusions: qtz/spar, lime only, equiaxed organic burnout, Fe_2O_3.
28:13	Jar, lip and body fragment; strap handles.	
28:14	Spouted vessel; spherical body; disc base; strap handle.	

PL#:	Method of Mfg:	Surf. Decor:	Firing:	State of Pres:
28:1	Thrown; fine circumferential marks 1.0 mm apart and deeper impressions 7-10 mm apart; pulled handle joined at lip and widest part of body with excess clay at bottom but not at top; the base has facets from hand-trimming.	Indented circumferential groove between body and lip.	Surfaces and interior light yellowish brown; medium degree of vitrification; (MOHS 4); no defects.	Good, no wear.
28:2		Brown banded decoration on body and lip.	Brownish grey body with oxidized surfaces.	Good.
28:3		Brown banded decoration on body and lip.	Reduced body with brownish grey surface.	Good.
28:4		Very faint traces of brown banding.	Oxidation.	Good.
28:5		Faint black banded decoration on body and lip.	Oxidized body and surface.	Good.
28:6		Faint black banded decoration on body and lip.	Reduced body with oxidized surfaces.	Good.
28:7	Thrown.	Red and brown banded decoration painted on interior and exterior of rim and upper body.	Mostly reduction.	Good.
28:8		Traces of brown banding on rim and upper body.	Oxidation.	Good.
28:9				
28:10			Oxidized body and surface.	Good.
28:11	Thrown; fine circumferential marks <1.0 mm apart and deeper impressions 7-10 mm apart.	Indented circumferential groove ~20 mm from lip.	Surfaces and interior light yellowish brown; medium degree of vitrification; (MOHS 4); no defects.	Int. surface worn.
28:12	Thrown.	Two incised lines at widest part of body.	Reduced light grey body with oxidized tan surfaces.	Good.
28:13				
28:14				

PLATE NO. 29

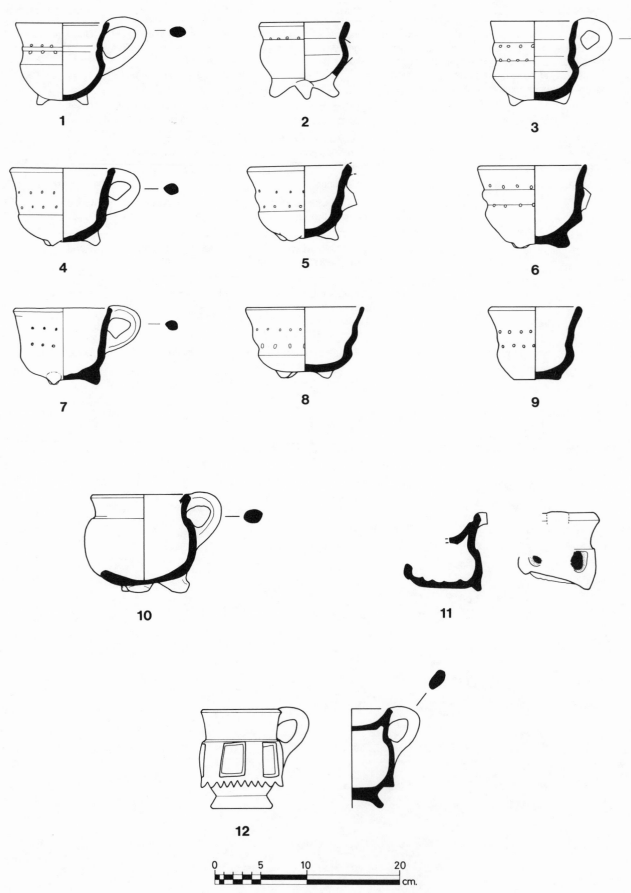

PLATE NO. 29

PL#:	Reg.#:	Date:	Prov:	Level:	Photo:	All:	Munsell References:
29:1						JAM	
29:2	264	4-4-38	Rm. 34	-1.30 m	541:3, 632:1, 1609:11	JAM	
29:3	340	4-7-38	Rm. 42	-1 m		JAM	
29:4	3060	4-27-39	Rm. 49A	-1 cm	651:16, 35	ASOR	
29:5	311	4-6-38	Rm. 41	-50 cm	1456:13	ASOR	
29:6	980	4-12-39	Rm. 60	-90 cm	612:6	ASOR	
29:7	3050	4-26-39	Rm. 49A	-1.40 m	589:5	ASOR	
29:8	5031	5-12-39	Rm. 49A		610:2	ASOR	
29:9	6097	3-18-40	Rm. 48		1456:14	ASOR	
29:10	233	4-2-38	Rm. 34	-50 cm	539:3, 541:4, 612:1, 1609:6	ASOR	
29:11	494	4-14-38	Rm. 35	-1 m	541:2	ASOR	
29:12	5087	3-11-40	Rm. 46		947, 1471:1,2, 1473:2	JAM	

PL#:	Description:	Body Comp. and Texture:
29:1	Perforated vessel, lip and base fragment; rounded base with knob feet; carinated; indented groove around upper body pierced with two rows of holes; elongated strap handle.	
29:2	Perforated vessel, lip and body fragment; carinated; one row of holes between rim and body; vestige of handle on upper body.	
29:3	Perforated vessel, lip and base fragment; double carination; pierced by a row of holes at each point of carination; stump legs; loop handle.	
29:4	Perforated vessel, lip and base fragment; three knob feet; two indented grooves around upper body pierced with a row of holes in each; strap handle.	Fine texture; some black and white inclusions.
29:5	Perforated vessel, lip and body fragment; three knob feet; two indented grooves around upper body pierced with a row of holes in each at distance of 10-15 mm; vestige of handle on upper body.	Fine textured calcareous clay; lightly tempered (10-20%); fine particle size (≤ 1.0 mm); inclusions: qtz/spar, lime, fine fibrous organic burnout, minor Fe_2O_3; very weak HCl reaction.
29:6	Perforated vessel, lip and base fragment; two thrown grooves with a row of punched perforations in each groove; carinated; vestige of handle on upper body; three knob feet.	Ferrugenous clay; heavily tempered (30%); coarse particles (≤ 3.0 mm); inclusions: qtz/spar, lime, Fe_2O_3, platey inclusions.
29:7	Perforated vessel, lip and base fragment; three knob feet; carinated; two indented grooves; punched perforations in each groove at distance of 10-15 mm; strap handle.	Fine textured calcareous clay; lightly tempered (10-20%); fine particle size (≤ 1.0 mm); inclusions: qtz/spar, lime, fine fibrous organic burnout, minor Fe_2O_3; very weak HCl reaction.
29:8	Perforated vessel, lip and base fragment; two thrown grooves with a row of punched perforations in each groove; carinated; three knob feet.	Ferrugenous clay; medium temper (20%); fine particle size (≤ 1.0 mm); inclusions: qtz/spar and lime, Fe_2O_3, platey inclusions.
29:9	Perforated vessel, lip and base fragment; flat base; two thrown grooves with a row of punched perforations in each groove; carinated.	Ferrugenous clay; heavily tempered (30%); coarse particle size (≤ 3.0 mm); inclusions: qtz/spar and lime, Fe_2O_3, platey inclusions.
29:10	Cup, lip and base fragment; knob feet; lip rolled inward; spherical body; strap handle.	Fine textured ferrugenous clay; medium temper (20-30%); angular inclusions.
29:11	Fenestrated vessel, lip and base fragment; double walled; body windows; broken handle fragment at rim.	Fine texture.
29:12	Fenestrated vessel; carinated; ring base; rectangular windows around body; denticulated fringe below windows.	

PL#:	Method of Mfg:	Surf. Decor:	Firing:	State of Pres:
29:1				
29:2				
29:3				
29:4	Thrown with added feet; two rows of holes pierced from exterior.		Mostly reduction with some oxidation at end of firing as shown in lighter color of exterior surface.	Accretion on interior.
29:5	Thrown; fine circumferential marks <1.0 mm apart and deeper impressions 7-10 mm apart; pulled handle joined at lip and in lower of 2 grooves; base hand-worked.	Two indented circumferential grooves placed one above and one below the handle.		Exterior base worn.
29:6	Thrown.		Reduced grey body with brown surfaces; (MOHS 3-3➤).	Good.
29:7	Thrown; fine circumferential marks 1.0 mm apart and deeper impressions 7-10 mm apart; pulled handle joined at lip and in lower of 2 grooves; base hand-worked.	Two indented circumferential grooves placed one above and one below the handle; each groove has punched perforations.	Surfaces and interior light yellowish brown; medium degree of vitrification; (MOHS 4); no defects.	Exterior base worn.
29:8	Thrown; not trimmed.		(MOHS 3-3➤).	Good.
29:9	Thrown.		(MOHS 3-3➤).	Good, interior accretions.
29:10	Thrown.		Oxidized inner body with surface layer reduction.	Surfaces worn.
29:11	Thrown.	None.	Oxidation.	Broken.
29:12				

PLATE NO. 30

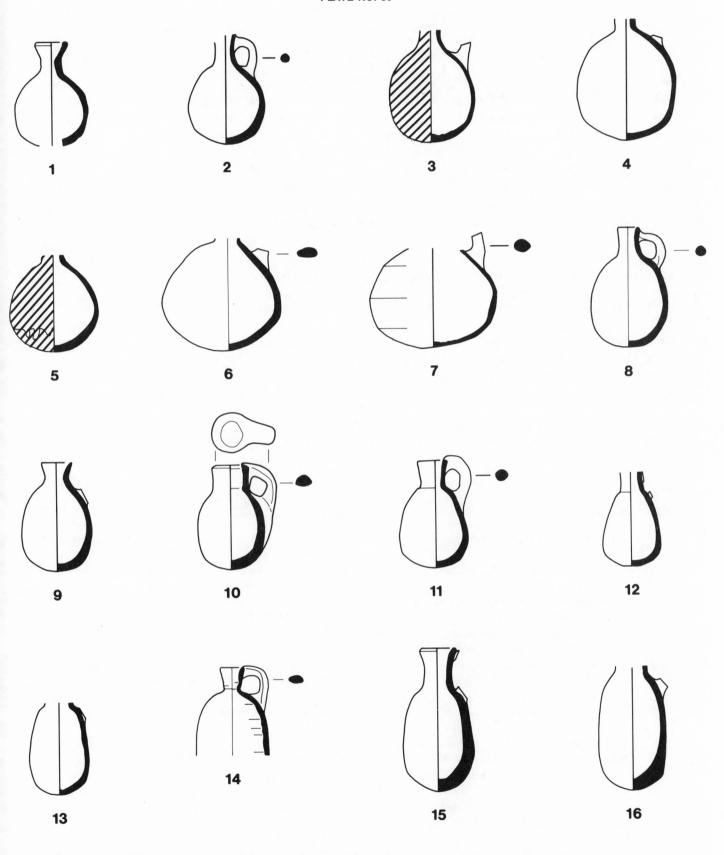

PLATE NO. 30

PL#:	Reg.#:	Date:	Prov:	Level:	Photo:	All:	Munsell References:
30:1	118	3-28-38	O:11	-1 m	518:4, 613:2, 1616:2	ASOR	
30:2	3038	4-26-39	Rm. 49B		615:5	ASOR	ext. 5 YR 6/4, sec. 5 YR 6/4
30:3	6023	3-13-40	Rm. 48		1450:11	ASOR	ext. 5 YR 6/4, sec. 5 YR 7/4
30:4	514	4-14-38	Rm. 25	-2 m	535:5, 640:6	ASOR	ext. 2.5 Y 8/2, sec. 2.5 Y 7/2
30:5	3087	4-29-39	Rm. 60	Surface	615:8	ASOR	ext. 5 YR 6/4, sec. 5 YR 6/3
30:6	2064	4-23-39	Rm. 50		617:3	ASOR	ext. 5 YR 5/3, sec. 2.5 YR 5/6
30:7	9052	4-6-40	Rm. 49		1454:16	ASOR	ext. 2.5 Y 6/2, sec. 10 YR 7/2
30:8	140	3-29-38	Rm. 19	-2 m	525:1, 614:3	ASOR	
30:9	5089A	3-11-40	Rm. 46		1450:1	ASOR	ext. 2.5 YR 6/6, sec. 5 YR 5/1
30:10	342	4-7-38	Rm. 39	-55 cm	518:1, 622:2	ASOR	ext. 7.5 YR 5/2, sec. 5 YR 4/1
30:11	392	4-9-38	Rm. 17A	-80 cm	518:5, 615:2	ASOR	ext. 2.5 Y 7/2, sec. 2.5 Y 7/2
30:12	6007	3-12-40	Rm. 48	-30 cm	1450:3	ASOR	
30:13	2041	4-22-39	Rm. 34	-1.70 m	615:1	ASOR	ext. 5 YR 6/3, sec. 5 YR 6/3
30:14	802	4-20-38	Rm. 28	-1.10 m	1450:13	ASOR	ext. 5 YR 6/3, int. 5 YR 6/1, sec. 5 YR 5/1
30:15	144	3-29-38	Rm. 21	-75 cm	518:6, 616:2, 1609:10	ASOR	ext. 2.5 YR 5/6, sec. 5 YR 5/3
30:16	260	4-4-38	Rm. 28	-2 m	518:2, 614:2, 1609:7	ASOR	ext. 5 YR 6/6, sec. 5 YR 4/2

PL#:	Description:	Body Comp. and Texture:
30:1	Juglet, lip and body fragment; ovoid shape.	Ferrugenous clay; particle size < 3.0 mm; inclusions: qtz/spar/lime, equiaxed organic burnout, very minor Fe_2O_3.
30:2	Juglet, lip, handle and body fragment; ovoid shape.	Ferrugenous clay; particle size <3.0 mm; inclusions: qtz/spar/lime, equiaxed organic burnout, very minor Fe_2O_3.
30:3	Juglet; ovoid shape; broken handle fragment on upper body; thin walled; burnished.	Ferrugenous clay; fine particle size (< 0.5 mm); inclusions: qtz/spar/lime, Fe_2O_3, Fe_3O_4.
30:4	Juglet, body and base fragment; ovoid shape; lip missing; vestige of handle on upper body.	
30:5	Juglet, lip missing; thin-walled; burnished.	Ferrugenous clay; vol. fraction of inclusions < 20%; fine particle size (< 0.5 mm); inclusions: qtz/spar/lime, Fe_2O_3, Fe_3O_4.
30:6	Juglet; spherical shape; carinated body; neck and rim missing; vestige of handle on upper body; rounded base.	Ferrugenous clay; particle size < 2.0 mm; inclusions: qtz/spar/lime, Fe_2O_3, Fe_3O_4, equiaxed burned out organic particles.
30:7	Juglet; spherical shape; neck and rim missing; broken handle fragment on upper body; rounded base.	Ferrugenous clay; particle size < 2.0 mm; inclusions: qtz/spar/lime, Fe_2O_3, Fe_3O_4, equiaxed burned out organic particles.
30:8	Juglet, much of rim missing; ovoid shape; flattened base; shoulder to rim handle.	White, brown and grey inclusions.
30:9	Juglet; part of neck and all of rim missing; elongated ovoid shape; vestige of handle on shoulder; rounded base.	Ferrugenous clay; particle size < 3.0 mm.
30:10	Juglet, complete; ovoid shape; shoulder to rim handle; dark grey; thick walls; rounded base.	Ferrugenous clay; particle size < 2.0 mm; inclusions: qtz/spar/lime, Fe_2O_3, Fe_3O_4, equiaxed burned out organic particles.

30:11	Juglet, complete; ovoid shape; rounded base; shoulder to rim handle; rim chipped, restored; narrow section at shoulder missing.	Calcareous clay; particle size < 2.0 mm; inclusions: qtz/spar/lime.
30:12	Juglet; elongated ovoid shape; lip and handle missing; rounded base.	Ferrugenous clay; particle size < 3.0 mm; inclusions: qtz/spar/lime, equiaxed organic burnout; very minor Fe_2O_3.
30:13	Juglet; elongated ovoid shape; carinated at shoulder; rounded base; neck and lip missing; vestige of handle on upper body.	Ferrugenous clay; particle size < 3 mm; inclusions: qtz/spar/lime, equiaxed organic burnout, very minor Fe_2O_3.
30:14	Juglet, lip and body fragment, handle from shoulder to rim, restored.	Ferrugenous clay; particle size < 2.0 mm; inclusions: qtz/spar/ lime, Fe_2O_3, Fe_3O_4, equiaxed burned out organic particles.
30:15	Juglet; elongated ovoid shape; carinated at shoulder; rounded base; vestige of handle at shoulder; neck and rim restored.	Ferrugenous clay; particle size < 3.0 mm; inclusions: qtz/spar/lime, equiaxed organic burnout, very minor Fe_2O_3.
30:16	Juglet; elongated ovoid shape; rounded base; vestige of handle at shoulder; lip missing.	Ferrugenous clay; particle size < 3.0 mm; inclusions: qtz/spar/lime, equiaxed organic burnout, very minor Fe_2O_3.

PL#:	Method of Mfg:	Surf. Decor:	Firing:	State of Pres:
30:1	Thrown; rounded base.		Oxidized red surface over light grey body; (MOHS 3-3➤); soft body.	Poor, pitting and surface wear.
30:2	Thrown; rounded base.		Oxidized red surface over light grey body; (MOHS 3-3➤); soft body.	Poor, pitting and surface wear.
30:3	Thrown; heavy throwing marks on interior.	Surface slipped and burnished.	Reduced grey body with reddish brown exterior surface layer.	Good.
30:4	Thrown.	None.	Medium oxidation.	Good.
30:5	Thrown; heavy throwing marks on interior.	Surface slipped and burnished; upper surface coated with red iron wash.	Reduced grey body with reddish brown exterior surface layer.	Good.
30:6	Thrown.		Reduced grey body with reddish brown surface layers.	Pitted and worn.
30:7	Thrown.		Reduced grey body with reddish brown surface layers.	Good.
30:8	Thrown; rolled coil handle.	None.	Medium, nearly neutral.	Good.
30:9	Thrown.		Oxidized surfaces; grey reduced body.	Poor, pitting and surface wear.
30:10	Thrown.		Reduced grey body with reddish brown surface layers.	
30:11	Thrown.		Oxidized tan surfaces and slightly more reduced greyish tan body.	Good but pitted.
30:12	Thrown.		Oxidized red surface over light grey body; (MOHS 3-3➤); soft body.	Poor, pitting and surface wear.
30:13	Thrown.		Oxidized red surface over light grey body; (MOHS 3-3➤); soft body.	Poor, pitting and surface wear.
30:14	Thrown.		Reduced grey body with reddish brown surface layers.	Pitted and worn.
30:15	Thrown.		Oxidized red surface over light grey body; (MOHS 3-3➤); soft body.	Poor, pitting and surface wear.
30:16	Thrown.		Oxidized red surface over dark grey body; (MOHS 3-3➤).	Poor, pitting and surface wear.

PLATE NO. 31

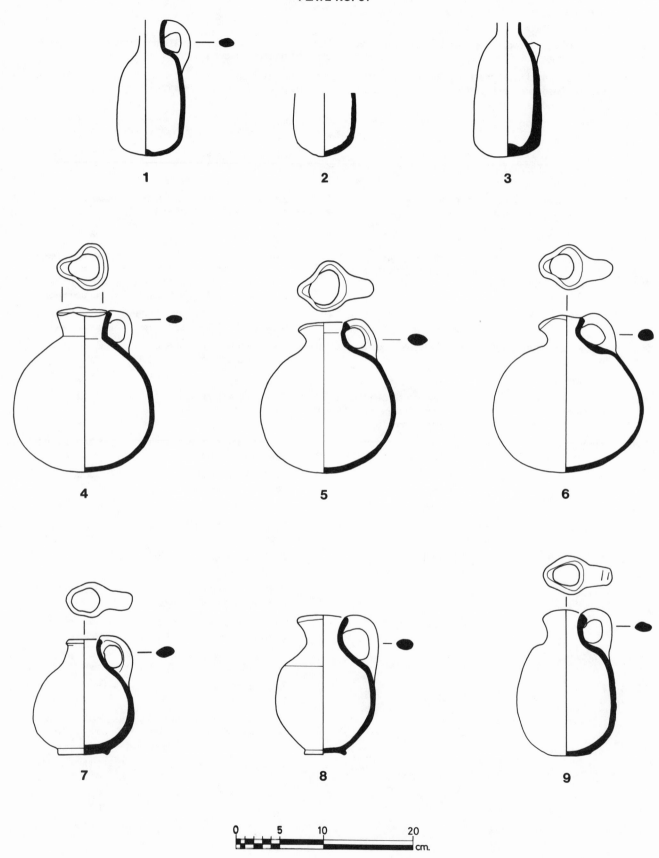

PLATE NO. 31

PL#:	Reg.#:	Date:	Prov:	Level:	Photo:	All:	Munsell References:
31:1	1075	4-19-39	Rm. 40	-1.110 m	615:3	JAM	
31:2	125	3-28-38	0:11	-75 cm	635:8, 1616:1	ASOR	ext. 5 YR 6/4, sec. 5 YR 6/4
31:3	5089 B	3-11-40	Rm. 51			ASOR	ext. 5 YR 6/4, sec. 5 YR 6/4
31:4	375	4-9-38	Rm. 49	-50 cm	520:1, 1625:2	JAM	
31:5	169	3-30-38	P:12	-75 cm	520:2, 618:3, 1628:1	JAM	ext. 10 R 5/2, sec. 10 R 4/1
31:6	170	3-30-38	P:12	-75 cm	520:6, 1628:2	ASOR	ext. 5 YR 5/3, sec. 5 YR 5/3
31:7	104	3-27-38	O:9	-50 cm	521:4, 1628:7	ASOR	
31:8	524	4-14-38	Rm. 35A	-60 cm	521:3	JAM	
31:9	119	3-28-38	Rm. 18	-1.50 m	521:2, 1628:3	ASOR	ext. 5 YR 6/6, sec. 2.5 YR 5/8

PL#:	Description:	Body Comp. and Texture:
31:1	Juglet; rectangular; rounded base; shoulder to rim handle; portion of rim missing.	
31:2	Juglet, base fragment; slightly pointed base.	Fine with a few white inclusions.
31:3	Juglet; elongated ovoid shape; rounded base; vestige of handle on shoulder; lip missing.	Ferrugenous clay; particle size < 3.0 mm; inclusions: qtz/spar/lime, equiaxed organic burnout, very minor Fe_2O_3.
31:4	Jug; pinched, pitcher-shaped lip; spherical body; rounded base; strap handle.	
31:5	Jug; pinched, pitcher-shaped lip; spherical body; rounded base; strap handle.	
31:6	Jug; pinched, pitcher-shaped lip; spherical body; rounded base; shoulder to rim handle; small sections of body missing.	Ferrugenous clay; particle size < 2.0 mm; inclusions: qtz/spar/lime, Fe_2O_3, Fe_3O_4, equiaxed burned out organic particles.
31:7	Jug; oval, pitcher-shaped lip; spherical body; ring base.	Ferrugenous clay; particle size < 2.0 mm; inclusions: qtz/spar/lime, Fe_2O_3, Fe_3O_4, equiaxed burned out organic particles.
31:8	Jug; flared rim; carinated; spherical body; ring base; shoulder to rim handle.	
31:9	Jug; elongated ovoid shape; pinched, pitcher-shaped lip; carinated at lower body; flat base; strap handle; restored, sections of body missing.	Ferrugenous clay; particle size < 3.0 mm.

PL#:	Method of Mfg:	Surf. Decor:	Firing:	State of Pres:
31:1				
31:2	Thrown; exterior trimmed.	Exterior partly burnished.	Medium firing; oxidation.	Good.
31:3	Thrown; rounded base.		Oxidized red surface over light grey body; soft body; (MOHS 3-3→).	Poor, pitting and surface wear.
31:4				
31:5				
31:6	Thrown; rounded base.		Reduced grey body with reddish brown surface layers.	
31:7	Thrown.		Reduced grey body with reddish brown surface layers.	
31:8				
31:9	Thrown.		Oxidized surfaces; oxidized red body; may have slip or paint layer not lime.	Poor, pitting and surface wear.

PLATE NO. 32

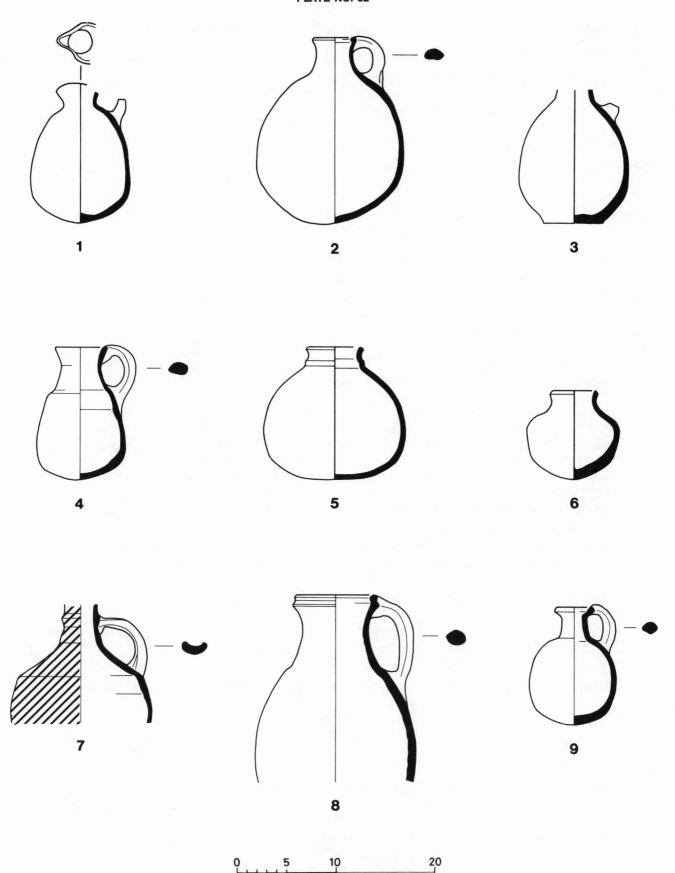

PLATE NO. 32

PL#:	Reg.#:	Date:	Prov:	Level:	Photo:	All:	Munsell References:
32:1	484	4-13-38	Rm. 38	-1.20 m	525:4, 615:9	ASOR	ext. 7.5 YR 6/4, sec. 2.5 YR 5/6
32:2	970	4-11-39	Rm. 49	-95 cm	617:1	ASOR	ext. 2.5 Y 7/2, int. 7.5 YR 5/2, sec. 10 R 6/1
32:3	116	3-28-38	O:11	-30 cm	521:5, 1628:4	ASOR	ext. 2.5 Y 7/2, sec. 7.5 YR 5/2
32:4	202	3-31-38	O:12	-120 cm	525:3, 614:7	ASOR	ext. 2.5 YR 6/6, sec. 2.5 YR 5/6
32:5	416	4-10-38	Rm. 37	-70 cm	522:1, 617:5, 1623:1	JAM	
32:6	327	4-6-38	Rm. 40	-1 m	535:4, 643:2, 1453:1	ASOR	ext. 7.5 YR 6/4, sec. 7.5 YR 6/4
32:7	3015	4-25-39	Rm. 60	-1 m	620:3	ASOR	
32:8	546	4-15-38	Rm. 35A	-2 m	678:1	ASOR	
32:9	6073	3-17-40	Rm. 32		1436:13	JAM	

PL#:	Description:	Body Comp. and Texture:
32:1	Juglet; pinched, pitcher-shaped lip; carinated at lower body; rounded base; broken handle at shoulder; restored; section of rim missing.	Medium coarse texture; white, red and black inclusions.
32:2	Jug; spherical body; rounded base; shoulder to rim handle; restored, large section of body and rim missing.	Ferrugenous clay; particle size < 2.0 mm; inclusions: qtz/spar/lime, Fe_2O_3, Fe_3O_4, equiaxed organic burnout.
32:3	Jug; ovoid shape; carinated at lower body; vestige of handle at shoulder; neck and rim missing.	Medium coarse texture; inclusions: transluscent and opaque, white, black and red grits.
32:4	Juglet; elongated ovoid shape; rounded base; carination on upper shoulder.	Ferrugenous clay; particle size < 3.0 mm
32:5	Small jar; spherical body flattened at base; grooved at neck.	
32:6	Small jar, complete; carinated; rounded base.	
32:7	Decanter, handle and body fragment; narrow neck, ridged.	Ferrugenous clay; particle size < 1%; inclusions: qtz/spar/lime.
32:8	Jug, lip and body fragment; carinated; handle from body to rim.	Medium texture; some white and red inclusions.
32:9	Juglet; spherical; rounded base; strap handle shoulder to rim.	

PL#:	Method of Mfg:	Surf. Decor:	Firing:	State of Pres:
32:1	Thrown.	None.	Oxidation, then reduction.	Good.
32:2	Thrown.		Reduced grey body with reddish brown surface layers.	Pitted and worn.
32:3	Thrown.	None.	Medium; partly oxidized and partly reduced.	Good.
32:4	Thrown.		Oxidized surfaces; oxidized red body.	Poor, pitting and surface wear.
32:5				
32:6	Thrown; bottom scraped.	None.	Medium; nearly neutral atmosphere.	Good.
32:7	Thrown.	Burnished.	Reduced grey body and surfaces; (MOHS 3-3 ➤).	Heavily worn and interior pitted.
32:8	Probably thrown.	None.	Medium; mostly oxidized.	Very worn.
32:9				

PLATE NO. 33

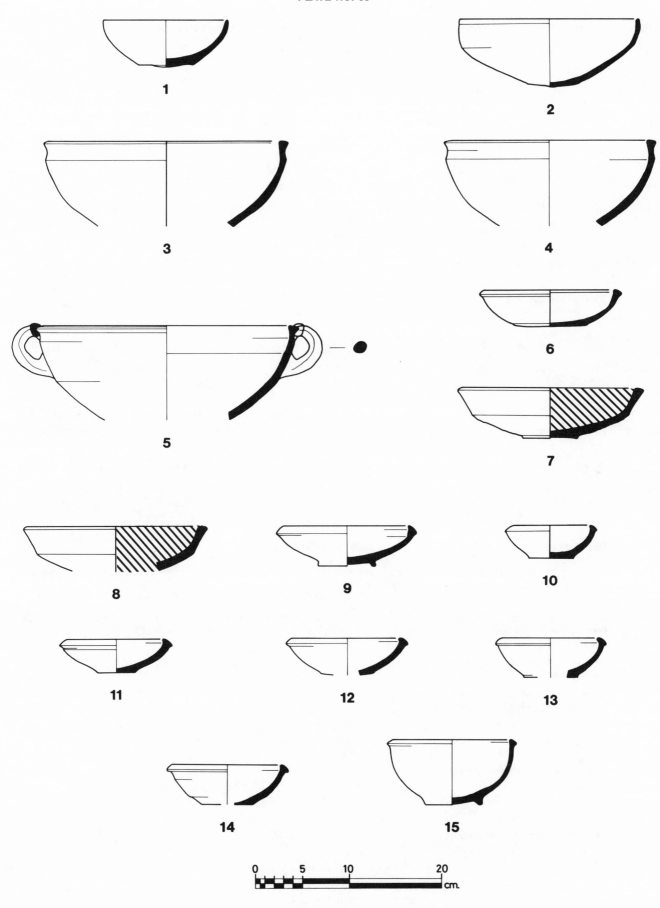

PLATE NO. 33

PL#:	Reg.#:	Date:	Prov:	Level:	Photo:	All:	Munsell References:
33:1	117	3-28-38	O:11	-1 m	528:2, 530:6, 621:7, 1463:10, 1627:3	ASOR	
33:2	295	4-4-38	M:12	-30 cm	523:6, 1451:9, 1613:2	ASOR	
33:3	10,078	4-13-40	Rm. 39		1462:15	JAM	
33:4						JAM	
33:5	160	3-29-38	P:11	-50 cm	550:2, 645:10, 1465:2, 1619:3	JAM	ext. 5 Y 8/2, int. 5 Y 8/2, sec. 5 Y 7/1
33:6	5024	5-12-39	110 C		593:30, 1461:22	JAM	
33:7	3048	4-26-39	Rm. 34	-2 m	624:2, 1463:1	ASOR	
33:8						JAM	
33:9	856	4-20-38	L:12	-1 m	1458:3	ASOR	ext. 7.5 YR 6/4, int. 5 YR 6/4, sec. 5 YR 6/1
33:10	141	3-29-38	Rm. 21	-70 cm	528:1, 530:7, 632:5	ASOR	ext. 10 YR 6/4, int. 10 YR 7/3
33:11	828	4-20-38	P:12		644:21	ASOR	ext. 7.5 YR 6/4, int. 7.5 YR 7/4, sec. 10 YR 6/2
33:12	722	4-18-38	Rm. 33		1458:2	ASOR	ext. 10 YR 4/2, int. 10 YR 7/2, sec. 7.5 YR 7/4
33:13						JAM	
33:14	9049	4-6-40	Rm. 46		1458:5	ASOR	ext. 10 YR 7/3, int. 7.5 YR 7/4, sec. 7.5 YR 8/2
33:15	189	3-31-38	Rm. 24A	-1.50 m	1458:15	ASOR	ext. 2.5 YR 6/6, int. 2.5 YR 6/6, sec. 2.5 YR 6/6

PL#:	Description:	Body Comp. and Texture:
33:1	Bowl, complete; simple rim; ring base; rounded walls.	Fine textured ferrugenous clay; medium temper (10-30%); fine and medium particle size; inclusions; (< 3.0 mm). inclusions: fibrous organic burnout (< 1.0 mm), qtz/spar
33:2	Bowl, complete; "X" marked on exterior near base; simple rim; flat base; restored, small section of body and rim missing.	Fine textured ferrugenous clay; lightly tempered (10%); fine particle size (1.0 mm); inclusions: qtz/spar, fibrous organic burnout.
33:3	Medium-size bowl, lip and body fragment; thickened rim; carinated just below rim.	
33:4	Medium-size bowl, lip and body fragment; thickened rim; carinated just below rim.	
33:5	Large bowl, lip and body fragment; flattened triangular rim; loop handle from shoulder to rim; knob at rim near handle.	Fine textured calcareous clay; heavily tempered (30-50%); fine particle size (≤1.0 mm); inclusions: qtz/spar, equiaxed organic burnout; weak HCl reaction.
33:6	Small bowl; triangular rim; disc base; slight body carination.	
33:7	Shallow bowl, lip and base fragment; flattened rim; flat base; carinated.	Fine texture; some white inclusions.
33:8	Medium-size bowl, lip and body fragment; shallow; carinated; slipped and burnished.	

33:9	Small bowl, lip and base fragment; ring base; triangular rim.	Fine textured ferrugenous clay; lightly tempered (10-20%); coarse particle size (≤3.0 mm); inclusions: qtz/spar, Fe_2O_3, Fe_3O_4, equiaxed organic burnout, weak HCl reaction.
33:10	Small bowl, intact; flattened, inverted rim; flat base.	Fine textured calcareous clay; lightly tempered (10-20%); fine particle size (≤1.0 mm); inclusions: qtz/spar, equiaxed organic burnout; weak HCl reaction.
33:11	Small bowl, lip and body fragment; flat base; flattened, inverted triangular rim; groove on exterior below rim.	Fine textured ferrugenous clay; lightly tempered (10-20%); fine particle size (≤1.0 mm); inclusions: qtz/spar, Fe_3O_4, Fe_2O_3, equiaxed organic burnout; weak HCl reaction.
33:12	Small bowl, lip and body fragment; flattened, inverted triangular rim; flat base.	Fine textured ferrugenous clay; lightly tempered (10-20%); fine particle size (≤1.0 mm); inclusions: qtz/spar, Fe_3O_4, Fe_2O_3, equiaxed organic burnout; weak HCl reaction.
33:13	Small bowl, lip and body fragment; flat base; inverted triangular rim.	Fine textured ferrugenous clay; lightly tempered (10-20%); fine particle size (≤1.0 mm); inclusions: qtz/spar, Fe_3O_4, Fe_2O_3, equiaxed organic burnout; weak HCl reaction.
33:14	Small bowl, lip and body fragment; flat base; inverted triangular rim.	Fine textured calcareous clay; lightly tempered (10-20%); fine particle size (≤1.0 mm); inclusions: qtz/spar, equiaxed organic burnout; weak HCl reaction.
33:15	Small bowl, lip and base fragment; flattened, triangular rim; ring base; restored.	Fine textured ferrugenous clay; lightly tempered (10-20%); fine particle size (≤1.0 mm); inclusions: Fe_3O_4, Fe_2O_3, equiaxed organic burnout; weak HCl reaction.

PL#:	Method of Mfg:	Surf. Decor:	Firing:	State of Pres:
33:1	Probably thrown.		Oxidized body and surface with thin reduced surface on interior of bowl.	Exterior spalling and heavily worn.
33:2	Thrown lip with probable handbuilt body; base trimmed and wiped flat.		Heavily oxidized surfaces.	Good.
33:3				
33:4				
33:5	Thrown; pulled handle and knob to right of handle.		Fired in oxidation; medium degree of vitrification; (MOHS 4-4→).	Good.
33:6				
33:7	Thrown; exterior trimmed to give solid, protruding base.	Red slip on interior; burnished probably on wheel.	Medium; oxidation.	Good.
33:8				
33:9	Thrown; wheel trimmed.		Grey reduced body with reddish brown surfaces.	Worn interior surface.
33:10	Thrown; base not trimmed.		Fired in oxidation; low degree of vitrification; (MOHS 3-3→).	Good.
33:11	Thrown; base trimmed flat by wheel.		Fired mainly in oxidation; (MOHS 4).	Good.
33:12	Thrown; base trimmed flat by wheel.		Fired in reduction; (MOHS 3→).	Good.
33:13	Thrown; base trimmed flat on wheel.		Fired in reduction; (MOHS 3).	Good.
33:14	Thrown; base trimmed flat.	Interior circumferential painted bands in brown.	Fired in oxidation; low degree of vitrification; (MOHS 3-3→).	Good.
33:15	Thrown; base ring trimmed when clay leather hard.		Fired in oxidation; (MOHS 3-3→).	Surfaces worn.

PLATE NO 34

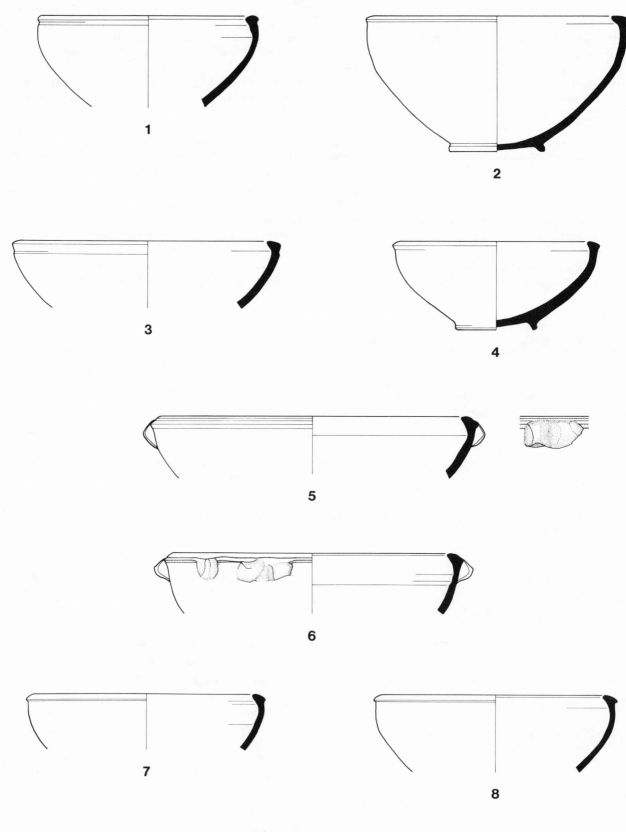

PLATE NO 34

PL#:	Reg.#:	Date:	Prov:	Level:	Photo:	All:	Munsell References:
34:1	5036						ext. 2.5 Y 8/2, int. 2.5 Y 8/2, sec. 2.5 Y 8/2
34:2	10,034	4-9-40	Rm. 125		1496:4	ASOR	ext. 5 Y 7/1, int. 5 Y 7/1, sec. 5 Y 7/1
34:3	296	4-4-38	Rm. 28	-1 m	590:15	ASOR	ext. 5 YR 6/6, int. 5 YR 7/4, sec. 5 YR 7/3
34:4	5035	5-12-39	Rm. 33	-2 m	642:7	ASOR	ext. 5 YR 6/3, int. 5 YR 6/2, sec. 5 YR 6/2
34:5	601	4-18-38	Rm. 35A		563:1	ASOR	
34:6	708	4-18-38	Rm. 29	-1 m	562:5	ASOR	ext. 10 YR 8/3, int. 10 YR 8/3, sec. 10 YR 7/4
34:7	1020	4-15-39	Rm. 60		625:2	ASOR	ext. 10 YR 7/3, int. 10 YR 7/4, sec. 5 YR 6/6
34:8	9045	4-6-40	Rm. 46		1482:7	ASOR	ext. 7.5 YR 7/4, int. 5 YR 6/4, sec. 5 YR 6/4

PL#:	Description:	Body Comp. and Texture:
34:1	Medium-size bowl, lip and body fragment; inverted rim.	Fine textured calcareous clay; lightly tempered (10-20%); fine particle size ($\leq$1.0 mm); inclusions: qtz/spar, equiaxed organic burnout; very weak HCl reaction.
34:2	Large bowl, lip and body fragment; flattened, inverted triangular rim; ring base; restored and later rebroken.	Fine textured calcareous clay; lightly tempered (10-20%); fine particle size ($\leq$1.0 mm); inclusions: qtz/spar, equiaxed organic burnout; weak HCl reaction.
34:3	Medium-size bowl, lip and body fragment; inverted, triangular rim.	Fine textured ferrugenous clay; lightly tempered (10-20%); coarse particle size ($\leq$ 3.0 mm); inclusions: qtz/spar, Fe_3O_4, Fe_2O_3, equiaxed oraganic burnout; weak HCl reaction.
34:4	Medium-size bowl, lip and base fragment; flattened, inverted, triangular rim; ring base.	Fine textured ferrugenous clay; lightly tempered (10-20%); fine particle size ($\leq$1.0 mm); inclusions: qtz/spar, Fe_3O_4, Fe_2O_3, equiaxed organic burnout; weak HCl reaction.
34:5	Large bowl, lip and body fragments; double knobbed handle at lip; another knob on one sherd at the lip to the left of the handle; flattened, inverted triangular rim.	Fine textured calcareous clay; medium tempered (20-30%); fine particle size ($\leq$1.0 mm); inclusions: qtz/spar, equiaxed organic burnout; very weak HCl reaction.
34:6	Large bowl, lip and body fragment; flattened, inverted triangular rim; knobs at rim; three-knobbed handle.	Fine textured calcareous clay; lightly tempered (10-20%); fine particle size ($\leq$1.0 mm); inclusions: qtz/spar, equiaxed organic burnout; weak HCl reaction.
34:7	Medium-size bowl, lip and body fragment; flattened, inverted triangular rim.	Fine textured ferrugenous clay; lightly tempered (10-20%); coarse particle size ($\leq$3.0 mm); inclusions: qtz/spar, Fe_3O_4, Fe_2O_3, equiaxed organic burnout; weak HCl reaction.
34:8	Medium-size bowl, lip and body fragment; flattened, inverted triangular rim; restored.	Fine textured ferrugenous clay; lightly tempered (10-20%); coarse particle size ($\leq$3.0 mm); inclusions: qtz/spar, Fe_3O_4, Fe_2O_3, equiaxed organic burnout; weak HCl reaction.

PL#:	Method of Mfg:	Surf. Decor:	Firing:	State of Pres:
34:1	Thrown.		Fired in oxidation; low degree of vitrification; (MOHS 3-3→).	Good.
34:2	Thrown; base trimmed on wheel and surface wiped.		Fired in oxidation; low degree of vitrification; (MOHS 3-3→).	Accretions on surfaces.
34:3	Thrown.		Fired mostly in oxidation; (MOHS 3→4).	Good.
34:4	Thrown; base rim trimmed when clay leather hard.		Fired in reduction; (MOHS 4-4→).	Surface pitted and worn on interior.
34:5	Thrown.	Holes drilled near lip.	Fired in oxidation; low degree of vitrification; (MOHS 3-3→).	Good.
34:6	Thrown.	Hole drilled near lip.	Fired in oxidation; low degree of vitrification; (MOHS 4).	Good.
34:7	Thrown.	White slipped.	Fired mostly in oxidation; (MOHS 3→4).	Good.
34:8	Thrown.		Fired mostly in oxidation; (MOHS 3→4).	Good.

PLATE NO. 35

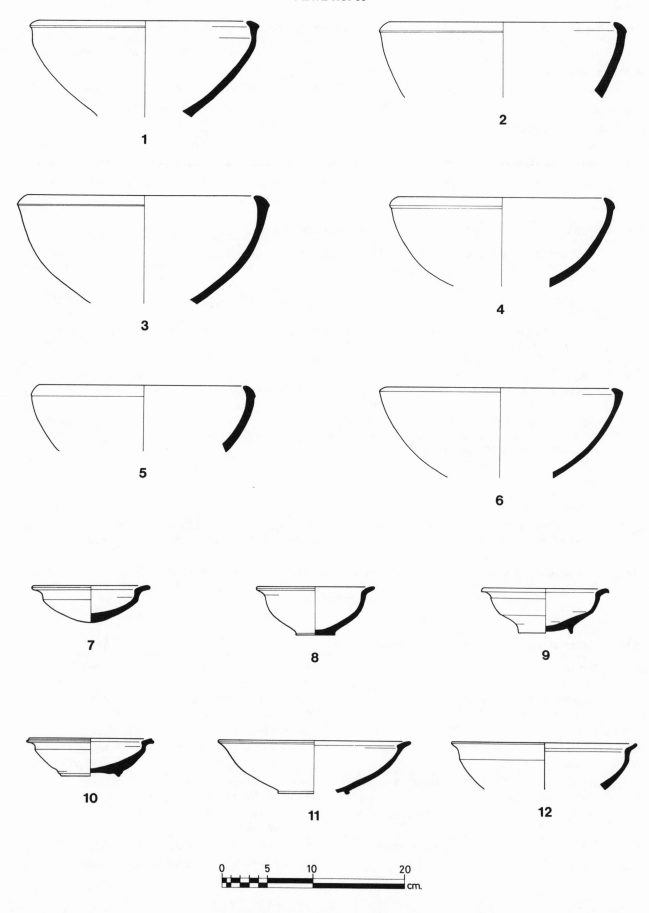

PLATE NO. 35

PL#:	Reg.#:	Date:	Prov:	Level:	Photo:	All:	Munsell References:
35:1	5037A	5-12-39	Rm. 33	-2 m	590:19	ASOR	ext. 7.5 YR 7/4, int. 7.5 YR 7/4, sec. 5 YR 6/4
35:2			Rm. 39			JAM	ext. 2.5 Y 7/2, int. 2.5 Y 8/2, sec. 5 YR 6/3
35:3	911	6-6-38	P:11			ASOR	ext. 2.5 YR 5/6, int. 2.5 YR 5/6, sec. 2.5 YR 5/6
35:4	575	4-16-38	O:9		644:7	ASOR	ext. 10 R 5/6, int. 2.5 YR 6/6, sec. 2.5 YR 6/4
35:5	92	3-17-38		Surface		ASOR	
35:6	6054	3-16-40	Rm. 55		1479:1, 1482:8	ASOR	ext. 10 R 5/6, int. 10 R 5/6
35:7	704	4-18-38	Rm. 11			ASOR	ext. 7.5 YR 7/4, int. 10 YR 8/3, sec. 5 YR 6/3
35:8	814	4-20-38	R:12	-30 cm	590:16	ASOR	ext. 5 Y 8/3, int. 5 Y 8/3, sec. 5 Y 8/2
35:9	188	3-31-38	Rm. 18	-1 m	1476:5, 1477:5	ASOR	ext. 5 YR 5/2, int. 5 YR 6/6, sec. 5 YR 6/1
35:10	849	4-20-38	N:12	-50 cm	532:6, 553:5, 590:12, 1456:1	ASOR	ext. 7.5 YR 6/4, int. 7.5 YR 6/4, sec. 7.5 YR 6/2
35:11				Debris			ext. 2.5 YR 5/6, int. 2.5 YR 6/6, sec. 2.5 YR 6/6
35:12	297	4-4-38	Rm. 28	-1 m	644:5, 20	ASOR	ext. 5 YR 6/6, int. 5 YR 6/6, sec. 5 YR 5/1

PL#:	Description:	Body Comp. and Texture:
35:1	Medium-size bowl, lip and body fragment; flattened, inverted triangular rim; carinated; restored.	Fine textured ferrugenous clay; lightly tempered (10-20%); coarse particle size ($\leq$3.0 mm); inclusions: qtz/spar, Fe_3O_4, Fe_2O_3, equiaxed organic burnout; weak HCl reaction.
35:2	Large bowl, lip and body fragment; inverted triangular rim.	
35:3	Large bowl, lip and body fragment; flattened, inverted triangular rim; restored.	Ferrugenous clay; heavily tempered; inclusions: unknown platey particles and fibrous organic burnout.
35:4	Medium-size bowl, lip and body fragment; flattened, inverted triangular rim; hole drilled in lower body.	Fine textured ferrugenous clay; lightly tempered (10-20%); coarse particle size ($\leq$3.0 mm); inclusions: qtz/spar, Fe_3O_4, Fe_2O_3, equiaxed organic burnout; weak HCl reaction.
35:5	Medium-size bowl, lip and body fragment; inverted triangular rim.	Fine textured ferrugenous clay; lightly tempered (10-20%); coarse particle size ($\leq$3.0 mm); inclusions: qtz/spar, Fe_3O_4, Fe_2O_3, equiaxed organic burnout; weak HCl reaction.
35:6	Large bowl, lip and body fragments; holes drilled along edges; inverted triangular rim; restored and rebroken.	Ferrugenous clay; heavily tempered; inclusions: unknown platey particles and fibrous burnout.
35:7	Small bowl, lip and body fragment; shallow; flared rim; carinated.	Fine textured ferrugenous clay; lightly tempered (10-20%); medium size particles (<2.0 mm); inclusions: qtz/spar/lime, Fe_2O_3, fibrous organic burnout.
35:8	Small bowl, lip and base fragment; flared rim; disc base.	Fine textured calcareous clay; lightly tempered (10-20%); fine particle size ($\leq$1.0 mm); inclusions: qtz/spar, equiaxed organic burnout; weak HCl reaction.
35:9	Small bowl, lip and base fragment; flared rim; ring base.	Fine textured ferrugenous clay; lightly tempered (10-20%); fine particle size ($\leq$1.0 mm); inclusions: qtz/spar, Fe_3O_4, Fe_2O_3, equiaxed organic burnout; weak HCl reaction.
35:10	Small bowl, lip and base fragment; flared rim; carinated; ring base.	Medium texture; white and a few red and black inclusions; some organic burnout.
35:11	Small bowl; flared rim, ring base.	Fine textured calcareous clay; lightly tempered (10-20%); fine particle size; inclusions: qtz/spar, equiaxed organic burnout; weak HCl reaction.
35:12	Small bowl, lip and body fragment; shallow; flared rim; carinated.	Fine textured ferrugenous clay; lightly tempered (10-20%); fine particle size ($\leq$1.0 mm); inclusions: qtz/spar, Fe_3O_4, Fe_2O_3, equiaxed organic burnout; weak HCl reaction.

PL#:	Method of Mfg:	Surf. Decor:	Firing:	State of Pres:
35:1	Thrown.		Fired mostly in oxidation; (MOHS 3→4).	Good.
35:2				
35:3	Handbuilt with fast-turned lip; diagonal marks from handbuilding.		Mixed oxidation state; splotching areas of grey and red; (MOHS 3).	
35:4	Thrown.		Fired mostly in oxidation; (MOHS 3→4).	Poor, exterior spalling.
35:5	Thrown.		Fired mostly in oxidation; (MOHS 3→4).	Good.
35:6	Probably lip thrown; poor particle alignment.		Grey interior reduced with red surface layers on interior and exterior; (MOHS 3).	Worn exterior surface.
35:7	Thrown; not trimmed.		Reduced grey body; tan exterior surfaces.	Good.
35:8	Thrown; raised base formed by turning wheel.		Carbonaceous matter; light grey and tan surface.	Worn surfaces and accretions.
35:9	Thrown and trimmed.		Fired in reduction; grey body and surfaces.	Worn surfaces.
35:10	Thrown; exterior trimmed.	Red and brown bands below rim on interior.	Mixed atmosphere; mostly reduced; medium firing.	Good.
35:11	Thrown.			Worn surfaces and accretions.
35:12	Thrown.		Fired in reduction; grey body and surfaces.	Worn surfaces.

PLATE NO. 36

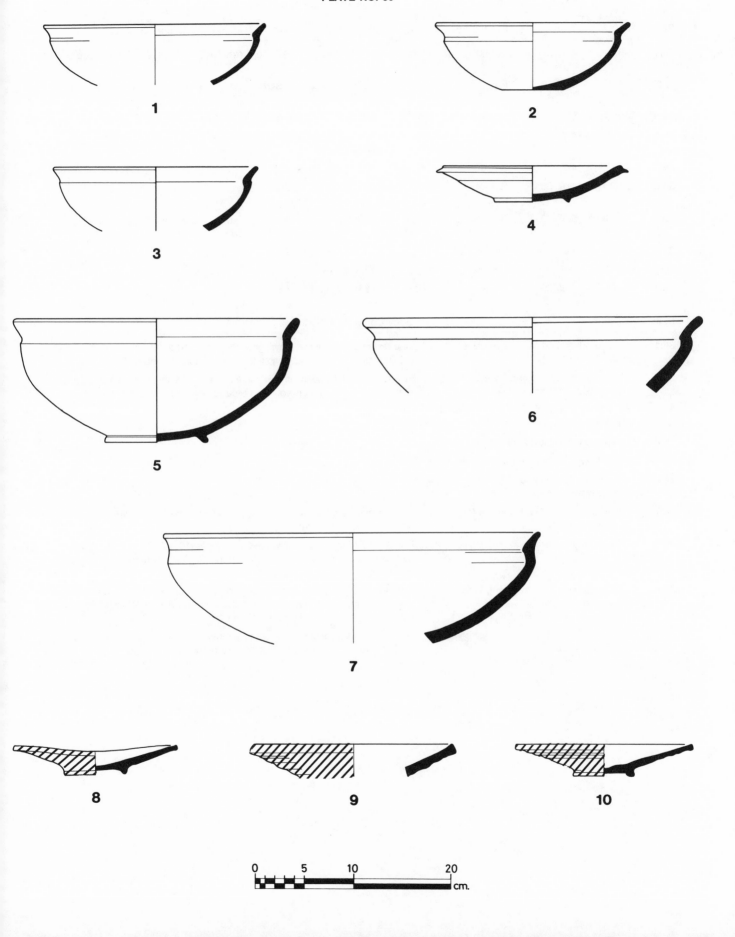

PLATE NO. 36

PL#:	Reg.#:	Date:	Prov:	Level:	Photo:	All:	Munsell References:
36:1	988	4-12-39	Rm 60	-50 cm	593:1, 1465:4	ASOR	ext. 10 YR 6/2, int. 2.5 YR 5/6, sec. 7.5 YR 6/2
36:2	153	3-29-38	Rm. 21	-40 cm	523:3	ASOR	ext. 2.5 Y 8/2, int. 2.5 Y 8/2, sec. 2.5 Y 8/2
36:3	4020	5-1-39	Rm. 40	-1 m	595:19	JAM	
36:4	258	4-4-38	Rm. 28	-2 m	549:7, 552:10, 645:1, 1462:7	JAM	
36:5	2066	4-23-39	Rm. 40	-1 m	601:16, 625:3	JAM	
36:6	716	4-18-38	Rm. 34; L:12	-1 m	567:10	JAM	
36:7	5038	5-12-39	Rm. 33	-2 m	642:3	ASOR	ext. 5 YR 6/3, int. 5 YR 6/4, sec. 2.5 YR 6/6
36:8	8015	3-26-40	Rm. 40		1476:1, 1477:1	ASOR	
36:9	10,031	4-9-40	Rm. 29		1476:2, 1477:2	ASOR	
36:10	3024	4-25-39	Rm. 49	-1.50 m	624:5, 1463:8	ASOR	

PL#:	Description:	Body Comp. and Texture:
36:1	Small bowl, lip and body fragment; everted triangular rim.	Fine textured ferrugenous clay; lightly tempered (10-20%); medium size particles (<2.0 mm); inclusions: qtz/spar/lime, Fe_2O_3, fibrous organic burnout.
36:2	Medium-size bowl, lip and base fragment; carinated; everted rim; flat base.	Fine textured calcareous clay; lightly tempered (10-20%); fine particle size (≤1.0 mm); inclusions: qtz/spar, equiaxed organic burnout; weak HCl reaction.
36:3	Medium-size bowl, lip and body fragment; carinated; everted rim.	
36:4	Small bowl; shallow; flared rim; ring base.	
36:5	Large bowl; carinated; everted rim; ring base.	
36:6	Large bowl, lip and body fragment; carinated; everted rim.	
36:7	Large bowl, lip and body fragment; everted triangular rim.	Ferrugenous clay; heavily tempered; coarse inclusions: unknown platey particles and fibrous organic burnout.
36:8	Saucer, lip and base fragment; ring base.	Fine textured ferrugenous clay; medium temper (10-30%); fine and medium particle size; inclusions: qtz/spar (<3.0 mm), Fe_2O_3, fibrous organic burnout (<1.0 mm).
36:9	Saucer, lip and body fragment; horizontal ridges around body.	Fine textured ferrugenous clay; heavily tempered (≤30%); medium particle size (1.0 - 2.0 mm, with some 4.0 mm); inclusions: qtz/spar, Fe_3O_4 and Fe_2O_3, equiaxed organic burnout; weak HCl reaction.
36:10	Saucer, lip and base fragment; flattened rim; ring base; restored.	Fine textured ferrugenous clay; lightly tempered (10%); fine particle size (1.0 mm); inclusions: qtz/spar, fibrous organic burnout.

PL#:	Method of Mfg:	Surf. Decor:	Firing:	State of Pres:
36:1	Thrown.	Wheel burnished interior and brown banded rim.	Grey reduced body with grey exterior and oxidized interior.	Good.
36:2	Thrown; base flattened by wheel turning.		Fired in oxidation; low degree of vitrification; (MOHS 3-3➤).	Good.
36:3				
36:4				
36:5				
36:6				
36:7	Probably handbuilt with thrown lip; poor particle alignment.	Residual traces of black painted design on lip.	Fired in oxidation; red body with grey reduced surfaces; (MOHS 3).	Worn surfaces.
36:8	Thrown.		Reduction firing; grey core with red surface layers; (MOHS 3-3➤).	Surfaces worn.
36:9	Thrown; rim thickened.	Exterior surface partly burnished.	Fired in mixed oxidation state; (MOHS 3-4).	Good.
36:10	Thrown; ridges on exterior beneath lip; base ring trimmed.	Painted brown slip band at rim.	Oxidation; incomplete oxidation of grey core; (MOHS 3-3➤).	Good.

PLATE NO. 37

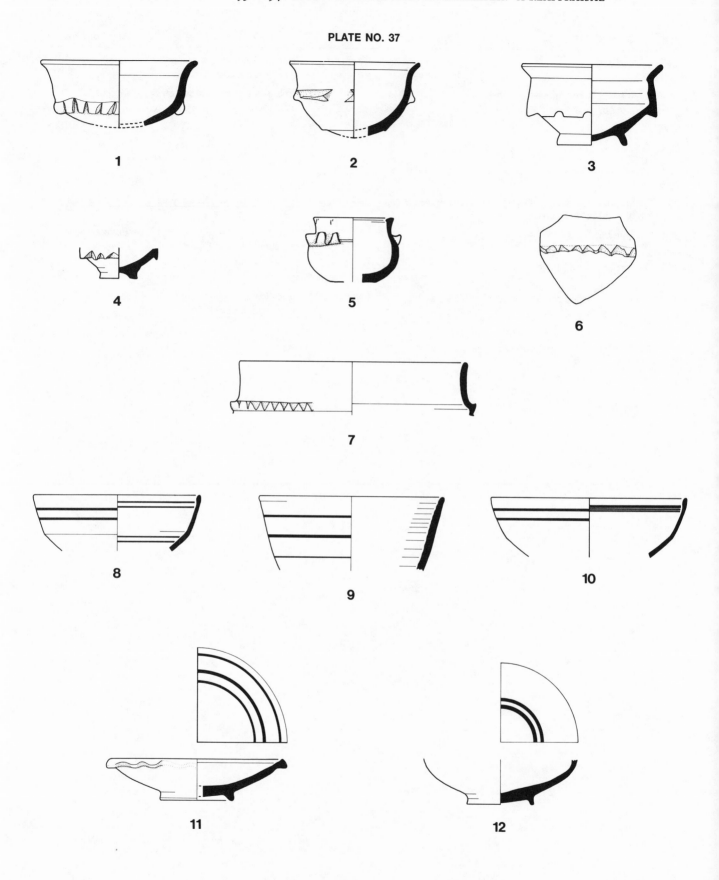

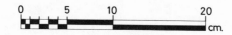

PLATE NO. 37

PL#:	Reg.#:	Date:	Prov:	Level:	Photo:	All:	Munsell References:
37:1	236	4-2-38	O:12	-1 m		ASOR	
37:2	571	4-16-38	O:9		571:3	JAM	
37:3						JAM	
37:4	9097	4-7-40	Rm. 49		1453:15	ASOR	
37:5	6066	3-16-40	Rm. 86		1454:8	JAM	
37:6	741	4-18-38	Rm. 30	Surface to 1 m	531:3, 597:18	ASOR	
37:7			Rm. 27			JAM	
37:8	660	4-18-38	Rm. 35	1 m to 1.90 m	549:3, 552:1, 593:21	ASOR	
37:9	3017	4-25-39	Rm. 60	-1 m	594:9, 1462:2	ASOR	
37:10	5022	5-12-39	Rm. 49A		593:8, 645:16, 1462:5	ASOR	
37:11	12,053	5-1-40	Rm. 38		1462:4	ASOR	
37:12	325	4-6-38	Rm. 37	Surface to 50 cm	549:6, 552:9, 645:2, 1426:6	ASOR	

PL#:	Description:	Body Comp. and Texture:
37:1	Crenelated bowl, lip and body fragment; everted rim; rounded base.	Calcareous clay; particle size < 2 mm; inclusions: qtz/spar/lime, Fe_2O_3, Fe_3O_4, equiaxed organic burnout.
37:2	Crenelated bowl, lip and base fragment; everted rim; rounded base.	
37:3	Crenelated bowl, lip and base fragment; everted rim; ring base.	
37:4	Small crenelated vessel, body and base fragment; ring base.	Calcareous clay; particle size less than 2 mm.
37:5	Small crenelated bowl, lip and base fragment; thickened rim; flat base.	
37:6	Crenelated vessel, body fragment.	Calcareous clay.
37:7	Bowl, lip and body fragment; row of crenelations at base of neck.	Calcareous clay; particle size < 2 mm.
37:8	Painted bowl, lip and body fragment; carinated; simple rim.	Fine textured ferrugenous clay; medium temper (10-30%); fine and medium particle size; inclusions: qtz/spar (< 3.0 mm), fibrous organic burnout (< 1.0 mm), Fe_3O_4.
37:9	Painted bowl, lip and body fragment; simple rim; restored.	Fine textured ferrugenous clay; medium temper (10-30%); fine and medium particle size; inclusions: qtz/spar (< 3.0 mm), fibrous organic burnout (< 1.0 mm).
37:10	Painted bowl, lip and body fragment; carinated; simple rim.	Fine textured ferrugenous clay; lightly tempered (10%); fine particle size (1.0 mm); inclusions: qtz/spar, fibrous organic burnout.
37:11	Painted saucer, lip and base fragment; fluted lip; ring base.	Fine textured ferrugenous clay; lightly tempered (10%); fine particle size (1.0 mm); inclusions: qtz/spar, fibrous organic burnout.
37:12	Painted bowl, base fragment; ring base.	Fine textured ferrugenous clay; medium temper (10-30%); fine and medium particle size; inclusions: qtz/spar (< 3.0 mm), fibrous organic burnout (< 1.0 mm).

PL#:	Method of Mfg:	Surf. Decor:	Firing:	State of Pres:
37:1	Thrown; crenelations folded over and cut out.	Crenelated frieze on body.	Greyish brown body and surfaces; (MOHS 3-3➤).	Worn surfaces.
37:2				
37:3				
37:4	Thrown; crenelations folded over and cut out.	Crenelated frieze on body.	Tan body and surfaces.	Good.
37:5				
37:6	Thrown; crenelations added as coil and cut out.	Crenelated frieze on body.	Tan body and surfaces.	Good.
37:7	Thrown; crenelations folded over and cut out.	Crenelated frieze on body.	Tan body and surfaces.	Good.
37:8	Thrown; uneven wall thickness (wall thick, base thin).	Painted on exterior and interior in red and brown bands.	Reduction firing; grey core with red surface layers; (MOHS 3-3➤).	Good.
37:9	Thrown.	Three black bands on exterior surface.	Reduction firing; grey core with red surface layers; (MOHS 3-3➤).	Worn surfaces.
37:10	Thrown; wheel trimmed.	Painted brown and red bands on exterior and interior.	Oxidation; incomplete oxidation of grey core; (MOHS 3-3➤).	Good.
37:11	Thrown with ridges beneath lip; thrown fluted lip; wheel-turned base rim.	Painted on interior in red and brown bands.	Oxidation; incomplete oxidation of grey core; (MOHS 3-3➤).	Good.
37:12	Thrown.	Painted brown and black bands on interior.	Reduction firing; grey core with red surface layers; (MOHS 3-3➤).	Good.

PLATE NO. 38

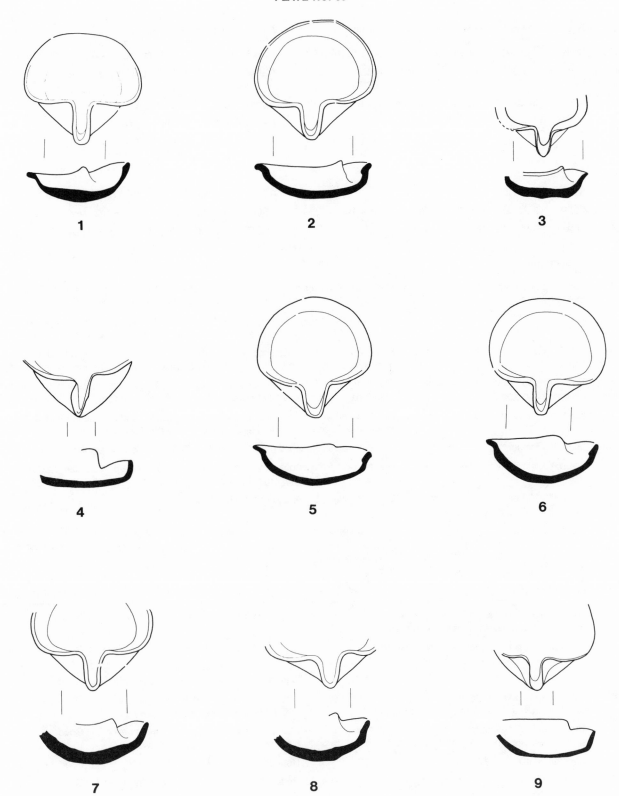

PLATE NO. 38

PL#:	Reg.#:	Date:	Prov:	Level:	Photo:	All:	Munsell References:
38:1	8039	3-29-40	Rm. 50		1452:5, 1452A:5	ASOR	ext. 10 YR 8/3, int. 10 YR 8/4, sec. 10 YR 7/2
38:2	261	4-4-38	Rm. 28	-1.85 m	1452:1, 1452A:1, 1609:1	ASOR	ext. 10 YR 8/3, int. 10 YR 8/3, sec. 5 YR 7/6
38:3	430	4-10-38	Rm. 39	Surface	531:6, 532:3, 626:6	ASOR	ext. 5 Y 5/1, int. 5 Y 6/1
38:4	526	4-14-38	Rm. 25A	Debris		ASOR	ext. 2.5 YR 6/6, int. 2.5 YR 6/6, sec. 2.5 YR 6/6
38:5	6009	3-12-40	Rm. 46		1452:21, 1453A:2	ASOR	ext. 10 YR 8/3, 5 YR 8/4, int. 5 YR 8/4, sec. 5 YR 6/1, 7.5 YR 8/4
38:6							
38:7	839	4-20-38	Q:9		639:2	ASOR	ext. 10 YR 7/1, int. 10 YR 7/2, sec. 2.5 Y N5/
38:8	7029	3-22-40	Rm. 74	Debris	1452:10	ASOR	ext. 2.5 Y 8/2, int. 10 YR 8/2, sec. 10 YR 6/1
38:9	109	3-27-38	Rm. 10	Surface		ASOR	ext. 7.5 YR N4/, int. 10 YR 6/1, sec. 2.5 Y N5/

PL#:	Description:	Body Comp. and Texture:
38:1	Lamp, lip and body fragments, black stain at spout.	Fine textured ferrugenous clay; some temper (10-20%); fine particle size ($\leq$1.0 mm); inclusions: qtz/spar/lime, Fe_2O_3, no organic; strong HCl reaction.
38:2	Lamp.	Fine textured ferrugenous clay; heavily tempered (30%); fine particle size ($\leq$1.0 mm); inclusions: $CaCo_3$, qtz/spar, Fe_2O_3 and organic; strong HCl reaction.
38:3	Small lamp, lip and body fragment; lip flange.	Fine textured ferrugenous clay; heavily tempered (30%); mostly fine particle size ($\leq$0.5 mm); inclusions: qtz/spar, Fe_2O_3, Fe_3O_4, equiaxed organic burnout; no HCl reaction.
38:4	Lamp, lip and body fragment; black stains around spout.	Fine textured ferrugenous clay; heavily tempered (30-40%); fine particle size ($\leq$1.0 mm); inclusions: qtz/spar, equiaxed organic burnout; no HCl reaction.
38:5	Lamp, lip and body fragment; restored.	Fine textured ferrugenous clay; heavily tempered (30%); fine particle size ($\leq$1.0 mm); inclusions: $CaCo_3$, qtz/spar, Fe_2O_3, organic; strong HCl reaction.
38:6	Lamp; lip flange.	Fine textured ferrugenous clay; fine temper ($\leq$0.5 mm); no HCl reaction.
38:7	Lamp, lip and body fragment.	Fine textured ferrugenous clay; some temper (10-20%); fine particle size ($\leq$1.0 mm); inclusions: qtz/spar/lime, organic; medium HCl reaction.
38:8	Lamp, lip and body fragment; restored; heavily stained black around spout.	Medium texture; black and some white inclusions.
38:9	Lamp, lip and body fragment.	Fine textured ferrugenous clay; some temper (10-20%); mostly fine particle size ($\leq$0.5 mm) with some larger inclusions up to 5 mm; inclusions: qtz/spar, some organic: no HCl reaction.

PL#:	Method of Mfg:	Surf. Decor:	Firing:	State of Pres:
38:1	Thrown with lip flange; folded in on sides of spout when wet; finger impressions remain.		Slightly reduced; light tan color; (MOHS 4).	Good.
38:2	Thrown with lip flange; folded in on sides of spout when wet; finger impressions remain.		Oxidation; (MOHS 3-3→).	Good.
38:3			Dark grey to black reduced body & surfaces.	Good.
38:4	Thrown with lip flange; folded in on sides of spout when wet, finger impressions remain.		Red oxidized body and surfaces, except where black near lip; (MOHS 3-3→).	Good.
38:5	Thrown with lip flange; folded in on sides of spout when wet; finger impressions remain.		Mixed oxidation state; interior and exterior have patches of red and grey; (MOHS 4).	Good.
38:6	Undeterminable.		Reduction.	Poor, spalling.
38:7	Thick base, thinning to lip; finger impressions.		Reduced black body with grey surfaces and layers near surface.	Good.
38:8	Probably thrown.		Reduction.	Surface smudged black especially at spout.
38:9	Thrown with lip flange; folded in on sides of spout when wet.		Dark grey to black reduced body and surfaces.	Good.

PLATE NO. 39

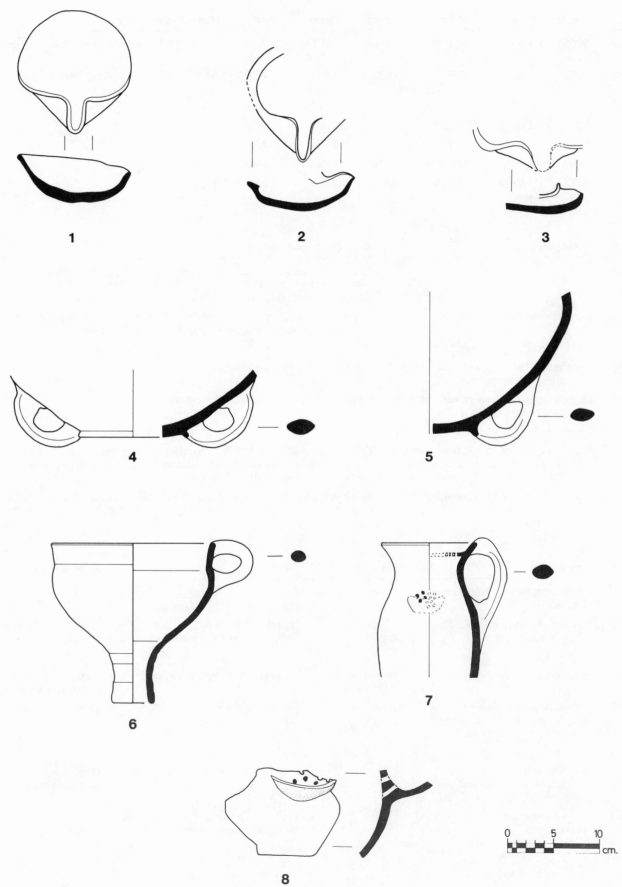

PLATE NO. 39

PL#:	Reg.#:	Date:	Prov:	Level:	Photo:	All:	Munsell References:
39:1	5053	3-7-40	Rm. 46	-34 cm	1452:4, 1452A:4	ASOR	ext. 2.5 YR 5/6, int. 2.5 YR 6/6, sec. 10 R 5/1
39:2	106	3-27-38	Q:9	Surface	1452:11, 1452A:11	ASOR	ext. 5 YR 6/2, int. 10 YR 5/2, sec. 7.5 YR N51
39:3						JAM	
39:4	731	4-18-38	Rm. 30	-1 m	676:2	ASOR	
39:5	668	4-18-38	Rm. 35	-1 m	527:5, 676:1	ASOR	
39:6	3097	4-29-39	Rm. 49A	-2.10 m	625:4	JAM	
39:7	527	4-15-38	Rm. 25A	Debris	677:1	ASOR	
39:8	855	4-20-38	L:12	-1 m	1455:8	ASOR	

PL#:	Description:	Body Comp. and Texture:
39:1	Lamp.	Fine textured ferrugenous clay; heavily tempered (50%); coarse particle size (≤ 3.0 mm); inclusions: qtz/spar, Fe_2O_3, equiaxed organic burnout and platey inclusions; no HCl reaction.
39:2	Lamp, lip and body fragment.	Fine textured ferrugenous clay; heavily tempered (30-50%); coarse particle size (~3.0 mm); inclusions: qtz/spar, Fe_3O_4, Fe_2O_3; no HCl reaction.
39:3	Lamp, lip and body fragment; lip flange.	
39:4	Large vessel, base fragment; handles as feet, from lower body to ring base.	Calcareous clay; particle size < 1mm.
39:5	Large vessel, base fragment; handles as feet from lower body to ring base.	Coarse texture; white, red and black inclusions.
39:6	Funnel; upper body to rim handle.	
39:7	Pitcher with strainer, lip and body fragment; pierced holes at spout and at closure just below rim.	Fine textured calcareous clay; lightly tempered (≤ 10%); fine particle size (most ≤ 10.0 mm, rare inclusion ≤ 3.0 mm); inclusions: qtz/spar and lime, other with yellow reaction ring; medium HCl reaction.
39:8	Pitcher with strainer spout, body fragment.	Fine textured ferrugenous clay; medium temper (20-30%); coarse particle size, up to 3 mm; inclusions: organic burnout, Fe_2O_3 and platey white particles; weak HCl reaction.

PL#:	Method of Mfg:	Surf. Decor:	Firing:	State of Pres:
39:1	Thick base; thinning to lip; finger impressions.		Red oxidized body with grey inner layer near vessel interior; (MOHS 3).	Good.
39:2	Thrown with lip flange; folded in on sides of spout when wet.		Dark grey to black reduced body and surfaces; no oxidized patch on bottom.	Exterior surface worn.
39:3				
39:4	Handformed using wheel.	Handle attached to small base rim.	Oxidation; tan body and surfaces.	Outer surface worn, accretions on interior.
39:5	Handbuilt; interior has vertical and diagonal scrape marks; exterior has horizontal scrape and wipe marks.		Medium; oxidation.	Good.
39:6				
39:7	Thrown; simple lip and narrow handle; holes for spout and closure were pierced into interior of body.		Fired in oxidation; (MOHS 4).	Worn exterior surface with accretions.
39:8	Thrown; handbuilt spout and pierced strainer holes.		Fired in reduction; grey with red surface layers interior and exterior; (MOHS 4).	Good.

PLATE NO. 40

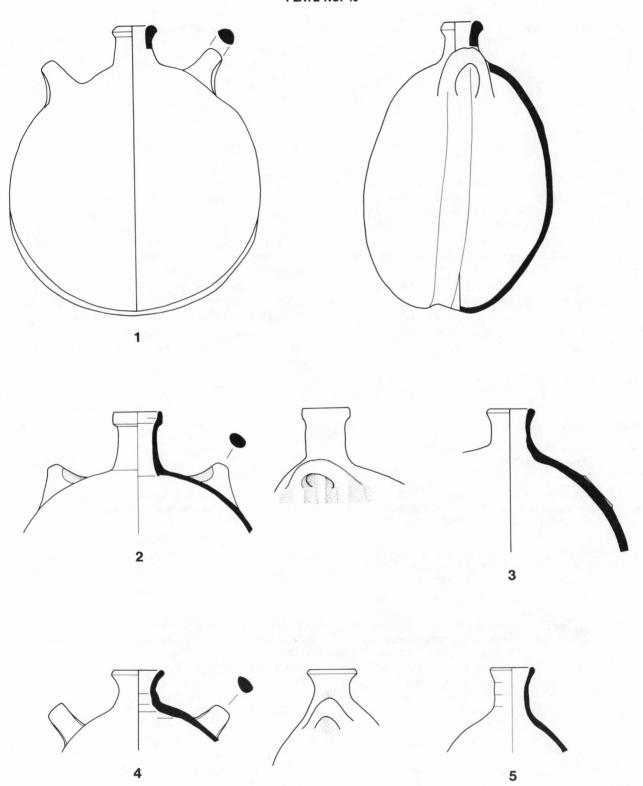

1

2

3

4

5

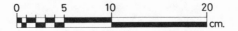

PLATE NO. 40

PL#:	Reg.#:	Date:	Prov:	Level:	Photo:	All:	Munsell References:
40:1	3037	4-26-39	Rm. 49A		625:1	ASOR	
40:2	544	4-15-38	Rm. 27	-2 m	526:4	ASOR	
40:3	10,039	4-9-40	Rm. 92		1455:7	ASOR	
40:4	771	4-20-38	Rm. 24	-1 m	526:3	ASOR	
40:5			Rm. 27			JAM	

PL#:	Description:	Body Comp. and Texture:
40:1	Canteen, complete; groove around circumference probably for a rope; restored, small sections of body and one handle missing; thickened rim.	Medium texture; white, red and a few black inclusions.
40:2	Canteen, lip, neck and body fragment; double groove around circumference probably for a rope; thickened rim.	Fine textured ferrugenous clay; heavily tempered; fairly coarse particle size (≤3.0 mm); inclusions: qtz/spar/lime, small amount of equiaxed burnout; no HCl reaction.
40:3	Canteen, body, neck and lip fragment; groove around circumference; thickened rim.	Fine textured ferrugenous clay; heavily tempered; fairly coarse particle size (≤3.0 mm); inclusions: lime, qtz/spar, small amount of organic equiaxed burnout; medium HCl reaction.
40:4	Canteen, body, neck and lip fragment; groove around circumference probably for a rope; everted rim.	Fine textured ferrugenous clay; lightly tempered (~10%); fine particle size; inclusions: qtz/spar, Fe_2O_3, organic burnout; no HCl reaction.
40:5	Canteen, lip and neck fragment; slightly thickened rim.	

PL#:	Method of Mfg:	Surf. Decor:	Firing:	State of Pres:
40:1	Thrown in two pieces and joined; thrown cylinder for neck and rim added.		Mixed.	Worn with surface encrustation.
40:2	Body thrown; separate thrown neck and lip joined onto body; handles have break at joint; exterior on bulbous side trimmed.		Heavily reduced body and surfaces; grey to black; medium degree of vitrification; (MOHS 4-4→).	Accretion on exterior surface.
40:3	Body thrown; separate thrown neck and lip joined onto body; exterior on bulbous side trimmed; single groove around circumference probably for rope handle.		Body reduced, then oxidized as black layer remains on interior of body near interior surface; (MOHS 4).	Good.
40:4	Thrown in two halves and joined along flatter side outer surface; lip and neck thrown as separate piece and joined to body; handles now broken where joined; pulled handles. This clay was quite short and tended to tear and crack as can be seen on interior surface.	Flatter side of canteen has circumferential incised line at base of each handle and of neck that is perpendicular to handle direction.	Red oxidized body with light grey layer on interior of body; medium degree of vitrification; (MOHS 3-3→).	Good.
40:5				

Plates

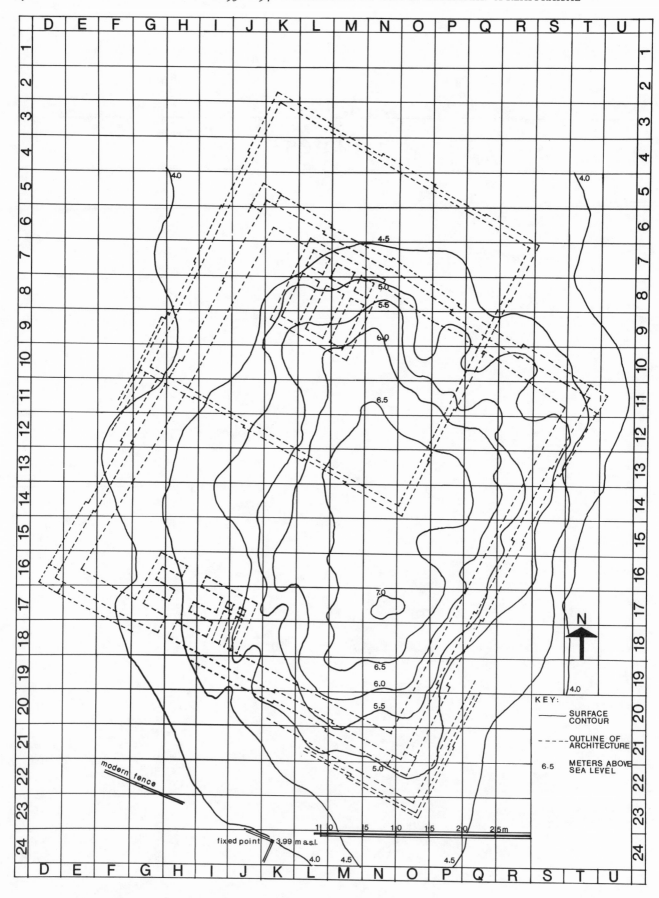

Pl. 1: Topographical plan of the site and immediate environs.

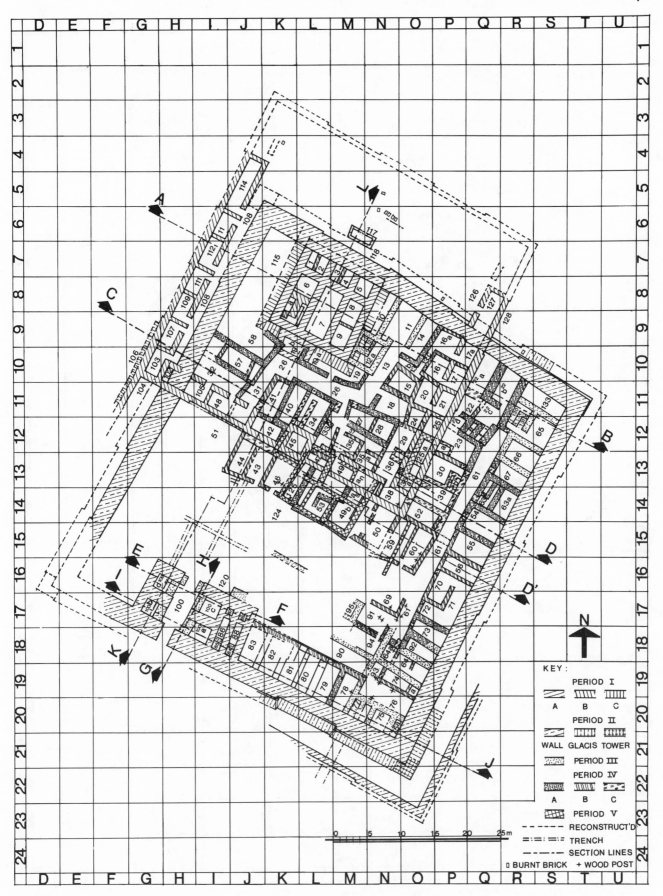

Pl. 2: General plan of Tell el-Kheleifeh.

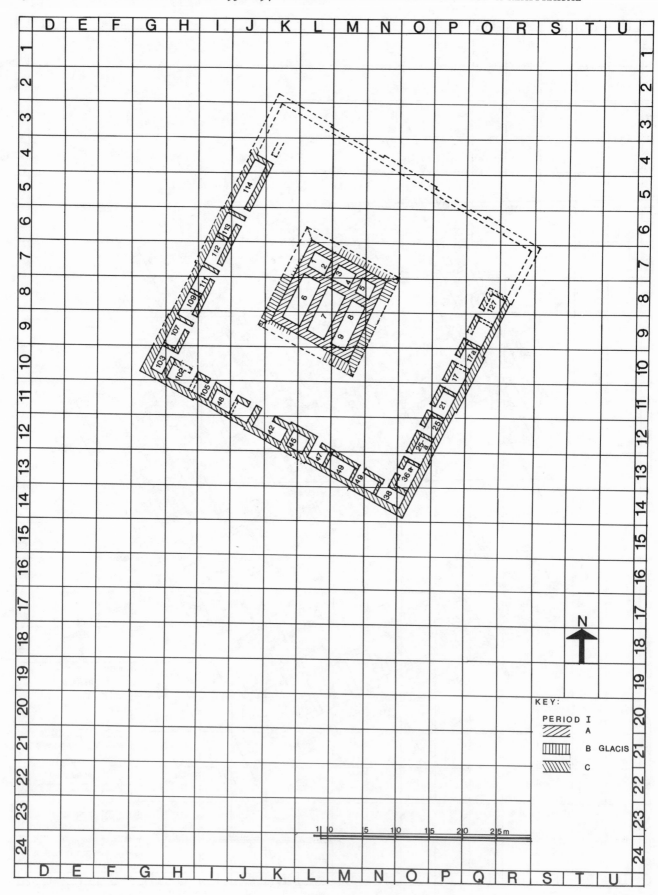

Pl. 3: The casemate fortress (Glueck's Period IC).

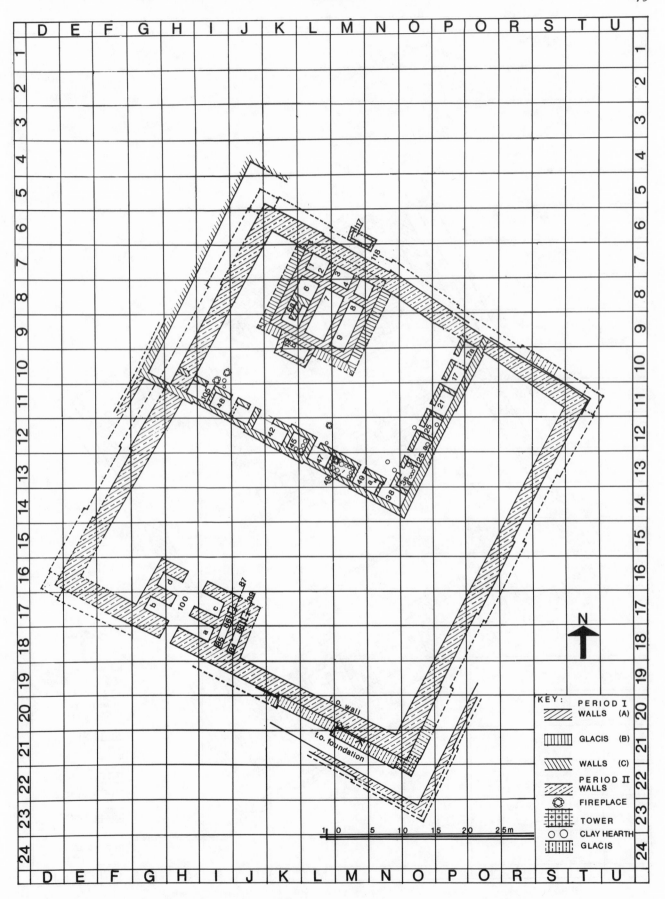

Pl. 4: The fortified settlement (Glueck's Periods I and II).

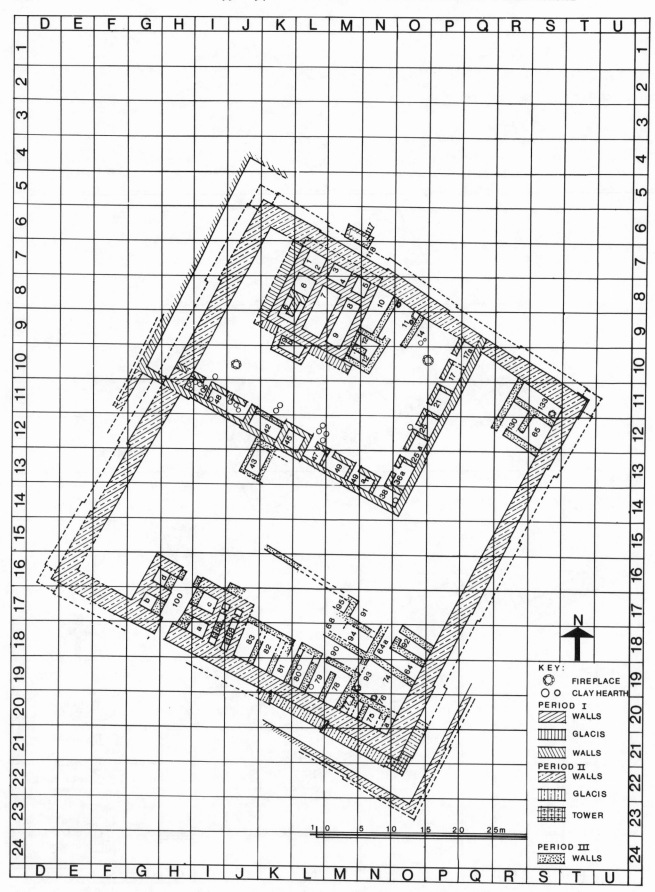

Pl. 5: The fortified settlement (Glueck's Periods I-III).

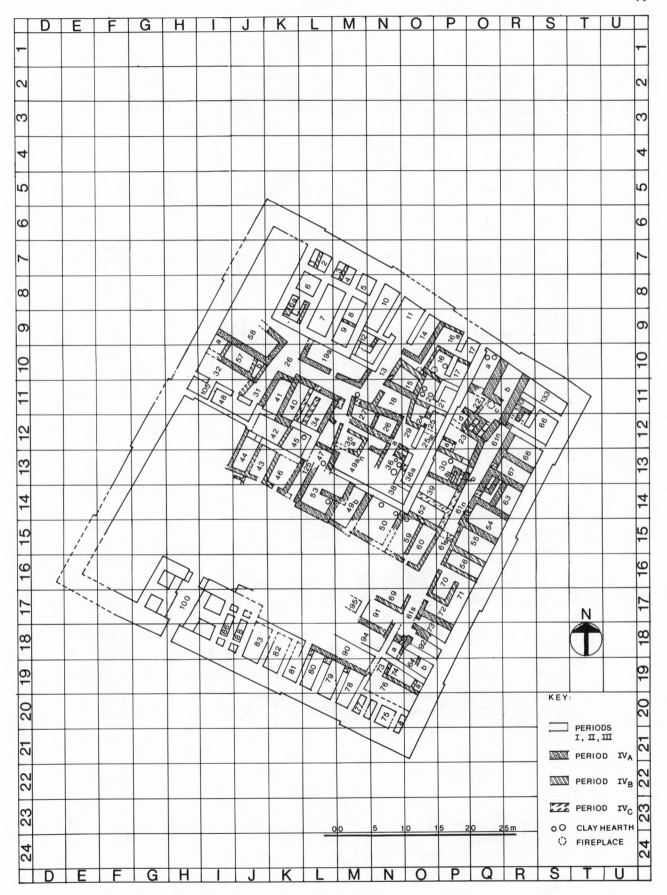

Pl. 6: The fortified settlement (Glueck's Periods IVA-C).

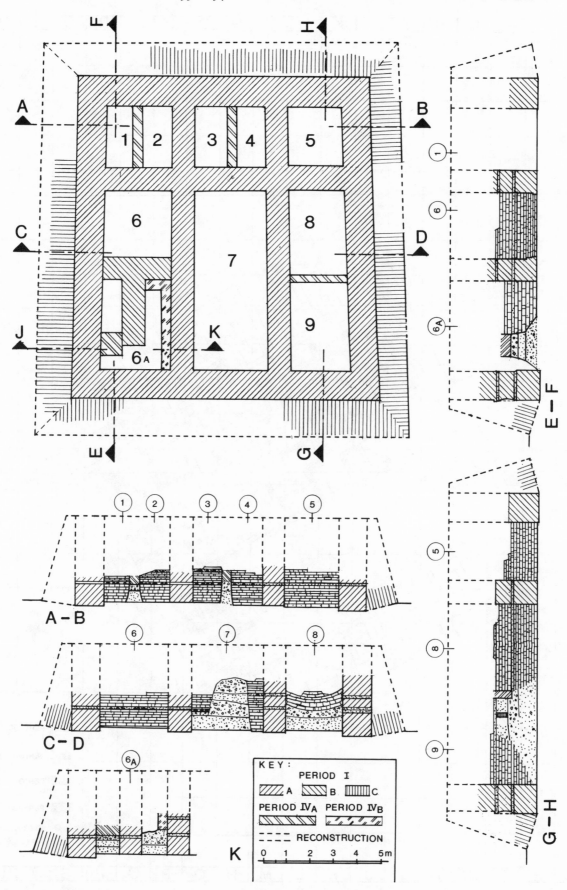

Pl. 7: Detail of the four-room building (Glueck's smelter/granary).

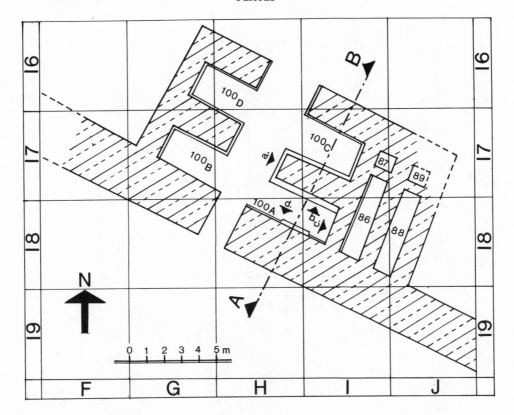

PLAN OF GATE,   PERIOD II

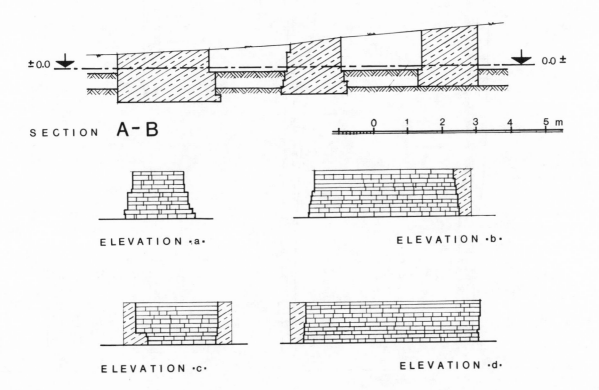

SECTION A-B

ELEVATION ·a·   ELEVATION ·b·

ELEVATION ·c·   ELEVATION ·d·

Pl. 8: Detail of the four-chambered gate.

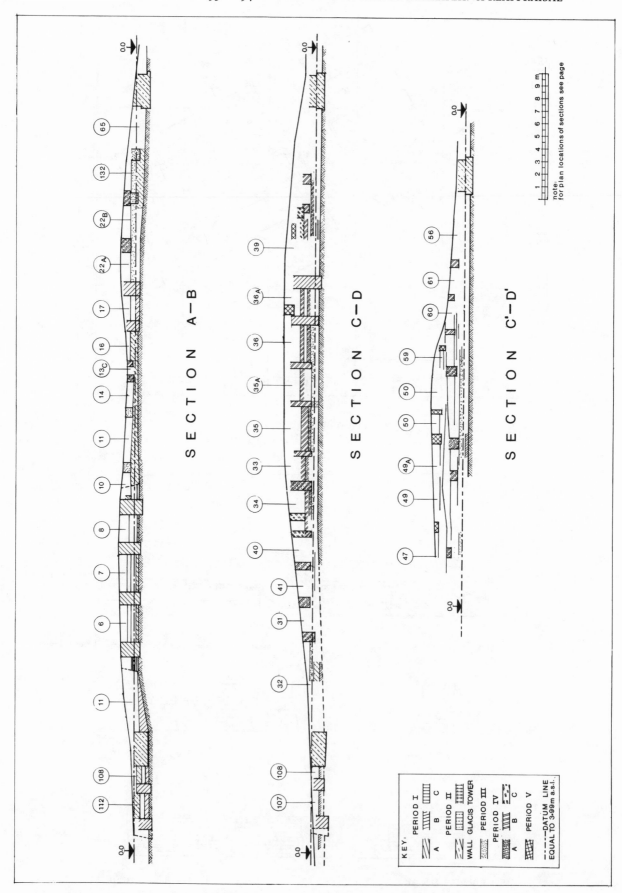

Pl. 9: Sections A-B, A'-B', C-D, and C'-D'.

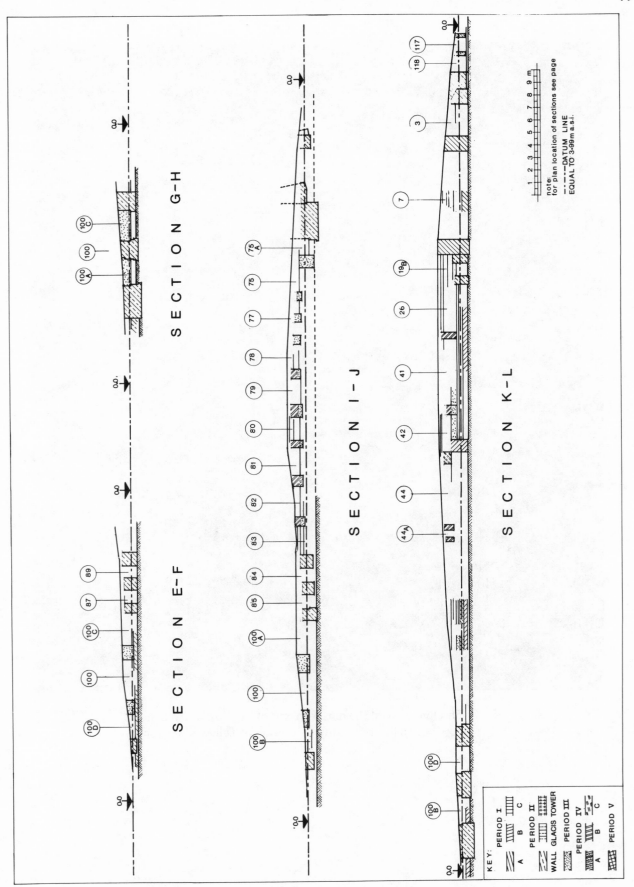

Pl. 10: Sections E-F, G-H, I-J and K-L.

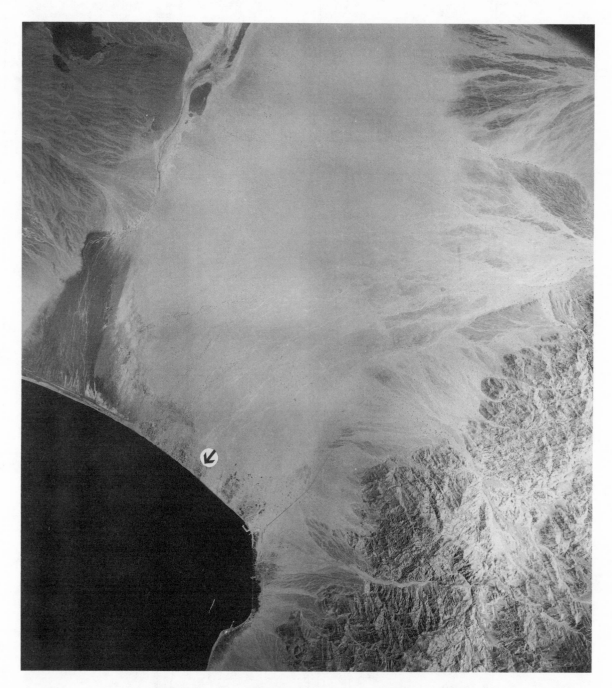

Pl. 41: Satellite view of the northern end of the Gulf of Aqaba.
The arrow marks the approximate location of Tell el-Kheleifeh.

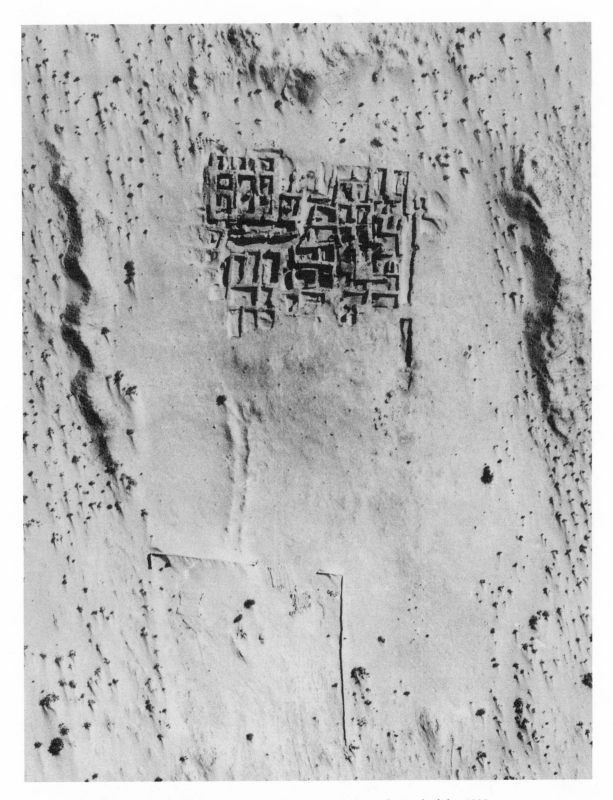

Pl. 42: Aerial photograph of Glueck's excavations at the end of the 1938 season.

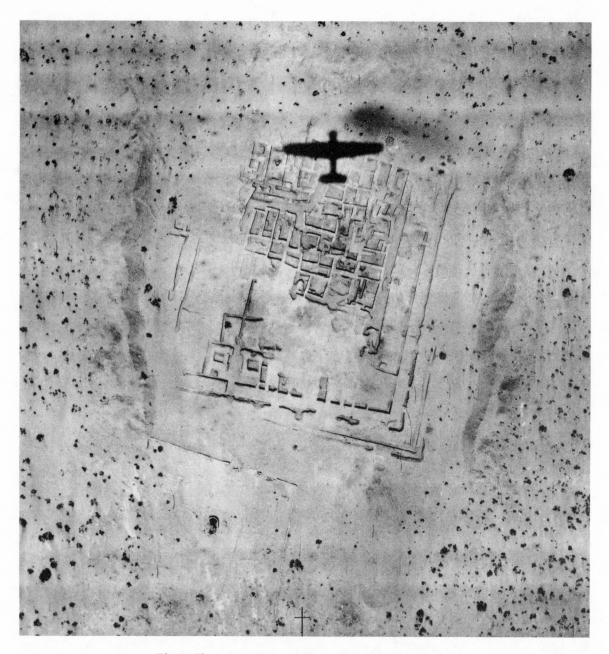

Pl. 43: The excavations at the end of the 1939 season.

Pl. 44: The excavations at the end of the 1939 season from the northwest.

Pl. 45: Aerial view of the excavations at the conclusion of the 1940 season.

Pl. 46A: The northern end of the Gulf of Aqaba and
the southern end of the Wadi Arabah. Neg. 1271

Pl. 46B: The northern shore of the Gulf of Aqaba from the west. Neg. 1691

Pl. 47A: View of Aqaba from the east. Neg. 230

Pl. 47B: The view from the southwestern side
of the tell, looking west-southwest. Neg. 937

Pl. 48A: Tell el-Kheleifeh from the south. Neg. B179

Pl. 48B: The modern gardens to the south of Tell el-Kheleifeh
(see the 1938 aerial photograph). Looking south.

Pl. 49A: A well near one of the gardens. Looking south. Neg. 113

Pl. 49B: The expedition en route to Aqaba, April 1939. Beginning second from the left: J. Pinkerfeld, N. Glueck, V. Glidden, military officer, and A. K. Henschel. Neg. 296

Pl. 50A: Nelson Glueck calling roll, April 1939. Neg. 289

Pl. 50B: Nelson Glueck (right) and Albert Henschel, Aqaba 1940. Neg. 1667

Pl. 51A: The four-room building from the north with Grave 117 in the foreground (A). The latter was constructed in Period II according to Glueck. Portions of Rooms 5, 7, and 8 are visible (marked B, C, and D respectively). The excavation trenches, running along the partially removed offsets/insets wall, are visible immediately to the south of Grave 117 (E). Neg. 1337

Pl. 51B: A view of the northwestern corner of the four-room building, looking southwest. Rooms 1 (A), 2 (B) and the northern portion of 6 (C) are visible. Two apertures can be seen in the southern wall of Room 1. Neg. B203

Pl. 52A: Apertures in
the southern wall of
Room 1. Neg. B193

Pl. 52B: Detail of two "ventilation" apertures. Neg. B50

Pl. 53A: Detail of apertures in the western wall of Room 7. Neg. B72

Pl. 53B: Two rows
of apertures in the
eastern wall of
Room 7. Neg. B200

Pl. 54A: The two rows of apertures in the exterior of the southern wall of the four-room building, looking northwest. The southern ends of Rooms 6 (A) and 7 (B) are visible. Glueck's Period IB "glaçis" is visible in the lower left (C). Neg. B143

Pl. 54B: Pictured in the center of this photograph (looking west) is the southern perimeter (A) and southeastern corner (B) of Glueck's Period IB "glaçis" which adjoins the southern wall of the four-room building (C). This supporting revetment is here enclosed on the south by the walls of Rooms 19 and 19A of later periods (D), visible on the left. Note the two rows of apertures in the southern wall of the citadel (E). Neg. 1421

Pl. 55A: The southern wall of Room 10 (A) is constructed over a section of the "glaçis" (B) built against the eastern side of the four-room building (C). The eastern revetment was not well-preserved. A missing section of some 15 m (D) was reconstructed on the plans (Squares H8 and H9). Neg. 1424

Pl. 55B: General view of the western perimeter of the casemate fortress (Glueck's Period IC) from the northeast. Rooms 114 (A), 113, 112, 111, 109, 107, and 103 are visible. Neg. 1087

Pl. 56A: The western row of casemates from the south (Glueck's Period IC). Neg. 1115

Pl. 56B: Detail of Room 114 from the south. The location of the northern dump prevented excavation of the casemate wall further to the north. Neg. 1197

Pl. 57A: Detail of Casemate 109 (Period IC) from the northeast. Neg. 1118

Pl. 57B: Casemates 111 (foreground), 109, 107, and 103 from the north. Neg. 1057

Pl. 58A: The entrance to Room 127 on the eastern side of the casemate fortress. Neg. 114

Pl. 58B: The orientation of this photograph, looking west, is closely aligned with that of Glueck's section C-D (see general plan and the 1940 aerial photograph). The western perimeter of the offsets/ insets wall runs from left to right (A), cutting the line of the earlier case-mate wall at Room 102 (B). The western end of this unit and adjoining Casemate 103 to the west (C) are located in the lower left of the photo-graph. Also clearly visible is the southern wall of the casemate fortress (D), with a salient and recess (E). Neg. 1365

Pl. 59A: Room 49 (Period II) from the west. This image depicts one of Glueck's "furnace rooms" with a series of clay hearths next to each other. Neg. 80

Pl. 59B: Hearths in the western end of Room 49. Neg. 72

Pl. 60A: Detail of apertures in the south wall of Room 49. Neg. 215

Pl. 60B: Apertures in the southern wall of Room 49A. Neg. 211

Pl. 61A: Apertures in the western wall of Room 52. Note the charcoal debris. Looking southwest. Neg. 1307

Pl. 61B: Apertures in the northern wall of Room 40. Neg. 68

Pl. 62A: A view of the exterior of the southern offsets/insets wall of Glueck's Periods II-IVB (Squares L21 and M21). Both the revetment with a salient (A) and the inner face of the wall with a salient (B) are visible. The line of the outer fortification element (Squares M22 and N22) can be seen on the right (C). Looking east. Neg. 1289

Pl. 62B: Detail of previous photograph. The "glaçis" salient of the offsets/insets wall (Square L21) is clear (A). The entire southeastern corner of the offsets/insets wall is here visible. Neg. 1313

Pl. 63A: Detail of the inner face salient (A), looking to the northwest across Rooms 78 (B), 79, 80, 81, and 82 (right to left). The sloping revetment is visible to the left (C). Its salient is somewhat obscured in this photograph (D). Neg. 1340

Pl. 63B: General view of the four-chambered gateway from the south (Periods II-IVB). The blockings of Rooms 100D and 100C are visible (labelled A and B respectively). The blockings of Rooms 100A and 100B have been removed. Neg. 184

Pl. 64A: The four-chambered gate from the north. Rooms 100A, 100B (labelled A and B respectively) and Glueck's Period III blocking of Room 100C (C) are visible. Water sources are located near the mound. Note the modern gardens and wells to the south. Neg. 219

Pl. 64B: The western side of the four-chambered gate from the northeast. The Period III blocking of Room 100D is clearly visible (A). Neg. 165

Pl. 65A: Detail of the innermost pier on the western side of the four-chambered gate. The innermost pier of the Period II gate appears beneath the visible architecture (A). Neg. 183

Pl. 65B: Room 100C (A) and the two innermost eastern piers (B) of the four-chambered gate. The northern portion of Room 100A (C) is to the right. Glueck's Period III blocking of Room 100C (D) has not been removed. Looking northeast. Neg. 228

Pl. 66A: Details of the north wall of Room 100A. Glueck's
Period III blocking has been removed. Neg. 178

Pl. 66B: Masonry detail of the eastern, outermost pier of the four-
chambered gate. The southern wall of Room 100A is visible on the left.
The Period III blocking of this guardroom has been removed. Neg. 180

Pl. 67A: General view of the excavations from the northeast. Rooms 63 and 63A (A and B respectively) are visible in the foreground. Neg. 1085

Pl. 67B: General view of the southeastern corner of the fortified settlement (Periods III-IVA) from the northeast. Rooms 75, 76, 74, 64, 92, 73, and 72 (left to right) are visible on the interior of the offsets/insets wall (A). Neg. 1086

Pl. 68A: Detail of Pl. 67B. Looking west across Rooms 75, 77, and 78 (A-C) which adjoin the inner face of the offsets/insets wall (D), visible on the left. Neg. 933

Pl. 68B: Looking north into Street 61 (A) on the eastern side of the settlement. Rooms 52 (B), 39, 30, and 23 are visible on the left (left to right). Architecture belonging to Periods IC-IVB is here visible, according to Glueck. Neg. 1383

Pl. 69A: Street 61 from the north, looking across Rooms
23 (A), 30, 39, and 52 (right to left). Neg. 1384

Pl. 69B: Looking down
Street 26 to the west. The
entrance to Room 19 is
visible on the right (A).
Neg. 123

Pl. 70A: View of Room 16 from the northwest. The site's stratigraphic complexity is here illustrated. The eastern wall of this room (A) was originally constructed as the western wall of Casemate 17 (B) in Glueck's Period IC. The southern wall (C) was constructed in Period IV according to Glueck. The northern (D) and western (E) walls were built in Period IVA. The doorway was blocked in IVB. Neg. 63

Pl. 70B: View of Room 16 (A) from the northeast. Room 17 adjoins to the left (B). The common wall between Rooms 16 and 17 (C) was originally constructed as the western wall of Casemate 17 in Period IC. Neg. 61

Pl. 71A: Detail of the previous photograph. The wall adjoining to the left (A) is the common wall of Rooms 17 and 17A, assigned to Period IVA by the excavator. Neg. 120

Pl. 71B: Doorway in the northwestern corner of Room 27. Glueck assigned the construction of this room to Period IV and a blocking of the doorway (here removed) to IVB. Neg. 23

Pl. 72A: Doorway in the
northwestern corner of
Room 35, looking to the
southwest. Note the use of
stones in the construction.
Glueck assigned this room
to Period IVB. Neg. 16

Pl. 72B:
Glueck's Period
IVB blocking of
the doorway in
Room 40. The
construction of
this room was
assigned to
Period IV. The
southern wall
of Room 19A is
visible on the
right (A). Street
26 separates
these units (B).
Neg. 934

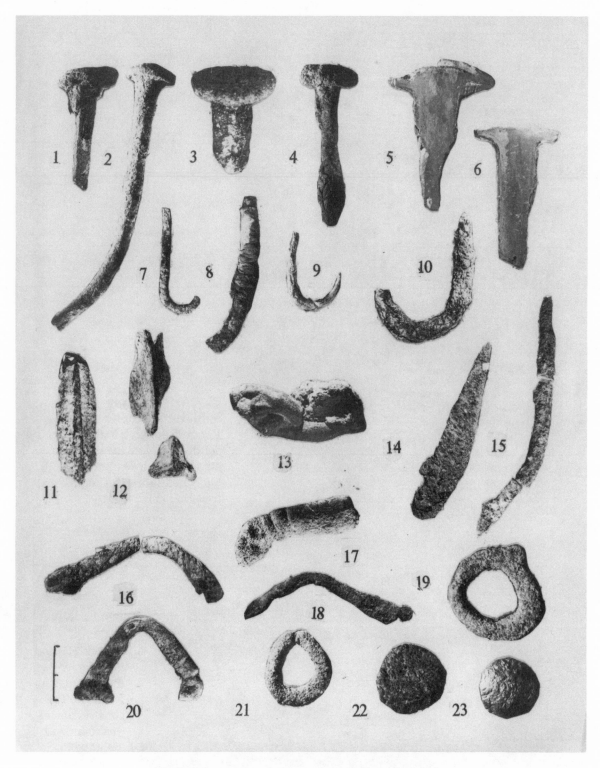

Pl. 73: Selected metal objects from Tell el-Kheleifeh.

215

241

Pl. 74: Seal impressions 215 and 241.

278

463

Pl. 75: Seal impressions 278 and 463.

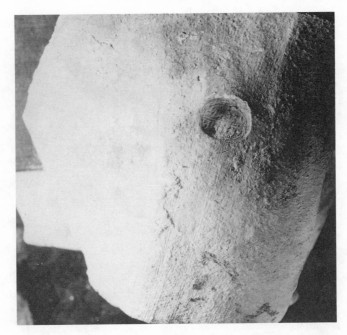

464

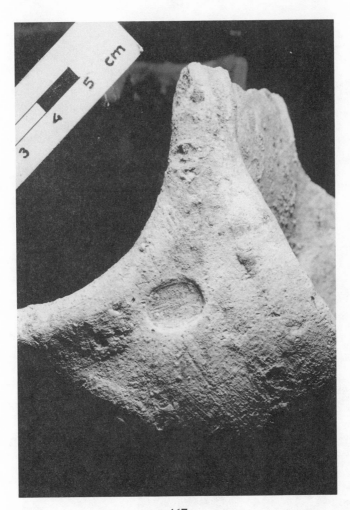

467

Pl. 76: Seal impressions 464 and 467.

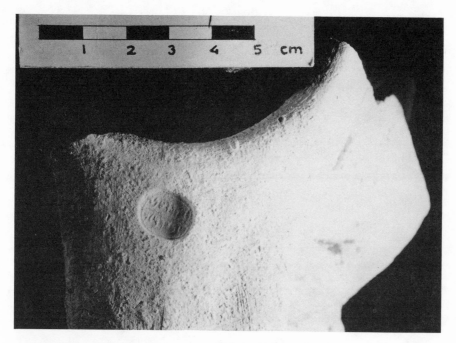

528

724

Pl. 77: Seal impressions 528 and 724.

2096

Pl. 78: Seal impressions 2096 and 2098.

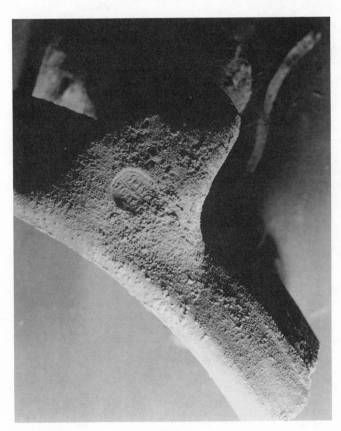

2098

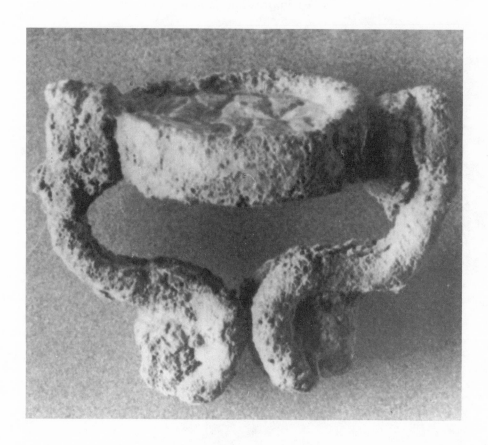

Pl. 79: Signet 7022.

80:A   374

80:B   469

Pl. 80: Jar graffito 374 and jar inscription 469.

81:A   2069

81:B (obverse)   2070

81:B (reverse)   2070

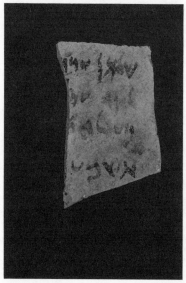

81:C   2071

Pl. 81: Ostraca 2069, 2070, and 2071.

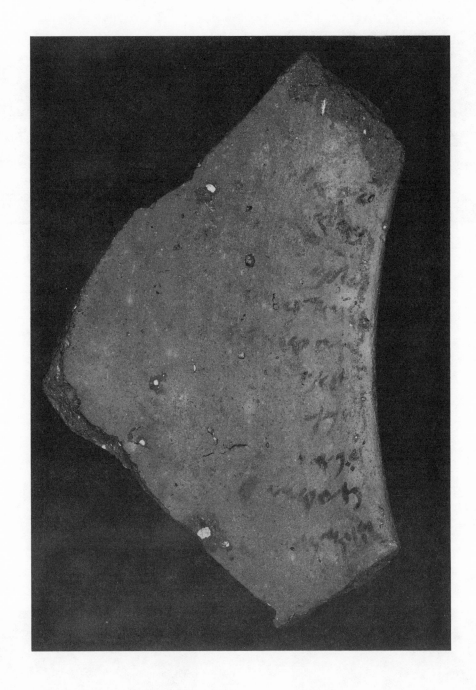

Pl. 82: Ostracon 6043.

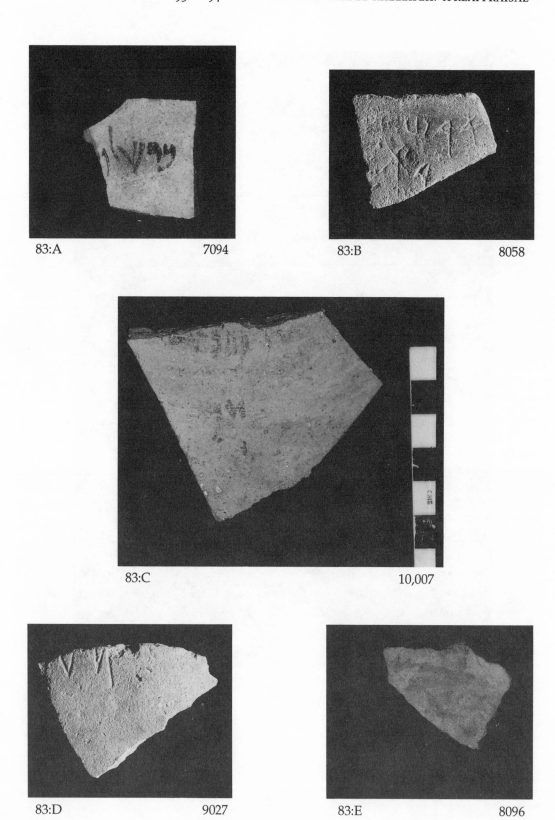

Pl. 83: Inscriptions 7094, 8058, 10,007, 9027, and Ostracon 8096.

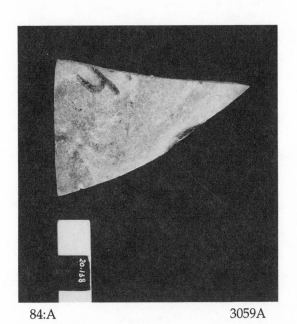

84:A 3059A

84:B 3059B

84:C Rhodian jar handle

Pl. 84: Ostraca 3059A, 3059B, and the Rhodian jar handle.